John Stevens

Check it!

Wortschatz- und
Grammatikfehler
erkennen
und vermeiden

Cornelsen

Check it!
Wortschatz- und Grammatikfehler erkennen und vermeiden

Erarbeitet von
John Stevens
und der Englischredaktion:
The author would like to express his special thanks to the editor in charge,
Hartmut Tschepe,
who made an enormous contribution to the book.

Projektleitung
Michael Ferguson

Beratung
Birgit Ohmsieder, Mervyn Whittaker

Illustrationen
Ed McLachlan

Gesamtgestaltung und technische Umsetzung
Stephan Hilleckenbach *sowie* Eva Schmidt

 http://www.cornelsen.de

1. Auflage, 1. Druck 2005

Alle Drucke dieser Auflage sind inhaltlich unverändert
und können im Unterricht nebeneinander verwendet werden.

Druck: CS-Druck CornelsenStürtz, Berlin

ISBN 3-464-31050-7

Bestellnummer 310507

 Gedruckt auf säurefreiem Papier,
umweltschonend hergestellt aus chlorfrei gebleichten Faserstoffen.

Inhaltsverzeichnis

FAQ (Frequently Asked Questions)

1 Welchen Nutzen habe ich von *Check it*?

Check it ist ein Nachschlagewerk und Übungsbuch zur Vermeidung von Wortschatz- und Grammatikfehlern, mit dem man sich selbst testen und sein Wissen gezielt wiederholen und erweitern kann. Es behandelt ca. 800 englische Wörter, die von Lernenden besonders häufig falsch verwendet werden, und insgesamt über 1000 Sprachfallen.

Check it hilft, die eigene Sprachproduktion zu verbessern und sprachlich korrekte Äußerungen und Texte zu formulieren.

Check it beantwortet u. a. folgende Fragen:

- Welche Grammatikstruktur kann ich mit einem bestimmten englischen Wort verwenden? Beispiel:
  Heißt es *she explained me the rule* oder *she explained the rule to me*?
  (Antwort auf Seite 81)

- Welches von mehreren ähnlichen englischen Wörtern ist das richtige oder passende? Beispiel:
  Heißt es *sit in the shade* oder *sit in the shadow*? (Antwort auf Seite 235)

- Kann ich ein bestimmtes englisches Wort genauso wie ein ähnliches deutsches Wort verwenden? Beispiel:
  Kann ich sagen *call me on my handy*?
  (Antwort auf Seite 107)

- Welche Präposition muss ich verwenden? Beispiel:
  Heißt es *welcome to Germany* oder *welcome in Germany*? (Antwort auf Seite 283)

- Welches Adjektiv/Adverb/Verb/Nomen passt zu einem bestimmten englischen Wort? Wie lautet die richtige Wortkombination (Kollokation)? Beispiel:
  Heißt es *my little finger* oder *my small finger*? (Antwort auf Seite 165)

- Wie bilde ich eine bestimmte Form richtig? Beispiel:
  Heißt es *I've hanged my coat up* oder *I've hung my coat up*? (Antwort auf Seite 109)

- Wie schreibt sich ein bestimmtes englisches Wort richtig? Beispiel:
  Schreibt man *my prefered option* oder *my preferred option*? (Antwort auf Seite 215)

2 Wie ist *Check it* aufgebaut?

- **Doppelseiten:**
  Übungsseite links + Informationsseite rechts

Check it ist alphabetisch wie ein Wörterbuch geordnet. Auf einer Doppelseite werden bis zu acht Stichwörter behandelt. (Nicht alphabetisch eingeordnete Stichwörter findet man mithilfe des *Wordfinder* am Ende des Buches.) Zu jedem Stichwort gibt es sowohl Übungen als auch Erklärungen und Regeln zur Form, Bedeutung und zum richtigen Gebrauch. Alle Erklärungen werden durch eine Vielzahl von Beispielsätzen, meist mit deutscher Übersetzung, illustriert.

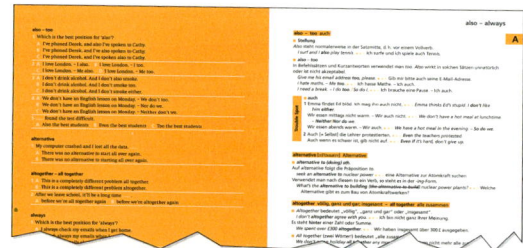

Links: Übungen – rechts: Erklärungen und Beispiele

- **Checkpoints: zusammenfassende Testaufgaben**

In der Mitte des Buches, zwischen den Buchstaben K und L, finden Sie 12 **Checkpoints**. Die **Checkpoints** bieten übergreifende Testaufgaben, in denen Wörter und Problemfälle aus verschiedenen Teilen des Buches zusammengefasst werden. Hier können Sie gezielt an Fehlerbereichen wie Wortwahl, Satzstellung und Präpositionen arbeiten.

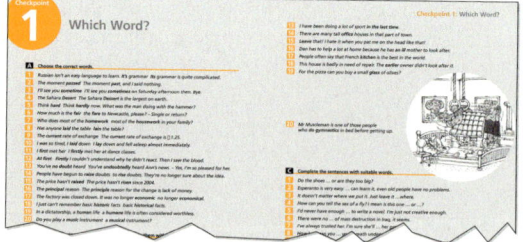

Checkpoints in der Mitte des Buches

- **Separates Lösungsheft zur Selbstkontrolle**

Die Lösungen zu allen Übungs- und Testsätzen des alphabetischen Hauptteils und der **Checkpoints** sind in dem Lösungsheft zu finden, das dem Buch beigelegt ist. Das Lösungsheft dient der Überprüfung der eigenen Lösungen.

FAQ (Frequently Asked Questions)

3   Wie arbeite ich mit *Check it*?

■ Arbeiten mit dem alphabetischen Hauptteil

■ *Check it* kann man sowohl zum Üben als auch zum Nachschlagen verwenden. Ob man zuerst nachschlägt und dann übt, oder ob man sich zuerst testet und dann kontrolliert, hängt vor allem davon ab, wie sicher man die betreffenden Wörter schon beherrscht: Sind Sie unsicher in Bezug auf die Verwendung eines Wortes, sollten Sie zuerst die Erklärungen und Beispiele lesen, bevor Sie die Übungssätze bearbeiten. Sind Sie jedoch recht sicher, wie ein bestimmtes Wort richtig verwendet wird, so können Sie auch mit den Übungssätzen beginnen (dabei die rechten Seiten abdecken!) und anschließend Ihre Lösungen anhand des Lösungsheftes und der Informationen auf der rechten Seite kontrollieren. Auf jeden Fall sollte man ein Stichwort immer sowohl links (Übungsseite) als auch rechts (Informationsseite) bearbeiten.
Die Lösungen der Übungsaufgaben sollten stets auf einem Blatt Papier oder in einem Heft notiert werden.

■ Alle Übungssätze sind als Multiple-Choice-Aufgaben angelegt, d. h., man wählt die richtige Lösung aus den angebotenen Möglichkeiten. Eine unterstrichene Satznummer (z. B. **2**) kennzeichnet Sätze, bei denen mehr als eine der vorgegebenen Antworten richtig ist. Versuchen Sie, alle richtigen Lösungen herauszufinden.

■ Arbeiten mit den *Checkpoints*

■ Die 12 *Checkpoints* bieten eine Vielzahl unterschiedlicher Testaufgaben zu bestimmten Fehlerbereichen. Die *Checkpoints* setzt man am besten zum übergreifenden Üben und Testen ein, nachdem man eine Weile mit *Check it* gearbeitet und den Blick für die verschiedenartigen Fehlergefahren geschärft hat. Die *Checkpoints* können in beliebiger Reihenfolge bearbeitet werden.

■ Anhand des Lösungsheftes können Sie überprüfen, ob Sie die Testaufgaben richtig gelöst haben. Wenn Sie Fehler gemacht haben oder eine angegebene Lösung nicht verstehen, sollten Sie erneut die Informationsseiten im alphabetischen Hauptteil heranziehen. Im Lösungsheft wird auf die entsprechenden Stichwörter mit den Erklärungen hingewiesen.

4   Was sind *Trouble Spots* und *False Friends*?

Bei den *Trouble Spots* („Problemgebiete") handelt es sich um ca. 100 deutsche Wörter, deren Wiedergabe im Englischen besondere Probleme bereitet, z. B. „als", „fahren", „früher", „groß", „wie". In den *Trouble Spots* finden Sie die passenden englischen Entsprechungen dieser deutschen „Problemwörter".

Eine Liste der in *Check it* behandelten *Trouble Spots* finden Sie ganz vorn im Buch. Testaufgaben zu verschiedenen *Trouble Spots* enthält u. a. der *Checkpoint 1*, S. 132–135.

False Friends („Falsche Freunde") sind englisch-deutsche Wortpaare wie *brave* und „brav", die ähnlich geschrieben werden, aber unterschiedliche Bedeutungen haben und somit leicht zur Sprachfalle werden können. Um Fehlern und Missverständnissen vorzubeugen, werden in den entsprechenden Abschnitten von *Check it* die richtigen Entsprechungen von beiden „Partnern" (also von *brave* und von „brav") anhand von Beispielen illustriert.

Eine Übersicht über die in *Check it* behandelten *False Friends* finden Sie ganz hinten im Buch. Testaufgaben zum richtigen Gebrauch der *False Friends* enthält der *Checkpoint 3*, S. 138/139.

5   Wozu dienen die *Topic Boxes*?

In den *Topic Boxes* („Themenkästen") richtet sich das Augenmerk nicht nur auf mögliche Fehlerquellen. Hier finden Sie außerdem besonders häufige und nützliche Wendungen zu ausgewählten Themenbereichen wie *Talking about the Internet*, *Talking about times of the day* und *Greetings and wishes*.

Die Themen aller *Topic Boxes* finden Sie ganz vorn im Buch. Testaufgaben zum Gebrauch der Wendungen aus den *Topic Boxes* enthält der *Checkpoint 11*, S. 152/153.

a – an

1 Which combinations are correct?

A an honest person   B an hour   C an university   D a MP   E a VIP   F a US president

2 What is the rule?

A We use 'an' before a word or abbreviation that starts with 'a', 'e', 'i', 'o' or 'u'.

B We use 'an' before a word or abbreviation that starts with a vowel sound.

C The use of 'a' and 'an' depends on how a word is spelt.

abroad

1 A My sister lives abroad.   B My sister lives in abroad.   C My sister lives in the abroad.

2 How many people in this company are ...... ?

A from abroad   B from the abroad   C out of the abroad

acceptable

1 We need a solution which is ...... in the conflict.

A acceptable by all sides   B acceptable to all sides   C acceptable with all sides

accident

1 A Tony was badly injured by a car accident last year.

B Tony was badly injured in a car accident last year.

C Tony was badly injured at a car accident last year.

2 There was ...... on Brands Hill Avenue last night. Two people were badly injured.

A a heavy accident   B an earnest accident   C a serious accident   D a bad accident

accommodation

1 ...... for the two days of the festival.

A I need an accommodation   B I need accommodation

2 A Sorry, all accommodations have been booked up for months.

B Sorry, all accommodation have been booked up for months.

C Sorry, all accommodation has been booked up for months.

according to

1 ...... computer games are bad for you.

A According to my parents   B According to my parents' opinion

account

1 I've just paid €120 ....

A into my account   B onto my account   C to my account

2 I now have over €1000 ....

A in my account   B on my account   C at my account

accuse

1 ...... confidential documents.

A The police accused him to have stolen   B The police accused him for stealing

C The police accused him of stealing   D The police accused him that he had stolen

A

a – an ein, eine

■ *a* oder *an* – die Aussprache entscheidet

Entscheidend für die Wahl von *a* oder *an* ist nicht die Schreibung, sondern die Aussprache des folgenden Wortes: *An* steht vor Wörtern, die mit einem Vokallaut am Wortanfang ausgesprochen werden – auch wenn der erste (geschriebene) Buchstabe ein Konsonant ist.

  an update [ən_'ʌpdeɪt], *an hour* [ən_'aʊə]

Andererseits steht *a* vor Wörtern mit der Lautkombination [juː] am Anfang, also Wörtern, die mit dem Buchstaben *u* geschrieben, aber mit dem Anfangslaut [j] ausgesprochen werden.

  a university [ə juːnɪ'vɜːsəti]

Diese Regeln gelten auch für Abkürzungen.

  an MP3 player [ən_ˌempiː'θriː ˌpleɪə], *a UN official* [ə juːn_ə'fɪʃl]

abroad im Ausland, ins Ausland

■ ohne *the*

Abroad ist ein Adverb wie *home* („zu Hause"), kein Nomen wie das deutsche Wort „Ausland". Deshalb wird *abroad* ohne Artikel verwendet.

  go abroad, live abroad ● ● ● ins Ausland gehen, im Ausland leben
  be from abroad ● ● ● aus dem Ausland sein

acceptable [ək'septəbl] akzeptabel, annehmbar

■ *be acceptable to* sb. ● ● ● für jmdn. annehmbar sein

accident Unfall

■ *be hurt/injured in an accident* ● ● ● bei einem Unfall verletzt werden
  a bad/major/serious/fatal ['feɪtl] *accident* ● ● ● ein schlimmer/größerer/schwerer/tödlicher Unfall

accommodation Unterkunft, Unterkünfte

■ ohne *a/an*

Accommodation ist im BE ein nicht zählbares Nomen. Man kann es also nicht mit *a/an* oder im Plural verwenden. Im AE ist die Pluralform *accommodations* jedoch möglich.

  (some) accommodation (~~an accommodation~~) ● ● ● (eine) Unterkunft
  Most of our accommodation is / (AE auch:) *accommodations are self-catering.* ● ● ● Die meisten unserer Unterkünfte sind mit Selbstversorgung.

according to laut, nach

■ nicht vor *opinion/view*

According to bedeutet „laut/nach einer bestimmten Informationsquelle".

  according to the dictionary ● ● ● laut Wörterbuch, dem Wörterbuch zufolge

Man kann *according to* nicht mit *opinion* oder *view* („Ansicht") verwenden.

  according to Hanif (~~according to Hanif's opinion~~) ● ● ● laut Hanif, nach Hanifs Ansicht

account Konto

■ *have an account with a bank* ● ● ● Geld bei einer Bank haben
  have money in an account ● ● ● Geld auf einem Konto haben
  pay money into an account ● ● ● Geld auf ein Konto einzahlen
  take money out of an account ● ● ● Geld von einem Konto abheben

accuse beschuldigen, vorwerfen

■ *accuse* sb. *of doing*

Nach *accuse* verwendet man *of* + die *-ing*-Form des Verbs, keinen *to*-Infinitiv und keinen *that*-Satz.

  He accused me of lying. ● ● ● Er beschuldigte mich zu lügen / gelogen zu haben.

actual ≠ „aktuell"

1 What is the correct translation of 'the actual birthday' in the following sentence?
The actual birthday is two days later.

   A der diesjährige Geburtstag   **B** der eigentliche Geburtstag   **C** der offizielle Geburtstag

2 [Die aktuellen Ereignisse] going on in Sierra Leone are the main topic in today's paper.
   A The actual events   **B** The current events   **C** The up-to-date events

3 This play is [sehr aktuell].
   A very actual   **B** very current   **C** very topical

4 [Das aktuelle Problem] is different from the one we had recently.
   A The actual problem   **B** The current problem   **C** The up-to-date problem

5 I'm afraid the prices you were quoted are [nicht mehr aktuell].
   A no longer actual   **B** no longer topical   **C** no longer valid   **D** not up to date

additional – in addition to

1 Six more people have just arrived. ......
   A We need additional six chairs.
   B We need an additional six chairs.
   C We need six additional chairs.

2 They lent me their car – ....
   A in addition to pay my flight   **B** in addition to paying my flight

admire

1 It was very brave of her. I didn't like her before, ...
   A but now I admire her   **B** but now I'm admiring her

2 **A** I've always admired my English teacher for her patience.
   B I've always admired my English teacher about her patience.
   C I've always admired my English teacher on her patience.

admit

1 **A** Tony admitted his brother his weakness.
   B Tony admitted his weakness to his brother.
   C Tony admitted his weakness his brother.

2 After further questioning ....
   A one of the men admitted planning the break-in
   B one of the men admitted to plan the break-in
   C one of the men admitted to planning the break-in
   D one of the men admitted that he had planned the break-in

advantage

1 What is ...... to be interviewed?
   A the advantage being the last person   **B** the advantage in being the last person
   C the advantage to being the last person   **D** the advantage to be the last person

2 You will always ...... if you have a good knowledge of English.
   A be at an advantage   **B** be in an advantage   **C** be to an advantage   **D** be with an advantage

actual [ˈæktʃuəl] wirklich, tatsächlich; eigentlich

! ■ **False Friend!**
! *Actual* bedeutet nicht „~~aktuell~~", sondern „wirklich", „tatsächlich", „eigentlich", „genau".
!   *It's a huge complex, but the **actual** reactor is small.* ● ● ● ... aber der eigentliche Reaktor ...
!   *I know it was sometime in May, but what was the **actual** date?* ● ● ● ... das genaue Datum?
! Beachte die englischen Entsprechungen von „aktuell":
!   die aktuelle Lage [gegenwärtig] ● ● ● *the **current** situation*
!   ein aktuelles Thema/Theaterstück [gegenwartsbezogen, von aktuellem Interesse] ● ● ●
!   *a **topical** issue/play*
!   aktuelle Zahlen/Daten/Informationen [auf dem neuesten Stand] ● ● ● ***up-to-date** figures/*
!   *data/information*
!   nicht (mehr) aktuell sein [nicht (mehr) gültig] ● ● ● *be no longer **valid** / be not **up to date***

additional zusätzlich – in addition to außer, zusätzlich zu

■ *an additional* **+ Plural** ▸ **estimated** ▸ **extra**
Wenn man das Adjektiv *additional* vor einem Zahlwort + Nomen im Plural verwendet (z. B. *three spoons*), setzt man – widersinnigerweise – den Artikel *an* davor, ähnlich wie bei *another*.
  *We need **an additional three spoons** (= another three spoons)/**three additional spoons**.* ● ● ● Wir
    brauchen drei weitere Löffel / drei zusätzliche Löffel / noch drei Löffel.

■ *in addition to doing*
In addition to ist eine zusammengesetzte Präposition. Ein Verb nach *in addition to* steht in der
-*ing*-Form, nicht im Infinitiv.
  ***In addition to doing** all the housework, the au pair also had to cut the grass.* ● ● ● Zusätzlich zu /
    Neben der ganzen Hausarbeit musste das Aupairmädchen auch noch den Rasen schneiden.

admire bewundern

■ **nicht in der Verlaufsform**
Admire wird normalerweise nicht in der Verlaufsform verwendet.
  *I really **admire** your work.* ● ● ● Ich bewundere Ihre Arbeit wirklich sehr.
Die Verlaufsform ist nur in der Bedeutung „bewundernd anschauen" möglich.
  *I **was** just **admiring** this painting.* ● ● ● Ich habe gerade dieses Bild bewundert.

■ *admire* sb. *for their skill* ● ● ● jmdn. wegen seiner Geschicklichkeit bewundern

admit zugeben, gestehen

■ *admit sth. to sb.*
Nach *admit* wird die Person, der man etwas gesteht, mit *to* angeschlossen.
  *admit sth. **to** your best friend* ● ● ● dem besten Freund etwas gestehen

■ *admit (to) doing / admit that …*
Ein Verb nach *admit* steht in der -*ing*-Form, wahlweise mit *to* davor („sich zu etwas bekennen").
  admit (to) breaking the window ● ● ● zugeben, dass man das Fenster zerbrochen hat
Ein *that*-Satz ist auch möglich, aber kein *to*-Infinitiv.
  *He **admitted that** he **had broken** the window.* ● ● ● Er gab zu, dass er das Fenster zerbrochen hatte.

advantage Vorteil

■ *advantage of/in doing*
Nach *advantage* verwendet man *of/in* + die -*ing*-Form des Verbs, keinen *to*-Infinitiv.
  *What are the **advantages of speaking** English?* ● ● ● Welche Vorteile hat man, wenn man …?
  *Is there any **advantage in getting** there early?* ● ● ● Bringt es was, früh da zu sein?
Ausnahme: Sätze, in denen der Infinitiv eine Subjektergänzung zu „leerem" *it* bildet.
  *It's an **advantage to know** the area.* ● ● ● Es ist von Vorteil, die Gegend zu kennen.

■ *be at an advantage (over sb.)* ● ● ● (jmdm. gegenüber) im Vorteil sein

advice – advise

1
  A What is your advice? What do you advice me to do?
  B What is your advice? What do you advise me to do?
  C What is your advise? What do you advice me to do?

2 The guidebook has …… for young travellers.
  A good advices **B** good advice **C** some good advice **D** some good pieces of advice

3 …… Whoever it was wasn't very well informed.
  A Whose advice did you do this at?
  B Whose advice did you do this from?
  C Whose advice did you do this on?

4
  A We don't advise take large amounts of cash.
  B We don't advise taking large amounts of cash.
  C We don't advise to take large amounts of cash.

5
  A We don't advise you taking large amounts of cash.
  B We don't advise you to take large amounts of cash.
  C We don't advise you to taking large amounts of cash.

6
  A I advise against to try to climb the mountain in this weather.
  B I advise against trying to climb the mountain in this weather.
  C I advise you against trying to climb the mountain in this weather.
  D I advise you not to try to climb the mountain in this weather.

7
  A He was advised to wear a suit for the interview, not jeans.
  B Him was advised to wear a suit for the interview, not jeans.
  C It was advised him to wear a suit for the interview, not jeans.

afraid: be afraid – frightened

1 The camps were full of ……
  A afraid refugees. Many were afraid that there would be further attacks.
  B frightened refugees. Many were afraid that there would be further attacks.
  C frightened refugees. Many were frightened that there would be further attacks.
  D afraid refugees. Many were frightened that there would be further attacks.

2 Have the results been put on the website yet? – ……
  A I'm afraid no. **B** I'm afraid not. **C** I'm not afraid so.

3 …… in case I say the wrong thing.
  A I'm afraid at opening my mouth
  B I'm afraid of opening my mouth
  C I'm afraid to open my mouth

4
  A I'm always afraid at losing my passport.
  B I'm always afraid of losing my passport.
  C I'm always afraid to lose my passport.

after all – after all that

1 Shall I call a taxi? ……
  A After all, it's late, and it's raining too. **B** After all that it's late, and it's raining too.

2 I worked hard all weekend, learning vocabulary, revising grammar, re-reading my notes, learning quotations by heart. ……
  A And then, after all, the test was cancelled because the teacher was ill.
  B And then, after all that, the test was cancelled because the teacher was ill.

advice [əd'vaɪs] Rat, Ratschlag – advise [əd'vaɪz] raten

■ **Nomen *advice* – Verb *advise***
Advice (mit „c") ist das Nomen („Rat"); *advise* (mit „s") ist das Verb („raten").

■ **nicht zählbares Nomen**
Advice ist ein nicht zählbares Nomen. Man kann es also nicht mit *a/an* oder im Plural verwenden.
  *(some) good **advice** (~~a good advice, some good advices~~)* ● ● ● ein guter Rat / gute Ratschläge
  *a good **piece of advice*** ● ● ● ein guter Rat(schlag)

■ **get *advice* about/on sth.** ● ● ● Rat über/zu etwas einholen
  *do sth. **on** sb.'s **advice*** ● ● ● etwas auf jmds. Rat hin tun

■ ***advise doing* – *advise <u>sb.</u> to do***
Wenn man die Person, der etwas geraten bzw. von etwas abgeraten wird, **nicht** nennt, verwendet man *advise (against)* + die *-ing*-Form des Verbs.
  *We **advise booking** early.* ● ● ● Wir raten dazu, früh zu buchen.
  *They **advised against coming** by car.* ● ● ● Sie haben davon abgeraten, mit dem Auto zu kommen.
Wenn man die Person nennt, verwendet man *advise* + Personenobjekt + *to*-Infinitiv.
  *They have **advised us to book** early / **advised us not to come** by car.* ● ● ● Sie haben uns geraten, früh zu buchen / nicht mit dem Auto zu kommen.

■ **Passiv mit persönlichem Subjekt**
Advise ist ein normales transitives Verb, also auch im Passiv möglich.
  *We **were advised** to wear a helmet.* ● ● ● Uns wurde geraten, einen Helm zu tragen.

afraid: be* afraid Angst haben, sich fürchten – frightened verängstigt

■ *Afraid* gehört zu den wenigen Adjektiven, die nur prädikativ, also nach einem Verb wie *be*, verwendet werden können.
  *The passengers **were afraid**.* ● ● ● Die Passagiere hatten Angst.

■ *Frightened* kann sowohl prädikativ verwendet werden als auch vor einem Nomen stehen.
  *The passengers **were frightened**.*
  *the **frightened** passengers (~~the afraid passengers~~)* ● ● ● die verängstigten Passagiere

■ ***I'm afraid so* / *I'm afraid not***
Die kurze Antwort *I'm afraid* im Sinne von „leider" verwendet man mit *so/not*, nicht mit *yes/no*.
  *Has Ann phoned yet? – **I'm afraid not**.* ● ● ● Hat Ann schon angerufen? – Leider nicht/nein.

■ ***afraid to do* – *afraid of doing***
Sowohl *afraid to do* als auch *afraid of doing* drücken aus, dass jemand etwas nicht machen will, weil er/sie unangenehme oder gefährliche Folgen befürchtet und diese vermeiden will.
  *I'm **afraid to drive** / **afraid of driving** fast in this icy weather.*
Nur *afraid of doing* kann verwendet werden, wenn man von etwas spricht, was einem ungewollt zustoßen kann, wie z. B. ein Unfall.
  *I'm **afraid of having** an accident. (~~I'm afraid to have an accident.~~)*

after all doch, schließlich, immerhin – after all that nach alledem, und dann   ▶ last: at last

■ *After all* bedeutet nicht „nach allem", sondern „doch", „schließlich (doch)", „immerhin".
  *The match was cancelled, but now it's going to take place **after all**.* ● ● ● Das Spiel wurde abgesagt, aber nun findet es (schließlich) doch statt.
  *I think we should go by coach. It is, **after all**, a lot cheaper.* ● ● ● … Schließlich/Immerhin ist es viel billiger.

■ Mit *after all that* sagt man, was nach einer Reihe von Ereignissen eintrat. Oft wird damit ein krönender Abschluss oder Höhepunkt beschrieben, der etwas verhindert oder zunichte macht.
  *We missed the bus, called a taxi, then got stuck in traffic and had to run the last 300 metres in the rain. And **after all that**, the concert had been cancelled.* ● ● ● … Und dann war das Konzert auch noch abgesagt worden.

against

1 I'm not going to vote for them. ......
  A They're against spending more on education.
  B They're against to spend more on education.

2 A I've always been against people cheating in exams.
  B I've always been against people to cheat in exams.
  C I've always been against that people cheat in exams.

3 I never take .... I wait till it gets better on its own.
  A medicine against a cold   B medicine for a cold   C medicine to a cold

4 The driver took the bend too fast ...... coming the other way.
  A and crashed against a bus   B and crashed in a bus
  C and crashed into a bus   D and crashed with a bus

5 This blouse is a little too small. ......
  A Can I exchange it against a larger size, please?   B Can I exchange it for a larger size, please?
  C Can I exchange it to a larger size, please?   D Can I exchange it with a larger size, please?

6 Let's meet this afternoon, ...
  A about five o'clock   B around five o'clock   C against five o'clock   D towards five o'clock

age

1 ...... What do you think?
  A What age has this building?   B What age is this building?

2 A At what age can you take your driving test in this country? – At 17.
  B In what age can you take your driving test in this country? – In the age of 17 years.
  C With what age can you take your driving test in this country? – With 17 years.

3 How old is the missing girl? – ......
  A She's 18.   B She's 18 years.   C She's 18 years of age.   D She's 18 years old.

ago

1 My grandmother died ....
  A ago two years   B before two years   C two years ago

2 This castle doesn't look very old. ......
  A Before how long was it built?
  B How long ago was it built?
  C How long was it built ago?

3 I was just too late. ......
  A They had sold the last remaining tickets before two minutes.
  B They had sold the last remaining tickets two minutes ago.
  C They had sold the last remaining tickets two minutes before.

agree

1 I'm sorry, ...
  A but I can't agree to you   B but I can't agree with you

2 Before we finish, ... for our next meeting.
  A we must agree at a date   B we must agree on a date   C we must agree to a date

A

against gegen

■ *against doing*

Against ist eine Präposition. Darauf folgt ein Verb als *-ing*-Form, nicht als Infinitiv. Es ist auch nicht möglich, einen *that*-Satz anzuschließen.

I'm **against building** a new airport. ● ● ● Ich bin dagegen, einen neuen Flughafen zu bauen.
I'm **against them building** it. ● ● ● Ich bin dagegen, dass sie ihn bauen.

Trouble Spot

■ **gegen**

ein Mittel gegen eine Krankheit ● ● ● *a cure/remedy* ['remədi] **for** *an illness*
gegen etwas fahren/krachen/stoßen ● ● ● *drive/crash/knock* **into** *sth.*
etwas gegen etwas tauschen ● ● ● *exchange/swap sth.* **for** *sth.*
gegen … Uhr [Uhrzeit] ● ● ● *(at)* **about/around** *… o'clock*
gegen Morgen/Mittag/… [Tageszeit] ● ● ● **towards** *morning/midday/…*

age Alter

Topic Box

■ *Talking about age* ▷ **old**

How old are you? / What age are you? ● ● ● Wie alt bist du?
How old is this building? / What age is this building? (~~What age has this building?~~) ● ● ● Wie alt ist dieses Gebäude?
He's 19 (years old). / He's 19 years of age. (~~He's 19 years.~~) ● ● ● Er ist 19 (Jahre / Jahre alt).
They are the same age. ● ● ● Sie sind gleichaltrig / gleich alt.
Wait till you're my age. ● ● ● Warte, bis du in meinem Alter bist / bis du so alt bist wie ich.
people (of) your age ● ● ● Leute deines Alters / in deinem Alter
at the age of 20 ● ● ● im Alter von 20 (Jahren)
at (age) 20 ● ● ● mit 20 (Jahren)
at your age ● ● ● in deinem Alter
a boy of 14 / a 14-year-old boy ● ● ● ein Junge von 14 / ein 14-jähriger Junge
girls aged 6 to 10 ● ● ● Mädchen im Alter von 6 bis 10
live to (fml:) a great age / (infml:) a ripe old age (~~a high age~~) ● ● ● ein hohes Alter erreichen

ago vor

■ *ago + past tense*

Ago wird mit dem *past tense* verwendet.

He **died** two years **ago**. ● ● ● Er starb vor zwei Jahren. / Er ist vor zwei Jahren gestorben.

■ **Stellung: nach der Zeitbestimmung**

Ago steht auch in einer Frage am Ende der Zeitbestimmung.

How long **ago** did you find out? ● ● ● Vor wie langer Zeit …? / Wie lang ist es her, dass …?

■ *ago – before*

Ago bedeutet „von jetzt zurückgerechnet". Wenn man von einem vergangenen Zeitpunkt zurückrechnet, verwendet man das *past perfect* mit *before*.

We got to the station at 10.07. The train **had left** on time at 10.05, two minutes **before** (~~ago~~).

agree zustimmen, übereinstimmen, sich einigen

■ **agree about** *the need for action* ● ● ● sich einig sein über die Notwendigkeit zu handeln
agree on *a date* ● ● ● sich auf ein Datum einigen
agree to *a proposal* ● ● ● einem Vorschlag zustimmen
agree with *sb.* ● ● ● jmdm. zustimmen, mit jmdm. übereinstimmen
agree with *sb.'s analysis* ● ● ● jmds. Analyse zustimmen, mit jmds. Analyse einverstanden sein

aim

1 Which is the generally accepted form?
She booked an intensive language course ....
   A with the aim of improving her speaking skills
   B with the aim to improve her speaking skills

alike – similar

1 A Supermarkets are very much alike all over the world.
   B Supermarkets are very much like all over the world.
   C Supermarkets are very similar all over the world.

2 The language schools all have ...... for their summer courses.
   A alike programmes   B similar programmes   C same programmes

alive – living

1 A Who is the greatest alive writer?
   B Who is the greatest writer alive today?
   C Who is the greatest living writer?

all

1 I had a wonderful trip. ......
   A All people I met were extremely friendly.
   B All the people I met were extremely friendly.
   C All of the people I met were extremely friendly.

2 A The apartments all have a balcony.
   B The apartments have all a balcony.
   C The apartments have all of them a balcony.

3 ...... She's great.
   A All of us like our new teacher.   B We all like our new teacher.   C We like all our new teacher.

4 A I've copied all the seven hundred pages. All of them.
   B I've copied the seven hundred pages all. All of them.
   C I've copied all the seven hundred pages. All.

5 There was a snowstorm, ...
   A and all in my class were late for school
   B and everyone in my class was late for school
   C and everybody in my class were late for school

6 The festival takes place [alljährlich im August].
   A all years in August   B every year in August   C every one year in August

7 There was a hole in the tent [und alles wurde nass].
   A and all got wet   B and anything got wet   C and everything got wet

aim Ziel, Absicht

A

■ **with the aim of doing**

With the aim verwendet man in der Regel mit *of* + der *-ing*-Form des Verbs.

*I went to London **with the aim of finding** a job.* ● ● ● … mit dem Ziel / um eine Stelle zu finden.

■ *work hard to **achieve** one's aims* ● ● ● hart arbeiten, um seine Ziele zu erreichen

alike – similar ähnlich

■ *Alike* gehört zu den wenigen Adjektiven, die nur prädikativ, also nach einem Verb wie *be*, verwendet werden können.

*The two brothers **are** very much **alike**.* ● ● ● Die beiden Brüder sind sich sehr ähnlich.

■ *Similar* kann sowohl prädikativ verwendet werden als auch vor einem Nomen stehen.

*The two brothers **are** very **similar**.* ● ● ● Die beiden Brüder sind sich sehr ähnlich.

*They have **similar tastes** in music.* ● ● ● Sie haben einen ähnlichen Musikgeschmack.

alive [ə'laɪv] am Leben, lebendig – living ['lɪvɪŋ] lebend

■ *Alive* gehört zu den wenigen Adjektiven, die nur prädikativ, also nach einem Verb wie *be*, verwendet werden können.

***Is** he still **alive**? I thought he died several years ago.* ● ● ● Lebt er noch? …

■ Vor einem Nomen kann man nur das Adjektiv *living* („lebend") verwenden.

*the world's greatest **living guitarist** [= the world's greatest guitarist (who is) alive now]*

all alle

■ **all (of) the**

Vor einem Nomen muss man *all* mit *(of) the* verwenden, wenn „alle aus einer bestimmten Anzahl" gemeint ist. Vergleiche:

***All babies** drink milk.* [ganz generell] ● ● ● Alle Babys trinken Milch.

***All (of) the babies** in the photo are crying.* [aus einer bestimmten Gruppe] ● ● ● Alle Babys auf dem Foto schreien.

■ **all of us / you / them**

Vor einem Personalpronomen muss die Form *all of* verwendet werden.

***All of us** (= We all) like pop music.* ● ● ● Wir alle mögen Popmusik.

Zum Rückbezug auf zuvor genannte Personen oder Sachen verwendet man *all of them*.

*We met **lots of people**. **All of them** spoke English.* ● ● ● … Alle sprachen Englisch.

*I phoned **eight hotels**. **All of them** were full.* ● ● ● … Alle waren voll / ausgebucht.

■ **Wortstellung**

Die Stellung von *all* ist sehr flexibel und oft wie im Deutschen.

***All (of) the shops** were shut. / The shops were **all** shut. / They were **all** shut. / **All of them** were shut.*

Beachte aber folgende Unterschiede zum Deutschen:

1 Wenn *all* dem Subjekt nachgestellt wird, steht es **vor** (nicht hinter!) einem Vollverb.

*The patients **all need** rest.* ● ● ● Die Patienten brauchen alle Ruhe.

*They **all need** rest.* ● ● ● Sie brauchen alle Ruhe.

2 Wenn *all* zum Objekt gehört, kann es nur **vor** einem Nomen stehen (nicht wahlweise auch dahinter!).

*I answered **all the questions** (the questions all).* ● ● ● Ich habe alle Fragen beantwortet. / Ich habe die Fragen alle beantwortet.

Trouble Spot

■ **alle**

Alle brauchen ein Visum. ● ● ● ***Everybody / Everyone needs*** [Singular!] *a visa.*

Die Busse fahren alle zehn Minuten. ● ● ● *The buses go **every** ten minutes.*

■ **alles**

Alles ist fertig. Wir können beginnen. ● ● ● ***Everything** is ready. We can begin.*

Ich bin zu allem [= egal was] bereit. ● ● ● *I'm ready for **anything**.*

allow – permit

1 In the maths exam, ... ?
   A do they allow to use a calculator
   B do they allow that you use a calculator
   C do they allow you to use a calculator

2 A It is not allowed to take bags into the museum.
   B It is not permitted to take bags into the museum.
   C You are not allowed to take bags into the museum.
   D People are not permitted to take bags into the museum.

alone – on my own / by myself

1 ...... Honestly, nobody helped me.
   A I did all the research for the project alone.
   B I did all the research for the project by myself.
   C I did all the research for the project on my own.

2 We received over 1000 emails [allein in den ersten drei Stunden].
   A alone in the first three hours
   B only in the first three hours
   C in the first three hours alone

already

1 Which is the best position for 'already'?
   A Already last Monday we had over 30 offers of help.
   B Last Monday we already had over 30 offers of help.
   C Last Monday already we had over 30 offers of help.

2 I've told my parents. ......
   A Have you told **your** parents already?   B Have you told **your** parents yet?

3 I'm still looking for a weekend job. ......
   A Pamela already found one – at the Western Hotel.
   B Pamela has already found one – at the Western Hotel.
   C Pamela had already found one – at the Western Hotel.

4 [Schon nach zwei Wochen] I knew that French was not my best choice of subjects.
   A Already after two weeks   B After only two weeks   C As early as two weeks

5 The noise of traffic wakes you [schon um fünf].
   A already at five   B as early as five   C even at five

6 We should hear the results [schon bald].
   A already soon   B very soon

7 [Schon in den achtziger Jahren] there were warnings about this terrorist group.
   A Already in the eighties   B As soon as the eighties   C As long ago as the eighties

8 [Schon damals] people knew that oil would not last for ever.
   A Already then   B Then already   C Even then

A

allow – permit erlauben, gestatten

■ **kein *that*-Satz nach *allow***

Nach *allow* verwendet man ein Personenobjekt + *to*-Infinitiv *(allow sb. to do)*, keinen *that*-Satz.
Das Personenobjekt darf nicht weggelassen werden.

> They **allow you to use** a dictionary (~~allow that you use a dictionary~~). ● ● ● Sie erlauben, dass man
> ein Wörterbuch benutzt. / Sie erlauben einem, ein Wörterbuch zu benutzen.

■ ***it is not permitted – it is not allowed***

„Leeres" *it* kann nur Subjekt von *be permitted* sein, nicht von *be allowed*.

> **It isn't permitted** to take photos. (~~It isn't allowed to take photos.~~) = **You** / **People aren't permitted** /
> **aren't allowed** to take photos. ● ● ● Es ist nicht gestattet/erlaubt zu fotografieren.

It is (not) allowed ist nur möglich, wenn *it* sich auf etwas zuvor Genanntes bezieht.

> **Smoking** is forbidden. **It** [= smoking] **isn't allowed** anywhere in the building. ● ● ● Rauchen ist
> verboten. Es ist an keinem Ort in diesem Gebäude erlaubt.

alone – on my own / by myself allein

■ *Alone* bedeutet „allein" im Sinne von „ohne Anwesenheit/Begleitung anderer".

> She lives **alone**. ● ● ● Sie lebt allein.

■ In der Bedeutung „ohne Hilfe anderer" verwendet man *on my own, on your own* usw. oder
by myself, by yourself usw.

> Who helped you? – Nobody. I solved the problem **on my own** / **by myself**. ● ● ● … Ich habe
> das Problem (ganz) allein gelöst.

■ **Stellung von *alone* bei Emphase**

Wenn man *alone* zur Betonung verwendet, steht es hinter dem Satzteil, auf den es sich bezieht.

> I've lost four kilos **in the last two weeks alone**. ● ● ● Allein in den letzten zwei Wochen …

already schon

■ **nicht direkt neben anderen Zeitbestimmungen**

Already sollte normalerweise nicht direkt neben eine andere Zeitbestimmung gestellt werden.

> **Ten years ago** people had **already** realized that … (~~Already ten years ago …~~) ● ● ● Schon vor zehn
> Jahren …

■ **nicht in Fragen**

In Fragen wird *yet* (nicht *already*) verwendet – außer wenn die Antwort *yes* erwartet wird.

> Are you ready **yet**? ● ● ● Bist du (schon) fertig?

Eine Frage mit *already* drückt oft Überraschung aus.

> Have you spent all that money **already**? ● ● ● Hast du das ganze Geld etwa schon ausgegeben?

■ **mit *present perfect* und *simple past***

Already verwendet man sowohl mit dem *present perfect* als auch mit dem *simple past*.
Der Gebrauch mit dem *simple past* findet sich überwiegend im AE.

> Toby **has already arrived**. (überwiegend BE) ● ● ● Toby ist schon angekommen / ist schon da.
> Toby **already arrived**. (überwiegend AE)

■ **schon**

> Es wird schon um vier Uhr hell. ● ● ● It gets light **as early as** four o'clock.
> Schon im Jahre 1928 / im 16. Jahrhundert … ● ● ● **As long ago as** 1928 / the 16th century …
> Du wirst dich schon bald besser fühlen. ● ● ● You'll feel better **very soon**.
> Schon als wir ankamen, fiel er mir auf. ● ● ● I noticed him **as soon as** we arrived.
> Schon bevor das Spiel anfing … ● ● ● **Even before** the match started …
> Schon jetzt/damals … ● ● ● **Even now** / **then** …
> Schon nach wenigen Wochen … ● ● ● **After only** a few weeks …

Unbetontes „schon" hat oft keine Entsprechung im Englischen.

> Ich bin schon neugierig, was sie sagen wird. ● ● ● **I'm curious** what she will say.
> Ich komme schon. ● ● ● **I'm coming.**

Trouble Spot

also – too

1 Which is the best position for 'also'?

  A I've phoned Derek, and also I've spoken to Cathy.

  B I've phoned Derek, and I've also spoken to Cathy.

  C I've phoned Derek, and I've spoken also to Cathy.

2 **A** I love London. – I also.   **B** I love London. – I too.

  C I love London. – Me also.   **D** I love London. – Me too.

3 **A** I don't drink alcohol. And I don't also smoke.

  B I don't drink alcohol. And I don't smoke too.

  C I don't drink alcohol. And I don't smoke either.

4 **A** We don't have an English lesson on Monday. – We don't too.

  B We don't have an English lesson on Monday. – Nor do we.

  C We don't have an English lesson on Monday. – Neither don't we.

5 ...... found the test difficult.

  A Also the best students   **B** Even the best students   **C** Too the best students

alternative

1 My computer crashed and I lost all the data. ......

  A There was no alternative to start all over again.

  B There was no alternative to starting all over again.

altogether – all together

1 **A** This is a completely different problem all together.

  B This is a completely different problem altogether.

2 After we leave school, it'll be a long time ....

  A before we're all together again   **B** before we're altogether again

always

1 Which is the best position for 'always'?

  A I always check my emails when I get home.

  B I check always my emails when I get home.

  C I check my emails always when I get home.

2 Which is more likely: A or B?

It's not that I'm a careless person, ... I don't lose other things.

  A but somehow I'm always losing my keys   **B** but somehow I always lose my keys

3 In the height of the summer, ...

  A the farmworkers always got up at 4.30   **B** the farmworkers were always getting up at 4.30

also – too auch

■ Stellung

Also steht normalerweise in der Satzmitte, d. h. vor einem Vollverb.

*I surf and I **also** play tennis.* ● ● ● Ich surfe und ich spiele auch Tennis.

■ also – too

In Befehlssätzen und Kurzantworten verwendet man *too*. *Also* wirkt in solchen Sätzen unnatürlich oder ist nicht akzeptabel.

*Give me his email address **too**, please.* ● ● ● Gib mir bitte auch seine E-Mail-Adresse.

*I hate maths. – Me **too**.* ● ● ● Ich hasse Mathe. – Ich auch.

*I need a break. – I do **too**. / So do I.* ● ● ● Ich brauche eine Pause. – Ich auch.

Trouble Spot

■ auch

1 Emma findet Ed blöd. Ich mag ihn auch nicht. ● ● ● *Emma thinks Ed's stupid. I **don't** like him **either**.*

Wir essen mittags nicht warm. – Wir auch nicht. ● ● ● *We don't have a hot meal at lunchtime. – **Neither/Nor do** we.*

Wir essen abends warm. – Wir auch. ● ● ● *We have a hot meal in the evening. – **So do** we.*

2 Auch [= Selbst] die Lehrer protestierten. ● ● ● ***Even** the teachers protested.*

Auch wenn es schwer ist, gib nicht auf. ● ● ● ***Even if** it's hard, don't give up.*

alternative [ɔːlˈtɜːnətɪv] Alternative

■ alternative to (doing) sth.

Auf *alternative* folgt die Präposition *to*.

*seek an **alternative to** nuclear power* ● ● ● eine Alternative zur Atomkraft suchen

Verwendet man nach diesem *to* ein Verb, so steht es in der *-ing*-Form.

*What's the **alternative to building** (the alternative to build) nuclear power plants?* ● ● ● Welche Alternative gibt es zum Bau von Atomkraftwerken?

altogether völlig, ganz und gar; insgesamt – all together alle zusammen

■ *Altogether* bedeutet „völlig", „ganz und gar" oder „insgesamt".

*I don't **altogether** agree with you.* ● ● ● Ich bin nicht ganz Ihrer Meinung.

Es steht **hinter** einer Zahl oder Summe.

*We spent over £300 **altogether**.* ● ● ● Wir haben insgesamt über 300 £ ausgegeben.

■ *All together* (zwei Wörter!) bedeutet „alle zusammen".

*We don't go on holiday **all together** any more.* ● ● ● Wir fahren nicht mehr alle zusammen in Urlaub.

always immer, ständig

■ Stellung

Always steht in der Satzmitte, d. h. vor einem Vollverb, aber nach *be*.

*I **always** read (I read always) the sports page.* ● ● ● Ich lese immer die Sportseite.

■ always + einfache Form des Verbs

In der Bedeutung „immer" [= jedes Mal, die ganze Zeit] steht *always* mit der einfachen Form des Verbs.

*I **always** sleep late on Sundays.* ● ● ● Ich schlafe sonntags immer aus.

*When I was small, it **always** seemed to rain on my birthday.* ● ● ● … schien es … immer zu regnen.

*I **always** thought you had children.* ● ● ● Ich habe immer gedacht, du hättest Kinder.

■ always + Verlaufsform

In der Bedeutung „ständig" [= zu oft, überraschend oft] steht *always* mit der Verlaufsform des Verbs.

*He's hopeless. He's **always losing** something.* ● ● ● … Ständig verliert er etwas.

*They got divorced. They **were always arguing** about something or other.* ● ● ● … Sie haben sich ständig über irgendetwas gestritten.

a.m. – p.m.

1 What time is the meeting? – ......

   A At 10.30 a.m.   **B** At half past ten.   **C** At half past ten in the morning.   **D** At half past ten a.m.

2 The best train is ....

   A at 13.43   **B** at 13.43 p.m.   **C** at 1.43 p.m.

ambulance ≠ „Ambulanz"

1 An ambulance is ....

   A a department in a hospital where sick people stay

   B a room in a doctor's practice

   C a vehicle for transporting sick people

2 *[Die Ambulanz]* was so full, I had to wait over an hour before I was seen by a doctor.

   A A & E   **B** The ambulance   **C** The ambulance department

amount

1 It won't take ....

   A a big amount of time or money   **B** a large amount of time or money

   C a huge amount of time or money   **D** a tremendous amount of time or money

angry

1 ...... They said they would never let me have another party at home.

   A My parents were so angry at me.   **B** My parents were so angry on me.

   C My parents were so angry over me.   **D** My parents were so angry with me.

annoyed

1 The builders made a real mess. ......

   A I was really annoyed at what they had done.

   B I was really annoyed on what they had done.

   C I was really annoyed over what they had done.

   D I was really annoyed with what they had done.

answer

1 ...... , I am pleased to tell you that we still have three vacancies.

   A As answer at your enquiry   **B** As an answer to your enquiry

   C In answer on your enquiry   **D** In answer to your enquiry

apologize/apologise

1 ...... It was our fault entirely.

   A We really must apologize to you because of what happened.

   B We really must apologize to you for what happened.

   C We really must apologize you because of what happened.

   D We really must apologize you for what happened.

2 **A** I apologize for keeping you waiting.

   B I apologize for that I kept you waiting.

   C I apologize to keep you waiting.

a.m. Uhr morgens/vormittags – p.m. Uhr nachmittags/abends

■ Bedeutung

a.m. (im BE oft auch ohne Punkt: *am*) steht für den lateinischen Ausdruck *ante meridiem* und bedeutet „vor Mittag"; *p.m./pm* steht für *post meridiem* und bedeutet „nach Mittag".

■ wann man *a.m.* und *p.m.* nicht verwenden kann

a.m. und *p.m.* werden nur mit Stundenangaben zwischen 1 und 12 verwendet: „15.00 Uhr" wird z. B. als *3.00 p.m.* oder (in Fahrplänen usw.) *15.00* wiedergegeben, nicht aber als *15.00 p.m.* *a.m.* und *p.m.* verwendet man nur mit „nackten" Zahlen, also nicht in Verbindung mit *o'clock/past/to/minutes*.

> *It's 6.00 a.m.* / *It's 6.23 a.m.* / *It's 6.40 a.m.*
> *It's 6 o'clock.* / *It's twenty-three minutes past six.* / *It's twenty to seven (in the morning).*

ambulance ['æmbjələns] Krankenwagen

■ False Friend!

Ambulance bedeutet nicht „~~Ambulanz~~", sondern „Krankenwagen".

> *The police arrived at the scene of the accident before the **ambulance.*** ● ● ● D Polizei war vor dem Krankenwagen an der Unfallstelle.

Beachte die englischen Entsprechungen von „Ambulanz" und „ambulant":

> Samstagabends ist die Ambulanz voll mit Betrunkenen. ● ● ● *On Saturday evenings* (BE:) ***A & E** [= the accident and emergency department]* / (AE:) ***the ER** [= the emergency room] is full of drunks.*
> Ich wurde ambulant behandelt. ● ● ● *I was treated **as an outpatient.***

amount Menge

> ■ *a **large**/**great**/**small** amount (~~a big~~/~~little amount~~) of gold* ● ● ● eine große/kleine Menge Gold
> *a **considerable** amount of money* ● ● ● eine beträchtliche Summe Geld
> *a **tremendous** amount of money* ● ● ● eine ungeheuer große Summe Geld
> ***huge** amounts of data* ● ● ● riesige Datenmengen

angry böse, ärgerlich

> ■ *be **angry with** sb.* ● ● ● auf jmdn. böse sein, jmdm. böse sein
> *be **angry at** the delay* ● ● ● ärgerlich sein wegen der / über die Verspätung

annoyed verärgert, ärgerlich

> ■ *be **annoyed with** sb.* ● ● ● sich über jmdn. ärgern
> *be **annoyed at** the delay* ● ● ● sich über die Verspätung ärgern

answer Antwort

> ■ ***In answer to** your criticism ...* ● ● ● Als Antwort auf Ihre Kritik ...

apologize / (BE auch:) apologise sich entschuldigen

■ nicht reflexiv

> *Why should I **apologize** (~~apologize myself~~)?* ● ● ● Warum soll ich mich entschuldigen?

■ *apologize to sb. for (doing) sth.*

Nach *apologize* wird die Person, bei der man sich entschuldigt, mit *to* angeschlossen. Der Umstand, für den man sich entschuldigt, wird mit *for* angeschlossen.

> *He **apologized to** his girlfriend **for** his mistake (~~because of his mistake~~).* ● ● ● Er entschuldigte sich bei seiner Freundin für seinen Fehler.

Ein Verb nach *apologize for* steht in der *-ing*-Form. Ein *that*-Satz ist nicht möglich.

> *He **apologized for being** late (~~apologized that he was late~~).* ● ● ● Er entschuldigte sich (dafür), dass er zu spät kam. / Er entschuldigte sich für sein Zuspätkommen.

appear

1 After all the discussions, ... that they don't have enough money for the project anyway.
  A it's now appearing   B it now appears

2 ...... than a generation ago.
  A Today's candidates appear more realistic   B Today's candidates appear more realistically

appetite

1 It smells delicious. *[Guten Appetit]*, everybody!
  A Bon appétit   B Good appetite   C Eat well

apply

1 ...... , and got three interviews.
  A Janet applied at four jobs   B Janet applied by four jobs
  C Janet applied for four jobs   D Janet applied to four jobs

approach

1 ...... , step by step, with their hands on their guns.
  A The cowboys approached each other slowly
  B The cowboys approached to each other slowly
  C The cowboys approached towards each other slowly

argue

1 A What are you two arguing about again?   B What are you two arguing at again?
  C What are you two arguing on again?   D What are you two arguing with again?

arms – weapons

1 They expected to find ...... in Iraq.
  A arms of mass destruction   B weapons of mass destruction

2 The judge asked the witness if she could identify ....
  A the murder arm   B the murder weapon

army

1 In this country young people don't have to ....
  A serve any time at the army   B serve any time by the army   C serve any time in the army

arrange

1 The articles at a flea market are not ...... or size or in any other order.
  A arranged after price   B arranged by price   C arranged from price   D arranged in price

arrest

1 Seven people have been arrested ....
  A because of planning a terrorist attack   B concerning planning a terrorist attack
  C for planning a terrorist attack   D to plan a terrorist attack

appear erscheinen; scheinen

■ In der Bedeutung „auftauchen", „in Sicht kommen" kann *appear* in der Verlaufsform stehen und mit einem *-ly*-Adverb verwendet werden.

> *The first signs of spring **were appearing** in the garden.* ● ● ● Die ersten Frühlingsboten tauchten im Garten auf.
> *An arm **appeared slowly** out of the hole, then a head.* ● ● ● Langsam kam aus dem Loch ein Arm, dann ein Kopf in Sicht.

■ In der übertragenen Bedeutung „den Anschein haben" ist der Gebrauch der Verlaufsform und die Kombination mit einem *-ly*-Adverb nicht möglich.

> *It now **appears** that the minister wasn't telling the truth.* ● ● ● Es hat jetzt den Anschein, als …
> *The game **appears easy**, but it is in fact very difficult.* ● ● ● Das Spiel scheint leicht zu sein …

appetite ['æpɪtaɪt] Appetit

■ **kein *Good appetite* als Tischgruß**

In Restaurants wünscht die Bedienung *Enjoy your meal*. Im privaten Kreis sagt man vor dem Essen *Bon appétit* oder verwendet einen Satz wie *Please start. / Don't wait. / Don't let it get cold. / Has everybody got everything?*

Good appetite findet man nur in Kontexten wie dem folgenden:

> *He **has a good appetite**.* ● ● ● Er hat einen guten [= kräftigen] Appetit.

apply sich bewerben

■ *He **applied to** an EU organization **for** a scholarship.* ● ● ● Er bewarb sich bei einer EU-Organisation um ein Stipendium.

approach sich nähern

■ **ohne Präposition**

Approach ist ein normales transitives Verb und wird ohne Präposition verwendet.

> *As you **approach the town**, there is a big hotel on the left.* ● ● ● Wenn man sich der Stadt nähert …

argue (sich) streiten

■ ***argue with** sb. **about/over** sth.* ● ● ● sich mit jmdm. wegen/über etwas streiten

arms – weapons ['wepənz] Waffen

■ *Arms* (nur Plural) sind Gegenstände, die zu Kriegs- und Kampfzwecken produziert werden.

> *The **arms** industry is a multi-billion-dollar business.* ● ● ● Die Waffenindustrie …

■ *Weapons* können alle Gegenstände sein, mit denen jemand kämpft oder sich verteidigt.

> *The police found the murder **weapon**.* ● ● ● … die Mordwaffe.

Daneben wird *weapons* aber auch in folgenden festen Wendungen verwendet:

> ***nuclear/atomic/conventional weapons*** ● ● ● Nuklear-/Kern-/konventionelle Waffen
> ***(semi-)automatic weapons*** ● ● ● (halb)automatische Waffen
> ***weapons of mass destruction (WMDs)*** ● ● ● Massenvernichtungswaffen

army Armee

■ *be **in the army*** ● ● ● bei der Armee sein

arrange (an)ordnen

■ ***arrange** things **by** age/size* ● ● ● Sachen nach Alter/Größe ordnen

arrest verhaften, festnehmen

■ ***arrest** sb. / **be arrested for** (doing) sth.* ● ● ● jmdn. verhaften / verhaftet werden wegen (einer Tat)

as – like

1 Choose a suitable synonym for 'as':
As darkness began to fall, people began to collect on the square in front of the cathedral.

A After darkness began to fall …
B Because darkness began to fall …
C When darkness began to fall …

2 Choose a suitable synonym for 'as':
I can go to the post office for you as I have to collect a parcel anyway.

A … because I have to collect a parcel anyway.
B … when I have to collect a parcel anyway.
C … while I have to collect a parcel anyway.

3 ......, I'm not very fond of dogs.

A As you   B Like you   C Similar to you

4 This empire will fall, its power will weaken, ...

A as has happened throughout history   B like has happened throughout history

5 To be honest, ...

A I was more surprised as shocked   B I was more surprised than shocked

6 They ate, *[als hätten sie wochenlang nichts gegessen]*.

A as they had eaten nothing for weeks
B as if they hadn't eaten anything for weeks
C as if they ate nothing for weeks

ask

1 A In the oral exam they don't ask every candidate the same questions.
B In the oral exam they don't ask the same questions to every candidate.
C In the oral exam they don't ask the same questions every candidate.

2 A There are some important details I still have to ask the organizers after.
B There are some important details I still have to ask the organizers about.

3 We got lost and had to ....

A ask after the way   B ask about the way   C ask for the way   D ask the way

4 Some people are very sensitive ....

A when you ask them after their age
B when you ask them for their age
C when you ask them their age

A

as wie; als; da, weil – like wie

■ **Bedeutungen von *as***

1 *Leave everything **as** it is, please.* [= in dem Zustand] ● ● ● Lass alles bitte (so), wie es ist.
*Tony won **as** he did last year.* [= in der Art und Weise] ● ● ● … (so) wie er es letztes Jahr getan hat.
***As** you all know, Dennis can't be here today.* [ergänzender Kommentar] ● ● ● Wie ihr alle wisst …

2 ***As** we approached the house, we saw signs of life.* [= während] ● ● ● Als wir uns dem Haus näherten …

3 *I'll inform Mr Barnes **as** I have to phone him anyway.* [= weil] ● ● ● … da ich ihn sowieso anrufen muss.

4 ***As** a taxi-driver I meet lots of strangers.* [= in der Funktion] ● ● ● Als Taxifahrer/-in …
[Beachte: *as* + unbestimmter Artikel *a/an*]

5 *This meat is **as** tough **as** an old boot.* [in gleichsetzenden Vergleichen] ● ● ● … so zäh wie ein alter Stiefel.

■ **Unterschied zu *like*** ▶ so

As ist in der Bedeutung „wie" immer eine Konjunktion und leitet Nebensätze ein.
Like dagegen ist eine Präposition und steht vor Nomen und Pronomen.
*You look **like** a scarecrow.* ● ● ● Du siehst wie eine Vogelscheuche aus.
***Like** you, I hate maths.* ● ● ● Wie du hasse ich Mathe.
Informell wird *like* auch als Konjunktion benutzt. Dieser Sprachgebrauch sollte aber in förmlicher Schriftsprache vermieden werden.
*Nobody can cook lasagne **like** you do.* ● ● ● Niemand kann Lasagne (so) wie du kochen.
***Like** I said, it all happened so fast.* ● ● ● Wie ich schon sagte, es geschah alles so schnell.

Trouble Spot

■ **als**

1 zeitlich: ein Geschehen löst ein anderes aus
Als wir ankamen, jubelten alle. ● ● ● ***When** we arrived, everybody cheered.*

2 zeitlich: zwei gleichzeitige, voneinander unabhängige Geschehen
Als wir ankamen, dämmerte es bereits. ● ● ● ***As** we arrived, dusk was falling.*

3 „als ob"
Die Mannschaft spielt, als wollte sie verlieren, nicht gewinnen. ● ● ● *The team is playing **as if**/**as though** it wanted to lose, not win.*

4 nach dem Komparativ
Ich bin älter als mein Bruder. ● ● ● *I'm older **than** my brother.*

ask fragen; bitten

■ ***ask sb. sth.***
Die Person oder Personen, an die sich eine Frage richtet, werden direkt an *ask* angeschlossen (ohne *to*!) – auch wenn das indirekte Objekt lang und kompliziert ist.
*The police **asked every man, woman and child in the street** the same five questions.* ● ● ● Die Polizei stellte an jeden Mann, jede Frau und jedes Kind … dieselben fünf Fragen./Die Polizei stellte jedem Mann, jeder Frau und jedem Kind … dieselben fünf Fragen.

■ **Wendungen mit Präposition**
*I couldn't do it on my own, I had to **ask for** help.* ● ● ● … um Hilfe bitten.
*I phoned the hospital and **asked about** the driver of the other car.* ● ● ● … erkundigte mich nach …
*We **asked about** the times of the trains.* ● ● ● … fragten nach …

■ **Wendungen ohne Präposition**
ask a question ● ● ● eine Frage stellen
ask the way**/**the time**/**the price ● ● ● nach dem Weg/der Zeit/dem Preis fragen
ask sb. their name**/**their address**/**their age**/**their date and place of birth ● ● ● jmdn. nach seinem Namen/seiner Adresse/seinem Alter/seinem Geburtsdatum und -ort fragen

assure – insure

1 For young people it usually costs a huge amount of money ....
   A to assure a car or motorbike   B to insure a car or motorbike

2 .... that everything possible would be done to prevent the same thing happening again.
   A The police assured us   B The police insured us

astronomic – astronomical

1 A The cost of German reunification has been astronomic.
   B The cost of German reunification has been astronomical.
   C The cost of German reunification has been astronomically.

2 To be able to study the stars and planets ....
   A you need an astronomic telescope   B you need an astronomical telescope

athletic – athletics

1 A Athletic isn't my favourite sport.
   B Athletics aren't my favourite sport.
   C Athletics isn't my favourite sport.

2 I don't know how old she is, ...
   A but she's still very fit and athletic   B but she's still very fit and athletical

attitude

1 .... is still not very welcoming.
   A The attitude of many people opposite having foreigners as neighbours
   B The attitude of many people to having foreigners as neighbours
   C The attitude of many people towards having foreigners as neighbours

average

1 A I study an average of seven hours a day.
   B I study averagely seven hours a day.
   C I study seven hours a day on average.

2 A A car costing less than €1000 is averagely at least ten years old.
   B A car costing less than €1000 is on average at least ten years old.

avoid

1 A We must avoid making too much noise.
   B We must avoid that we make too much noise.
   C We must avoid to make too much noise.

aware – conscious

1 .... when we started.
   A We were aware to the problems   B We were aware of the problems
   C We were conscious to the problems   D We were conscious of the problems

2 You mean you made .... to fail the exam?!
   A an aware decision   B a conscious decision

assure – insure versichern

■ „Versichern" im Sinne von „eindringlich bestätigen" heißt auf Englisch *assure*.
  *I **assure** you I did not take the money.* ● ● ● Ich versichere Ihnen, dass ich …

■ „Versichern" im Sinne von „einen Versicherungsvertrag abschließen" heißt *insure*.
  *These old books are worth a lot of money; they are all **insured**.* ● ● ● … sie sind alle versichert.

astronomic – astronomical astronomisch

■ *Astronomic* kann nur im übertragenen Sinn („sehr groß") verwendet werden.
  *The cost of reconstruction is **astronomic**.* ● ● ● Die Wiederaufbaukosten sind astronomisch.

■ *Astronomical* bedeutet sowohl „sehr groß" als auch „das Weltall betreffend".
  *The cost of reconstruction is **astronomical**.*
  *What does **astronomical** research tell us about black holes?* ● ● ● Was sagt uns die Astronomie-
  forschung über schwarze Löcher?

athletic [æθˈletɪk] athletisch, sportlich – athletics Leichtathletik

■ **Adjektiv** *athletic*
  *She's over 60, but still very **athletic**.* ● ● ● Sie ist über 60, aber immer noch sehr athletisch.

■ **Nomen** *athletics* **(Singular!)**
  *I don't like **athletics**, I prefer to play games.* ● ● ● Ich mag Leichtathletik nicht …
  Wie *statistics, aerobics, economics* ist *athletics* trotz der *-s*-Endung ein Singularnomen.
  ***Athletics is** of course one of the most important Olympic disciplines.*

attitude [ˈætɪtjuːd] Einstellung

■ ***attitude to/towards** sb./sth.* ● ● ● Einstellung zu/gegenüber jmdm./etwas

average [ˈæv(ə)rɪdʒ] Durchschnitts-, durchschnittlich

■ ***The average** cost of a roll is 50c.* ● ● ● Der Durchschnittspreis eines Brötchens beträgt 50 Cent.
  *My **average** working day is eight hours.* ● ● ● Mein durchschnittlicher Arbeitstag dauert acht
  Stunden.

■ *average:* **kein Adverb**
  Anders als das deutsche Wort „durchschnittlich" kann *average* nicht als Adverb verwendet werden.
  Stattdessen verwendet man *on average* („im Durchschnitt", „durchschnittlich") oder *an average of*.
  *A roll costs 50c **on average**. / A roll costs **an average of** 50c.* ● ● ● … kostet durchschnittlich 50 Cent.
  *I work eight hours a day **on average**. / I work **an average of** eight hours a day.* ● ● ● Im Durchschnitt
  arbeite ich acht Stunden am Tag.

■ *be (well) **above/below average*** ● ● ● (weit) über/unter dem Durchschnitt liegen

avoid vermeiden

■ *avoid doing*
  Nach *avoid* verwendet man die *-ing*-Form des Verbs, keinen *to*-Infinitiv und keinen *that*-Satz.
  *I try to **avoid working** (~~avoid to work~~ / ~~avoid that I work~~) on Sundays.* ● ● ● Ich versuche es
  zu vermeiden, sonntags zu arbeiten.

aware – conscious [ˈkɒnʃəs] bewusst

■ *Aware* gehört zu den wenigen Adjektiven, die nur prädikativ, also nach einem Verb wie *be*,
  verwendet werden können.
  *I'm **aware of** the difficulties.* ● ● ● Ich bin mir der Schwierigkeiten bewusst.

■ *Conscious* kann sowohl prädikativ verwendet werden als auch vor einem Nomen stehen.
  *I'm **conscious of** the difficulties.* ● ● ● Ich bin mir der Schwierigkeiten bewusst.
  *I made a **conscious decision** to leave.* ● ● ● Ich traf die bewusste Entscheidung zu gehen.

away – gone – off

1 I was only in the shop two minutes, but when I came out, ...
  A my bike was away   **B** my bike was gone   **C** my bike was off

2 That's mine! ......
  A Hands away!   **B** Hands gone!   **C** Hands off!

baby

1 Our English teacher will be away for several months. ......
  A She's going to become a baby.   **B** She's going to get a baby.   **C** She's going to have a baby.

back

1 I want to sit ...... so that I can get away quickly at the end of the talk.
  A at the back of the room   **B** back in the room   **C** in the back of the room

backside ≠ „Rückseite"

1 'Backside' is a word for ....
  A the part of a building away from the road
  B the part of your body below your shoulders
  C the part of your body that you sit on

2 The plan was sketched ...... after some official dinner.
  A at the back of an envelope   **B** on the back of an envelope
  C at the backside of an envelope   **D** on the backside of an envelope

3 There's a car park ....
  A at the back of the building   **B** on the back of the building
  C at the backside of the building   **D** on the backside of the building

bad

1 A I'm very bad at remembering jokes.
  B I'm very bad in remembering jokes.
  C I'm very bad to remember jokes.

2 Can I go to the toilet, please? *[Mir ist schlecht.]*
  A I'm bad.   **B** I'm sick.   **C** I feel sick.

bank

1 How much money do you have ...... ?
  A at the bank   **B** in the bank   **C** on the bank

be: I've been to … – I was in … – I went to …

1 ...... – No, but I know Ireland quite well.
  A Have you ever been in Scotland?
  B Have you ever been to Scotland?

2 Last summer, ... , I saw a Shakespeare play at the Globe.
  A when I've been in London   **B** when I've been to London
  C when I was in London   **D** when I went to London

away – gone – off weg ▷ distance ▷ far

■ „verschwunden" = *gone*
*Our car was **gone**. They had towed it **away**.* ● ● ● Unser Auto war weg. Man hatte es abgeschleppt.

■ ***Hands off!*** ● ● ● Hände weg!

baby Baby

■ ***have a baby*** ● ● ● ein Baby bekommen

back Rücken; hinterer Teil ▷ backside

■ *sit **at the back** of the theatre* ● ● ● hinten im Theater sitzen
*sit **in the back** /* (AE:) ***in back** of the car* ● ● ● hinten (im Auto) sitzen

backside (infml) Hintern

!
!
!
!

■ **False Friend!**
Backside bedeutet nicht „~~Rückseite~~", sondern „Hintern".
*After ten hours on a horse anybody's **backside** [= bottom] would hurt.* ● ● ● Nach einem Zehnstundenritt würde jedem der Hintern wehtun.
Beachte die englischen Entsprechungen von „Rückseite", „hinterer Teil":
Bitte schreiben Sie Ihren Namen auf die Rückseite. ● ● ● *Please write your name on the **back**.*
Geh zur Rückseite des Gebäudes! ● ● ● *Go to the **back**/**rear** of the building.*

bad schlecht; schlimm ▷ good

■ *I'm **bad at** maths.* ● ● ● Ich bin schlecht in Mathe.
*I'm **bad at remembering** names.* ● ● ● Ich kann mir Namen schlecht merken.

■ **schlecht**
Mir ist schlecht. ● ● ● *I **feel sick**.*
Die Milch ist schlecht geworden. ● ● ● *The milk has **gone off**.*
Mein Englisch ist schlecht. ● ● ● *My English is **poor**.*
Das Konzert war schlecht besucht. ● ● ● *The concert was **poorly attended**.*
Heute Abend ist schlecht / passt es mir schlecht. Kannst du morgen? ● ● ● *This evening is **difficult**. Can you make it tomorrow?*
Das kann ich schlecht sagen. ● ● ● *I **can't really say**.*

Trouble Spot

bank Bank [Geldinstitut]

■ *have money **in the bank*** ● ● ● Geld auf der Bank haben
*put money **in the bank*** ● ● ● Geld auf die Bank bringen / Geld einzahlen
*take money **out of the bank*** ● ● ● Geld von der Bank abheben

be: I've been to … – I was in … – I went to … ich war in …

■ *I've been to a place / country* bedeutet, dass der Ort / das Land zu denen gehört, die ich kenne, weil ich dort gewesen bin.
***Have** you (ever) **been to** Canada?* ● ● ● Waren Sie schon mal in Kanada?
*I've **been to** Paris, but not **to** Bordeaux.* ● ● ● Ich war schon mal in Paris, aber nicht in Bordeaux.

■ *I was in a place / country* bedeutet, dass ich mich (zu einem bestimmten vergangenen Zeitpunkt) in dem genannten Ort / Land aufgehalten habe.
*I **was in** Paris / France last year.* ● ● ● Ich war letztes Jahr in Paris / Frankreich.

■ *I went to a place / country* bedeutet, dass ich eine Reise dorthin gemacht habe.
*I **went to** Paris / France last year.* ● ● ● Ich bin letztes Jahr nach Paris / Frankreich gefahren / geflogen / gereist.

beach – beech

1 It was a glorious day, ... taking it easy, chatting, going for the occasional swim.

  A and we just sat at the beach   B and we just sat at the beech

  C and we just sat on the beach   D and we just sat on the beech

beautiful – handsome – good-looking

1 People admired the actor Marlon Brando, ...

  A but I don't know how many found him beautiful

  B but I don't know how many found him good-looking

  C but I don't know how many found him handsome

2 Who can be described as beautiful?

  A female children   B female adults   C male children   D male adults

become

1 We can see the effects of global warming. ......

  A Our summers are becoming warmer and wetter.   B Our summers become warmer and wetter.

2 Choose the best collocation:

[Was will er mal werden] when he grows up? – I don't think he knows.

  A What does he want to be   B What does he want to become   C What does he want to get

3 Choose the best collocation:

[Ich wurde sehr böse] when I heard that he hadn't even read my email.

  A I got very angry   B I turned very angry   C I went very angry

4 Choose the best collocation:

Joanne Rowling [wurde die reichste Frau] in Britain.

  A became the richest woman   B got the richest woman

  C went the richest woman   D turned the richest woman

5 Choose the best collocation:

At what age [wurde Vincent van Gogh wahnsinnig]?

  A did Vincent Van Gogh get mad   B did Vincent Van Gogh go mad

  C did Vincent Van Gogh grow mad   D did Vincent Van Gogh turn mad

6 Choose the best collocation:

My father's hair is beginning ....

  A to become grey   B to go grey   C to grow grey

7 Choose the best collocation:

After a wet start, ...

  A the day got nice and sunny   B the day grew nice and sunny

  C the day turned out nice and sunny   D the day went nice and sunny

8 Choose the best collocation:

So many old people say that it's hard ....

  A becoming old   B going old   C growing old   D turning old

beach Strand – beech Buche

- *go **to the beach*** ● ● ● zum Strand gehen
  *sit **on the beach*** ● ● ● am Strand sitzen
- *sit under a beautiful **beech (tree)*** ● ● ● unter einer wunderschönen Buche sitzen

beautiful – handsome ['hænsəm] – good-looking schön

- ***beautiful*** **nur bei Frauen und Kindern**
  *a **beautiful** girl / woman / child / little boy*
- **bei Männern: *handsome*/*good-looking***
  Statt *beautiful* wird für Männer und männliche Jugendliche *handsome* („gut aussehend") oder
  good-looking verwendet.
  *a **handsome**/**good-looking** (young) man*

become* werden

- **Verlaufsform bei Entwicklungen und Veränderungen**
  Become verwendet man in der Verlaufsform, wenn man eine Entwicklung oder Veränderung
  beschreibt, die noch nicht abgeschlossen, also immer noch im Gange ist.
  *The traffic situation on our roads **is becoming** worse and worse.* ● ● ● Die Verkehrslage auf unseren
    Straßen wird immer schlimmer.
  *I's **becoming** difficult for grandma to walk without a stick.* ● ● ● Es wird allmählich schwierig für
    Oma, ohne Stock zu laufen.
- *What has **become** of Steffi Graf?* ● ● ● Was ist aus Steffi Graf geworden?

Trouble Spot

- **werden**
  1 berufliche Zukunftspläne
    Was willst du werden, wenn du groß bist? ● ● ● *What do you want to **be** when you're
      grown up?*
    Ich will Ärztin werden. ● ● ● *I want to **be**/**become** a doctor.*
    Ich werde Lehrer. ● ● ● *I'm going to **be**/**become** a teacher.*
    [Vergangenheit:] Albert Schweitzer wurde Arzt. ● ● ● *Albert Schweitzer **became** a doctor.*
  2 die meisten Zustandsveränderungen: *get* / (more fml:) *become*
    get angry/*excited*/*interested*/*nervous*/*dark*/*bigger*/*better*/*tired*/*wet*/*seasick*/...
    become famous / *more unlikely* / *ill* / ...

    Vor Nomen steht nur *become*:
    ***become** law* / *the richest woman in the world* / *a hotel* / ...
  3 negative, nicht aufzuhaltende Veränderungen: *go*
    [bei Lebensmitteln:] schlecht werden ● ● ● *go bad*/*off*
    verrückt/blind werden ● ● ● *go mad*/*blind*
    kahl werden, eine Glatze kriegen/bekommen ● ● ● *go bald*
    grau werden, graue Haare kriegen/bekommen ● ● ● *go grey*

    Aber:
    alt werden ● ● ● *get*/*grow old*
  4 Farbveränderungen: *go*/*turn*
    go/*turn brown*/*yellow*/*red*/...
  5 Wetterveränderungen: *turn*
    turn cold/*warm*
    turn out nice/*sunny*

before

1 We need to book flights, ...
   A but before we should find out about visas   B but beforehand we should find out about visas
   C but before that we should find out about visas   D but first we should find out about visas

2 I bought this camera *[vor zwei Jahren]*.
   A before two years   B for two years   C two years ago   D two years before

3 It's your turn. *[Sie waren vor mir da.]*
   A You were here before me.   B You were here in front of me.

4 I'll wait for you *[vor der Schule]*.
   A at the front of the school   B before the school   C outside the school

5 Go along here, and you'll see a chemist's *[direkt vor der nächsten Kreuzung]*.
   A just at the front of the next crossroads   B just before the next crossroads
   C just in front of the next crossroads   D just outside the next crossroads

6 You're looking at the wrong page. ....
   A 'I' comes above 'J'.   B 'I' comes before 'J'.   C 'I' comes in front of 'J'.

7 In the middle of the season, ...
   A the Bristol team were two places above their local rivals
   B the Bristol team were two places before their local rivals

8 The argument took place *[direkt vor meinen Augen]*. I was speechless.
   A before my very eyes   B in my very eyes

9 My mother used to try and .... , but we always found it.
   A hide chocolate before us   B hide chocolate for us   C hide chocolate from us

10 A The poor man was shivering before cold.
    B The poor man was shivering for cold.
    C The poor man was shivering with cold.

11 Let me explain ....
    A the background against which these tragic developments are taking place
    B the background in front of which these tragic developments are taking place
    C the background to which these tragic developments are taking place

beginning

1 Some pupils are never there ....
   A at the beginning of the lesson   B in the beginning of the lesson

2 A At the beginning God created the heaven and the earth.
   B In the beginning God created the heaven and the earth.

before 1 vor **2** bevor, ehe **3** vorher   ▶ ago

B

■ **Bedeutungen von *before***

1 ***before*** *six o'clock* [zeitlich] ● ● ● vor sechs Uhr
  *You were here **before** me.* ● ● ● Sie waren vor mir hier.

2 *The bank is on the left **before** the Argent Hotel.* [Wegbeschreibung] ● ● ● Die Bank ist links
    (noch) vor dem Hotel Argent.
  *Turn right **before** the bridge.* ● ● ● Biegen Sie vor der Brücke rechts ab!

3 *A comes **before** B in the alphabet.* [in einer Reihenfolge] ● ● ● A kommt vor B …
  *Who's next, please? – This lady is **before** me.* ● ● ● … – Diese Dame ist vor mir an der Reihe.
  *Age **before** beauty.* ● ● ● Alter vor Schönheit.

4 *appear **before** a judge* [= in Anwesenheit von] ● ● ● vor einem Richter / einer Richterin erscheinen
  *It happened **before** my very eyes.* ● ● ● Es geschah direkt vor meinen Augen.

5 ***Before*** *we start, I have some announcements.* ● ● ● Bevor / Ehe wir anfangen …

6 *I've seen this film **before**.* ● ● ● Ich habe den Film (früher) schon einmal gesehen.
  *We had met **before**.* ● ● ● Wir hatten uns (schon) früher getroffen.

■ **„zuerst", „davor", „vorher" = *first, before that, beforehand***
Man verwendet nicht *before*, sondern *first, before that* oder *beforehand* in der Bedeutung „zuerst",
„davor", „vorher", wenn man von Vorbereitungen spricht.
  *Building work starts next week. But **first** / **before that** they are going to fell the trees.* ● ● ● … Aber
    zuerst / davor werden sie die Bäume fällen.
  *Don't start immediately. Always do some warm-up exercises **first** / **beforehand**.* ● ● ● … Mach immer
    zuerst / vorher ein paar Aufwärmübungen.

Trouble Spot

■ **vor**

1 **„vor" als Präposition der Zeit** (s. auch oben)
  vor zehn Jahren ● ● ● *ten years **ago***

2 **„vor" als Präposition des Ortes**
  Die Katze lief vors Auto. ● ● ● *The cat ran out **in front of** the car.*
  Ich legte meinen Pass auf den Tisch vor mir. ● ● ● *I put my passport on the table*
    ***in front of** me.*
  Warte (draußen) vor dem Bahnhof auf mich! ● ● ● *Wait for me **outside** the station.*
  Arsenal steht zwei Plätze vor Chelsea. [Auflistung, Tabelle] ● ● ● *Arsenal is two places*
    ***above** Chelsea.*

3 **„vor" bei Verben des Versteckens, Rettens und Schützens**
  jmdn. / etwas vor der Geheimpolizei verstecken ● ● ● *hide sb. / sth. **from** the secret police*
  jmdn. vor dem sicheren Tod retten ● ● ● *save / rescue sb. **from** certain death*
  jmdn. vor dessen Feinden schützen ● ● ● *protect sb. **from** their enemies*

4 **sonstige Verwendungen von „vor"**
  bis vor den Eingang fahren ● ● ● *drive **right up to** the entrance*
  vor diesem Hintergrund ● ● ● ***against** this background*
  zittern vor Angst / zittern vor Kälte ● ● ● *tremble **with** fear / shiver **with** cold*

beginning Anfang, Beginn

■ ***at the beginning***
  At the beginning, *they played a jazz piece.* ● ● ● Am Anfang / Zu Beginn [eines Zeitraums /
    einer Veranstaltung usw.] spielten sie ein Jazzstück.
  *I pay my rent **at the beginning of** the month.* ● ● ● Ich zahle meine Miete (am) Anfang des Monats.
  at the beginning of *the chapter* ● ● ● am Anfang / zu Beginn des Kapitels

■ ***in the beginning***
  In the beginning, *mobile phones were big and heavy.* ● ● ● Zuerst / Zunächst / In der Anfangszeit
    waren Handys groß und schwer. [*In the beginning* deutet auf einen Gegensatz zu später hin.]

behaviour/behavior

1 You need to change your attitude. ...... doesn't help.

   A Your behaviour at your fellow students   **B** Your behaviour on your fellow students

   C Your behaviour opposite your fellow students   **D** Your behaviour towards your fellow students

behind

1 ...... , but he disappeared into the crowd.

   A I ran after the man   **B** I ran behind the man   **C** I ran beyond the man

2 Turn the page. ......

   A 'Smithson' comes after 'Smith'.

   B 'Smithson' comes behind 'Smith'.

   C 'Smithson' comes beyond 'Smith'.

believe

1 I didn't believe them when they first told me, ...

   A but I'm believing them now   **B** but I believe them now

2 A large number of Americans don't ....

   A believe at Darwin's theory of evolution   **B** believe in Darwin's theory of evolution

   C believe on Darwin's theory of evolution   **D** believe to Darwin's theory of evolution

belong to

1 I think ....

   A the building is now belonging to the state

   B the building now belongs to the state

   C the building now belongs the state

beside – besides

1 **A** Come and sit beside me.   **B** Come and sit besides me.

2 What do people do here all day ...... ?

   A beside eating   **B** besides eating   **C** beside to eat   **D** besides to eat

3 It's done nothing *[außer zu regnen]* since we've been here.

   A beside rain   **B** besides rain   **C** but rain   **D** than rain

4 I'll be there at six *[außer es ruft jemand an]* and tells me not to come.

   A beside someone calls   **B** besides someone calls

   C except someone calls   **D** unless someone calls

5 Everybody arrived on time *[außer unser Reiseführer]*.

   A beside our guide   **B** except our guide   **C** unless our guide

bet

1 ...... that we lose.

   A I bet five euros with you   **B** I bet with you for five euros   **C** I bet you five euros

behaviour (BE) / behavior (AE) Verhalten

■ *His **behaviour towards** her was awful.* ● ● ● Sein Verhalten ihr gegenüber …

behind hinter

■ *Stay close **behind** me.* ● ● ● Bleib dicht hinter mir!

Trouble Spot

■ **hinter**
hinter jmdm. herrennen ● ● ● *run **after** sb.*
In der Wortliste steht „facility" hinter „face". ● ● ● *In the wordlist 'facility' comes **after** 'face'.*
Die Buchstaben „MP" hinter einem Namen bedeuten „Member of Parliament". ● ● ● *The
letters 'MP' **after** somebody's name stand for 'Member of Parliament'.*

believe glauben

■ **nicht in der Verlaufsform**
*I thought you were lying, but I **believe** (~~I'm believing~~) you now.* ● ● ● … aber jetzt glaube ich dir.

■ ***believe in** God* ● ● ● an Gott glauben

belong to gehören

■ **nicht in der Verlaufsform**
*The hotel has been sold and now **belongs** (~~is belonging~~) to an American company.* ● ● ● Das Hotel
ist verkauft worden und gehört jetzt (zu) einem amerikanischen Unternehmen.

beside neben – besides neben, außer

■ ***beside***
Beside bedeutet „neben" im räumlichen Sinn.
*Ann sat **beside** me [= next to me].* ● ● ● Ann saß neben mir.

■ ***besides***
Besides bedeutet „neben" im Sinne von „außer", „zusätzlich zu".
*Have you read any other of his novels **besides** this one?* ● ● ● Hast du außer diesem noch andere
seiner Romane gelesen?
Ein Verb nach *besides* steht in der *-ing*-Form.
***Besides acting**, she also teaches drama.* ● ● ● Außer zu schauspielern …

Trouble Spot

■ **außer**
1 „mit Ausnahme von"
Alle außer Peter haben bezahlt. ● ● ● *Everybody's paid **except** Peter.*

Nach *any, anything, no, nothing* steht *but*:
Er spielte nichts außer/als Schnulzen. ● ● ● *He played **nothing but** slushy songs.*
Sie macht nichts anderes, als sich dauernd nur zu beschweren. ● ● ● *She does **nothing but**
complain.*

2 „neben", „zusätzlich zu"
Außer mir gehen (noch) fünf andere. ● ● ● *Five others are going **besides** me.*

3 „außer wenn", „es sei denn" ▷ unless
Wir spielen definitiv – außer es gießt. ● ● ● *We'll definitely play **unless** it pours with rain.*

bet* wetten

■ **Verb mit zwei Objekten**
Die Person, mit der man um etwas wettet, wird im Englischen direkt, d. h. ohne Präposition,
angeschlossen. Die Person steht dabei immer vor dem Wettbetrag.
*I **bet you ten euros** that Phil will be late again.* ● ● ● Ich wette mit dir um zehn Euro, dass …
*She **bet me 50 euros** that I wouldn't do it.* ● ● ● Sie hat mit mir um 50 Euro gewettet, dass …

between – among

1 I found a ten-pound note ....
   A among two books on my aunt's bookshelf   **B** between two books on my aunt's bookshelf

2 .... are some first-edition Harry Potters.
   A Among the books on her bookshelf   **B** Between the books on her bookshelf

big – large – tall – great

1 Look at that guy over there. ....
   A He must be at least two metres big.   **B** He must be at least two metres large.
   C He must be at least two metres tall.   **D** He must be at least two metres great.

2 It's a very narrow building, ... , towering high above the rest of the town.
   A but very big   **B** but very large   **C** but very tall   **D** but very great

3 .... , just a couple of thousand euros!
   A It didn't cost a big amount of money   **B** It didn't cost a large amount of money
   C It didn't cost a tall amount of money   **D** It didn't cost a great amount of money

4 .... when developing a software program.
   A You need a big deal of patience   **B** You need a large deal of patience
   C You need a tall deal of patience   **D** You need a great deal of patience

5 **A** You need big patience.   **B** You need large patience.
   C You need tall patience.   **D** You need great patience.

6 **A** The festival was a big success.   **B** The festival was a large success.
   C The festival was a tall success.   **D** The festival was a great success.

7 **A** She's a woman of big intelligence.   **B** She's a woman of large intelligence.
   C She's a woman of tall intelligence.   **D** She's a woman of great intelligence.

8 **A** This is a big moment in our country's history.
   B This is a large moment in our country's history.
   C This is tall moment in our country's history.
   D This is a great moment in our country's history.

9 With the population ageing, ...
   A care for the elderly has become big business   **B** care for the elderly has become large business
   C care for the elderly has become tall business   **D** care for the elderly has become great business

bike

1 I didn't drive, ...
   A I went by bike   **B** I went by a bike   **C** I went with a bike
   D I went on a bike   **E** I went by Tom's bike   **F** I went on Tom's bike

birth

1 **A** The baby weighed only 1650 grams at birth.
   B The baby weighed only 1650 grams at the birth.
   C The baby weighed only 1650 grams by birth.
   D The baby weighed only 1650 grams by the birth.

2 **A** My neighbour is Moroccan by birth.
   B My neighbour is Moroccan from birth.
   C My neighbour is Moroccan with birth.

between zwischen – **among** unter, zwischen

■ *between*

Between bezieht sich auf zwei (oder mehrere) einzelne Punkte.

*I was sitting **between** my mother and father.* ● ● ● … zwischen meiner Mutter und meinem Vater.

*What's the difference **between** these words?* ● ● ● … der Unterschied zwischen diesen Wörtern?

■ *among*

Among bezieht sich auf eine Einheit oder eine als Einheit empfundene Gruppe.

*The President walked **among** the crowd.* ● ● ● … in der Menge.

***Among** the books in his study was a guide to Timbuktu.* ● ● ● Zwischen/Unter den Büchern …

big – large – tall – great groß ▷ strong

■ **groß**

1 „körperlich groß", „physisch umfangreich"

Personen: *big* (selten: *large*); Sachen: *big*/*large*

*a **big** boy*/*girl*/*man*

*a **big**/**large** country*/*house*/*pair of shoes*/*dog*

Bei Betonung der vertikalen Größe von Personen bzw. Höhe von Sachen: *tall*

*a **tall** police officer*/*tree*/*building*

*be 1.82 metres **tall***

2 „politisch/wirtschaftlich potent"

*a **big**/**large** organization*/*company*/*player in the market*

3 Mengen

*a **large** quantity (of)*

*a **large**/**great** amount (of)*

*a **large**/**great** number (of)*

4 „beträchtlich"

*a **big**/**great** advantage*/*success*/*mistake*/*difference*/*improvement*

Bei nicht zählbaren Nomen (oft Bezeichnungen für Eigenschaften und Gefühle) nur *great*:

great joy/*intelligence*/*concentration*/*speed*/*courage*/*danger*

5 „bedeutend", „hervorragend", „wichtig", „von großer Tragweite"

*a **great** writer*/*leader*/*event*/*victory*

6 feste Wendungen mit *big*

*my **big** sister* [= my older sister]

***Big** Brother* („der Große Bruder, der die Menschen beobachtet und überwacht")

***big** business, **big** money*

***big** trouble*

*a **big** star, a **big** name*

a/*the **big*** [auch: ***great***] *moment*

Trouble Spot

bike Rad

■ *He comes to school **by bike**/**on a bike**/**on his bike** (~~by a bike~~/~~by his bike~~/~~with a bike~~/ ~~with his bike~~).* ● ● ● Er kommt mit dem/seinem Fahrrad zur Schule.

*How did you get here? – I came **on Al's bike** (~~by Al's bike~~).* ● ● ● … – Ich bin mit Als Rad gekommen.

birth Geburt

■ **Präpositionen + *birth* (ohne *the*)**

*How much did he weigh **at birth**?* ● ● ● … bei der Geburt?

*She has two passports. **By birth** she's Venezuelan, but she's also German, by marriage.* ● ● ● … Von Geburt ist sie Venezolanerin/Sie ist gebürtige Venezolanerin, aber …

*He's been handicapped **since**/**from birth**.* ● ● ● … seit der Geburt/von Geburt an behindert.

blame ≠ „blamieren"

1 What does the following sentence mean?
You have no one to blame but yourself.
   A It's your fault and nobody else's.
   B There is no one you can play a joke on.
   C You will only hurt yourself.

2 I just wanted to leave the room there and then. *[Ich habe mich wirklich blamiert.]*
   A I really accused myself.   B I really blamed myself.
   C I really made a fool of myself.   D I really made me a fool.

blind

1 Was Blunkett ...... to become a government minister?
   A the first blind   B the first blinder   C the first blind person

2 I couldn't find the way, but someone helped me, ...
   A a blind   B a blind boy   C a blind girl   D a blind one

book

1 It's ...... who was very close to the President: the author is his daughter.
   A a book by someone   B a book from someone   C a book of someone

border

1 I was born in a small town ....
   A at the border with Poland   B on the border to Poland   C on the border with Poland

2 Manned flights to Mars: these are ....
   A today's borders of science and civilization   B today's boundaries of science and civilization
   C today's frontiers of science and civilization   D today's limits of science and civilization

3 ...... have you set yourself? – €150.
   A What price border   B What price boundary   C What price frontier   D What price limit

4 ...... on highways in Florida?
   A What's the limit on speed   B What's the limit of speed   C What's the speed limit

bored: be/get bored

1 A I'm getting bored at sitting at home all day.
   B I'm getting bored to sit at home all day.
   C I'm getting bored with sitting at home all day.

born

1 ...... – In Munich.
   A Where are you born?   B Where have you been born?   C Where were you born?

borrow – lend

1 A I'm happy to borrow you my leather coat – if you want to borrow it, that is.
   B I'm happy to borrow you my leather coat – if you want to lend it, that is.
   C I'm happy to lend you my leather coat – if you want to borrow it, that is.
   D I'm happy to lend you my leather coat – if you want to lend it, that is.

B

blame Vorwürfe machen, die Schuld geben

> **!**
> **!**
> **!**
>
> ■ **False Friend!**
> *Blame* bedeutet nicht „~~blamieren~~", sondern „Vorwürfe machen", „die Schuld geben".
>   *I **blame** myself for the accident. It was my fault.* ● ● ● Ich bin selbst schuld an dem Unfall. …
> Beachte die englische Entsprechung von „sich blamieren":
>   Er blamierte sich vor der ganzen Schule. ● ● ● *He **made a fool of himself** in front of the entire school.*

blind [blaɪnd] blind

■ **als Nomen nur zur Bezeichnung einer Gesamtgruppe**
The blind kann nur zur Bezeichnung der Gesamtgruppe der Blinden verwendet werden.
   ***the blind** and the sick* ● ● ● die Blinden und die Kranken
Aber:
   *a **blind person** with a guide dog* ● ● ● ein Blinder / eine Blinde mit einem Blindenhund
   ***Blind people** often have a good sense of hearing.* ● ● ● Blinde haben oft ein gutes Gehör.
   ***The blind man** was reading a book in Braille* [breɪl]. ● ● ● Der Blinde las ein Buch in Blindenschrift.

book Buch

■ *a **book** (written) **by** Cornelia Funke* ● ● ● ein Buch von Cornelia Funke [= sie hat es geschrieben]
   *a **book** (I got) **from** Ann* ● ● ● ein Buch von Ann [= von ihr habe ich es bekommen]

border Grenze

■ *a place **on the border with / to** Canada* ● ● ● ein Ort an der Grenze zu Kanada
   *stop a thief **at the border*** ● ● ● einen Dieb an der Grenze / bei der Grenzkontrolle stoppen

> ■ **Grenze**
> **1 „Grenze von Grund und Boden"**
>   die Grenze zwischen zwei Ländern ● ● ● *the **border** between two countries*
>   die Grenze eines US-Bundesstaats ● ● ● *the **boundary** of a US state*
>   die Grenze zwischen zwei Grundstücken ● ● ● *the **boundary** between two plots of land*
> **2 „Grenze als weitester erreichter Punkt oder als schwer zu überwindendes Hindernis"**
>   die Grenzen der Wissenschaft/Zivilisation ● ● ● *the **frontiers** of science / civilization*
> **3 „Grenze eines Sperrgebiets"**
>   die Grenzen der Flugverbotszone ● ● ● *the **limits** of the no-fly zone*
> **4 „zumutbare Grenze"**
>   Preisgrenze ● ● ● *price **limit***
> **5 „zulässige Grenze"**
>   Geschwindigkeitsbegrenzung ● ● ● *speed **limit***

(Trouble Spot)

bored: be* / get* bored sich langweilen

■ ***bored with** (doing) sth.*
   *I'm **bored with** (playing) that game.* ● ● ● Das Spiel langweilt mich. / Das Spiel ist mir über.

born geboren

■ *Where **were** you **born**? (~~Where are you born?~~)* ● ● ● Wo bist du geboren?
   *I **was born** in Canada. (~~I'm born in Canada.~~)* ● ● ● Ich bin in Kanada geboren.

borrow – lend* leihen

■ ***borrow** sth. **from** sb.* ● ● ● (sich) etwas von jmdm. (aus)leihen
■ ***lend** sth. **to** sb.* ● ● ● jmdm. etwas (aus)leihen, etwas an jmdn. verleihen

both

1 A Both windows were open. B Both the windows were open.
  C The windows both were open. D The windows were both open.

2 A Both Julia's parents agreed. B Julia's parents both agreed. C Julia's parents agreed both.

3 A Both her parents agreed. B Her both parents agreed.
  C Her parents both agreed. D Her parents agreed both.

4 A I like Julia's parents, both. B I like Julia's parents, both of them.

5 A I can't see both of them. Where are they sitting?
  B I can't see either of them. Where are they sitting?
  C I can see neither of them. Where are they sitting?

brave ≠ „brav"

1 Which words are synonyms of 'brave'?
  A boring B bold C courageous D uninteresting E fearless

2 *[Sei brav!]* Don't do anything I wouldn't do.
  A Be brave! B Be correct! C Be good!

3 I want someone with a bit of style, a bit of pep. Justin is just *[zu brav]*.
  A too brave B too conventional C too good

bread – sandwich

1 We'll be 14 for breakfast, so buy *[drei Weißbrote]*, please.
  A three white breads B three loaves of white bread C three white loaves

2 My mother used to make me *[ein Käsebrot]* every morning, and I used to feed it to the dog every lunchtime.
  A a cheese bread B a cheese loaf C a cheese roll D a cheese sandwich

both beide

■ Wortstellung

Die Stellung von *both* ist sehr flexibel und oft wie im Deutschen.

   Both (the) shops were shut. | *The shops were **both** shut.* | *They were **both** shut.* | *Both were shut.*

Beachte aber folgende Unterschiede zum Deutschen:

1 Wenn *both* dem Subjekt nachgestellt wird, steht es **vor** (nicht hinter!) einem Vollverb.

   The brothers both passed their driving test. (~~The brothers passed both their driving test.~~ |
   ~~The brothers passed their driving test both.~~) ● ● ● Die Brüder bestanden beide den Führerschein.

   They both passed their driving test. ● ● ● Sie bestanden beide den Führerschein.

2 *Both* steht **vor** (nicht hinter!) einem weiteren Begleiter (+ Nomen).

   Both the parents are dead. ● ● ● Beide Eltern sind tot.

   Both her parents are dead. (~~Her both parents are dead.~~) ● ● ● Ihre beiden Eltern sind tot.

■ *both of*

Als nachgestellte Ergänzung zum Subjekt bzw. Objekt steht *both of* + Objektform des Personal-
pronomens.

   *We played well, **both of us** (~~both~~).* ● ● ● Wir haben gut gespielt, beide.

   *I know her sisters, **both of them** (~~both~~).* ● ● ● Ich kenne ihre Schwestern, alle beide.

■ beide

1 both – either – neither

   Anna und Willi kennen beide den Weg. ● ● ● *Anna and Willi **both** know the way.* [A und B]

   Du kannst beide fragen. ● ● ● *You can ask **either**.* [A oder B]

   Aber beide sind heute nicht da. ● ● ● *But **neither (of them)** is here today.*
   [A nicht und B nicht; weder A noch B – als Subjekt]

   Ich kenne beide nicht. ● ● ● *I don't know **either (of them)**.* | *I know **neither (of them)**.*
   [A nicht und B nicht; weder A noch B – als Objekt]

2 both – the two

   Both bedeutet „alle beide" [betont], „zwei zusammengehörige Personen/Dinge":

   (Alle) beide Mannschaften sind gut. Das wird ein gutes Spiel. ● ● ● ***Both (the) teams** are good.*
   It'll be a good match.

   The two bedeutet „die zwei" [unbetont], „zwei von mehreren Personen/Dingen":

   Die beiden Tische auf der linken Seite sind reserviert, aber die anderen sind frei. ● ● ●
   ***The two tables** on the left are reserved, but the others are free.*

brave mutig, tapfer

■ False Friend!

! *Brave* bedeutet nicht „~~brav~~", sondern „mutig".

!   *It was a **brave** decision.* ● ● ● Es war eine mutige Entscheidung.

Beachte die englischen Entsprechungen von „brav":

!   Braver Hund! ● ● ● ***Good** dog!*

!   Die Kinder waren brav. ● ● ● *The children were **good**/**well-behaved**.*

   Diese Bluse ist mir zu brav. ● ● ● *I find this blouse too **plain**/**conventional**.*

bread – sandwich ['sænwɪtʃ, 'sænwɪdʒ] Brot

■ *bread:* nicht zählbares Nomen

Bread ist nicht zählbar, kann also nicht mit *a* stehen. Stattdessen verwendet man *loaf* („Laib").

   *Go to the baker's and buy **a loaf of bread** (~~a bread~~), please.* ● ● ● … und kaufe bitte ein Brot.

   ***three loaves (of bread)** and two fishes* ● ● ● drei Brote und zwei Fische

■ „belegtes Brot" = *sandwich*

Ein Brot im Sinne von „belegtes Brot" ist im Englischen ein *sandwich*.

   *a cheese **sandwich*** ● ● ● ein Käsebrot

breakfast

1 A My favourite meal of the day is breakfast.   B My favourite meal of the day is the breakfast.

2 I'm not a morning person. ......
   A I hate conversation at breakfast.   B I hate conversation at the breakfast.
   C I hate conversation by breakfast.   D I hate conversation by the breakfast.

breast – chest

1 When did Tony start feeling ...... ?
   A these pains in his breast   B these pains in his breast area   C these pains in his chest

2 Aunt Sarah was a motherly woman, ...
   A with big breasts, pudgy arms, and a friendly smile
   B with a big chest, pudgy arms, and a friendly smile

bring – take

1 Can I ask you a favour? ......
   A Could you bring me to the airport tomorrow morning?
   B Could you take me to the airport tomorrow morning?

2 Husband: I'm going shopping. – Wife: ......
   A Could you bring me some ink cartridges?
   B Could you take me some ink cartridges?

3 It's getting very late. ......
   A It's time to bring the children to bed.
   B It's time to put the children to bed.
   C It's time to take the children to bed.

4 ...... immediately after this bulletin of news.
   A We'll be bringing the full interview
   B We'll be broadcasting the full interview
   C We'll be taking the full interview

broken – broken down – not working – have had it

1 ...... , so could you give me a lift?
   A Our car is broken   B Our car is off the road

2 ...... and there's chaos.
   A The traffic lights are broken
   B The traffic lights are broken down
   C The traffic lights aren't working

3 That washing machine is over 15 years old. ...... It's just not worth repairing.
   A It's not working.   B It's had it.   C It's completely gone broken.

breakfast Frühstück ▶ lunch

■ **meist ohne** *the*
Breakfast steht – wie *lunch* und *dinner* – in der Regel ohne Artikel.
   Breakfast is from 7.30 to 9.30. ● ● ● Frühstück gibt es von 7.30 Uhr bis 9.30 Uhr.

■ **At breakfast** you said … ● ● ● Beim Frühstück hast du gesagt …
   I drink tea **for breakfast.** ● ● ● Ich trinke Tee zum Frühstück.

breast [brest] Brust, Brüste – **chest** Brust(korb)

■ Mit *breast* wird die weibliche Brust bezeichnet.
   a woman's **breast** ● ● ● die Brust einer Frau
   a woman's **breasts** ● ● ● die Brüste / der Busen einer Frau

■ *Chest* wird in Bezug auf männliche Wesen und in medizinischen Zusammenhängen im Sinne von „Brustbereich", „Brustkorb" verwendet.
   a man's **chest** ● ● ● die Brust / der Brustkorb eines Mannes
   Before a heart attack people often have pain in their **chest** (~~breast~~). ● ● ● Vor einem Herzinfarkt hat man oft Schmerzen in der Brust.

bring* – take* bringen

■ *bring* = „(her)bringen", „mitbringen"
   Bring me a cloth, quick! ● ● ● Bring mir einen Lappen, schnell!
   It's a megaparty. **Bring** all your friends! ● ● ● Es ist eine Riesenparty. Bring alle deine Freunde mit!

■ *take* = „(hin)bringen", „(weg)bringen"
   The ambulance **took** him to hospital. ● ● ● Der Krankenwagen brachte ihn ins Krankenhaus.
   It's OK, I'll **take** you to the station. ● ● ● Ist schon gut, ich bringe dich zum Bahnhof.

Trouble Spot

   ■ **bringen**
   Er bringt gerade die Kinder ins Bett. ● ● ● He's just **putting** the children **to bed.**
   Sie bringen ein Interview mit ihr nach den Nachrichten. ● ● ● They're **broadcasting/showing** an interview with her after the news.
   Heute Abend bringen/zeigen sie einen tollen Film. ● ● ● There's a great film **on** this evening.
   Die Zeitung brachte es auf Seite 1. ● ● ● The newspaper **had/printed/published/carried** it on page 1.

broken – broken down – not working – have had it kaputt (sein)

Trouble Spot

   ■ **kaputt sein**
   1 „zerbrochen sein"
      In der letzten Nacht hatten wir einen Sturm, und zwei Fenster sind kaputt(gegangen). ● ● ● We had a storm last night, and two windows **are/have broken**.
   2 „nicht mehr funktionieren, ersatz- oder reparaturbedürftig sein" [Autoteil, kleines Gerät]
      Die Kupplung/Fernbedienung ist kaputt. ● ● ● The clutch / remote control **is broken.**
   3 „liegen geblieben sein", „eine Panne haben" [Auto]
      Ich fahre zzt. mit dem Fahrrad zur Arbeit, weil mein Auto kaputt ist. ● ● ● I'm cycling to work because my car **has broken down / is off the road.**
   4 „[vorübergehend] außer Betrieb sein"
      Der Fahrstuhl ist kaputt. Wir müssen laufen. ● ● ● The lift's **not working**. We'll have to walk.
   5 „hin sein"
      Unser Auto/Fernseher ist [endgültig] kaputt. Wir müssen ein neues/einen neuen kaufen.
      ● ● ● Our car/television (infml:) **has had it.** We have to buy a new one.

bus – coach

1 A I usually come by the number 19 bus.

  B I usually come on the number 19 bus.

  C I usually come with the number 19 bus.

2 What's the cheapest way of getting from London to Scotland? – ......

  A By coach. B On the coach. C With coach.

by – near

1 A She lived in a big house at the sea.

  B She lived in a big house by the sea.

  C She lived in a big house next to the sea.

2 A Siegburg is a town by Bonn and Cologne.

  B Siegburg is a town in the near of Bonn and Cologne.

  C Siegburg is a town near Bonn and Cologne.

3 Let's meet at ten to seven ....

  A at Sue B at Sue's place C at Sue's D by Sue E by Sue's place

4 We're not staying in a hotel, ...

  A we're staying at friends B we're staying by friends C we're staying with friends

5 A I wouldn't want to work by a very small company.

  B I wouldn't want to work for a very small company.

6 A Our cat got injured at a fight.

  B Our cat got injured by a fight.

  C Our cat got injured in a fight.

7 A It's impossible to work at this temperature.

  B It's impossible to work by this temperature.

  C It's impossible to work with this temperature.

8 ...... A passport or driving licence?

  A Do you have any means of identification at you?

  B Do you have any means of identification by you?

  C Do you have any means of identification on you?

  D Do you have any means of identification with you?

can

1 A Can you Spanish? B Can you speak Spanish?

capable

1 Don't trust him. ......

  A He's capable at selling his own grandmother!

  B He's capable of selling his own grandmother!

  C He's capable to sell his own grandmother!

car

1 A We all came by Anthea's car. B We all came in Anthea's car.

  C We all came on Anthea's car. D We all came with Anthea's car.

C

bus – coach Bus

■ Im BE unterscheidet man meist zwischen *bus* („örtlicher Linienbus") und *coach* („Fernreisebus").
  take the **bus** to school ● ● ● den Bus zur Schule nehmen / mit dem Bus zur Schule fahren
  go from London to Scotland by **coach** from Victoria **Coach** Station ● ● ● … mit dem Reisebus …
Bus hat die Pluralform *buses* oder (nur im AE:) *busses*.

■ **Präpositionen**
  He comes to school **by bus** / **on the bus** (~~by the bus~~). ● ● ● Er kommt mit dem Bus zur Schule.
  How did you get here? – I came **on the number 22 bus** / **on the school bus** (~~by / with the … bus~~).
   ● ● ● … – Ich bin mit dem 22er-Bus / mit dem Schulbus gekommen.
  I'm going to Rome **by coach** / **on a coach** (~~by the coach~~). ● ● ● Ich fahre mit dem Reisebus nach Rom.

by – near neben, an   ▶ from   ▶ until

■ *By* bedeutet in Ortsbestimmungen „neben" oder „an".
  I live **by** the sea / **by** the river Thames / **by** the church. ● ● ● … am Meer / an der Themse / neben der
    Kirche.

■ Nicht *by*, sondern *near* verwendet man vor Ortsnamen.   ▶ **near**
  I live in a small town **near** Paris (~~by Paris~~). ● ● ● … bei / in der Nähe von Paris.

Trouble Spot

■ **bei**
  bei mir zu Hause ● ● ● **at** my place
  bei meiner Tante / bei Graham ● ● ● **at** my aunt's (place) / **at** Graham's (place)
  beim Bäcker ● ● ● **at** the baker's
  bei einem Treffen / einer Versammlung ● ● ● **at** a meeting
  bei Sonnenaufgang ● ● ● **at** sunrise
  bei einer Temperatur von 270 Grad ● ● ● **at** a temperature of 270 degrees
  bei jmdm. wohnen / übernachten ● ● ● live / stay **with** sb. / live / stay **at** sb.'s house / place
  bei einer Bank arbeiten ● ● ● work **for** / **at** a bank
  kein Geld / keinen Ausweis bei sich haben ● ● ● have no money / no passport **on** / **with** you
  bei dieser Gelegenheit ● ● ● **on** this occasion
  sich bei einer Tasse Kaffee unterhalten ● ● ● chat **over** a cup of coffee
  sich bei einem Unfall verletzen ● ● ● get injured **in** an accident
  sich bei einem Kampf verletzen ● ● ● get injured **in** a battle / fight
  Es wird schwierig bei [= in Anbetracht von] so vielen Problemen und so hohen Kosten. ● ● ●
    It'll be difficult **with** so many problems and such high costs.
  bei [= im Falle von] schönem Wetter / bei Regen ● ● ● **if** the weather is nice / **if** it rains

can können   ▶ may

■ *can speak, can do*
Die Fähigkeit, eine Sprache zu sprechen bzw. etwas zu tun, kann nicht durch *can* allein ausgedrückt werden.
  How come you **can speak** Italian so well? ● ● ● Woher kannst du so gut Italienisch?
  You write such wonderful letters. You **can do** it so well. ● ● ● … Du kannst es so gut.

capable ['keɪpəbl] fähig

■ *capable of doing*
Auf *capable* folgt *of* + die *-ing*-Form des Verbs.
  I'm quite **capable of looking** after myself. [= I'm able to look after myself.] ● ● ● Ich kann gut selbst
    auf mich aufpassen.

car Auto

■ He comes to school **by car**. ● ● ● … mit dem Auto. [allgemeine Angabe des Transportmittels]
  How did you get here? – I came **in Ed's car** (~~by Ed's car / with Ed's car~~). ● ● ● … mit / in Eds Auto …

carry – wear – support – bear

1 British people don't normally carry means of identification *[bei sich]*.
  A by them   B by themselves   C with them   D on them

2 Is she the woman who always goes around ...... ?
  A carrying dark glasses   B wearing dark glasses

3 Do these two little towers ...... ?
  A bear the whole bridge   B carry the whole bridge
  C support the whole bridge   D wear the whole bridge

4 The river is frozen, ...
  A but it won't bear the weight of a car
  B but it won't carry the weight of a car
  C but it won't wear the weight of a car

5 ...... for this whole risky enterprise? Not me!
  A Who is going to bear the cost
  B Who is going to support the cost
  C Who is going to wear the cost

cattle

1 A The cattle in that field belong to Lord Northumberland.
  B The cattle in that field belongs to Lord Northumberland.

certain(ly) – sure(ly)

1 ...... She always supports organizations like ours.
  A I'm certain that she'll support us.   B She's certain to support us.
  C She's sure to support us.

2 The weather during the festival has been so awful, ...
  A it's certain that the organizers will make a loss
  B it's sure that the organizers will make a loss

3 I don't think I've ever seen so many people. – ......
  A No, it's certain very busy today.   B No, it's certainly very busy today.
  C No, it's surely very busy today.

change

1 We're leaving tomorrow ....
  A and I don't really want to change any more money for dollars now
  B and I don't really want to change any more money in dollars now
  C and I don't really want to change any more money into dollars now
  D and I don't really want to change any more money to dollars now

2 Somebody bought me this as a present, ...
  A but I'd like to change it for another colour, please
  B but I'd like to change it in another colour, please
  C but I'd like to change it into another colour, please
  D but I'd like to change it to another colour, please

3 The next station is Salisbury. ......
  A Change at Salisbury for Southampton.   B Change at Salisbury to Southampton.
  C Change at Salisbury towards Southampton.

carry – wear* – support – bear* tragen

■ **tragen**

1 „befördern"
Ich trage den Koffer für dich. ● ● ● *I'll* **carry** *the suitcase for you.*

2 „bei sich haben", „mitführen"
Britische Polizisten tragen normalerweise keine Waffe (bei sich). ● ● *British police officers don't normally* **carry** *a gun (on/with them).*

3 „direkt am Körper tragen"
Wer trägt denn heute schon eine Krawatte? ● ● ● *Who* **wears** *a tie these days?*
Kann man Pilot werden, wenn man eine Brille trägt? ● ● ● *Can you become a pilot if you* **wear** *glasses?*

4 „von unten stützen"
Ein Pfeiler trägt das ganze Dach. ● ● ● *One pillar* **supports** *the whole roof.*

5 „das Gewicht von etwas aushalten"
Das Eis wird dein Gewicht nicht tragen. ● ● ● *The ice won't* **bear** *your weight.*

6 „etwas Unangenehmes übernehmen"
die Kosten / die Last tragen ● ● ● **bear/carry** *the cost / the burden*

7 feste Wendung
Früchte tragen ● ● ● **bear fruit**

cattle Vieh

■ **Pluralnomen**
Begleiter und Verben, die mit *cattle* verbunden werden, stehen im Plural.
What **are those cattle** *doing on the road?* ● ● ● *Was macht dieses Vieh auf der Straße?*
The **cattle were** *being milked.* ● ● ● *Das Vieh wurde (gerade) gemolken.*

certain(ly) – sure(ly) sicher

■ **certain/sure to do – certain/sure that ...**
Die Bedeutung und Konstruktionsmöglichkeiten von *certain* und *sure* sind fast, aber nicht völlig gleich.
I'm **certain/sure that I left** *the keys here.* ● ● ● *Ich bin (mir) sicher, dass …*
We're **certain/sure to meet** *Anna at the party.* ● ● ● *Wir werden sicher/bestimmt …*
In der Wendung *it is … that* kann nur *certain* stehen.
It is **certain that** (~~It is sure that~~) **she'll be** *there.* ● ● ● *Es ist sicher/klar, dass …*

■ **certainly – surely**
Certainly bedeutet „sicher" im Sinne von „definitiv".
It's **certainly** *much colder today. Look at the frost.*
Surely bedeutet „doch (wohl)" und wird verwendet, wenn man sich beim Gesprächspartner rückversichern oder Überraschung zum Ausdruck bringen will.
Surely *you don't believe that?!* ● ● ● *Das glaubst du doch wohl (selber) nicht!*

change wechseln, tauschen; umsteigen; verwandeln

■ **change into** *more comfortable clothes* ● ● ● in bequemere Kleidung wechseln / sich bequemere Sachen anziehen
change *dollars* **into** *euros* ● ● ● Dollar in Euro wechseln/umtauschen
change *sth.* **for** *sth. else (at a shop)* ● ● ● etwas gegen etwas anderes (um)tauschen
change *at Oxford* **for** *Banbury* ● ● ● in Oxford nach Banbury umsteigen
change *sb.* **into** *a frog* ● ● ● jmdn. in einen Frosch verwandeln

chaos

1 You can hardly get into the room. ......
   A It's a chaos!   B It's chaos!

chef ≠ „Chef/-in"

1 What is the best synonym for 'chef'?
   A boss   B cook   C guide   D manager   E police officer

2 *[Die Chefin]* I had in my last holiday job was really nice.
   A The boss   B The chef   C The leader

choose – select – elect – vote

1 How often do voters in this country ...... ?
   A elect a new president   B vote a new president

2 ...... in the elections next Sunday?
   A Which party are you going to choose   B Which party are you going to select
   C Which party are you going to vote   D Which party are you going to vote for

3 I think I probably clicked on the wrong icon ....
   A and elected the wrong menu item
   B and selected the wrong menu item
   C and voted for the wrong menu item

Christ – Christian

1 A Do all Christs believe in life after death?   B Do all Christians believe in life after death?

city ≠ „City"

1 Let's meet somewhere *[in der City]*.
   A in the city   B in the centre   C in the central town

2 ...... is one of the most exciting places I know.
   A The city from New Orleans   B The city of New Orleans   C The city New Orleans

classic – classical

1 A Do you like classic music?   B Do you like classical music?

2 Everybody has seen it. ......
   A It's a Hollywood classic.   B It's a Hollywood classical.   C It's a classic Hollywood.

clock – watch

1 When I'm on holiday, ...
   A I try not to wear a clock   B I try not to wear a watch

2 ...... Mine says 8.27.
   A What's the time according your watch?   B What's the time at your watch?
   C What's the time by your watch?   D What's the time on your watch?

chaos [ˈkeɪɒs] Chaos

■ **nicht zählbares Nomen: ohne *a***
Chaos ist nicht zählbar, kann also nicht mit *a* verwendet werden.
   *What **chaos**! (~~What a chaos!~~)* ● ● ● Was für ein Chaos!

chef [ʃef] Berufskoch/-köchin, Küchenchef/-in

!
!
!
■ **False Friend!**
Chef bedeutet nicht „~~Chef~~", sondern „Koch" [als Beruf].
   *He worked as a **chef** in hotels in France and Italy.* ● ● ● Er hat als Koch … gearbeitet.
Beachte die englische Entsprechung von „Chef/-in":
   Die Chefin hat heute schlechte Laune. ● ● ● *The **boss** is in a bad mood today.*

choose* – select – elect – vote (aus)wählen

Trouble Spot

■ **wählen**
1 „auswählen"
   zwischen zwei Farben (aus)wählen ● ● ● ***choose between** two colours*
   im Menü Bearbeiten „Kopieren" wählen ● ● ● ***select** 'copy' in the Edit menu*

2 „bei Wahlen abstimmen"
   einen Vorsitzenden wählen [= durch eine Wahl bestimmen] ● ● ● ***elect** a chairperson*
   jmdn. zum Präsidenten wählen ● ● ● ***elect** sb. President*
   Ich wähle nur Frauen. [= stimmen für] ● ● ● *I only **vote for** women.*
   Wann gehst du wählen? ● ● ● *When are you going to **vote**?*

Christ [kraɪst] Christus – Christian [ˈkrɪstʃən] 1 Christ/-in 2 christlich

■ ***Christ** died on the cross.* ● ● ● Christus starb am Kreuz.

■ *He's a Muslim, not **a Christian**.* ● ● ● Er ist Muslim, kein Christ.
   *the **Christian** religion* ● ● ● die christliche Religion

city (Groß-)Stadt

!
!
!
■ **False Friend!**
City bedeutet nicht „~~City~~", sondern „Großstadt".
   *London was once the largest **city** in the world.* ● ● ● … die größte Stadt der Welt.
   *live in **the city of** Bristol (~~the city Bristol~~)* ● ● ● in der Stadt Bristol wohnen
Beachte die englischen Entsprechungen von „City":
   ein Geschäft in der City ● ● ● (BE:) *a shop in the **(town) centre*** / (AE:) *a **downtown** store*

classic 1 klassisch 2 Klassiker – classical klassisch

■ *classic* = „dauerhaft gut"; „typisch"
   *a **classic** Hollywood film* ● ● ● … ein klassischer Hollywoodfilm
   *a Hollywood **classic*** ● ● ● … ein Hollywoodklassiker
   *a **classic** case of bad communication* ● ● ● ein klassischer Fall schlechter Kommunikation

■ *classical* = „zur Antike gehörend"; „zur klassischen Musik gehörend"
   classical architecture in Athens and Rome ● ● ● klassische Architektur in Athen und Rom
   classical music ● ● ● klassische Musik

clock – watch Uhr

■ *the kitchen/school/station **clock***

■ *wear a gold **watch**, a pocket **watch*** [= am Körper getragene Uhr]
   *What's the time **by/on** your **watch**?* ● ● ● Wie spät ist es nach/auf deiner Uhr?

close – shut

1 ...... There's been a serious accident.
   A The road is closed.   B The road is shut.

2 Some books say ...... with 'Looking foward to hearing from you'.
   A you shouldn't close your letter   B you shouldn't shut your letter

3 ...... , cut off from the rest of society around them.
   A The monks live in a closed world   B The monks live in a shut world

coast

1 ...... in southern England.
   A Bere is the name of a town at the coast   B Bere is the name of a town by the coast
   C Bere is the name of a town next to the coast   D Bere is the name of a town on the coast

colour/color

1 ...... Is it red?
   A What colour has it?   B What colour is it?   C Which colour has it?   D Which colour is it?

come

1 A My family comes from the south of Germany.
   B My family is coming from the south of Germany.

2 ...... on the left on the first floor.
   A Those boxes come in the first room   B Those boxes get in the first room
   C Those boxes go in the first room

3 It's two days' drive. ...... , you'll have done well.
   A If you come as far as Ohio on the first day   B If you get as far as Ohio on the first day
   C If you reach as far as Ohio on the first day

4 A Which class will you be in next year?   B Which class will you come in next year?
   C Which class will you get in next year?   D Which class will you go in next year?

comment

1 I'm afraid ....
   A I can't comment at that report   B I can't comment on that report
   C I can't comment to that report   D I can't comment that report

complain

1 ...... , but it made no difference.
   A I complained my neighbour about the noise   B I complained to my neighbour about the noise
   C I complained by my neighbour about the noise

concentrate

1 At the moment ....
   A I'm concentrating on passing my maths exam   B I'm concentrating to pass my maths exam
   C I concentrate on passing my maths exam   D I concentrate to pass my maths exam

2 ...... It was a difficult text to understand.
   A We were all listening very concentrated.   B We were all listening very concentratedly.
   C We were all listening with great concentration.

50

C

close [kləʊz] – shut* schließen, zumachen

- *Close* und *shut* sind austauschbar in der Bedeutung „zumachen".
  Close/Shut *your eyes/the door/your books.* ● ● ● Schließt …!/Macht … zu!
Aber bei einer zeitweiligen Sperrung wird nur *close* verwendet.
  The airport has been **closed** *because of a bomb alert.* ● ● ● Der Flughafen wurde … geschlossen.
In der Bedeutung „beenden" wird ebenfalls nur *close* verwendet.
  close *a letter/a meeting/a speech/a discussion* ● ● ● einen Brief/… (ab)schließen/beenden
- Nur *closed* kann als Adjektiv vor einem Nomen stehen.
  Closed *doors everywhere: nobody was willing to help.* ● ● ● Überall geschlossene Türen: …

coast Küste

- *a town* **on the coast/ by the coast** (~~at the coast~~ / ~~next to the coast~~) ● ● ● eine Stadt an der Küste

colour (BE)/color (AE) Farbe

- **What colour is** (~~Which colour has~~) *your car?* ● ● ● Welche Farbe/Was für eine Farbe hat …?

come* kommen

- **come from** nicht in der Verlaufsform
In der Bedeutung „herstammen" steht *come* nicht in der Verlaufsform.
  I **come from** *York. Where* **do** *you* **come from**? ● ● ● Ich komme/bin aus York. Woher kommst du?

<table>
<tr><td rowspan="7">Trouble Spot</td><td>■ kommen</td></tr>
<tr><td>Die Gläser kommen ins Wohnzimmer. [= hingehören] ● ● ● The cups go in the living room.</td></tr>
<tr><td>Wie komme ich zum Zentrum? [= hinkommen, gelangen] ● ● ● How do I get to the centre?</td></tr>
<tr><td>Wir sind nicht weit gekommen. ● ● ● We didn't get far.</td></tr>
<tr><td>Ich musste den Arzt kommen lassen. ● ● ● I had to send for the doctor.</td></tr>
<tr><td>Bald komme ich in eine neue Klasse. ● ● ● I'll soon be in a new class.</td></tr>
<tr><td>Das kommt gar nicht infrage. ● ● ● That is quite out of the question.</td></tr>
</table>

comment ['kɒment] kommentieren

- **comment on sth.**
Ein Objekt nach dem Verb *comment* wird mit der Präposition *on* angeschlossen.
  He refused to **comment on** *the matter.* ● ● ● Er weigerte sich, die Angelegenheit zu kommentieren.

complain sich beschweren

- *We* **complained to** *the manager* **about** *the meal.* ● ● ● Wir beschwerten uns bei der Geschäftsführerin wegen des Essens/über das Essen.

concentrate ['kɒnsntreɪt] sich konzentrieren

- **concentrate on doing**
  concentrate on reducing *costs* ● ● ● sich darauf konzentrieren, die Kosten zu senken
Concentrate ist im Englischen kein reflexives Verb.
  This is difficult. I must **concentrate** *hard.* ● ● ● … Ich muss mich sehr konzentrieren.
- Adjektiv *concentrated* nur vor Nomen
Das Adjektiv *concentrated* kann nur vor Nomen stehen.
  make a **concentrated effort** ● ● ● gezielte/energische Anstrengungen unternehmen
„Konzentriert sein" entspricht *concentrate* oder *be concentrating*.
  Chang is playing well. He's **concentrating** *hard.* ● ● ● Er ist sehr konzentriert.
- Adverb *concentratedly* unüblich
„Konzentriert" im Sinne von „auf konzentrierte Art und Weise" wird normalerweise nicht durch ein -*ly*-Adverb ausgedrückt.
  Everybody was listening **with great concentration**. ● ● ● Alle hörten sehr konzentriert zu.

concept ≠ „Konzept"

1 What is the best synonym for 'concept' in the following sentence?
The concept of free will is being undermined by psychological research.
  A belief   B idea   C power   D thought

2 The marketing experts are still working out *[ihr Konzept]*.
  A their campaign   B their concept   C their plan   D their project

concerned

1 *[Die betroffenen Klassen]* have been informed by the school secretary.
  A The classes concerned   B The concerned classes

condition

1 What is the best synonym for 'condition' in the following sentence?
Is the condition of the building OK?
  A heating   B state

2 We will only support the plan ....
  A below the condition that we have a say in how the money is spent
  B on condition that we have a say in how the money is spent
  C under condition that we have a say in how the money is spent

confess

1 A He confessed her his love.   B He confessed his love to her.

2 A I confess that I've known about the problem for at least two months.
  B I confess to know about the problem for at least two months.
  C I confess to having known about the problem for at least two months.

confession ≠ „Konfession"

1 What is the correct German translation of the following sentence?
I have a confession to make.
  A *Ich muss ein Gebet sprechen.*
  B *Ich habe einen Bericht zu machen.*
  C *Ich muss etwas beichten.*

2 We have students *[mit acht verschiedenen Konfessionen]*.
  A of eight different believes   B of eight different confessions
  C of eight different denominations   D of eight different religions

confident

1 .... when they dig deeper.
  A The archaeologists are confident at finding more gold ornaments
  B The archaeologists are confident of finding more gold ornaments
  C The archaeologists are confident to find more gold ornaments
  D The archaeologists are confident that they will find more gold ornaments

concept ['kɒnsept] **Begriff**

> ■ **False Friend!**
> *Concept* bedeutet nicht „~~Konzept~~", sondern „Begriff", „grundlegende Idee", „Gedanke".
> > The **concept** of freedom is a very Western idea. ● ● ● Der Freiheitsbegriff / Die Idee der Freiheit / Die Vorstellung von Freiheit …
> Beachte die englischen Entsprechungen von „Konzept" [= Entwurf; erste Fassung; grober Plan]:
> > Das Konzept wird noch entwickelt. ● ● ● The **plan** is still being developed.
> > Ich habe erst ein Konzept geschrieben. ● ● ● I've just written an **outline**.

C

concerned **betreffend, betroffen**

■ **nach einem Nomen**
Das Adjektiv *concerned* (wie auch *involved*) steht in der Bedeutung „betreffend", „betroffen" **nicht vor** einem Nomen, sondern dahinter.
> **The people concerned** are requested to contact the police. ● ● ● Die betreffenden Personen …

condition [kən'dɪʃn] **Zustand; Kondition; Bedingung**

■ *The used car was* **in (a) good condition**. ● ● ● … in gutem Zustand.
I haven't trained for weeks. I'm **out of condition**. ● ● ● … Ich habe keine Kondition.

■ *do sth.* **on condition that** … ● ● ● etwas unter der Bedingung machen, dass …

confess **zugeben, gestehen, beichten**

■ **confess to sb.**
Nach *confess* wird die Person, der etwas gebeichtet wird, mit *to* angeschlossen.
> He **confessed to** his boss that he had made a big mistake. ● ● ● Er gestand seiner Chefin, dass …
> He **confessed** his mistake **to** his boss. ● ● ● Er gestand seiner Chefin seinen Fehler.

■ **confess to a crime**
Nach *confess* wird das Verbrechen, das man gesteht, mit *to* angeschlossen, wenn das förmliche Eingestehen vor der Polizei gemeint ist.
> He **confessed to** the murder. ● ● ● Er gab den Mord zu. / Er gestand den Mord.

■ **confess to doing / confess that …**
Anstelle eines *that*-Satzes kann *confess to doing* (nicht *confess to do*) verwendet werden.
> He **confessed to not understanding** what I meant. ● ● ● Er gestand, nicht zu verstehen …
> = He **confessed that he didn't understand** what I meant. ● ● ● Er gestand, dass er nicht verstand …

confession [kən'feʃn] **Geständnis, Beichte**

> ■ **False Friend!**
> *Confession* bedeutet nicht „~~Konfession~~", sondern ist das zum Verb *confess* gehörige Nomen mit der Bedeutung „Geständnis", „Beichte".
> > *make a full* **confession** *to the police* ● ● ● ein umfassendes Geständnis … ablegen
> Beachte die englischen Entsprechungen von „Konfession":
> > Welche Konfession haben Sie? ● ● ● What **religion / denomination** are you?

confident ['kɒnfɪdənt] **zuversichtlich**

■ **confident of doing / confident that …**
Confident kann man mit *of* + der *-ing*-Form des Verbs oder mit einem *that*-Satz verbinden – nicht aber mit einem *to*-Infinitiv.
> I'm **confident of passing** (~~confident to pass~~) my driving test. ● ● ● Ich bin zuversichtlich, meine Fahrprüfung zu bestehen.
> I'm **confident (that) I'll pass** my driving test. ● ● ● Ich bin zuversichtlich, dass ich meine Fahrprüfung bestehe.

consist of

1 ...... I'm full already!
   A How many courses does this meal consist at?
   B How many courses does this meal consist for?
   C How many courses does this meal consist in?
   D How many courses does this meal consist of?

content – contents

1 What is more important – ...... ?
   A the content or the structure of my essay   B the contents or the structure of my essay

2 You'd be surprised at ....
   A the content of some people's pockets and handbags
   B the contents of some people's pockets and handbags

continue

1 A We've continued making progress this year.
   B We've continued on making progress this year.
   C We've continued to make progress this year.

control ≠ „kontrollieren"

1 What is the best synonym for 'control' in the following sentence?
   Traffic lights control the flow of traffic.
   A check   B manage   C order   D interrupt

2 Passports *[werden dreimal kontrolliert]* before you actually board the plane.
   A are checked three times   B are controlled three times   C are tested three times

cook

1 ...... Shall I make the tea?
   A The water is boiling.   B The water is cooking.

2 I don't like fried eggs, but I don't mind ....
   A boiled eggs   B boiling eggs   C cooked eggs

3 I think I'll probably ...... of what's left.
   A boil soup   B cook soup   C make soup

cost

1 A Norway has a very high cost of living.   B Norway has very high costs of living.

2 ...... really shocked me.
   A The cost of repairing the car   B The costs of repairing the car

3 If you want to eat somewhere else, you'll have to do it *[auf eigene Kosten]*.
   A at your own costs   B at your own expense
   C on your own cost   D on your own expenses

4 We'll just have a quick snack. A proper meal *[kostet zu viel Zeit]*.
   A will cost too much time   B will spend too much time   C will take too much time

consist of bestehen aus

■ The festival **consists of** 12 one-act plays. ● ● ● Das Festival besteht aus 12 Einaktern.

content – contents ['kɒntents] Inhalt

■ Content (Singular) bedeutet „Inhalt" im Sinne von „(thematischer/chemischer) Gehalt".
   The way you present your argument is as important as the actual **content**. ● ● ● … wie der
      eigentliche Inhalt.
   a drink with a low alcohol **content** ● ● ● … mit einem geringen Alkoholgehalt

■ Contents (Plural) bedeutet „Inhalt" im Sinne von „enthaltene Sachen" oder „Inhaltsverzeichnis".
   He emptied the **contents** of the suitcase onto the bed. ● ● ● … den Inhalt des Koffers …
   This book has seven pages of **contents**. ● ● ● … ein siebenseitiges Inhaltsverzeichnis.

continue fortfahren (mit), weiter[machen]   ▷ go on

■ Auf continue kann ein to-Infinitiv oder eine -ing-Form folgen.
   I **continued to ask**/**continued asking** questions. ● ● ● Ich stellte immer weiter Fragen.

control beherrschen, regeln

> ! ! ! !

■ **False Friend!**
Control entspricht dem deutschen „kontrollieren" nur im Sinne von „beherrschen",
„überwachen", „steuern", „regeln".
   Multinational companies **control** the market. [= beherrschen] ● ● ● … beherrschen den Markt.
   Thermostats **control** the heating. [= regeln] ● ● ● Thermostate regeln die Heizung.
Beachte die englische Entsprechung von „kontrollieren" im Sinne von „überprüfen", „prüfen":
   Unsere Pässe wurden drei Mal kontrolliert. ● ● ● Our passports were **checked** three times.

cook kochen

■ Who's going to **cook**/**do the cooking** this evening? ● ● ● Wer kocht heute Abend?
   How do you **cook** seaweed? ● ● ● Wie kocht man Seetang?

Trouble Spot

■ **kochen**
1 Das Wasser kocht. [= sieden] ● ● ● The water's **boiling**.
   ein gekochtes Ei [= in siedendem Wasser gekocht] ● ● ● a **boiled** egg
2 Tee/Kaffee/Suppe kochen ● ● ● **make** tea/coffee/soup
3 Er kocht gut. ● ● ● He **is a good cook**.

cost [kɒst] 1 Kosten 2* kosten

Trouble Spot

■ **Kosten**
„Kosten" im Sinne von „der Geldbetrag oder der Aufwand, der notwendig ist, um etwas zu
kaufen oder zu tun" wird durch die Singularform cost wiedergegeben.
   Die Lebensmittelkosten sind gestiegen. ● ● ● The **cost** of food **has** risen.
   Die Lebenshaltungskosten sind gestiegen. ● ● ● The **cost** of living **has** risen.
   Die menschlichen Kosten des Krieges sind gewaltig. ● ● ● The human **cost** of the war **is**
      enormous.
Die Pluralform costs bezeichnet die Kosten in einem Unternehmen.
   Produktionskosten, Arbeitskosten ● ● ● production **costs**, labour **costs**
Wendung:
   etwas auf eigene Kosten reparieren ● ● ● repair sth. **at** one's **own expense** [Singular!]

■ **kosten**
   Wie viel kostet es? ● ● ● How much does it **cost**?/How much **is** it?
   Ich fürchte, das kostet zu viel Zeit. ● ● ● I'm afraid it will **take** too much **time**.

credit – loan

1 What's the bank's usual policy? ......
   A Do they give credit to students?
   B Do they give credits to students?
   C Do they give loans to students?

crime

1 A A report last week said that crime had gone up in country areas.
   B A report last week said that the crime had gone up in country areas.
   C A report last week said that the criminality had gone up in country areas.

critic ≠ „Kritik"

1 'Critic' is ....
   A an adjective that means *kritisch*
   B a noun that means *Kritiker/-in*
   C a verb that means *kritisieren*

2 I thought Joanne was really unfair *[mit ihrer Kritik]*.
   A with her critic   B with her critics   C with her criticism   D with her criticisms

3 I thought the play was really good, but it didn't get *[eine gute Kritik]* in the paper.
   A a good critic   B a good criticism   C a good report   D a good review

criticize/criticise

1 A The report criticized the prime minister because not informing parliament.
   B The report criticized the prime minister for not informing parliament.
   C The report criticized the prime minister on account that he didn't inform parliament.

currant – current

1 A currant is ....
   A a very recent event   B a development   C a modern trend   D a piece of fruit

2 ...... It's less than 240 volts, isn't it?
   A What voltage is the electric currant in the USA?
   B What voltage is the electric current in the USA?
   C What voltage is the electric stream in the USA?

damage

1 A How many damages did the storm cause?   B How much damage did the storm cause?

2 A The storm caused a great damage.   B The storm caused great damage.
   C The storm caused great damages.   D The storm caused a lot of damages.

credit ['krɛdɪt] – loan Kredit

■ **nicht zählbares Nomen**

Credit im Sinne von „Kredit" ist nicht zählbar, kann also – im Gegensatz zu *loan* – nicht mit *a* oder im Plural verwendet werden.

*The bank won't give me **any credit**.* = *The bank won't give me **a loan**.* ● ● ● … keinen Kredit.

D

crime Kriminalität; Verbrechen

■ ***crime* als nicht zählbares Nomen**

Crime kann als nicht zählbares oder als zählbares Nomen verwendet werden.

Als nicht zählbares Nomen bedeutet *crime* „Kriminalität" (das Wort *criminality* [ˌkrɪmɪ'næləti] ist in der Alltagssprache unüblich). In dieser Bedeutung steht *crime* (als abstraktes Nomen) meist ohne den bestimmten Artikel.

Crime / *The amount of **crime** has gone down.* ● ● ● Die Kriminalität ist zurückgegangen.

■ ***crime* als zählbares Nomen**

Als zählbares Nomen bedeutet *crime* „Verbrechen" im Sinne von „einzelne Taten oder Fälle".

*How many **crimes** were committed last year?* ● ● ● Wie viele Verbrechen wurden letztes Jahr begangen?

critic ['krɪtɪk] Kritiker/-in

■ **False Friend!**

Critic bedeutet nicht „~~Kritik~~", sondern bezeichnet eine Person und bedeutet „Kritiker/-in".

*My brother is one of my harshest **critics**.* ● ● ● … einer meiner schärfsten Kritiker.

Beachte die englischen Entsprechungen von „Kritik":

Deine Kritik hat mich sehr getroffen. ● ● ● *Your **criticism(s)*** ['krɪtɪsɪzəm(z)] *really hurt me.*

Die Kritik [= Besprechung von Büchern, Filmen und kulturellen Veranstaltungen] in der Zeitung war sehr positiv. ● ● ● *The **review** [rɪ'vjuː] in the paper was very positive.*

criticize / (BE auch:) criticise ['krɪtɪsaɪz] kritisieren

■ ***criticize sb. for doing***

*The government was **criticized for failing** to react sooner to the crisis.* ● ● ● Die Regierung wurde kritisiert, weil sie nicht früher auf die Krise reagierte / reagiert hatte.

currant Rosine; Johannisbeere – current 1 Strom 2 aktuell   ▶ actual

■ *Currant* ist ein Nomen und bedeutet „Rosine" oder „Johannisbeere".

*a **currant** cake* ● ● ● ein Rosinenkuchen

blackcurrant / ***redcurrant** jam* ● ● ● schwarze / rote Johannisbeerkonfitüre

■ *Current* ist ein Nomen mit der Bedeutung „Strom", „Strömung" oder ein Adjektiv mit der Bedeutung „aktuell".

*electric **current*** ● ● ● elektrischer Strom

*the **current** in a river* ● ● ● die Strömung in einem Fluss

*at **current** prices* ● ● ● bei den aktuellen Preisen

damage ['dæmɪdʒ] Schaden, Schäden

■ **nicht zählbares Nomen**

Damage ist ein nicht zählbares Nomen und kann daher nicht mit *a* oder im Plural verwendet werden.

*The floods caused **great damage** (~~a great damage~~).* ● ● ● Die Überschwemmungen verursachten (einen) großen Schaden.

*The floods caused **a lot of damage** (~~a lot of damages~~).* ● ● ● Die Überschwemmungen verursachten viele Schäden.

danger

1 That man drives like a maniac. ......

  A He's a danger to everyone on the road.

  B He's a danger towards everyone on the road.

2 ...... Don't do that.

  A You're in danger to lose a friend.   B You're in danger of losing a friend.

  C You're running the danger to lose a friend.   D You're running the danger of losing a friend.

3 I'm not going to help. ......

  A You do that at your own danger.   B You do that at your own risk.

  C You do that on your own danger.

4 ...... , I have to say I think it would be a foolish thing to do.

  A At the danger to sound like our father   B At the danger of sounding like our father

  C At the risk of sounding like our father   D On the danger to sound like our father

data

1 ...... that there has been a reduction in the number of unemployed.

  A The most recent data show   B The most recent datas show   C The most recent data shows

date

1 Half the players had flu, ...

  A so the match has been postponed at a later date

  B so the match has been postponed on a later date

  C so the match has been postponed to a later date

  D so the match has been postponed towards a later date

dead

1 [Der Tote] was wearing a very unusual green amulet round his neck.

  A The dead   B The died   C The dead man   D The died man

deadly – fatal

1 Is the cobra ...... ?

  A a deadly snake   B a fatal snake

2 They didn't know at the time, but the decision to go north was ....

  A a deadly mistake   B a fatal mistake

decide

1 With so many people involved, ...

  A we must decide at a date for our next meeting soon

  B we must decide for a date for our next meeting soon

  C we must decide on a date for our next meeting soon

  D we must decide to a date for our next meeting soon

decision

1 Have you ...... yet?

  A arrived at a decision   B fallen a decision   C felled a decision   D reached a decision

  E taken a decision   F made a decision   G come to a decision

danger Gefahr

■ *Smoking is **a danger to** your health.* ● ● ● Rauchen ist eine Gefahr für die Gesundheit.
*You're **in danger of losing** your job.* ● ● ● Du läufst Gefahr, deine Arbeitsstelle zu verlieren.

Trouble Spot

■ **Gefahr**
etwas auf eigene Gefahr tun ● ● ● *do sth. **at** one's **own risk***
Selbst auf die Gefahr hin, unhöflich zu erscheinen / Auch wenn es unhöflich erscheinen mag,
muss ich sagen … ● ● ● ***At the risk of seeming** rude, I have to say …*
Es besteht die Gefahr, dass er sich ansteckt. ● ● ● ***There's a risk** that he might become infected.*

data Daten

■ **nicht zählbares Nomen oder Pluralnomen**
Data kann (ohne Bedeutungsunterschied) als nicht zählbares Nomen oder als Nomen im Plural
verwendet werden.
This data shows** / **These data show *that …* ● ● ● Diese Daten zeigen, dass …

date Datum

■ *We'll discuss this **at** a later **date**.* ● ● ● Wir besprechen das zu einem späteren Zeitpunkt.
*We'll postpone this **to** a later **date**.* ● ● ● Wir verschieben das auf einen späteren Zeitpunkt.

Topic Box

■ *Talking about dates and seasons*
1 Schreibung des Datums
6 June 2005 / 6th June(,) 2005 / June 6, 2005 / June 6th, 2005

2 gesprochene Formen des Datums
What's the date (today)? – It's the sixth. / It's the sixth of June. / It's June the sixth.
The D-Day landings happened on the sixth of June 1944 / on June the sixth 1944 /
(AE:) on June six(th) 1944.

3 Jahreszeiten
Spring / The spring is my favourite season. ● ● ● Der Frühling ist meine Lieblingsjahreszeit.
I was born in (the) spring. ● ● ● Ich bin / wurde im Frühling geboren.
I was born in the spring of 1982. ● ● ● Ich bin im Frühling 1982 geboren.

dead tot

■ **als Nomen nur zur Bezeichnung einer Gruppe**
The dead (ohne Plural-*s*) bezeichnet eine Gruppe von Toten (oft im Sinne von „alle Toten").
*pray for the souls of **the dead*** ● ● ● für die Seelen der Toten beten
Aber:
***The dead person** (The died person) has been identified.* ● ● ● Der / Die Tote ist identifiziert worden.

deadly – fatal ['feɪtl] tödlich

■ *Deadly* und *fatal* werden mit unterschiedlichen Nomen verwendet.
Faustregel: *Deadly* setzt eine Absicht oder einen persönlichen Angriff voraus. *Fatal* bezeichnet unwillentlich oder zufällig tödliche Begebenheiten.
*a **deadly** enemy / poison / snake / blow*
*a **fatal** accident / illness / mistake*

decide (sich) entscheiden

■ ***decide on** a date* ● ● ● sich für ein Datum entscheiden

decision Entscheidung

■ ***make / take / arrive at / come to / reach** a decison* ● ● ● eine Entscheidung treffen

deep – deeply

1 ......, you can make use of thermal energy.
  A If you dig deep enough   **B** If you dig deeply enough

2 You're going to be alright. Now just calm down, ...
  A breathe deep and relax a bit   **B** breathe deeply and relax a bit

defect – defective

1 ...... leading to the starter motor.
  A The problem was a defect cable   **B** The problem was a defective cable

degree

1 ......, it's very pleasant.
  A It's 22 degree outside this afternoon   **B** It's 22 degrees outside this afternoon

democracy

1 People always say ......, but it's the best form of government we have.
  A democracy is not perfect   **B** the democracy is not perfect

2 Freedom of speech is ....
  A one of the most precious rights in democracy
  B one of the most precious rights in the democracy

deny

1 A He denied having any contact with the man.
  B He denied having had any contact with the man.
  C He denied to have any contact with the man.
  D He denied to have had any contact with the man.
  E He denied that he had any contact with the man.
  F He denied that he had had any contact with the man.

depend

1 Who is going to win? ...... which candidate can mobilize her core voters on the day.
  A It all depends now   **B** It's all depending now

describe

1 ...... It was amazing.
  A I'll describe you the scene.   **B** I'll describe the scene to you.   **C** I'll describe the scene for you.

desert – dessert

1 ...... – Chocolate mousse, please.
  A What would you like for desert?   **B** What would you like for dessert?

2 Gill has gone on another trekking holiday, this time to ....
  A the Gobi Desert   **B** the Gobi Dessert

D

deep – deeply tief

■ Sowohl *deep* als auch *deeply* werden als Adverb verwendet. Faustregel: *deep* im wörtlichen, *deeply* im übertragenen Sinn.

The submarine went **deep** below the surface. ● ● ● … tief unter die Wasseroberfläche.

be **deeply** hurt by sb.'s criticism ● ● ● tief/schwer gekränkt sein durch die Kritik von jmdm.

breathe **deeply** / sleep **deeply** ● ● ● tief atmen / tief schlafen

defect ['diːfekt; dɪ'fekt] Defekt, Fehler [an Maschine usw.] – defective [dɪ'fektɪv] defekt

■ *Defect* ist ein Nomen.

There is a **defect** in the system somewhere. ● ● ● Irgendwo im System steckt ein Fehler.

■ Das dazugehörige Adjektiv *defective* gehört der fachsprachlichen Ebene an.

The temperature control was **defective**. ● ● ● Die Temperaturregelung war defekt.

Allgemeinsprachliche Entsprechungen für „defekt" sind z.B. *faulty* ['fɒlti] und *broken*. ▷ broken

degree Grad   ▷ minus   ▷ temperature

■ **bei Temperaturangaben:** *degrees* **mit Singularverb**

Degree ist ein zählbares Nomen mit der Pluralform *degrees*.

Water freezes **at zero degrees** Celsius (0°C). ● ● ● Wasser gefriert bei null Grad Celsius (0 °C).

Bei Temperaturangaben steht das Verb jedoch im Singular.

It's 32 **degrees** in the shade. ● ● ● Es sind 32 Grad im Schatten.

democracy [dɪ'mɒkrəsi] Demokratie

■ **ohne** *the* **in Aussagen allgemeiner Art**

Democracy gehört zu den abstrakten Nomen, die in Aussagen allgemeiner Art ohne den bestimmten Artikel verwendet werden.

We must defend **democracy** (the democracy). ● ● ● Wir müssen die Demokratie verteidigen.

deny leugnen, abstreiten

■ *deny doing* / *deny that* …

Auf *deny* folgt die *-ing*-Form des Verbs oder ein *that*-Satz, aber kein *to*-Infinitiv.

He **denied** stealing / **denied** having stolen (denied to have stolen) the ring. ● ● ● Er leugnete, den Ring gestohlen zu haben.

He **denied** that he stole / **denied** that he had stolen the ring. ● ● ● Er leugnete, dass er den Ring gestohlen habe.

depend abhängen

■ *it* / *that depends:* **nicht in der Verlaufsform**

Will you help me? – **It depends** (is depending) what you want me to do. ● ● ● … Das hängt davon ab, was ich für dich machen soll.

describe beschreiben

■ *describe sth. to* / *for sb.*

Die Person, der man etwas beschreibt, muss mit *to* (oder *for*) angeschlossen werden.

They **described** the man **to** the police. ● ● ● Sie beschrieben der Polizei den Mann.

Can you **describe** the house **to** / **for** me? ● ● ● Können Sie mir das Haus beschreiben?

desert ['dezət] Wüste – dessert [dɪ'zɜːt] Dessert, Nachtisch

■ the Sahara **Desert** ● ● ● die Wüste Sahara

■ the **dessert** menu ● ● ● die Dessertkarte

What's **for dessert**? ● ● ● Was gibt's zum Nachtisch?

deserve

1 What do you think? ......
   A Are we deserving the prize or not?   B Do we deserve the prize or not?

develop

1 I still have one of those old-fashioned non-digital cameras where you have to have your film
   ...... before you can view the pictures.
   A developed   B develloped   C developped   D devellopped

2 ...... if she continues training hard.
   A Susan will develop in a very powerful player
   B Susan will develop into a very powerful player
   C Susan will develop to a very powerful player

dictate

1 I'm sorry, ... I can't formulate it on my own.
   A but you're going to have to dictate me that   B but you're going to have to dictate that to me

die

1 A This town is slowly dieing.   B This town is slowly dying.

2 ...... two years before Sonia was born, so Sonia never knew her.
   A Sonia's grandmother died   B Sonia's grandmother dyed

3 ...... if I don't get a drink soon.
   A I'm going to die at thirst   B I'm going to die because of thirst
   C I'm going to die of thirst   D I'm going to die on thirst

different

1 Choose the best preposition to use with 'different'.
   A My life is so different from my grandmother's.
   B My life is so different than my grandmother's.
   C My life is so different to my grandmother's.

2 Over the next few months ...... to see how the building work was progressing.
   A we made different trips   B we made various trips

3 They both taste the same to me. ......
   A I can't realize the difference between them.   B I can't tell the difference between them.

4 A Can you differ between a British and an American speaker of English?
   B Can you distinguish between a British and an American speaker of English?

difficulty

1 ...... what we should do next.
   A We had difficulty deciding   B We had difficulty in deciding   C We had difficulty to decide

D

deserve verdienen

■ **nicht in der Verlaufsform**

Deserve zählt zu den Verben, die man normalerweise nicht in der Verlaufsform verwenden kann.

> *We **deserve** (~~We're deserving~~) a break now, after all this hard work.* ● ● ● Wir haben uns jetzt eine Pause verdient …

develop (sich) entwickeln

■ ***-ing-*Form und *-ed-*Form mit <u>einem</u> „p"**
developing, developed

■ ***develop from*** *a small town **into** a big city* ● ● ● sich aus einer Kleinstadt zu einer Großstadt entwickeln

> *Spamming has **developed into** a big problem.* ● ● ● Spammen ist zu einem großen Problem geworden.

dictate diktieren

■ ***dictate sth. to sb.***

Die Person, der man etwas diktiert, wird mit *to* angeschlossen.

> *Can you **dictate** the exact text **to** me?* ● ● ● Können Sie mir den genauen Text diktieren?

die sterben

■ **Schreibung**
die, dies, dying, died

■ ***die of*** *hunger / thirst / old age* ● ● ● verhungern / verdursten / an Altersschwäche sterben

> ***die of / from*** *cancer / a knife wound* [Krankheit, Verletzung] ● ● ● an Krebs / an einer Messerverletzung sterben

different anders; verschieden, unterschiedlich ▷ other

■ **Präpositionen**

Nach *different* verwendet man am besten *from*, auch wenn im BE teilweise *different to* (stilistisch fragwürdig) und im AE teilweise *different than* verwendet wird.

> *The weather is very **different from** last year.* ● ● ● Das Wetter ist ganz anders als im letzten Jahr.

Trouble Spot

■ **verschieden**

Anna und Bernd sind sehr verschieden [= unterschiedlich]. ● ● ● *Anna and Bernd are very **different**.*

Ich hatte verschiedene [= mehrere] Gründe, nicht nur einen. ● ● ● *I had **various** reasons, not just one.*

■ **Unterschied**

einen Unterschied zwischen zwei Dingen machen ● ● ● ***make a difference, make / draw a distinction*** *between two things*

Erkennst du den Unterschied? ● ● ● *Can you **tell the difference**?*

■ **sich unterscheiden; etwas / jmdn. (von etwas / jmdm.) unterscheiden**

Die zwei Länder unterscheiden sich sehr. ● ● ● *The two countries **differ** greatly.*

links und rechts unterscheiden ● ● ● ***distinguish between*** *left and right /* ***distinguish*** *left **from** right*

difficulty Schwierigkeit

■ ***have difficulty (in) doing***

Have difficulty (meist Singular!) verwendet man mit einer nachfolgenden *-ing-*Form (mit oder ohne *in*), nicht mit einem *to-*Infinitiv.

> *I **had difficulty (in) finding** (~~had difficulty to find~~) the house.* ● ● ● Ich hatte Schwierigkeiten, das Haus zu finden.

discriminate

1 A Women have been discriminated for centuries.
B Women have been discriminated against for centuries.
C Women have been discriminated from for centuries.
D Women have been discriminated to for centuries.

discuss

1 We spent a long time ....
A discussing Emily's project   B discussing about Emily's project
C discussing on Emily's project   D discussing over Emily's project

2 A We discussed for a long time.
B We discussed it for a long time.
C We had a long discussion.

dislike

1 .... , especially on Sunday mornings.
A I dislike to work at weekends   B I dislike working at weekends

distance

1 I don't recognize him. ......
A At this distance it could be anyone.
B From this distance it could be anyone.
C Out of this distance it could be anyone.

2 A How is the distance from the earth to the moon?
B How big is the distance from the earth to the moon?
C What's the distance from the earth to the moon?

3 A How far away is the moon?   B How far distant is the moon?   C How distant is the moon?

4 A The sun is 93 million miles away.
B The sun is 93 million miles distant.
C The sun is 93 million miles wide away.

5 A It is 93 million miles from here to the sun.
B There are 93 million miles from here to the sun.
C They are 93 million miles from here to the sun.

6 A My old school is only ten minutes on foot away.
B My old school is only a ten-minute walk away.
C My old school is only ten minutes on foot distant.

divide

1 A How do you divide £99 equally among four people?
B How do you divide £99 equally between four people?
C How do you divide £99 equally by four people?
D How do you divide £99 equally into four people?

discriminate diskriminieren

■ **discriminate against sb.**
Nach *discriminate* in der Bedeutung „jmdn. ungleich behandeln", „jmdn. benachteiligen" muss ein Objekt mit *against* angeschlossen werden.
*It is illegal to **discriminate against** blacks.* ● ● ● Es ist illegal, Schwarze zu diskriminieren.
*Blacks have been **discriminated against** for a long time.* ● ● ● Schwarze werden schon lange diskriminiert.

D

discuss diskutieren über, besprechen

■ **discuss sth.**
Discuss ist ein transitives Verb und wird immer mit Objekt verwendet. Zwischen *discuss* und dem Objekt steht keine Präposition.
*I'd like to **discuss our holiday plans** (~~discuss about our holiday plans~~) for the summer.* ● ● ● Ich würde gern über unsere Urlaubspläne für den Sommer sprechen.
*We **discussed the topic** for a long time.* ● ● ● Wir haben lange über das Thema diskutiert.
Beachte aber:
Wir haben lange diskutiert. [ohne Objekt] ● ● ● *We **had** a long **discussion**. / We **talked** for a long time.* (~~We discussed for a long time.~~)

dislike nicht mögen

■ **nur mit -*Ing*-Form**
Im Gegensatz zu *like* kann *dislike* nicht mit einem *to*-Infinitiv verwendet werden.
*I **dislike sitting** (~~dislike to sit~~) in smoky rooms.* ● ● ● Ich sitze ungern in verrauchten Räumen.

distance ['dɪstəns] Entfernung

■ *At/**From** this **distance** it's impossible to see exactly what's going on.* ● ● ● Aus dieser Entfernung …

> **Topic Box**
>
> ■ **Talking about distance** ▶ far
> *What's the distance (~~How (big) is the distance~~) from here to London?* ● ● ● Wie (groß) ist die Entfernung von hier bis London?
> *How **far** is it from here to London?* ● ● ● Wie weit ist es von hier nach London?
> *It's a hundred and ten miles.* ● ● ● Es sind hundertzehn Meilen.
> *How **far away** (~~How distant~~) is London?* ● ● ● Wie weit ist London entfernt?
> *London is 110 miles **away** (~~110 miles distant~~).* ● ● ● London ist 110 Meilen entfernt.
> *It's quite a (long) **way away**.* ● ● ● Es ist ziemlich weit weg/entfernt.
> *It's quite a (long) **way from here**.* ● ● ● Es ist ziemlich weit weg/entfernt von hier.
> *It's 200 km **from here**.* ● ● ● Es sind 200 km von hier.
> *It's (a) two hours' **drive** / a two-hour **drive**.* ● ● ● Es sind zwei Autostunden. / Es sind zwei Stunden mit dem Auto.
> *It's two hours **by car**.* ● ● ● Es sind zwei Stunden mit dem Auto.
> *It's a long **way** from Paris to Moscow.* ● ● ● Es ist ein weiter Weg von Paris nach Moskau.
> *We live about ten minutes' **walk** from the station.* ● ● ● Wir wohnen ca. zehn Minuten zu Fuß vom Bahnhof.
> *The office is a ten-minute bus **ride** from here.* ● ● ● Das Büro ist zehn Minuten mit dem Bus von hier (entfernt).

divide teilen, aufteilen ▶ multiply

■ ***Divide** the cake **into** four.* ● ● ● Teile den Kuchen in vier Teile.
***Divide** the cake **between**/**among** the four of us.* ● ● ● Teile den Kuchen unter uns vieren auf.

doctor – PhD/doctorate

1 This is our head teacher, *[Frau Dr. Mertens]*.
  A Dr Mertens   B Mrs Mertens   C Mrs Dr Mertens

2 A What's she doing her doctorate in?   B What's she making her doctorate in?

door

1 I thought I just heard someone *[an der Haustür]*. Could you go and look?
  A at the door   B at the front door   C at the house door

double

1 There was so much traffic, ...
  A it took us double as long that it took last time
  B it took us double the time that it took last time
  C it took us the double time that it took last time

2 A London is at least double as big as Cologne.
  B London is at least double the size of Cologne.
  C London is at least the double size of Cologne.

3 A This hotel is double the price of that B & B place down the road.
  B This hotel is double as expensive as that B & B place down the road.

doubt – no doubt – without doubt

1 ...... that we can finish this project by June.
  A I'm now doubting   B I now doubt

2 Do you think Germany will win? – ......
  A I'm very doubting.   B I doubt it much.   C I doubt it very much.

3 Pansy and Toby are getting married, ...
  A but no doubt you've already heard
  B but without doubt you've already heard
  C but doubtless you've already heard

4 A Everyone agrees that this year's festival was no doubt the best yet.
  B Everyone agrees that this year's festival was without doubt the best yet.
  C Everyone agrees that this year's festival was doubtless the best yet.
  D Everyone agrees that this year's festival was undoubtedly the best yet.

dozen

1 It was very disappointing. ......
  A There were not more than a dozen class members there.
  B There were not more than a dozen of class members there.
  C There were not more than dozen class members there.

doctor Arzt/Ärztin; Doktor **– PhD** [ˌpiː eɪtʃ ˈdiː] / **doctorate** [ˈdɒktərət] Doktortitel

■ **nicht zusammen mit** *Mr/Mrs/Ms*

Der Titel *Dr* wird nicht zusammen mit *Mr/Mrs/Ms* verwendet.

Can I introduce you to Dr Myers / Mrs Myers (Mrs Dr Myers)? ● ● ● Darf ich Ihnen (Frau) Dr. Myers/ Frau Myers vorstellen?

■ **Doktortitel**

She has (got) a PhD / a Ph.D. / a doctorate. ● ● ● Sie hat einen Doktor(titel).

He's doing his PhD / his Ph.D. / his doctorate. ● ● ● Er macht seinen Doktor / promoviert.

door Tür

■ **„Haustür" = (front) door**

There's someone at the (front) door (house door). ● ● ● … an der Haustür/Vordertür.

There's someone at the back door. ● ● ● … an der Hintertür.

double [ˈdʌbl] doppelt

■ **unterschiedliche Stellung und Verwendung von** *double* **und „doppelt"**

Double kann ein Adjektiv sein (z. B. in dem Ausdruck *a double bed*) und entspricht dann dem deutschen „Doppel-".

Der Gebrauch des Begleiters *double* und seiner deutschen Entsprechung „doppelt" ist jedoch unterschiedlich:

1 *Double* steht **vor** *the, this, my, your* usw., nicht dahinter.

It's now double the price (the double price)! ● ● ● Es kostet jetzt das Doppelte!

2 *Double* kann nicht vor *as* + Adjektiv stehen.

It's double the price (that) it was last week (double as expensive as …). ● ● ● Es kostet jetzt doppelt so viel wie letzte Woche.

His new flat is double this size (double as big). ● ● ● Seine neue Wohnung ist doppelt so groß (wie diese).

He's almost double your age (double as old as you). ● ● ● Er ist fast doppelt so alt wie du.

My mum earns double what my dad gets (double as much as …). ● ● ● Meine Mutter verdient doppelt so viel wie mein Vater.

doubt [daʊt] (be)zweifeln **– no doubt** höchstwahrscheinlich **– without doubt** zweifellos

■ **Verb** *doubt* **nicht in der Verlaufsform**

Doubt gehört zu den Verben, die man normalerweise nicht in der Verlaufsform verwenden kann.

I doubt (I'm doubting) now that they will come, after what's happened. ● ● ● Ich bezweifle jetzt, dass sie kommen werden …

■ *doubt very much*

Das Verb *doubt* verwendet man mit *very much*, nicht mit *very* oder nur *much*.

I very much doubt (very doubt / much doubt) they will pay that amount. ● ● ● Ich bezweifle sehr …

I doubt it very much. ● ● ● Ich bezweifle es sehr.

■ *no doubt – without doubt*

No doubt (oder *doubtless*) bedeutet „gewiss", „sicherlich", „höchstwahrscheinlich".

No doubt / Doubtless he'll phone as soon as he finds out. ● ● ● Bestimmt ruft er an, sobald er es herausgefunden hat.

Dem deutschen „zweifellos" / „ohne Zweifel" entspricht *without doubt* (oder *undoubtedly*).

The meeting of the two former presidents was without doubt / undoubtedly a historic event. ● ● ● Das Treffen der beiden ehemaligen Präsidenten war zweifellos ein historisches Ereignis.

dozen [ˈdʌzn] Dutzend

■ *a dozen*

Dozen wird wie *hundred* mit dem unbestimmten Artikel verwendet (*a dozen, a hundred*).

There were over a dozen people (dozen people) there. ● ● ● … über ein Dutzend Leute …

drive

1 I wasn't looking where I was going ....

  A and drove against the garage door   **B** and drove at the garage door

  C and drove in the garage door   **D** and drove into the garage door

2 When we were children, ...

  A we usually drove on holiday   **B** we usually drove away on holiday

  C we usually went on holiday by car   **D** we usually went on holiday with our car

3 A Does this bus drive to Beamer End?   **B** Does this bus go to Beamer End?

  C Does this bus ride to Beamer End?   **D** Does this bus run to Beamer End?

4 A How often do the buses drive to Beamer End?   **B** How often do the buses go to Beamer End?

  C How often do the buses ride to Beamer End?   **D** How often do the buses run to Beamer End?

5 Would you like me to ...... ?

  A drive you to the station   **B** go by car with you to the station

  C bring you to the station   **D** take you to the station

6 Her younger sister is now 15 ....

  A and drives moped   **B** and drives a moped   **C** and rides moped   **D** and rides a moped

7 He was going downhill on his skateboard ....

  A and was doing at least 20 km/h   **B** and drove at least 20 km/h

  C and went at least 20 km/h   **D** and was travelling at least 20 km/h

8 How fast can you ...... ?

  A drive on a skateboard   **B** do on a skateboard   **C** go on a skateboard   **D** run on a skateboard

driving licence / driver's license

1 Toby can't drive, he's only 15! ......

  A He hasn't got the driving licence.   **B** He hasn't got a driving licence.

2 ...... , my parents are going to buy me a car.

  A When I have a driving licence   **B** When I have the driving licence

  C When I've passed my driving exam   **D** When I've passed my driving test

3 He's 18 now ....

  A and is doing his driving licence   **B** and is making his driving licence

  C and is taking driving lessons

drunk – drunken

1 A It was a chaotic party and everybody was drunk.

  B It was a chaotic party and everybody was drunken.

2 A It was a really drunk party.   **B** It was really drunken party.

during – while

1 Which of the following rules is correct?

  A 'During' is a conjunction, and 'while' is a preposition.

  B 'While' is a conjunction, and 'during' is a preposition.

2 My cat usually sleeps ....

  A during much of the day   **B** while much of the day

3 ...... and broke a tooth.

  A He had an accident during skateboarding   **B** He had an accident while skateboarding

drive* fahren ▶ **journey**

■ *He was going too fast and **drove into** (~~drove against~~) a tree.* ● ● ● *… und fuhr gegen einen Baum.*

Trouble Spot

■ **fahren**
1 „von A nach B gelangen"
Wir fahren nach Luxemburg, um Freunde zu besuchen. ● ● ● *We're **going** to Luxembourg to visit some friends.*
Meist fahren wir mit dem Auto/Zug/Bus. ● ● ● *We usually **go by** car/train/coach.*
Fährt dieser Zug nach Westbury? ● ● ● *Does this train **go** to Westbury?*

2 „Auto fahren", „am Steuer sitzen"; „jmdn. fahren"
Ich fahre (mit dem Auto) zur Arbeit. ● ● ● *I **drive** to work.*
Soll ich dich nach Hause fahren? ● ● ● *Would you like me to **drive**/**take** you home?*

3 „Zweirad fahren"
Rad/Motorrad/Moped fahren ● ● ● ***ride** a bike / a motorbike / a moped*

4 „fahren" [mit Geschwindigkeitsangabe]
Die neuen Züge fahren mit 260 km/h. ● ● ● *The new trains **travel** at 260 km/h.*
Wir fuhren mit über 110 km/h. ● ● ● *We were **doing** over 110 km/h.*
Ich bin nur langsam gefahren. ● ● ● *I was only **going** very slowly.*

5 Fahreigenschaften eines Fahrzeugs
Dieses alte Auto fährt nicht sehr schnell. ● ● ● *This old car can't **go** very fast.*

6 „verkehren", „fahren" [nach Fahrplan]
Wie oft fahren die Züge? ● ● ● *How often do the trains **run**/**go**?*

driving licence (BE) / **driver's license** (AE) ['laɪsns] Führerschein, Fahrerlaubnis

■ *Can I see your **driving licence** / **driver's license**, please?*

Trouble Spot

■ **Führerschein**
Ich habe keinen Führerschein. ● ● ● *I **don't**/**can't drive**. / I **don't have a driving licence**.*
Willi macht den/seinen Führerschein. ● ● ● *Willi **is taking driving lessons**. (~~Willi is making/doing his driving licence.~~)*
Inge ist jetzt 18 und hat den Führerschein. ● ● ● *Inge is now 18 and **has passed her (driving) test** / **has a (driving) licence** / **has her (driving) licence** (~~has the driving licence~~).*

drunk – drunken betrunken

■ *Drunk* wird in aller Regel nur prädikativ, also nach einem Verb wie *be* oder *get*, verwendet.
be/**get drunk** ● ● ● betrunken sein/werden
Ausnahme:
***drunk**/**drunken** drivers* ● ● ● betrunkene Fahrer/-innen

■ *Drunken* kann nur attributiv, d. h. vor einem Nomen, stehen.
***drunken** fans / **drunken** singing* ● ● ● betrunkene Fans / betrunkener Gesang

during – while während

■ *during* **+ Nomen**
During ist eine Präposition und steht vor einem Nomen.
***During** the summer I usually walk to work.* ● ● ● Im Sommer / Während des Sommers …

■ *while* **+ Satz**
While ist eine Konjunktion und leitet einen (Neben-)Satz ein.
***While** the teacher fetched the video, I wrote a text message.* ● ● ● Während der Lehrer … holte …
While kann auch vor einem Partizip oder Nomen stehen, wenn das Verb *be* ergänzt werden kann.
***While** (I was) **waiting** at the dentist's, I sent a text message to Di.* ● ● ● Während ich … wartete …
***While** (I was) **a student**, I did some work for a small firm in Ulm.* ● ● ● Während meines Studiums …

each – every

1 Choose the better word – 'each' or 'every':
A We had sunshine each day, for the entire trip.
B We had sunshine every day, for the entire trip.

2 Choose the better word – 'each' or 'every':
A In the oral exam each student has a separate interview with the examiner.
B In the oral exam every student has a separate interview with the examiner.

3 She's read ...... , hasn't she?
A practically each book in the library   B practically every book in the library

4 The same thing happens ....
A each single time   B every single time

5 She has ten very capable people in her team. ......
A Each was very carefully selected.   B Every was very carefully selected.

6 A The groups each presented their results to the rest of the course.
B The groups presented each their results to the rest of the course.
C The groups presented their results each to the rest of the course.

7 A Each has a mobile phone these days.   B Every has a mobile phone these days.
C All have a mobile phone these days.   D Everybody has a mobile phone these days.
E Everyone has a mobile phone these days.

8 The technique isn't difficult to learn. ......
A All can master it in the space of two or three weeks.
B Anybody can master it in the space of two or three weeks.
C Each person can master it in the space of two or three weeks.

9 I don't mind what we go and see. You choose. ......
A All movies are OK for me.   B Any movie is OK for me.
C Each movie is OK for me.   D Every movie is OK for me.

10 We have nice neighbours [an jeder Seite].
A on both sides   B on either side   C on every side   D on either sides

earlier

1 My grandfather [lebte früher auf einer Ranch in Montana].
A lived earlier on a ranch in Montana
B once lived on a ranch in Montana
C used to live on a ranch in Montana

2 Is the thriller writer John Le Carré [ein früherer Geheimagent]?
A an ex-secret agent   B an earlier secret agent
C a former secret agent   D a previous secret agent

3 We've moved ...... when the baby arrived.
A because our earlier flat wasn't big enough
B because our ex-flat wasn't big enough
C because our previous flat wasn't big enough

4 I'm sorry. ......
A I should have told you earlier.
B I should have told you sooner.
C I should have told you former.

each – every jede(r/s)

■ **Bedeutungsunterschied**

Mit *each* betrachtet man jede Person oder Sache aus einer bestimmten Menge einzeln („jede[r/s] einzelne").

*The police interview **each** witness separately.* ● ● ● Die Polizei befragt jeden Zeugen einzeln/ getrennt.

Mit *every* betrachtet man die genannten Personen oder Sachen alle zusammen als eine Gruppe („alle").

*He sees **every** speck of dust.* ● ● ● Er sieht jedes Staubkörnchen.

Oft kann man sowohl *each* als auch *every* verwenden.

***Each**/**Every** time you log on, you have to wait.* ● ● ● Jedes Mal wenn man sich einloggt …

■ **Wortkombinationen mit *every***

Nur *every* kann mit *almost, nearly, practically* oder *single* („einzeln") verwendet werden.

***Almost**/**Nearly**/**Practically** every house had a swimming pool in the garden.*
*I checked **every single** connection, but I couldn't find the problem.*

■ **als Pronomen nur *each***

Each und *every* können beide als Begleiter **vor** einem Nomen oder dem Stützwort *one* stehen.

*There are six flats in the building. **Each flat**/**Every flat**/**Each one**/**Every one** is different.*

Aber nur *each* kann allein als Pronomen stehen.

*There are six flats in the building. **Each** (~~Every~~) is different.* ● ● ● … Jede ist anders.

■ **Stellung von *each***

Wenn *each* dem Subjekt nachgestellt wird, steht es **vor** (nicht hinter!) einem Vollverb.

***We each** gave (~~We gave each~~) a short talk.* ● ● ● Wir hielten jeder ein kurzes Referat.

Trouble Spot

■ **jeder**

1 „jedermann", „alle Welt" ▶ all ▶ everybody

Es ist kein Geheimnis mehr. Jeder weiß es. ● ● ● *It's no longer a secret. **Everybody**/**Everyone** knows.*

2 „jedermann", „egal wer"; „jede(r/s) x-beliebige", „egal welche(r/s)"

Die Veranstaltung ist offen. Jeder kann kommen. ● ● ● *The event is open to all. **Anybody**/ **Anyone** can come.*

Der Schuss war so schwach, dass jeder Torwart ihn gehalten hätte. ● ● ● *It was such a weak shot, **any** goalkeeper would have saved it.*

3 „jede(r/s) von zweien", „beide" ▶ both

Er hatte einen Bodyguard an jeder Seite. ● ● ● *He had a bodyguard on **either** side/ on **both** sides.*

---

earlier früher, eher

■ *Why didn't you come **earlier** [auch: **sooner**]?* ● ● ● Warum bist du nicht früher gekommen?

Trouble Spot

■ **früher** ▶ used to

Früher (einmal) war dies ein Hotel. ● ● ● *This was **once**/ This **used to** be a hotel.*

Wir sind früher (immer) nach Italien gefahren. ● ● ● *We (always) **used to** go to Italy.*

■ **frühere(r/s)**

1 „ehemalig", „einstig"

Unsere früheren [= ehemaligen] Nachbarn wohnen jetzt in Afrika. ● ● ● *Our **ex-neighbours** (fml: Our **former** neighbours) live in Africa now.*

Wer war Gladstone? – Ein früherer [= einstiger] britischer Premierminister ● ● ● *Who was Gladstone? – A **former** British prime minister.*

2 „vorhergehend"

Seine Frau ist Ärztin. Seine frühere [= letzte] Frau war Zahnärztin. ● ● ● *His wife's a doctor. His **previous** wife was a dentist.*

economic – economical

1 Elections are often decided ....
  A by the economic climate at the time   **B** by the economical climate at the time

2 ...... There were just too few visitors.
  A It wasn't economic to keep the place open.   **B** It wasn't economical to keep the place open.

3 ...... And with petrol prices as high as they are, I've decided to sell it.
  A This car isn't very economic.   **B** This car isn't very economical.

educate – bring up

1 Jan lost both her parents in a car accident .... Jan lived with her until she was 18.
  A and was educated by her mother's sister   **B** and was brought up by her mother's sister

effect – affect

1 **A** How will these changes affect the ordinary man or woman in the street?
  B How will these changes effect the ordinary man or woman in the street?

2 Things didn't improve at all. ......
  A In fact the new system had the effect of making things worse.
  B In fact the new system had the effect on making things worse.
  C In fact the new system had the effect to make things worse.

either

1 Would you like us to meet on Friday or Saturday? – ......
  A Either days suit me.   **B** Either day suits me.

else

1 So you met Yan and Wenwen at the party. ......
  A Who did you see else?   **B** Who did you else see?   **C** Who else did you see?

end

1 A book can have a detailed table of contents, ...
  A and/or an extensive appendix at the end   **B** and/or an extensive appendix in the end

2 There were complications after the operation, ...
  A and at the end he died   **B** and in the end he died

3 The phrase 'at the end of the day' is used ....
  A to introduce the last point in a list
  B to introduce the most important fact that must not be forgotten

4 Will there never be ...... ?
  A an end for this hopeless situation   **B** an end of this hopeless situation
  C an end to this hopeless situation

5 Sorry, does your name ...... ?
  A end with 't' or 'd'   **B** end in 't' or 'd'   **C** end on 't' or 'd'

engaged

1 Have you heard? ...... he met in Poland.
  A Mark is getting engaged for someone   **B** Mark is getting engaged to someone
  C Mark is getting engaged with someone

economic [ˌiːkəˈnɒmɪk] – economical [ˌiːkəˈnɒmɪkl] wirtschaftlich

■ *Economic* bedeutet „wirtschaftlich" im Sinne von „die Wirtschaft betreffend" und im Sinne von „rentabel".

*The country is in the middle of an **economic** crisis* [= die Wirtschaft betreffend, Wirtschafts-].
*Many of the old factories were no longer **economic*** [= rentabel] *and had to be closed.*

■ *Economical* bedeutet „wirtschaftlich" im Sinne von „sparsam", „günstig".

*Our new car is very **economical**. It's a diesel.* ● ● ● Unser neues Auto ist sehr sparsam. …
*It's more **economical** to buy in large quantities.* ● ● ● Es ist günstiger, große Mengen zu kaufen.

E

educate – bring* up erziehen

■ *Children are **educated** at school and **brought up** at home.* ● ● ● Kinder werden in der Schule ausgebildet und zu Hause erzogen.

effect [ɪˈfekt] Wirkung, Auswirkung – affect [əˈfekt] beeinflussen, sich auswirken auf

■ **Nomen: *effect* – Verb: *affect***

*What will be the **effect** of the new system? How will it **affect** us?* ● ● ● Was für Auswirkungen wird das neue System haben? Wie wird es sich auf uns auswirken?

■ ***effect* of doing**

Nach *effect* verwendet man *of* + die *-ing*-Form des Verbs, keinen *to*-Infinitiv.

*The new law should have **the effect of reducing** (the effect to reduce) greenhouse gases.* ● ● ● Das neue Gesetz müsste die Reduzierung von Treibhausgasen bewirken.

either [ˈaɪðə, ˈiːðə] eine(r/s) (von zweien), jede(r/s) (von zweien), beide ▶ also

■ **Unterschied zu *both* und *each/every*** ▶ both ▶ each

■ ***either* + Singular**

Either steht vor einem Nomen im Singular, auf das ein Verb im Singular folgt.

***Either** room **is** (Either rooms are) big enough for the meeting.* ● ● ● Beide Räume sind / Jeder der beiden Räume ist groß genug für die Sitzung.

else sonst [noch]

■ **Stellung: direkt hinter dem Bezugswort**

*Where **else** did you go?* (Where did you else go?) ● ● ● Wo bist du sonst noch hingegangen?
*There is **nobody else** we could ask.* (There is nobody we could else ask.) ● ● ● Es gibt sonst niemanden, den wir fragen könnten. / Es gibt niemanden, den wir sonst noch fragen könnten.

end 1 Ende 2 enden; beenden

■ ***at the end* – *in the end*** ▶ last: at last

At the end bedeutet „am Ende" im Sinne von „am Schluss(punkt)".

***At the end** (of the film) the cowboys always ride off into the sunset.* ● ● ● Am Ende/Schluss …
*We know it's difficult, but **at the end of the day**, you have to decide for yourself.* [Wendung]
● ● ● Wir wissen, dass es schwierig ist, aber letzten Endes musst du selbst entscheiden.

In the end bedeutet „am Ende" im Sinne von „schließlich".

*I spent two hours trying to persuade Jill, but **in the end** I gave up.* ● ● ● … aber schließlich …

■ ***end* + Präposition**

*an **end** to* (end of) *this situation/development* ● ● ● ein Ende dieser Situation/Entwicklung
*a word that **ends** in 'y'* ● ● ● ein Wort, das auf „y" endet

engaged [ɪnˈgeɪdʒd] verlobt

■ *be **engaged** to sb.* (engaged with sb.) ● ● ● mit jmdm. verlobt sein
*get **engaged** to sb.* ● ● ● sich mit jmdm. verloben

enjoy

1 ...... for two weeks.
   A We really enjoyed doing nothing   B We really enjoyed to do nothing

2 ...... so far to your work?
   A Do you enjoy not having to travel
   B Do you enjoy not to have to travel
   C Do you enjoy that you don't have to travel
   D Do you enjoy the fact that you don't have to travel

enough

1 We have to make sure .... We'll have extra things to bring back.
   A that we take a big enough suitcase   B that we take an enough big suitcase

2 Will there be enough money left ...... ?
   A for me to be able to buy that T-shirt I saw   B that I can buy that T-shirt I saw

envy

1 Toby is so mean. He has to be best at everything. ......
   A He even envies me this little success.   B He even envys me this little success.
   C He even envies me for this little success.   D He even envys me for this little success.

2 ...... who are old and ill all the time. I don't think I could do a job like that.
   A I don't envy you that you work with people
   B I don't envy you for working with people
   C I don't envy you working with people

especially – specially

1 A I especially like the southwest of the country.
   B I like especially the southwest of the country.
   C I like specially the southwest of the country.

2 ...... , but at least it's a job.
   A It's not especially well paid   B It's not specially well paid   C It's not special well paid

3 I fixed the meeting for 7.30, rather than 6.30, ...
   A especially for you   B specially for you

estimated

1 A There are estimated 10,000 illegal immigrants working in the hotel and restaurant business.
   B There are an estimated 10,000 illegal immigrants working in the hotel and restaurant business.
   C There is an estimated 10,000 illegal immigrants working in the hotel and restaurant business.

enjoy genießen, mögen, gern tun

■ *enjoy doing*

Auf *enjoy* folgt eine *-ing*-Form, kein *to*-Infinitiv.

*I **enjoyed meeting** (enjoyed to meet) your aunt.* ● ● ● Es war schön, deine Tante kennen zu lernen.

*I **enjoy** not **having** to get up so early.* ● ● ● Ich genieße es, nicht so früh aufstehen zu müssen.

■ *enjoy the fact that ...*

Ein *that*-Satz ist nur in Verbindung mit *the fact that* möglich.

*I **enjoy the fact that** (I enjoy that) I don't have to get up so early.* ● ● ● Ich genieße es, dass …

enough genug

■ **Stellung**

Enough steht hinter einem Adjektiv.

*Is this piece of paper **big enough**?* ● ● ● Ist dieses Blatt Papier groß genug?

Adjektiv + *enough* können auch vor einem Nomen stehen, aber ebenfalls nur in dieser Reihenfolge.

*Is this a **big enough** piece of paper?* ● ● ● Ist dies ein ausreichend großes Blatt Papier?

■ *enough ... for sb. to do*

Nach *enough* kann man einen *to*-Infinitiv, aber keinen *that*-Satz verwenden.

*Is there **enough** time **for me to go** (that I can go) to the bank before the train goes?* ● ● ● Habe ich noch genug Zeit, um zur Bank zu gehen / dass ich zur Bank gehen kann …?

envy ['envi] beneiden

■ **Schreibung**

envy, envies, envied

■ *envy sb. sth.*

Im Englischen steht keine Präposition, wenn man sagt, dass man jemanden um etwas beneidet.

*I **envy** you **your lovely flat**.* ● ● ● Ich beneide dich um deine schöne Wohnung.

■ *envy sb. doing*

Der Grund, warum man jemanden beneidet, kann auch als *-ing*-Form ausgedrückt werden.

*I **envy** you **living** (envy you that you live) in Venice.* ● ● ● Ich beneide dich (darum), dass du …

especially – specially besonders

■ **Stellung von** *especially*

Wenn sich *especially* auf das Subjekt bezieht, wird es nachgestellt. Es steht nicht am Satzanfang.

*Pets need attention. Dogs **especially** (Especially dogs) need regular human contact.* ● ● ●
… Besonders Hunde brauchen regelmäßigen menschlichen Kontakt.

Especially steht nicht zwischen Verb und Objekt.

*I love fruit. I **especially** like kiwis. / I like **kiwis** especially. (I like especially kiwis.)* ● ● ● Ich esse liebend gern Obst. Besonders Kiwis mag ich. / Ich mag besonders Kiwis. / Ich mag Kiwis besonders.

■ **Gebrauch von** *especially* **und** *specially* ▶ **extra**

Vor einem Adjektiv sind *especially* und *specially* austauschbar.

*It wasn't a **specially** good / an **especially** good film.* ● ● ● … kein besonders guter Film.

Faustregel zum sonstigen Gebrauch von *especially* und *specially*: *Especially* bedeutet „vor allem".
Specially bedeutet „extra", „speziell".

*I often get up late at the weekend, **especially** on Sunday.* ● ● ● … besonders am Sonntag.

*I cooked this **specially** for you.* ● ● ● Ich habe das extra für dich gekocht.

estimated geschätzt

■ *an estimated* + **Plural** ▶ **additional** ▶ **extra**

Wenn man das Adjektiv *estimated* vor einem Zahlwort + Nomen im Plural (mit Verb im Plural) verwendet, setzt man – widersinnigerweise – den Artikel *an* davor, ähnlich wie bei *another*.

***An estimated six million people** watch the show.* ● ● ● Geschätzte sechs Millionen Menschen …

eventual/eventually ≠ „eventuell"

1 What is the best translation?

The teacher said she would overlook *[eventuelle Schreibfehler]*.

A any spelling mistakes **B** eventual spelling mistakes
C maybe spelling mistakes **D** occasional spelling mistakes

2 I'm not sure which train I'll be able to get. *[Ich komme eventuell sehr spät.]*

A I'm eventually very late. **B** I may be very late. **C** I'll eventually be very late.

everybody/everyone

1 Are we all agreed? ......

A Are everybody of the same opinion? **B** Are everyone of the same opinion?
C Is everybody of the same opinion? **D** Is everyone of the same opinion?

everyday – every day

1 A The traffic is like this almost all day. Traffic jams are an almost every day occurrence.
B The traffic is like this almost every day. Traffic jams are an almost everyday occurrence.
C The traffic is like this almost every day. Traffic jams are an almost all day occurrence.

everywhere – anywhere – all over

1 A Is it true that in Finland you can camp anywhere?
B Is it true that in Finland you can camp all over?

2 A Harry Potter is familiar to children all over in the world.
B Harry Potter is familiar to children all over the world.

3 During the festival, the streets are crowded with tourists, ... selling anything from pots and pans to computer software.

A and there are stalls anywhere **B** and there are stalls everywhere

evidence – proof

1 A President Bush's 'evidences' of weapons of mass destruction were not believed by a lot of people.
B President Bush's 'evidence' of weapons of mass destruction was not believed by a lot of people.
C President Bush's 'proofs' of weapons of mass destruction were not believed by a lot of people.

exact

1 ...... It surely can't be 24 degrees in here. It's freezing!

A How accurate is this thermometer? **B** How exact is this thermometer?

2 There are going to be some major changes, ...

A but I don't know anything definite yet
B but I know nothing exact yet
C but I know nothing exactly yet

3 A They don't even know the accurate year.
B They don't even know the exact year.

E

---

eventual [ɪˈventʃuəl] / **eventually** letztendlich, schließlich ▷ last: at last

> ■ **False Friend!**
> *Eventual(ly)* bedeutet nicht „~~eventuell~~", sondern „letztendlich", „schließlich", „mit der Zeit".
> *The **eventual** total cost, when the project is finished, will be over $42,000,000.* ● ● ● Die letztendlichen Gesamtkosten …
> ***Eventually** all this area will be built on.* ● ● ● Irgendwann einmal / Eines Tages / Mit der Zeit …
> Beachte die englischen Entsprechungen von „eventuell":
> Wir müssen eventuelle Risiken hinnehmen. ● ● ● *We must accept **any (possible)** risks.*
> Peter kommt eventuell später. ● ● ● *Peter **may** / **might** come later.*

---

everybody / everyone alle, jeder(mann) ▷ all ▷ each

■ *everybody / everyone* + Verb im Singular
Nach *everybody* (bzw. – bedeutungsgleich – *everyone*) steht das Verb im Singular.
***Everybody / Everyone is** ready.* ● ● ● Alle sind fertig.

---

everyday alltäglich – **every day** jeden Tag, an jedem Tag

■ Das Adjektiv *everyday* („alltäglich") wird zusammengeschrieben.
*Computers and mobile phones are now **everyday** objects.* ● ● ● … alltägliche Gegenstände.
■ Die Wendung *every day* („jeden Tag", „an jedem Tag") wird in zwei Wörtern geschrieben.
*We use computers and mobile phones **every day**.* ● ● ● … täglich / jeden Tag.

---

everywhere – anywhere – all over überall

■ *Everywhere* bedeutet „überall" im Sinne von „an jedem Ort".
*I've looked **everywhere**, but I can't find it.* ● ● ● Ich habe überall geschaut …
■ *Anywhere* bedeutet „überall" im Sinne von „an jedem beliebigen Ort".
*On Sundays you can park **anywhere**. It's never a problem.* ● ● ● Sonntags kann man überall parken. …
■ Statt *everywhere / anywhere* + Präposition verwendet man oft *all over*.
*English is spoken **all over** the world (= **everywhere in** the world).* ● ● ● Englisch wird überall auf der Welt / auf der ganzen Welt gesprochen.

---

evidence [ˈevɪdəns] – **proof** Beweis(e)

■ nicht zählbare Nomen
Evidence („Beweismaterial", „Indizien", „Hinweise") und *proof* („Beweis" / „Beweise") sind nicht zählbare Nomen. Man kann sie also nicht mit *a / an* oder im Plural verwenden.
*The **evidence was** (~~The evidences were~~) overwhelming.* ● ● ● Die Beweise waren überwältigend.
*We have no **evidence of** life on Mars.* ● ● ● Wir haben keine Beweise für Leben auf dem Mars.
*Is there any positive **proof**?* ● ● ● Gibt es einen eindeutigen Beweis? / Gibt es eindeutige Beweise?

---

exact [ɪɡˈzækt] genau

■ *What's the **exact** time?* ● ● ● Wie spät ist es genau?

Trouble Spot
■ genau
Meine Uhr ist / geht ganz genau. ● ● ● *My watch is very **accurate** [ˈækjərət].*
Ich weiß nichts Genau(er)es. ● ● ● *I don't know anything **definite** [ˈdefɪnət].*
Ich weiß genau, dass ich abgeschlossen habe. ● ● ● *I know **for certain** that I locked up.*
Hör genau zu! ● ● ● *Listen **closely**.*
Die Post ist genau gegenüber. ● ● ● *The post office is **right** opposite.*

exam/examination

1 ...... before you qualify?

  A How many exams do you have to do   **B** How many exams do you have to make
  C How many exams do you have to sit   **D** How many exams do you have to take

2 I'm sorry to say ....

  A that you didn't stand the exam   **B** that you didn't pass the exam   **C** that you failed the exam

example

1 ...... you're thinking of?

  A Can you give me an example for the sort of animal
  B Can you give me an example of the sort of animal
  C Can you name me an example for the sort of animal
  D Can you name me an example of the sort of animal

excuse – apology – note

1 ...... It was unforgivable.

  A I really have no apology for what went wrong.
  B I really have no excuse for what went wrong.

2 If you are ill and miss a day, ...

  A you have to bring an apology from your parents
  B you have to bring an excuse from your parents
  C you have to bring a note from your parents

excuse me – sorry

1 What are you doing with my umbrella?! – ......

  A Excuse, I thought it was mine.
  B Excuse me, I thought it was mine.
  C Sorry, I thought it was mine.

2 We should be there by 6.30, ...

  A excuse me not 6.30, I mean 7.30   **B** sorry not 6.30, I mean 7.30

exist

1 ...... It's in the local museum.

  A The original document is still existing.   **B** The original document still exists.

expect

1 He was drunk *[und ich erwarte von ihm, dass er sich entschuldigt]*, not just to me but to everyone.

  A and I'm expecting that he apologizes
  B and I expect that he apologizes
  C and I expect him to apologize

2 *[Ich glaube, dass wir dieses Mal nicht kommen können.]* Tom is ill, you see.

  A I'm expecting that we won't be able to come this time.
  B I expect that we won't be able to come this time.

3 Will Schumacher win again? – *[Ich glaube ja.]*

  A I expect it.   **B** I expect so.   **C** I expect yes.

exam [ɪgˈzæm] / **examination** [ɪgˌzæmɪˈneɪʃn] Prüfung

- *do* / *sit* / *take* an *exam(ination)* ● ● ● eine Prüfung machen/ablegen
  pass an *exam(ination)* ● ● ● eine Prüfung bestehen
  fail an *exam(ination)* ● ● ● bei einer Prüfung durchfallen

example [ɪgˈzɑːmpl] Beispiel

- *gIve* sb. an *example of* sth. (~~name an example for sth.~~) ● ● ● jmdm. ein Beispiel für etwas geben/
  nennen

excuse [ɪkˈskjuːs] – **apology** [əˈpɒlədʒi] – **note** Entschuldigung   ▶ apologize

Trouble Spot

- **(eine) Entschuldigung**

1 Es gibt keine Entschuldigung [= Rechtfertigung, Ausrede] für sein Verhalten. ● ● ● *There's
   no **excuse** for his behaviour.*

2 Das ist ja unerhört! Ich verlange eine [persönliche] Entschuldigung. ● ● ● *This is outrageous!
   I demand an **apology**.*

3 Wenn man in der Schule fehlt, braucht man eine [schriftliche] Entschuldigung von den Eltern.
   ● ● ● *If you miss school, you need a **note** from your parents.*

excuse me [ɪkˈskjuːz mi] – **sorry** Entschuldigung!, entschuldigen Sie!

Trouble Spot

- **Entschuldigung!**

Excuse me sagt man, bevor man etwas tut.
  Entschuldigung / Entschuldigen Sie, ist dieser Platz noch frei? ● ● ● ***Excuse me**, is this seat
  taken?*
Wenn man sich entschuldigt, nachdem man etwas getan hat, verwendet man meist *sorry*,
besonders im AE aber auch *excuse me*.
  Sitze ich auf Ihrem Platz? Entschuldigung / Entschuldigen Sie! ● ● ● *Am I sitting in your seat?
  Sorry. /* (besonders AE auch:) ***Excuse me**.*
Sorry verwendet man auch, wenn man sich korrigiert.
  Es hat 65 £, Entschuldigung, 56 £ gekostet. ● ● ● *It cost £65, **sorry**, £56.*

exist [ɪgˈzɪst] existieren

- **nicht in der Verlaufsform**

Exist verwendet man in der Regel nicht in der Verlaufsform.
  *The original building **doesn't exist** (~~isn't existing~~) any more.* ● ● ● Das ursprüngliche Gebäude
  existiert nicht mehr.

expect [ɪkˈspekt] erwarten; annehmen

- **Konstruktionen in der Bedeutung „fest rechnen mit"**
  *We **expect** / We're **expecting** at least 20 guests.* ● ● ● Wir erwarten mindestens 20 Gäste.
  *We all **expected** you to win / **expected** (that) you'd win.* ● ● ● Wir haben alle (fest) damit
  gerechnet, dass du gewinnst. / Wir sind alle (fest) davon ausgegangen, dass du gewinnst.

- **Konstruktion in der Bedeutung „verlangen"**
  *You're late again. I **expect** you to be here (~~expect that you are here~~) by 8.30 at the latest.* ● ● ●
  … Ich erwarte, dass du bis spätestens 8.30 Uhr da bist.

- **Konstruktionen in der Bedeutung „annehmen", „vermuten", „glauben"**
  *I **expect** (~~I'm expecting~~) (that) he's missed the train again.* ● ● ● Ich nehme an, dass er wieder
  den Zug verpasst hat.
  *Will Asif be coming? – I **expect** so. (~~I expect it~~ / ~~yes.~~)* ● ● ● … – Ich nehme es an. / Ich glaube schon.
  *Who has eaten all the biscuits? – Sally, I **expect**.* ● ● ● … – Sally vermutlich. / Sally, glaube ich.

experience

1 ...... that people often underestimate the amount of time they will need.

  A We know from experience   B We know from the experience
  C We know out of experience   D We know out of the experience

2 ...... that people are prepared to help if you ask them politely.

  A I've often found   B I've often had the experience   C I've often made the experience

explain – explanation

1 ...... exactly how you came to have a frog in your bag, please?

  A Can you explain me   B Can you explain to me

express

1 You use the phrase "My mind's a complete blank" ....

  A to express that you can't think of anything
  B to express the idea that you can't think of anything

extra

1 A They're giving us an extra two weeks' holiday!
  B They're giving us extra two weeks' holiday!
  C They're giving us two extra weeks' holiday!

2 I don't believe you. ......

  A You did it extra!   B You did it on purpose!   C You did it with purpose!

3 We'd like the other T-shirt, too, ...

  A but my friend is going to pay for that apart
  B but my friend is going to pay for that extra
  C but my friend is going to pay for that separately

4 Oh, what beautiful flowers! – ......

  A I picked them extra for you.   B I picked them just for you.
  C I picked them on purpose for you.   D I picked them specially for you.

extract

1 A We want to read you an extract from one of Scott's letters.
  B We want to read you an extract of one of Scott's letters.

face

1 ...... What's so funny?

  A Why do you have that great big silly smile at your face?
  B Why do you have that great big silly smile in your face?
  C Why do you have that great big silly smile on your face?

2 A The two leaders first met from face to face at the Tokyo summit.
  B The two leaders first met from the face to the face at the Tokyo summit.
  C The two leaders first met face to face at the Tokyo summit.

experience [ɪk'spɪərɪəns] Erfahrung, Erlebnis

■ *I know from experience (from the experience) how hard this must be for you.* ● ● ● Ich weiß aus Erfahrung, wie schwierig das jetzt für dich sein muss.
I've had (I've made) an interesting new experience. ● ● ● Ich habe eine interessante neue Erfahrung gemacht.
gain experience / pick up experience ● ● ● Erfahrung(en) sammeln
Beachte die Konstruktion mit einem *that*-Satz.
I've found (I've had / made the experience) that it's not worth it. = My experience is that it's not worth it. ● ● ● Ich habe die Erfahrung gemacht [= weiß aus Erfahrung], dass es sich nicht lohnt.

explain [ɪk'spleɪn] erklären, erläutern – explanation [ˌeksplə'neɪʃn] Erklärung

■ **Schreibung**
expla<u>i</u>n – expla<u>na</u>tion

■ *explain sth. to sb.*
Die Person, der etwas erklärt wird, muss mit *to* stehen.
The teacher explained the rule to us (explained us the rule). ● ● ● Die Lehrerin erklärte uns die Regel.
Let me explain to you (explain you) what I mean. ● ● ● Ich will dir erklären, was ich meine.

express [ɪk'spres] ausdrücken

■ *express the fact / idea that …*
Einen *that*-Satz kann man nicht direkt an *express* anschließen. Dazwischen muss ein Ausdruck wie *the fact / the idea* stehen.
In this stanza the poet expresses the idea that (expresses that) youth is short. ● ● ● In dieser Strophe drückt der Dichter aus, dass die Jugend von kurzer Dauer ist.

extra ['ekstrə] zusätzlich, Extra-; besonders

■ *an extra* + Plural ▶ additional ▶ estimated
Wenn man *extra* vor einem Zahlwort + Nomen im Plural (mit Verb im Plural) verwendet, setzt man – widersinnigerweise – den Artikel *an* davor, ähnlich wie bei *another*.
An extra three chairs are needed. ● ● ● Es werden drei zusätzliche / noch drei Stühle benötigt.
Das Adjektiv *extra* kann aber auch (ohne *an*) zwischen Zahlwort und Nomen stehen.
We need three extra chairs. ● ● ● Wir brauchen drei zusätzliche / noch drei Stühle.

Trouble Spot

■ **extra** ▶ especially
Getränke kosten extra [= zusätzlich]. ● ● ● *Drinks are extra.*
Ich bezahle dieses Teil extra [= getrennt]. ● ● ● *I'm paying for this item separately* ['seprətli].
extra [= eigens / speziell] für dich ● ● ● *just / specially for you*
Das hast du extra [= absichtlich] gemacht! ● ● ● *You did that on purpose* ['pɜːpəs].

extract ['ekstrækt] Auszug, Ausschnitt [aus Buch, Film]

■ *This is an extract from one of the early dramas.* ● ● ● Dies ist ein Auszug aus einem der frühen Dramen.

face Gesicht

■ *have chocolate on your face* ● ● ● Schokolade im Gesicht haben
have a smile on your face ● ● ● ein Lächeln im Gesicht haben / tragen
make / pull a face ● ● ● ein Gesicht machen / ziehen
make / pull faces ● ● ● Grimassen schneiden
say sth. to sb.'s face ● ● ● jmdm. etwas ins Gesicht sagen
save / lose face ● ● ● das Gesicht wahren / verlieren
face to face (with sb.) ● ● ● von Angesicht zu Angesicht, persönlich

F

fair – fare

1 ...... is always in October.

  A The Frankfurt Book Fair   **B** The Frankfurt Book Fare

2 How much is ...... from London to New York?

  A the first-class fair   **B** the first-class fare

3 Which is the correct synonym for 'fair' in the following sentence?
Lars has short fair hair.

  A blond   **B** neat   **C** nice   **D** straight

fall

1 My grandma has had an accident. ......

  A She's fallen down and broken an arm. She felt down once before.

  B She's felt down and broken an arm. She fell down once before.

  C She's fallen down and broken an arm. She fell down once before.

false – wrong

1 ...... There must be another Grange Road, somewhere else.

  A We've come to the false address.   **B** We've come to the wrong address.

2 **A** She phoned him in the false hope that he might invite her round.

  B She phoned him in the wrong hope that he might invite her round.

3 ...... Can anyone spot the mistakes?

  A What's false in this sentence?   **B** What's wrong in this sentence?

family

1 Do you know who we met on holiday? ......

  A Family Stewart from down the road.   **B** The Stewart family from down the road.

2 ...... and the children had few friends.

  A The family was new to the area   **B** The family were new to the area

  C The families were new to the area

famous

1 This part of France has been ...... for centuries.

  A famous about its wine   **B** famous by its wine

  C famous from its wine   **D** famous for its wine

fancy

1 It's going to rain, ... Come on, let's go home.

  A and I don't fancy getting wet   **B** and I don't fancy to get wet

fantasy – imagination

1 Is becoming a children's author ...... ?

  A a way of living out your childhood fantasies

  B a way of living out your childhood imagination

2 Was J. K. Rowling ...... , do you think?

  A a child with a lot of fantasy   **B** a child with a lot of imagination

3 **A** Come on, now. Use your fantasy!   **B** Come on, now. Use your imagination!

fair 1 fair; blond, hell; schön, heiter **2** Kirmes, Jahrmarkt; Messe – **fare** Fahrpreis

- *Fair* ist ein Adjektiv mit vielen Bedeutungen, u. a. „fair" oder „blond", „hell".
  *a **fair** decision by the referee* ● ● ● eine faire Entscheidung des Schiedsrichters
  ***fair** hair* ● ● ● blondes Haar
  ***fair** skin* ● ● ● helle Haut
  ***fair** weather* ● ● ● schönes Wetter

- *Fair* ist außerdem ein Nomen mit der Bedeutung „Kirmes" oder „Messe".
  *the Frankfurt Book **Fair*** ● ● ● die Frankfurter Buchmesse

- *Fare* ist ein Nomen mit der Bedeutung „Fahrpreis" oder „Fahrgeld".
  *the cheapest bus **fare** / train **fare** / air **fare*** ● ● ● der günstigste Bus(fahr)preis / Bahn(fahr)preis /
    Flugpreis

F

fall* fallen

- ***fall – fell – fallen***
Nicht verwechseln mit: *feel* („fühlen") – *felt – felt*

false [fɔːls] – **wrong** falsch

- *False* ist das Gegenteil von *true* und von *genuine* [ˈdʒenjuɪn] („echt") oder *real*. Es bedeutet „falsch"
im Sinne von „unwahr", „unecht", „gefälscht", „irreführend".
  *Read the text and decide if statements 1–8 are true or **false**.*
  *He tried to enter the country with a **false** passport containing a **false** name and address.*
  *The patient was OK. It was a **false** alarm.*
  *English 'become' and German 'bekommen' are **false** friends – they don't mean the same.*
  *I don't want to give you any **false** ideas or **false** hopes.*

- *Wrong* ist das Gegenteil von *right* / *correct*. Es bedeutet „falsch" im Sinne von „unrichtig",
„inkorrekt".
  *Sorry, this sentence is **wrong**. It has two mistakes in it.*
  *Jamie went on the **wrong** day at the **wrong** time on the **wrong** road to the **wrong** place.*

family Familie

- ***The Smith family** (~~Family Smith~~) **has** / (BE auch:) **have** bought a new car.* ● ● ● (Die) Familie Smith
    hat sich ein neues Auto gekauft.

famous [ˈfeɪməs] berühmt

- ***famous for** sth.*
  *The town of Gouda is **famous for** its cheese.* ● ● ● … ist berühmt für ihren Käse / wegen ihres Käses.

fancy Lust haben

- ***fancy** doing*
  *Do you **fancy** going out (~~fancy to go out~~) tonight?* ● ● ● Hast du Lust, heute Abend auszugehen?

fantasy [ˈfæntəsi] – **imagination** [ɪˌmædʒɪˈneɪʃn] Fantasie

- *Fantasy* bedeutet „Fantasie" im Sinne von „[bildhafte Fantasie-]Vorstellung", „Fantasiegebilde".
  *have childhood **fantasies** / sexual **fantasies*** ● ● ● Kindheitsfantasien / sexuelle Fantasien haben
  *live in a **fantasy** world* ● ● ● in einer Fantasie-/Traumwelt leben

- *Imagination* bedeutet „Fantasie" im Sinne von „Vorstellungskraft", „Einbildungsvermögen",
„Bereich der Vorstellung [im Gegensatz zur Realität]". *Imagination* steht in der Regel nicht im Plural.
  *a child with a lot of **imagination*** ● ● ● ein Kind mit viel Fantasie
  *The Rolls Royce which he said he had existed only in his **imagination**.* ● ● ● … nur in seiner Fantasie.

far – a long way – away

1 How far is it? – ...... , about 800 kilometres.
  A Oh, it's a long way   B Oh, it's far

2 ...... I should take a taxi.
  A It's a long way.   B It's far.   C It's quite far.

3 The nearest village is ....
  A 170 kilometres far away   B 170 kilometres distant   C 170 kilometres away

farther – further

1 ...... I don't think I can keep going much longer.
  A How much farther is it?   B How much further is it?   C How much wider is it?

2 ...... , I declare this meeting closed.
  A If there are no farther questions   B If there are no further questions

fast – quick

1 A Gareth loves fast cars.   B Gareth loves quick cars.

2 ...... We should be there in time for lunch.
  A It's a good fast road.   B It's a good quick road.

3 A Would you like a fast drink before you go?   B Would you like a quick drink before you go?

fear

1 ...... can stop you doing your best in tests.
  A The fear of making mistakes   B The fear to make mistakes

2 ...... as the earthquake struck at a time of day when many people were asleep.
  A It's to be feared that a lot of lives have been lost
  B It's to fear that a lot of lives have been lost

fed up: be fed up

1 A We're fed up of listening to you moaning and complaining all the time.
  B We're fed up with listening to you moaning and complaining all the time.
  C We're fed up to listen to you moaning and complaining all the time.

feel

1 ...... I think we'll win.
  A I feel confident.   B I feel confidently.   C I'm feeling confident.

2 It's made of cashmere ....
  A and feels lovely and softly   B and feels lovely and soft   C and is feeling lovely and soft

3 ...... Someone must have opened a door or window on the other side of the building.
  A I'm feeling a draught.   B I can feel a draught.   C I feel a draught.

4 In our English lessons I used to hate working with CDs. But after my trip to England ....
  A I'm now feeling listening comprehension is one of the most important skills
  B I now feel listening comprehension is one of the most important skills

far – a long way – away weit, weit weg

■ *far* **in Fragen und verneinten Sätzen**
Faustregel: *Far* steht in Fragen und verneinten Sätzen; in bejahten Sätzen steht *a long way*.
   How far still to go? – **Not far.** – Good. I thought it was still **a long way**. ● ● ● Wie weit noch? –
     Nicht mehr weit. – Gut. Ich dachte, es wäre noch weit.
Wenn *far* näher bestimmt wird, kann es jedoch auch in bejahten Sätzen stehen.
   It's **quite far** / **so far** / **too far** / **awfully far** to walk. We'd better get the bus.
   I looked and saw something red **far above me** / **far below us** / **far away** / **far off in the distance**.

■ *Far* kann nicht in Verbindung mit einer Entfernungsangabe stehen.
   My school is **12 kilometres away** (~~12 kilometres far~~ / ~~12 kilometres far away~~).

F

farther – further weiter

■ *Farther* kann man nur im räumlichen Sinn verwenden.
   Dennis lives **farther** away from school than I do. ● ● ● … weiter weg/entfernt von der Schule …

■ *Further* kann man sowohl im räumlichen als auch im übertragenen Sinn verwenden.
   Dennis lives **further** away from school than I do. ● ● ● … weiter weg/entfernt von der Schule …
   Are there any **further** comments/questions? ● ● ● … noch weitere Kommentare/Fragen?

fast – quick schnell

■ *Fast* bezieht sich in der Regel auf Geschwindigkeit.
   a **fast** car/train/race/runner
   a **fast** road/journey

■ *Quick* bezieht sich in der Regel auf die Zeit, die etwas in Anspruch nimmt.
   a **quick** look/reply/decision/method/drink [Aber feste Wendung: **fast food**]

fear Furcht; fürchten

■ **fear of doing**
   The fear of losing (~~the fear to lose~~) his mother made the boy very frightened. ● ● ● Die Angst,
     seine Mutter zu verlieren …
   A lot of people have **a fear of flying** (~~a fear to fly~~). ● ● ● … haben Angst vorm Fliegen/Flugangst.

■ It is **to be feared** (~~It is to fear~~) that terrorist attacks will increase. ● ● ● Es ist/steht zu befürchten …

fed up: be fed up es satt haben

■ **fed up with doing**
   I'm **fed up with waiting** (~~fed up to wait~~) for you. ● ● ● Ich habe es satt, auf dich zu warten.

feel* (sich) (an)fühlen; meinen

■ **„sich fühlen"**
Nicht reflexiv: I **feel** / I'm **feeling** ill. (~~I feel myself~~ / ~~I'm feeling myself ill.~~) ● ● ● Ich fühle mich krank.
Feel + Adjektiv, nicht Adverb: I **feel sad**. (~~I feel sadly.~~) ● ● ● Ich bin traurig. / Mir ist traurig zumute.

■ **„sich anfühlen"**
Nicht reflexiv, nicht in der Verlaufsform: It **feels** like leather. ● ● ● Es fühlt sich an wie Leder.
Feel + Adjektiv, nicht Adverb: It **feels rough**. (~~It feels roughly.~~) ● ● ● Es fühlt sich rau an.

■ **„wahrnehmen", „spüren", „bemerken"**
Nicht in der Verlaufsform, oft mit *can*:
   Can you **feel** how the wind is blowing us out to sea now? ● ● ● Kannst du spüren, wie …?
Feel + Nomen + Partizip Präsens/Infinitiv:
   I **felt** an insect **crawling**/**crawl** up my back. ● ● ● Ich fühlte/bemerkte, wie …

■ **„finden", „glauben", „meinen"**
Nicht in der Verlaufsform:
   I **feel** that (~~I'm feeling that~~) this decision is a mistake. ● ● ● Ich finde/glaube/meine, dass …

female – feminine

1 What do you call ...... ? – A she wolf.
  A a female wolf   **B** a feminine wolf

2 Do piano players usually have ...... ?
  A female hands   **B** feminine hands

fever – temperature

1 ...... , call the doctor immediately.
  A If the child has more than 40 fever
  B If the child has a temperature of more than 40

2 He claims ...... just by feeling their ears!
  A he can measure fever by a patient
  B he can measure a patient's fever
  C he can take a patient's temperature

field

1 Can you see that animal ...... ? It looks like a lion, but it can't be, can it?
  A at the field over there   **B** in the field over there   **C** on the field over there

fight

1 ...... with another cat in the neighbourhood.
  A My cat was hurt by a fight   **B** My cat was hurt from a fight   **C** My cat was hurt in a fight

find

1 We've looked everywhere, ...
  A but he's nowhere to find   **B** but he's nowhere to be found

fine

1 I'm on holiday this week ....
  A and feel just fine   **B** and feel very fine

finish

1 ...... , can I have it back, please?
  A If you've finished to use my dictionary   **B** If you've finished using my dictionary

first

1 ...... – Yes, and I think she has an absolutely fantastic voice.
  A Is this the first time you're hearing this singer?
  B Is this the first time you hear this singer?
  C Is this the first time you've heard this singer?

2 A For the first time I cooked rice, it all stuck to the bottom of the pan.
  B At the first time I cooked rice, it all stuck to the bottom of the pan.
  C The first time I cooked rice, it all stuck to the bottom of the pan.

3 You'll never believe it: our team *[wurde Erster]*. We beat them all!
  A became first   **B** came first   **C** got first

female – feminine ['femənɪn] weiblich ▷ male

- *Female* bedeutet „weiblich" im Sinne von „weiblichen Geschlechts".
  Is the animal male or female? ● ● ● Ist das Tier männlich oder weiblich?
- *Feminine* bezeichnet das sprachliche Genus.
  'His' is masculine, 'her' is feminine. ● ● ● „His" ist männlich, „her" ist weiblich.
Feminine bedeutet außerdem „weiblich" im Sinne von „feminin", „typisch für eine Frau".
  His face is very feminine. ● ● ● Sein Gesicht hat sehr weibliche Züge.

fever ['fiːvə] – temperature ['temprətʃə] Fieber

- *Tanja's in bed with a fever / with a temperature.* ● ● ● Tanja liegt mit Fieber im Bett.
- Nicht *fever*, sondern *temperature* ist die übliche Entsprechung von „Fieber", wenn man vom Fiebermessen spricht.
  She has a temperature of 39 (degrees). / She's running a temperature of 39 (degrees). ● ● ●
    Sie hat 39° Fieber.
  He's got a high temperature / a slight temperature. ● ● ● Er hat hohes Fieber / leichtes Fieber.
  I just want to take your temperature. ● ● ● Ich will nur mal eben bei dir Fieber messen.

F

field Feld, Wiese; Gebiet

- *cows in the field* ● ● ● Kühe auf der Wiese
  work in the field of microbiology ● ● ● auf dem Gebiet der Mikrobiologie arbeiten

fight Kampf, Schlägerei

- *get hurt in a fight* ● ● ● bei einer Schlägerei verletzt werden

find* finden

- *find – found – found*
Nicht verwechseln mit: *found* („gründen") – *founded – founded*
- *The key was nowhere to be found (~~nowhere to find~~).* ● ● ● Der Schlüssel war nirgends zu finden.

fine gut, fein

- **Verstärkung mit *just***
Fine in der Bedeutung „gut" wird nicht mit *very*, sondern mit *just* verstärkt.
  How are you (doing)? – I'm fine thanks, just fine (~~very fine~~). ● ● ● Danke, mir geht's gut, ganz gut.
  Tuesday at 3.30 is just fine. ● ● ● Dienstag um 15.30 Uhr ist sehr gut / ganz recht.

finish beenden, zu Ende machen, aufhören mit ▷ ready ▷ stop

- *finish doing*
Nach *finish* steht die *-ing*-Form des Verbs, nicht der *to*-Infinitiv.
  Has he finished talking (~~finished to talk~~) yet? ● ● ● Hat er schon aufgehört zu reden?

first erste(r/s)

- *it's the first time (that) + present perfect*
Nach … *is the first time (that)* folgt das *present perfect*, keine Gegenwartsform.
  It/This is the first time I have been (~~It/This is the first time I am~~) to New York. ● ● ● Es/Dies ist
    das erste Mal, dass ich in New York bin.
- **Wendungen**
  I was in love for the first time in my life. ● ● ● Zum ersten Mal in meinem Leben war ich verliebt.
  I didn't notice anything the first time. ● ● ● Beim ersten Mal ist mir nichts aufgefallen.
  I'll do it first thing tomorrow. ● ● ● Ich mache es gleich morgen früh (als Erstes).
- *Marc came first (~~became first~~) in the race.* ● ● ● Marc wurde Erster in dem Rennen.

first – firstly – at first

1 ...... when I came across their website.
   A I at first became interested in the organization
   B I first became interested in the organization
   C I firstly became interested in the organization

2 ...... , but then Markus came and joined us.
   A At first there were only three of us
   B Firstly there were only three of us

3 But I tried to phone him *[erst heute Morgen]*, and there was no reply.
   A first this morning   B firstly this morning   C only this morning

4 *[Ich kann erst nächste Woche sagen]* what the trip will probably cost.
   A I can tell you first next week
   B I can't tell you till next week
   C I can only next week tell you
   D It'll be next week before I can tell you

fit – suit – go with – match

1 We're almost the same size and her clothes *[passen mir fast immer]*.
   A nearly always fit me   B nearly always suit me   C nearly always match me

2 A The shoes don't fit the rest of your outfit.
   B The shoes don't go with the rest of your outfit.
   C The shoes don't suit the rest of your outfit.

3 A Green has never fit me.   B Green has never fitted me.   C Green has never gone with me.
   D Green has never matched me.   E Green has never suited me.

flee – escape

1 The situation is critical. ......
   A Tens of thousands of people have escaped from their homes.
   B Tens of thousands of people have fled from their homes.
   C Tens of thousands of people have fleed from their homes.
   D Tens of thousands of people have flown from their homes.

2 A Two lions have escaped from the zoo.
   B Two lions have escaped out of the zoo.
   C Two lions have fled from the zoo.
   D Two lions have fled out of the zoo.

first – firstly – at first zuerst   ▸ before

■ **first = „als Erstes"; „das erste Mal"**
First (of all) we must make a list of all the things we need to buy. ● ● ● Als Erstes / Zunächst (einmal) müssen wir eine Liste all der Dinge machen …
*We **first** met at a party.* ● ● ● Wir haben uns das erste Mal auf einer Party getroffen.

■ **firstly = „erstens"**
*There are three good reasons: **firstly** …, secondly …, and thirdly …* ● ● ● Es gibt drei gute Gründe: erstens …, zweitens … , und drittens …

■ **at first = „zu / am Anfang (… aber dann)", „anfangs"**
***At first** I thought she wasn't there, **but then** I saw her at the buffet.* ● ● ● Zuerst dachte ich, sie wäre nicht da, aber dann sah ich sie am Büfett.

F

Trouble Spot

■ **erst**
1 „zuerst", „zuvor"
Ich muss erst meine Eltern fragen. ● ● ● *I have to ask my parents **first**.*

2 „vor kurzem", „nicht später als"; „bloß", „nicht mehr als"
Ich habe es erst gestern gekauft. ● ● ● *I bought it **only** yesterday.*
Meine Tochter ist erst fünf. ● ● ● *My daughter is **only** five.*

3 „nicht früher als", „nicht vor"
Wir kommen erst um 23.00 Uhr an. ● ● ● *We don't arrive **until** / **till** 11 p.m.*
Ich sehe dich erst in vier Wochen wieder. ● ● ● *It'll be four weeks **before** I see you again.*

fit (*) – suit [suːt] – go* with – match passen

Trouble Spot

■ **passen**
1 „in der Größe / in den Raum passen": fit – fitted – fitted / (AE meist:) fit – fit – fit
Der Rock passt mir genau. ● ● ● *The skirt **fits** me exactly.*
Ich habe das Inhaltsverzeichnis anders gestaltet, sodass es auf die Seite passte. ● ● ●
  *I redesigned the table of contents so that it **fit(ted)** onto the page.*
Die Schuhe passen nicht in den Koffer. ● ● ● *The shoes won't **fit** in the suitcase.*
Passt der Schlüssel? ● ● ● *Does the key **fit**?*

2 „im Stil / in der Farbe passen"
Dunkelblau passt zu dir. ● ● ● *Dark blue **suits** you.*

3 „in den Plan passen"
Dienstag passt mir gut. ● ● ● *Tuesday **suits** me **fine**.*
Passt es dir morgen Abend? ● ● ● *Does tomorrow evening **suit** you?*

4 „im Stil zueinander passen"
Die Vorhänge passen zum Teppich. ● ● ● *The curtains **go with** / **match** the carpet.*

flee* – escape fliehen

■ **flee – fled – fled**

■ *Flee* bedeutet „fliehen" im Sinne von „sich (aus Angst) vor Gefahr retten". Es steht mit der Präposition *from.*
*Tens of thousands of refugees **fled from** the city, as the war came closer.* ● ● ● Zehntausende von Flüchtlingen flohen aus der Stadt …

■ *Escape* bedeutet „fliehen" im Sinne von „sich befreien und entkommen". Es steht ebenfalls mit der Präposition *from.*
*How did they **escape from** a high-security prison?* ● ● ● Wie sind sie denn aus einem Hochsicherheitsgefängnis entkommen?

floor

1 ...... , but it's OK: there's a lift.
   A Our flat is at the sixth floor   B Our flat is in the sixth floor   C Our flat is on the sixth floor

2 We didn't have a tent. We just put our sleeping bags ....
   A on the bare bottom   B on the bare floor   C on the bare ground   D on the bare soil

3 You can see by the size of the farmhouses ....
   A that the bottom in this area is very good   B that the floor in this area is very good
   C that the ground in this area is very good   D that the soil in this area is very good

4 .... I'm not going to drink this.
   A There's something in the bottom of my glass.
   B There's something on the floor of my glass.
   C There's something on the ground of my glass.

flu

1 Angela is ill. ......
   A She has a flu.   B She has the flu.   C She has flu.
   D She has a bad flu.   E She has a bad bout of flu.   F She has a bad dose of flu.

follow

1 [Auf die Hitze folgten Gewitter.]
   A The heat followed thunderstorms.
   B The heat was followed by thunderstorms.
   C Thunderstorms followed after the heat.

2 I'm sorry, but I have no time [das weiterzuverfolgen].
   A to follow this any further   B to persecute this any further   C to pursue this any further

3 Dissidents are often ....
   A followed by the regimes they oppose
   B persecuted by the regimes they oppose
   C pursued by the regimes they oppose

foot

1 I can't walk another step. ......
   A My foot are terribly sore.   B My foots are terribly sore.   C My feet are terribly sore.

2 How did you get here? – ......
   A By foot.   B By feet.   C On foot.   D To foot.   E I went.   F I walked.

for

1 A I shall need your help for collecting all the information.
   B I shall need your help to collect all the information.

2 A This button is for calling the nurse.   B This button is for to call the nurse.

F

floor Etage, Stock(werk); Boden

■ *My office is on the* (BE:) ***ground floor*** / (AE:) ***first floor****.* ● ● ● Mein Büro ist im Erdgeschoss.

Trouble Spot

■ **Boden**

1 „Fußboden"
Das Zimmer hatte einen Holzboden. ● ● ● *The room had a wooden* ***floor****.*

2 „Boden draußen", „Erdboden"
Er schlief draußen auf dem nackten Boden. ● ● ● *He slept outdoors on the bare* ***ground.***

3 „Erdreich", „Erde, in der Pflanzen wachsen"
Der Boden ist fruchtbar. ● ● ● *The* ***soil*** *is fertile.*

4 „Boden eines Gefäßes oder Behältnisses"
Zuckerreste auf dem Boden der Tasse ● ● ● *remains of sugar in* / *at the* ***bottom*** *of the cup*

5 „Meeresboden"
Das Tier lebt auf dem Meeresboden. ● ● ● *The animal lives at the* ***bottom of the sea*** /
on the ***seabed.***

6 „Dachboden"
oben auf dem Dachboden ● ● ● *up in the* ***attic***

flu Grippe

■ **nicht zählbares Nomen**
Flu ist ein nicht zählbares Nomen. Man kann also nicht von *a flu* sprechen.
have ***(the) flu*** *(~~have a flu~~)* ● ● ● (die/eine) Grippe haben
have ***a bad bout*** / ***dose*** [dəʊs] ***of flu*** *(~~have a bad flu~~)* ● ● ● eine schlimme/schwere Grippe haben

follow folgen; verfolgen

■ Nach *follow* steht ein direktes Objekt, das zum Subjekt eines Passivsatzes werden kann.
Did anyone ***follow*** *you?* / ***Were you followed*** *(by anyone)?* ● ● ● Ist dir jemand gefolgt? /
Ist dir jemand nachgegangen? / Hat dich jemand verfolgt?

Trouble Spot

■ **verfolgen**

1 „Dieb, Tier usw. verfolgen"
Passanten verfolgten den Dieb durch das Einkaufszentrum. ● ● ● *Passers-by* ***chased*** [tʃeɪst] /
pursued [pə'sjuːd] *the thief through the shopping centre.*

2 „aktiv weiterbetreiben"
Wir verfolgen die Sache weiter. ● ● ● *We shall continue to* ***pursue*** *the matter.*

3 „religiös oder politisch verfolgen"
Im Mittelalter wurden viele Frauen als Hexen verfolgt. ● ● ● *In the Middle Ages*
a lot of women were ***persecuted*** ['pɜːsɪkjuːtɪd] *as witches.*

foot [fʊt] Fuß

■ *one* ***foot*** *– two* ***feet***

■ ***go*** *somewhere* ***on foot*** *(~~by foot~~)* *[=* ***walk*** *somewhere]* ● ● ● irgendwohin zu Fuß gehen

for für

■ *for doing*
Mit *for* + der *-ing*-Form des Verbs kann man den Zweck eines Gegenstands beschreiben, nicht aber
den Zweck oder Grund einer menschlichen Handlung.
Scissors are ***for cutting*** *things.* ● ● ● Scheren sind / Eine Schere ist zum Schneiden da.
Aber:
I phoned Angela ***to discuss*** *(~~for discussing~~) the problem.* ● ● ● … um das Problem zu besprechen.

forbid

1 Julia's father never forgave her. ......

  A He forbad her ever to enter his house again.

  B He forbade her ever to enter his house again.

  C He forbidded her ever to enter his house again.

2 A They want to forbid riding a bike in the pedestrian zone.

  B They want to forbid to ride a bike in the pedestrian zone.

3 Which is most likely way to end this sentence, A or B?

Lila's parents are so strict. She wanted to come to the disco with us, ...

  A but her parents forbid it

  B but her parents won't let her

foresee

1 ...... is a formal way of saying 'I knew this would happen'.

  A 'This was to foresee'   B 'This was to be foreseen'

forever – for ever

1 He's getting old and boring. ......

  A He's ever going on about how wonderful life was when he was young.

  B He's forever going on about how wonderful life was when he was young.

  C He's for ever going on about how wonderful life was when he was young.

forget

1 ...... It was such an exciting match.

  A I'll never forget to watch the 2002 men's final.

  B I'll never forget watching the 2002 men's final.

2 What will it cost? Do you remember, Frank? – No, sorry. ......

  A I'm afraid I've forgotten.   B I'm afraid I've forgotten it.   C I'm afraid I've forgotten so.

3 ...... We've got to go back and get it.

  A Tony's forgotten his camera in the car.   B Tony's left his camera in the car.

forgive

1 I don't think ....

  A she'll ever forgive me because of forgetting her birthday

  B she'll ever forgive me for forgetting her birthday

  C she'll ever forgive me that I forgot her birthday

  D she'll ever forgive me after forgetting her birthday

forbid* verbieten

■ **forbid – forbade** [fə'bæd, fə'beɪd] **– forbidden**

■ **forbid sb. to do – forbid sb. from doing**
They're going to **forbid** *us* **to use** / **forbid** *us* **from using** *a dictionary.* ● ● ● Sie wollen (es) uns
verbieten, ein Wörterbuch zu benutzen.
In der Umgangssprache verwendet man häufig *not let sb. do.*
He won't let me do it. ● ● ● Er hat's mir verboten.

■ **forbid doing**
Wird kein Personenobjekt nach *forbid* genannt, so kann man keinen *to*-Infinitiv anschließen.
They're going to **forbid using** (~~forbid to use~~) *a dictionary.* ● ● ● Sie wollen (es) verbieten,
ein Wörterbuch zu benutzen. / Sie wollen die Verwendung eines Wörterbuches verbieten.

F

foresee* [Ereignis usw.] vorhersehen, voraussehen

■ *It was* **to be foreseen** (~~It was to foresee~~) *that there'd be problems.* ● ● ● Es war vorauszusehen …

forever – for ever (für) immer, ständig

■ **forever** / (BE auch:) **for ever** = „für immer", „ewig"
I could sit here **forever** / **for ever.** ● ● ● Ich könnte (für) immer hier sitzen.

■ **forever** [+ Verlaufsform] = „(aber auch) immer", „ständig"
He's **forever** (~~for ever~~) *complaining.* ● ● ● Er beklagt sich ständig.

forget* vergessen

■ **forget to do**
Man verwendet *forget* + *to*-Infinitiv, um zu sagen, was zu tun jemand nicht vergessen darf oder
sollte.
I mustn't **forget to phone** *Jimmy this evening.* ● ● ● Ich darf nicht vergessen, Jimmy … anzurufen.

■ **forget doing**
Man verwendet *forget* + die *-ing*-Form des Verbs, wenn das Verb nach *forget* etwas Vergangenes
beschreibt, das geschehen ist.
I'm sorry, but I've completely **forgotten promising** *that.* ● ● ● … ich habe komplett vergessen, dass
ich das versprochen hatte.
I shall never **forget seeing** *her for the first time.* ● ● ● Ich werde nie vergessen, wie ich sie das erste
Mal gesehen habe.

■ **forget (it)**
It kann sich als Objekt von *forget* nur auf etwas Konkretes beziehen.
He said he'd bring me the CD, but he **forgot (it)** [= the CD]. ● ● ● … aber er hat sie vergessen.
When did he say he would be here? – I **forget** / I've **forgotten** (~~I forget it~~ / ~~I've forgotten it~~).
● ● ● … – Ich habe es vergessen.
They said they would phone, but they **forgot (to)** (~~forgot it~~). ● ● ● … aber sie haben es vergessen.
Aber:
Forget it! *We don't have a chance.* ● ● ● Vergiss es! …

■ **forget – leave**
Wenn man den Ort nennt, wo jemand etwas hat liegen lassen, verwendet man normalerweise
leave (nicht *forget*).
Damn! I've **forgotten** *my passport. I* **left** *it in the hotel.* ● ● ● … Ich habe meinen Pass vergessen.
Ich habe ihn im Hotel liegen lassen / gelassen / vergessen.

forgive* vergeben, verzeihen

■ **forgive sb. for doing**
Nach *forgive* verwendet man *for* + die *-ing*-Form des Verbs, keinen *that*-Satz.
I'll never **forgive** *him* **for lying** (~~that he lied~~) *to me.* ● ● ● Ich werde es ihm nie verzeihen, dass er
mich angelogen hat.

formula ≠ „Formular"

1 What is the best synonym for 'formula' in the following sentence?

They still haven't found the right formula to end the strike.

A analysis   B mixture   C text   D solution

2 I'm afraid you'll have to fill in [dieses Formular] before I can do anything to help you.

A this application   B this paper   C this form   D this formula

forward – forwards

1 A We need to do some forward planning.   B We need to do some forwards planning.

freeze – freezing

1 I hate this building. ......

A It's always freezing cold.   B It's always freezing.   C It's always icing.

2 It was a bitterly cold night, ...

A and the poor man freezed dead

B and the poor man froze dead

C and the poor man froze to death

fresh – cool – cold

1 ...... Come on, let's go inside.

A It's too cold out here.   B It's too fresh out here.

2 There's a washing machine, so I'm not going to take more than ....

A two lots of clean underwear   B two lots of fresh underwear   C two lots of pure underwear

3 Next to the sign [„Frisch gestrichen!"] there was a beautiful imprint of someone's hand.

A 'Freshly painted'   B 'Fresh paint'   C 'Wet paint'

friend – boyfriend – girlfriend

1 Timo says he's not [Tinas (fester) Freund, bloß einer von ihren Freunden und Bekannten].

A Tina's boyfriend, just one of her friends   B Tina's friend, just one of her boyfriends

2 ...... He was a loner.

A Dave was someone who didn't have many boyfriends.

B Dave was someone who didn't have many friends.

formula [ˈfɔːmjələ] Formel

> **!**
> **!** ■ **False Friend!**
> **!** *Formula* bedeutet nicht „~~Formular~~", sondern „Formel".
>   *a mathematical/chemical **formula*** ● ● ● eine mathematische/chemische Formel
>   *I have no magic **formula**.* ● ● ● Ich habe keine Zauberformel/Patentlösung.
>   Beachte die englische Entsprechung von „Formular":
>   ein Formular ausfüllen ● ● ● *fill in/out a **form***

forward – forwards vorwärts

■ Das Adverb kann ohne oder mit *-s* stehen.
   *We moved **forward/forwards**.* ● ● ● Wir bewegten uns vorwärts.

■ Das Adjektiv steht immer ohne *-s*.
   *a sudden **forward** movement* ● ● ● eine plötzliche Vorwärtsbewegung

freeze* (ge)frieren – freezing eiskalt

■ *freeze – froze – frozen*

■ *be **freezing** als Verlaufsform*
Freezing kann Teil der Verlaufsform des Verbs *freeze* sein.
   *It's already **freezing** outside.* ● ● ● Es gefriert schon draußen. [= Es ist unter null Grad.]

■ *freezing = „eiskalt"*
Freezing kann ein Adjektiv mit der Bedeutung „eiskalt" sein.
   *Turn the heating on! It's **freezing** (cold) in here!* ● ● ● … Es ist eiskalt hier drin.
   *I need a hot drink. I'm **freezing** / I'm **frozen**.* ● ● ● Mir ist eiskalt. / Ich friere.

■ *The two climbers **froze to death**.* ● ● ● Die beiden Bergsteiger sind erfroren.
   ***frozen** food* ● ● ● Tiefkühlkost

fresh – cool – cold frisch, kühl

■ *it's **fresh***
Man kann *it's fresh* sagen, um das Wetter zu beschreiben.
   *It's pretty **fresh** out there. Six degrees below!* ● ● ● Es ist ganz schön frisch/kühl da draußen.
      Sechs Grad unter null.

■ *it's too **cool/cold** for me*
Um auszudrücken, dass es einem zu frisch/kühl ist, verwendet man *cool* oder *cold*.
   *It's too **cool/cold** for me out here. I'm going inside.* ● ● ● Mir ist es hier draußen zu frisch. …

> **Trouble Spot**
> ■ **frisch**
> 1 drei Paar frische Socken einpacken ● ● ● *pack three pairs of **clean** socks*
>   das Bett frisch beziehen ● ● ● *put **clean** sheets on the bed*
> 2 Frisch gestrichen! ● ● ● ***Wet** paint!*
> 3 sich frisch machen ● ● ● ***freshen** (yourself) up*

friend Freund/-in – boyfriend Freund [eines Mädchens] – girlfriend Freundin

■ *friend = „Freund"/„Freundin"*
   *Asif is my best **friend**.* ● ● ● Asif ist mein bester Freund.
   *Bina is my best **friend**.* ● ● ● Bina ist meine beste Freundin.

■ ***boyfriend** nur bei Liebesbeziehung*
   *Jenny phoned one of her **(girl)friends** to tell her about her new **boyfriend**.*
   *Max phoned one of his **friends** (~~boyfriends~~) to tell him about his new **girlfriend**.*

■ *a **friend** of mine (~~a friend of me~~)* ● ● ● ein Freund/eine Freundin von mir

F

friendly

1 ...... , paused, then handed me back my passport.
- **A** The official looked at me in a not unfriendly way
- **B** The official looked at me not unfriendly
- **C** The official looked at me not unfriendlily

2 Thank you very much. ......
- **A** That was very friendly from you.   **B** That was very friendly of you.
- **C** That was very kind from you.   **D** That was very kind of you.   **E** That was very good of you.

3 **A** You should finish a letter of this type with 'friendly greetings'.
- **B** You should finish a letter of this type with 'kind greetings'.
- **C** You should finish a letter of this type with 'your sincerely'.
- **D** You should finish a letter of this type with 'yours sincerely'.

from – of – off – by – out of

1 **A** He was blind by birth.   **B** He was blind from birth.   **C** He was blind from the birth.

2 There has been ...... to stop his re-election.
- **A** an attempt by his critics   **B** an attempt from his critics

3 At this year's festival ....
- **A** we saw an interesting new play by an unknown playwright
- **B** we saw an interesting new play from an unknown playwright
- **C** we saw an interesting new play of an unknown playwright

4 We were all sitting there in class, ...
- **A** when suddenly this picture fell down the wall
- **B** when suddenly this picture fell from the wall down
- **C** when suddenly this picture fell off the wall

5 **A** Dusseldorf is north from Cologne.
- **B** Dusseldorf is north of Cologne.
- **C** Dusseldorf is north to Cologne.

6 **A** Two from three new cars on the road are now diesels.
- **B** Two of three new cars on the road are now diesels.
- **C** Two out of three new cars on the road are now diesels.

7 Who was that person who waved at us? – ......
- **A** It was a friend of me.   **B** It was a friend of mine.
- **C** It was a friend from me.   **D** It was a friend from mine.

8 **A** The room of my brother is bigger than mine.
- **B** The room from my brother is bigger than mine.
- **C** My brother's room is bigger than mine.

fry – roast – grill

1 I was too lazy to cook a proper meal. ......
- **A** I just fried an egg.   **B** I just roasted an egg.   **C** I just grilled an egg.

2 At Thanksgiving, the family I was with .... It only just fit in the oven.
- **A** fried a 12-pound turkey   **B** roasted a 12-pound turkey   **C** grilled a 12-pound turkey

friendly freundlich

■ **friendly = Adjektiv**

Friendly ist nur ein Adjektiv (*friendly, friendlier, friendliest*). Ein Adverb *friendly* oder ~~friendlily~~ gibt es nicht. Man verwendet stattdessen eine Umschreibung.

The beggar looked at me **in a friendly way**. ● ● ● Der Bettler hat mich freundlich angeschaut.

■ **Wortkombinationen**

The new model is even more **user-friendly**. ● ● ● Das neue Modell ist noch benutzerfreundlicher.

environmentally friendly / **eco-friendly** packaging ● ● ● umweltfreundliche Verpackung

F

Trouble Spot

■ **freundlich**

1 Das ist sehr freundlich von Ihnen. ● ● ● That's very **kind** [kaɪnd] / **good** of you.

Würden Sie bitte so freundlich sein und mich durchlassen? ● ● ● Would you be **so kind** / **good as to** let me through?

2 mit freundlichen Grüßen ● ● ● **Yours sincerely**

from – of – off – by – out of von

Trouble Spot

■ **von**

1 „von" zum Ausdruck eines räumlichen Verhältnisses

von links / rechts / hinten / oben ● ● ● **from** the left / the right / the back / above

nördlich von Berlin ● ● ● north **of** Berlin

links / rechts von der Lampe ● ● ● to the left / to the right **of** the lamp

2 „von [einer Fläche] herunter"

vom Tisch / von der Wand (herunter)fallen ● ● ● fall **off** the table / wall

3 „von" in Zeitbestimmungen

von zehn bis zwölf ● ● ● **from** ten to twelve

von heute an / ab heute ● ● ● **from** today

von Geburt (an) / seit der Geburt ● ● ● **from** birth

4 „von" + Urheber

ein Buch / Stück (von) einer berühmten Autorin ● ● ● a book / play **by** a famous author

5 „von" zum Ausdruck eines Zahlenverhältnisses

Neun von zehn Menschen würden den Unterschied nicht erkennen. ● ● ● Nine **out of** ten people wouldn't know the difference.

Aber:

Nur zwei von ihnen überlebten. ● ● ● Only two **of** them survived.

6 sonstige Wendungen

eine Freundin von mir ● ● ● a friend **of** mine

die Katze von meinem Onkel / meines Onkels ● ● ● my uncle**'s** cat

Das ist sehr freundlich von Ihnen. ● ● ● That's very kind / good **of** you.

fry – roast – grill braten   ▷ grill

Trouble Spot

■ **braten**

1 „in der Pfanne (oben auf dem Herd) braten"

ein Ei braten ● ● ● **fry** an egg [**fried** eggs = Spiegeleier]

Bratkartoffeln ● ● ● **fried** potatoes

Bratpfanne ● ● ● **frying** pan

2 „im Backofen oder am Spieß braten"

ein großes Stück Fleisch braten ● ● ● **roast** a big piece of meat

3 „auf dem Rost braten"

Steaks zum Abendessen auf dem Rost braten ● ● ● **grill** steaks for dinner

full

1 ...... It was awful.

  A The place was full tourists. **B** The place was full from tourists.

  C The place was full of tourists. **D** The place was full with tourists.

fully – completely

1 I'm sorry, but that is *[völlig unmöglich]*.

  A completely impossible **B** full impossible **C** fully impossible

fun

1 **A** The party was a huge fun. **B** The party was a big fun. **C** The party was great fun.

furniture

1 When my grandma died, ... We were only able to keep a few pieces.

  A we had to throw much of her furniture away **B** we had to throw many of her furnitures away

game – match – play

1 Anybody for tennis? – Yes, OK, ... , but I'm not any good.

  A I'll play a game with you **B** I'll play a match with you

2 How often do you go into a home nowadays and see a family ...... ? Never!

  A having a game of cards **B** making a card game **C** playing a game of cards

3 ...... always produce a lot of interest.

  A The England-Germany football games **B** The England-Germany football matches

German

1 The mother of the family I stayed with ....

  A spoke a really good German **B** spoke really good German

get

1 *[Kann ich bitte noch ein Brötchen bekommen?]* – Sure, just help yourself.

  A Can I become another roll, please?

  B Can I get another roll, please?

  C Can I have another roll, please?

get in / get on – get out of / get off

1 They said they couldn't find any steps, ... for a full half hour after we landed.

  A and we didn't get off the plane **B** and we didn't get out of the plane

2 It took the pop star, her publicity agent and bodyguards 15 minutes ...... , drive 200 metres up the road to the restaurant where they were dining, ...

  A to get in their limousine outside the hotel ... and get out of it again

  B to get into their limousine outside the hotel ... and get out of it again

  C to get on their limousine outside the hotel ... and get off it again

full voll

- *The room was **full of** people.* ● ● ● Der Raum war voll (von/mit) Menschen / voller Menschen.

fully – completely völlig, voll, ganz

- ***fully** aware/comprehensible* ● ● ● völlig bewusst/verständlich
  ***fully** automatic* ● ● ● vollautomatisch

- **nicht mit Negativbedeutung**
Fully kann man nicht vor Adjektive stellen, die eine negative Bedeutung haben.
  ***completely** (~~fully~~) unaware/incomprehensible* ● ● ● völlig unbewusst/unverständlich

fun Spaß

- **nicht zählbares Nomen**
Fun ist nicht zählbar, kann also nicht mit *a* verwendet werden.
  *The children had **great fun** (~~a great fun~~).* ● ● ● Die Kinder hatten einen Riesenspaß / großen Spaß.

furniture Möbel

- **nicht zählbares Nomen**
Furniture ist nicht zählbar, hat also keine Pluralform.
  *In a one-room flat you don't need **much furniture** (~~many furnitures~~).* ● ● ● … nicht viele Möbel.

game Spiel – match Spiel, Wettkampf – play (Theater-)Stück, Schauspiel

- *Game* ist das allgemeine Wort für „Spiel".
  *a **ball**/**board**/**computer** game* ● ● ● ein Ball-/Brett-/Computerspiel
  *Skat is a German **card game** completely unknown in the English-speaking world.* ● ● ● Skat ist ein
      deutsches Kartenspiel …
  *Let's **have**/**play** (~~make~~) **a game of cards** (~~a card game~~).* ● ● ● Spielen wir Karten / ein Kartenspiel.
  *How about **a game of volleyball**?* ● ● ● Wie wär's mit einer Runde Volleyball?

- Ein „offizielles" Wettkampfspiel heißt *match*.
  *a **volleyball match***
  *There's a big **football match** on TV this evening.*
  Ausnahmen im AE: *a big **baseball**/**football game***

- Ein *play* ist ein Theaterstück oder Schauspiel.
  *Our class is going to **put on a play**.* ● ● ● Unsere Klasse will ein Stück aufführen.
  *a **radio play*** ● ● ● ein Hörspiel

German Deutsch

- **nicht zählbares Nomen**
Wie andere Sprachennamen ist *German* nicht zählbar, d. h., man kann es nicht mit *a/an* verwenden.
  *She spoke excellent **German** (~~an excellent German~~).* ● ● ● … (ein) ausgezeichnetes Deutsch.

get* bekommen ▷ become ▷ come

- **nicht in Bitten**
Get sollte man nicht in höflichen Bitten verwenden.
  *Can I **have** (~~Can I get~~) another potato, please?* ● ● ● Kann ich bitte noch eine Kartoffel bekommen/
  haben?

get* in / get* on einsteigen – get* out of / get* off aussteigen

- ***get in(to)** a car / a taxi* ● ● ● in ein Auto / ein Taxi einsteigen
  ***get on(to)** a bus / a train / a plane* ● ● ● in einen Bus / einen Zug / ein Flugzeug einsteigen

- ***get out of** a car / a taxi* ● ● ● aus einem Auto / einem Taxi aussteigen
  ***get off** a bus / a train / a plane* ● ● ● aus einem Bus / einem Zug / einem Flugzeug aussteigen

G

glass – jar

1 Can you put ...... on the shopping list, please?
   A a new glass of honey   B a new jar of honey

glasses

1 'If you can't read this,' the bumper sticker said, ...
   A 'you need a glasses'   B 'you need a pair of glasses'   C 'you need glasses'

go

1 You can't drive all the way. You have to *[die letzten 300 Meter zu Fuß gehen]*.
   A go the last 300 metres   B walk the last 300 metres

2 What's the matter? – The light *[geht irgendwie nicht]*.
   A isn't somehow going   B isn't working somehow

go on

1 The teacher stood there in the doorway, ...
   A but people just went on talking   B but people just went on to talk

2 We have to agree both the text and the design. I suggest we discuss the text first, ...
   A then go on planning the design   B then go on to plan the design

good

1 ...... when a cake is done or not?
   A How good are you at telling   B How good are you in telling   C How good are you to tell

greatly – largely

1 A Prices vary greatly, by as much as 100%.   B Prices vary largely, by as much as 100%.

2 A The problem is now greatly under control.   B The problem is now largely under control.

3 ...... I don't think it would ever happen.
   A That is extremely unlikely.   B That is greatly unlikely.
   C That is highly unlikely.   D That is largely unlikely.

glass – jar Glas

- a **glass** of milk ● ● ● ein Glas Milch
  two **glasses of** wine ● ● ● zwei Glas Wein

- a **jar of** jam/olives [ˈɒlɪvz] /… ● ● ● ein [verschlossenes] Glas Marmelade/Oliven/…

glasses Brille

Pluralnomen, keine Singularform

Glasses („Brille") gibt es nur als Pluralnomen (mit einem Verb im Plural).
  My **glasses were** here a moment ago. Where **are they** now? ● ● ● Meine Brille war doch eben noch hier. Wo ist sie jetzt?
Um daraus eine Singularform zu machen, muss man a pair of glasses verwenden.
  I need a new **pair of glasses**. (= I need **(some)** new **glasses**.) ● ● ● Ich brauche eine neue Brille.

G

go* gehen ▷ become ▷ come ▷ drive ▷ visit

- Let's **go**. ● ● ● Gehen wir!

Trouble Spot

■ **gehen**
  Der Fuß tut mir so weh, dass ich kaum gehen [= zu Fuß gehen, laufen] kann. ● ● ● My foot hurts so much, I can hardly **walk**.
  Pass auf, wenn du über die Straße gehst. ● ● ● Be careful when you **cross the road**.
  Der rechte Blinker geht [= funktioniert] nicht. ● ● ● The right indicator isn't **working**
  Das Stück geht [= dauert] mindestens zwei Stunden. ● ● ● The play **lasts** at least two hours.
  Wie geht's dir/Ihnen? ● ● ● How **are you**?
  Das geht nicht. ● ● ● That's **impossible**.

go on weitermachen ▷ continue

■ **go on doing**
Go on doing bedeutet „fortfahren mit (dem, was man gerade tut)", „weitertun".
  People came and went, but we just **went on working**. ● ● ● … aber wir haben einfach weitergearbeitet.

■ **go on to do**
Go on to do bedeutet „dazu übergehen, zu tun".
  After lunch we **went on to discuss** the budget. ● ● ● Nach dem Essen machten wir uns daran, den Haushaltsplan zu besprechen.

good gut ▷ bad

■ **good at (doing) sth.**
  I'm (no) **good at** maths. ● ● ● Ich bin (nicht) gut in Mathe.
  I'm (no) **good at remembering** jokes. ● ● ● Ich kann mir Witze (nicht) gut merken.

greatly sehr, höchst – largely großenteils, größtenteils

■ **greatly – largely**
Greatly bedeutet „sehr", „höchst".
  Temperatures there can vary **greatly**. ● ● ● Die Temperaturen dort können sehr schwanken.
Largely bedeutet „zum größten Teil".
  The region is still **largely** unexplored. ● ● ● Das Gebiet ist noch zum größten Teil unerforscht.

■ **greatly** nur mit Partizipien
Greatly kann man nur vor Partizipien, nicht vor normalen Adjektiven (z. B. unusual) verwenden.
  a **greatly improved** performance ● ● ● eine deutlich verbesserte Leistung
  a **greatly increased** risk ● ● ● ein stark gestiegenes Risiko
Aber mit Adjektiv:
  a **very/highly/extremely** unusual request ● ● ● eine sehr/höchst/äußerst ungewöhnliche Bitte

greet – say hello

1 ...... if I don't know the person's name?
   A How do I greet   B How do I greet someone   C How do I say hello

2 If I don't see you again, [schöne Ferien].
   A happy holidays   B have a nice holiday   C nice holiday

3 [Grüß Bernd von mir] if you see him.
   A Greet Bernd from me   B Say hello to Bernd for me   C Say hello to Bernd from me

4 [Grüß die Tanja ganz lieb von uns], don't forget!
   A Greet Tanja from us kindly
   B Say hello to Tanja from us lovingly
   C Give our love to Tanja

5 ...... I hope you get the job.
   A Good luck by your interview!
   B Good luck on your interview!
   C Good luck with your interview!

grill – broiler/broil – barbecue

1 A The smell from the barbecue on the balcony below made me feel really hungry.
   B The smell from the grill on the balcony below made me feel really hungry.

2 It was a lovely summer evening. ...... , inside there was a wonderful salad buffet.
   A Outside they barbecued meat   B Outside they grilled meat   C Outside they broilered meat

ground ≠ „gründen"

1 To ground something means ....
   A to begin it   B to give reasons for it   C to not let it fly

2 A The organization was found at the end of the 19th century.
   B The organization was founded at the end of the 19th century.
   C The organization was grounded at the end of the 19th century.

guest – customer – visitor

1 It's only a very small restaurant ....
   A with room for not more than about 30 customers
   B with room for not more than about 30 guests
   C with room for not more than about 30 visitors

greet – say* hello grüßen

■ **greet sb.**
Greet muss immer ein Objekt haben.
> I **greet him** every morning, but he never **says hello** back. ● ● ● Ich grüße ihn jeden Morgen, aber er grüßt nie zurück.

> ■ **Greetings and wishes**
> *Good Morning.* / *Good Afternoon.* / *Good Evening.* ● ● ● Guten Morgen! / Guten Tag! / Guten Abend!
> (infml:) *Morning.* / *Afternoon.* / *Evening.* ● ● ● Morgen! / Tag! / 'n Abend!
> *Happy birthday.* / *Many happy returns (of the day).* ● ● ● Herzlichen Glückwunsch zum Geburtstag!
> *Happy* / *Merry Christmas.* ● ● ● Frohe / Fröhliche Weihnachten!
> *(A) Happy New Year.* ● ● ● (Ein) gutes neues Jahr!
> *Happy Easter.* ● ● ● Frohe Ostern!
> *Happy holidays.* / *Have a nice holiday.* ● ● ● Schöne Ferien!
> *Say hello to Tina for* / *from me.* ● ● ● Grüß mir Tina. / Grüß Tina von mir.
> *Give my love to Janet.* ● ● ● Grüß Janet ganz lieb von mir. / Ganz liebe Grüße an Janet.
> *Give my best wishes to your parents.* ● ● ● Grüß deine Eltern (herzlich) von mir.
> *Congratulations on (passing) your driving test!* ● ● ● Herzlichen Glückwunsch zur (bestandenen) Fahrprüfung / zum Führerschein!
> *Good luck with your exam!* ● ● ● Viel Glück bei deiner / für deine Prüfung!

Topic Box

G

grill – broiler – barbecue Grill – **grill – broil – barbecue** grillen ▶ **fry**

■ **grill** nur beim Kochen im Haus
> a gas stove with an electric (BE:) **grill** / (AE:) **broiler** ● ● ● ein Gasherd mit einem Elektrogrill
> turn on the extractor fan when (BE:) **grilling** / (AE:) **broiling** ● ● ● die Dunstabzugshaube beim Grillen einschalten

■ **barbecue** = „Grill(en) im Garten"
Wenn von Grillen draußen im Freien gesprochen wird, verwendet man im BE das Wort *barbecue*, nicht *grill*.
> Who left the **barbecue** / **BBQ** out in the rain? ● ● ● Wer hat den Grill draußen im Regen gelassen?
> It was a lovely evening, so we **had a barbecue**. ● ● ● … also haben wir gegrillt.
> **barbecue** / (AE auch:) **grill** cutlets for 50 people at a summer party ● ● ● Koteletts für 50 Personen auf einer Sommerparty grillen

ground: be grounded nicht starten können [Flugzeug usw.]

! ■ **False Friend!**
Ground bedeutet nicht „~~gründen~~", sondern „[einem Flugzeug] Startverbot erteilen".
> There was a terrific snowstorm and all planes **were grounded**. ● ● ● … und alle Flugzeuge konnten nicht starten.
Beachte die englischen Entsprechungen von „gründen":
> einen Verein gründen ● ● ● **found** a club
> eine Firma gründen ● ● ● **set up** a company
> eine Familie gründen ● ● ● **start** a family

guest [gest] – **customer – visitor** Gast

■ a hotel **guest** ● ● ● ein Hotelgast

■ Der Gast in einem Restaurant wird als *customer*, nicht als *guest* bezeichnet.
> a **customer** (~~guest~~) in a restaurant ● ● ● ein Gast in einem Restaurant

■ have **visitors** ● ● ● Gäste / Besucher haben

guesthouse ≠ „Gasthaus"

1 A guesthouse is ....
   A a place that serves beer and food
   B a sort of bed and breakfast

2 The *Goldener Löwe* is *[das beste Gasthaus]* in the area.
   A the best bed and breakfast   B the best canteen   C the best guesthouse
   D the best hostel   E the best restaurant

gymnasium ≠ „Gymnasium"

1 A gymnasium is ....
   A a place where people learn Latin
   B a place where people do gymnastics or fitness training
   C a place where people sit quietly and read

2 There are *[nicht so viele Gymnasien]* in Britain as in Germany.
   A not so many advanced schools
   B not so many higher schools
   C not so many grammar schools

gymnastics – exercises – fitness

1 My grandfather goes *[zu einem Gymnastikkurs]* for the over-sixties.
   A to a fitness class   B to a gymnastic class   C to a gymnastic course

2 One of my New Year's resolutions is *[ein bisschen Gymnastik zu machen]* each morning before I have breakfast.
   A to do some exercises   B to do some gymnastics

habit

1 A Mr Smith has the annoying habit of parking outside our house.
   B Mr Smith has the annoying habit parking outside our house.
   C Mr Smith has the annoying habit to park outside our house.

2 A It's so easy to make it to a habit to get up late.
   B It's so easy to make a habit of getting up late.
   C It's so easy to make the habit to get up late.

had: I had better

1 Don't you think ...... ?
   A you had better telling them now
   B you had better tell them now
   C you had better to tell them now

2 Is it OK to leave now? – ......
   A We better hadn't.   B We'd better not.   C We hadn't better.

hair

1 Will you go bald ...... like your father, do you think?
   A and lose all your hair   B and lose all your hairs   C and lose all your hair's

guesthouse Pension, kleines Hotel

> ! ! ! ■ **False Friend!**
> *Guesthouse* bedeutet nicht „~~Gasthaus~~", sondern bezeichnet ein kleines Hotel oder eine Frühstückspension.
>   *We stayed in a private* **guesthouse**. ● ● ● Wir haben in einer Privatpension gewohnt.
> Beachte die englische Entsprechung von „Gasthaus":
>   im Gasthaus essen ● ● ● *eat in a* **restaurant** / **pub**

gymnasium [dʒɪmˈneɪziəm] Turnhalle

> ! ! ! ■ **False Friend!**
> *Gymnasium* bedeutet nicht „~~Gymnasium~~", sondern „Turnhalle".
>   *have a PE (= 'physical education') lesson in the* **gymnasium** ● ● ● eine Sportstunde in der Turnhalle haben
> Beachte die englische Entsprechung von „Gymnasium":
>   aufs Gymnasium gehen ● ● ● *go to (a)* **grammar school** / (fml:) *attend (a)* **grammar school** (BE)

H

gymnastics [dʒɪmˈnæstɪks] – **exercises** – **fitness** Gymnastik

■ Mit *gymnastics* bezeichnet man kunstvolles Körperturnen als Wettkampfdisziplin.
   win a gold medal in **gymnastics** *at the Olympic Games*

■ „Private" Gymnastik nennt man *exercises* oder – in Wortkombinationen – *fitness*.
   do **exercises** *every morning* ● ● ● jeden Morgen Gymnastik machen
   On Tuesday evenings my mother goes to a **fitness class**. ● ● ● Dienstagabends geht meine Mutter zur Gymnastik / zum Fitnesstraining.

habit (An-)Gewohnheit

■ *a* / *the habit of doing*
In folgenden Wendungen steht nach *habit* die Präposition *of* + die *-ing*-Form des Verbs, kein *to*-Infinitiv:
   He **has a** / **the habit of interrupting** (*has a* / ~~the habit to interrupt~~) *people*. ● ● ● Er hat die Angewohnheit, anderen ins Wort zu fallen.
   He has **made a habit of watching** (~~has made a habit to watch~~) *TV at breakfast*. ● ● ● Er hat es sich zur Gewohnheit gemacht / Er hat sich angewöhnt, beim Frühstück fernzusehen.

had: I had better … ich sollte lieber …; es wäre besser, wenn ich …

■ *had better do*
Had better ist eine feste Wendung, bei der *had* immer in der Vergangenheitsform steht. Darauf folgt ein Infinitiv ohne *to*.
   *It's getting late. We***'d better go**. ● ● ● … Wir sollten lieber gehen.
Die Verneinung heißt *had better not*.
   *We***'d better not wait** *any longer*. ● ● ● Wir sollten lieber nicht länger warten.
Nur in verneinten Fragen wird *not* an *had* angeschlossen.
   Hadn't *we* **better phone** *first?* ● ● ● Sollten wir nicht lieber zuerst anrufen?

hair Haar(e)

■ *hair* (= „Haarschopf") immer Singular
Den Haarschopf als Ganzes bezeichnet man immer mit der Singularform *hair*.
   Anna's **hair is** *beautiful. It's shoulder-length* (~~shoulder-long~~) *and blonde*. ● ● ● Annas Haare sind / Annas Haar ist wunderschön. Sie sind / Es ist schulterlang und blond.
Von einzelnen Haaren kann man jedoch als *hairs* sprechen.
   Ugh! There are dog **hairs** *on my plate*. ● ● ● Igitt! Auf meinem Teller sind Hundehaare.

half

1 The journey only takes ....
   A a half hour   **B** an half hour   **C** half a hour   **D** half an hour

2 We won, ...
   A even though half our team was ill
   B even though our half team was ill
   C even though the half of our team was ill

3 We've already spent .... We must be more careful.
   A half our money   **B** the half of our money   **C** half of our money

4 When the boat overturned, ...
   A they swam the one and a half mile to the shore
   B they swam the one and a half miles to the shore
   C they swam the one and half mile to the shore
   D they swam the one and half miles to the shore

5 .... , it won't be so boring, and we'll be finished sooner.
   A If we do the half each   **B** If we do half each   **C** If we do each the half

hall

1 A hall can be ....
   A a part of a house
   B a room in a public building where people meet
   C a factory building

2 When I got back to the hotel, there was a party of tourists .... checking in.
   A in the foyer   **B** in the hall

3 Is it true that Microsoft started [in einer alten Halle] that belonged to a gas station?
   A in an old hall   **B** in an old shed

hand

1 [Hände weg!] I don't want that broken!
   A Hands away!   **B** Hands off!   **C** Hands up!

2 This traditional boat is still ....
   A made by hand   **B** made per hand   **C** made with hand

handy ≠ „Handy"

1 What is the best synonym for 'handy' in the following sentence?
A Swiss Army knife is a handy thing to have.
   A compact   **B** easy to use   **C** useful

2 The hotel is ....
   A close to the Kensington museums   **B** handy for the Kensington museums
   C handy to the Kensington museums   **D** near the Kensington museums

3 What's [deine Handynummer]?
   A your cell phone number   **B** your handy number   **C** your mobile number

half 1 halb 2 Hälfte

■ *half + Begleiter*
Half steht in aller Regel **vor** einem Begleiter, nicht dahinter.
  *I waited for **half an** hour, but nothing happened.* ● ● ● … eine halbe Stunde (lang) …
  *We slept **half the** time.* ● ● ● … die halbe Zeit / die Hälfte der Zeit …

■ *half of*
Vor *half of* im Sinne von „die Hälfte von", „50% von" wird *the* nicht verwendet.
  ***Half of** my friends (The half of my friends) are away on holiday.* ● ● ● Die Hälfte meiner Freunde
    sind verreist.
  ***Half of** them are away.* ● ● ● Die Hälfte von ihnen ist/sind weg.

■ **Sonstiges**
  *The sports field is **one and a half** kilometres from the school.* ● ● ● … anderthalb Kilometer …
  *The pizza was huge, so we ate **half each** (each the half).* ● ● ● … also aßen wir jeder die Hälfte.
  *I've got more than enough, you can have **half** (the half) if you want.* ● ● ● … du kannst
    die Hälfte (ab)haben, wenn du willst.

hall Flur; Halle, Saal

■ *Hall* kann einen Hausflur oder einen (größeren) Versammlungsraum bezeichnen.
  *walk through the narrow **hall** to the front door* ● ● ● durch den schmalen Hausflur … gehen
  *a concert in the **school hall*** ● ● ● ein Konzert in der Aula
  *The course will take place in the **village hall**.* ● ● ● … im Dorfgemeinschaftssaal …

Trouble Spot

  ■ **Halle**
  1 „öffentliches Gebäude"
    Warte auf mich in der (Eingangs-)Halle. ● ● ● *Wait for me in the **entrance hall** /*
      [im Hotel/Theater:] ***foyer*** ['fɔɪeɪ].
    Sie bauen eine neue Sporthalle. ● ● ● *They're building a new **sports hall**.*
    [Sport:] in der Halle spielen ● ● ● *play **indoors***
  2 „gewerbliches Gebäude"
    Die alte Fabrikhalle ist jetzt ein Kulturzentrum. ● ● ● *The old **factory building** is now*
      an arts centre.
    Diese Halle dort ist das Ersatzteillager. ● ● ● *That **shed** / **building** there is the spare parts store.*

hand Hand

■ ***Hands off**, that's mine!* ● ● ● Hände weg, das ist meins!
  *take sb. **by the hand*** ● ● ● jmdn. an der / die Hand nehmen
  *make sth. **by hand*** ● ● ● etwas von Hand / mit der Hand anfertigen

handy praktisch, handlich; griffbereit

  ■ **False Friend!**
  Handy ist kein Nomen und bedeutet nicht „Handy", sondern ist ein Adjektiv mit den Bedeu-
  tungen „praktisch" / „nützlich" bzw. „günstig" / „leicht erreichbar" / „griffbereit" / „greifbar".
    *It's a **handy** little tool, especially for campers.* ● ● ● Es ist ein praktisches kleines Werkzeug …
    *We live in west London, which is very **handy** for the airport.* ● ● ● … was sehr günstig ist,
      wenn man zum Flughafen muss.
    *The box will **come in handy** when we move.* ● ● ● Die Kiste können wir gebrauchen / wird
      sich als nützlich erweisen, wenn wir umziehen.
  Beachte die englischen Entsprechungen von „Handy":
    eine SIM-Karte für mein Handy ● ● ● *a SIM card for my **mobile (phone)*** [ˌməʊbaɪl 'fəʊn] /
      (besonders AE:) ***cellphone** / **cell(ular) phone***

H

hang

1 The furniture is in place, we've unpacked all the boxes ....
   A and hanged all the pictures   B and hung all the pictures

2 The plotters were arrested ...... the following day.
   A and hanged on Tower Hill   B and hung on Tower Hill

happen

1 Don't worry. ......

   A This sort of mistake can happen the best of us.
   B This sort of mistake can happen to the best of us.

harbour/harbor – port

1 A Rotterdam is the largest harbour in Europe.   B Rotterdam is the largest port in Europe.

hard – hardly

1 ...... and deserves all the success she's had.
   A Samira worked very hard   B Samira worked very hardly

2 A I know hardly people here.
   B I know hardly any people here.
   C I know hardly some people here.

3 A Hardly the barbecue party had started when it started to rain.
   B Hardly had the barbecue party started when it started to rain.
   C No sooner had the barbecue party started when it started to rain.
   D No sooner had the barbecue party started than it started to rain.

hate

1 We used to be friends, ... I can't forgive him for what he's done.
   A but now I'm hating him   B but now I hate him

2 A I hate having to work when it's so hot.
   B I hate to have to work when it's so hot.
   C I hate have to work when it's so hot.

3 Please hurry up. ......

   A I'd hate to miss the beginning of the film.
   B I'd hate missing the beginning of the film.

hang (*) (auf-, er)hängen

■ **hang – hung – hung**
In den meisten Bedeutungen ist *hang* ein unregelmäßiges Verb mit der Form *hung*.
  *A chandelier **hung** from the ceiling.* ● ● ● Von der Decke hing ein Kronleuchter.
  *We've **hung** our coats up.* ● ● ● Wir haben unsere Mäntel aufgehängt.

■ **hang – hanged – hanged**
In der Bedeutung „jmdn. erhängen" ist *hang* jedoch regelmäßig (*hang – hanged – hanged*).
  *He was **hanged** for murder.* ● ● ● Er wurde wegen Mordes erhängt/gehängt.

happen geschehen

■ *What's **happened to** (~~happened with~~) you? You're all wet.* ● ● ● Was ist denn mit dir passiert? …

harbour (BE) / harbor (AE) – port Hafen

■ Mit *harbour* bezeichnet man ein Hafenbecken allgemein.
  *watch fishing boats in the **harbour*** ● ● ● Fischerboote im Hafen beobachten
  *take a trip round Hamburg **harbour*** ● ● ● eine Rundfahrt durch den Hamburger Hafen machen

■ Mit *port* bezeichnet man einen (See-)Hafen als Handelsplatz oder Verkehrsknotenpunkt bzw. eine
Stadt, wo sich ein solcher Hafen befindet.
  *the **port** of Dover/Antwerp* ● ● ● die Hafenstadt Dover/Antwerpen

H

hard hart – hardly kaum ▷ heavy

■ **Adjektiv und Adverb: *hard***
Das zum Adjektiv *hard* gehörige Adverb heißt ebenfalls *hard*.
  *She's a **hard** worker. She works **hard**.* ● ● ● Sie ist eine harte Arbeiterin. Sie arbeitet hart.

■ **Adverb *hardly***
Das Adverb *hardly* bedeutet „kaum".
  *I could **hardly** believe it.* ● ● ● Ich konnte es kaum glauben.
Hardly ist vom Sinn her negativ („fast nicht", „fast kein") und wird daher mit *any* und mit bejahten
Frageanhängseln verwendet.
  *I'm sorry, I have **hardly any** time.* ● ● ● Ich habe leider kaum Zeit.
  *It's **hardly** worth it, is it (~~isn't it~~)?* ● ● ● Es lohnt sich kaum, nicht wahr?
Wie bei anderen Adverbien mit Negativbedeutung werden Subjekt und Verb umgestellt (wie in
einer Frage), wenn *hardly* – im förmlichen Englisch – am Satzanfang steht. Vergleiche:
  *Ed had **hardly** spoken her name when Di came through the door.* ● ● ● Ed hatte kaum …, als …
  ***Hardly** had Ed spoken her name when Di came through the door.* ● ● ● Kaum hatte Ed …, da …
Anstelle von *hardly* kann man auch den Ausdruck *no sooner* verwenden. In diesem Fall steht danach
nicht *when*, sondern *than*.
  ***No sooner** had Ed spoken her name **than** Di came through the door.* ● ● ● Kaum hatte Ed …, da …

hate hassen, gar nicht mögen

■ **normalerweise nicht in der Verlaufsform**
  *I used to like hot weather, but now I **hate** it.* ● ● ● … aber jetzt kann ich es überhaupt nicht leiden.
Hate steht nur dann in der Verlaufsform, wenn eine vorübergehende Einzelsituation gemeint ist.
  *This hot weather is awful. **I'm hating** every minute of it.* ● ● ● … Ich hasse jede einzelne Minute.

■ **hate doing – hate to do**
Nach *hate* kann man entweder die *-ing*-Form des Verbs oder einen *to*-Infinitiv verwenden.
  *I **hate going** / **hate to go** to the dentist's.* ● ● ● Ich hasse es, zum Zahnarzt zu gehen. / Ich gehe
      äußerst ungern zum Zahnarzt.

■ **would hate (sb. / sth.) to do**
Nach *would hate* steht nur der *to*-Infinitiv, nicht die *-ing*-Form.
  *I'd **hate** anything **to happen** to her.* ● ● ● Ich könnte es nicht ertragen, wenn ihr etwas zustieße.

headache

1 I'm sorry, but I have to go and lie down. ......
  A I have headache. **B** I have a headache.

healthy – (fit and) well – better – good for

1 Until he had the accident, ...
  A he was always a very healthy person   **B** he was always a very well person

2 *[Werde bald wieder gesund!]*
  A Become healthy again soon. **B** Get well soon. **C** Get healthy again soon.

3 I had flu last week, ...
  A but I'm better now **B** but I'm healthy again now

4 Eat lots of green vegetables. ......
  A They're good for you. **B** They're healthy for you. **C** They're well for you.

hear

1 I'm sorry, ... Could you repeat what you just said?
  A but we're not hearing what you're saying
  B but we can't hear what you're saying
  C but we don't hear what you're saying

2 ...... , this wouldn't have happened.
  A If you had heard my advice
  B If you had heard on my advice
  C If you had listened to my advice

3 ...... Where is it?
  A I've never heard from a place called Marlow.   **B** I've never heard of a place called Marlow.

4 ...... People say you're related to Bob Marley. Are you?
  A I've heard a lot about you, and now I want to know if it's all true.
  B I've heard a lot from you, and now I want to know if it's all true.

heaven – hell

1 "Where's grandma?" asked the little boy. ...... said his mother.
  A "At heaven, dear," **B** "At the heaven, dear,"
  C "In heaven, dear," **D** "In the heaven, dear,"

2 Religious fanatics are always telling you ....
  A that you will go to hell **B** that you will go to the hell
  C that you will go into the hell **D** that you will come in the hell

headache [ˈhedeɪk] Kopfschmerzen

■ **Singular mit** *a*

Headache ist ein normales zählbares Nomen mit Singularform („einmal auftretende Kopfschmerzen") und Pluralform („mehrmals auftretende Kopfschmerzen").

*Have you got an aspirin? I've got **a** terrible **headache**.* ● ● ● … Ich habe furchtbare Kopfschmerzen.

*I suffer from **headaches** a lot.* ● ● ● Ich leide sehr an Kopfschmerzen.

healthy [ˈhelθi] – (fit and) well – better – good (for) gesund

Trouble Spot

■ **gesund**

1 „robust", „kräftig"

Mein Opa ist 94 und noch ganz gesund. ● ● ● *My grandad is 94 and still **healthy** / **fit and well**.*

Sie ist ein gesunder Mensch, nie krank. ● ● ● *She's a **healthy** person, never ill.* [vor Nomen nur *healthy*]

2 „nicht (mehr) krank"

Werde bald wieder gesund! ● ● ● ***Get well** soon.* [feste Wendung]

Ist er wieder gesund [= genesen]? ● ● ● *Is he **better**?*

Er ist nicht gesund [= ständig krank]. Er hat Zucker. ● ● ● *He's not **well**. He has diabetes.*

3 „gesundheitsfördernd"

Sport ist gesund. ● ● ● *Sport is **good for you**.*

Eine gesunde Ernährungsweise verhindert viele Krankheiten. ● ● ● *A **healthy** diet prevents many illnesses.* [vor Nomen: nur *healthy*]

hear* hören   ▶ overhear   ▶ understand

■ *can hear*

Das Hören in einer konkreten Situation wird normalerweise mit *can hear* ausgedrückt.

Hear kann man bis auf seltene Ausnahmen nicht in der Verlaufsform verwenden.

*I **can hear** the sea. / I **hear** the sea. (~~I'm hearing the sea.~~)* ● ● ● Ich höre das Meer.

***Can** you **hear** it? / **Do** you **hear** it?* ● ● ● Kannst du es hören? / Hörst du es?

*I'm sorry. I **can't hear** you. (~~I don't hear you.~~ / ~~I'm not hearing you.~~) Can you speak a bit louder?*
● ● ● Tut mir leid. Ich kann dich nicht hören / [akustisch] nicht verstehen. …

Trouble Spot

■ **hören**

1 Musik / Radio hören ● ● ● ***listen to music** / **to the radio***

auf jmds. Rat hören ● ● ● ***listen to** sb.'s **advice***

Hör genau zu / hin! ● ● ● ***Listen** carefully.*

2 Was macht Opa? – Er hört gerade (die) Nachrichten. ● ● ● *What's grandad doing? – He's **listening to the news**.* [Vorgang steht im Mittelpunkt]

Hast du die Nachrichten(sendung) gehört? ● ● ● *Have you **heard the news**?* [Ergebnis steht im Mittelpunkt]

3 Ich habe nie von dieser Band gehört. [= (nicht) kennen] ● ● ● *I've never **heard of** this band.*

Hast du von Pias Unfall gehört? [= erfahren] ● ● ● *Have you **heard about** Pia's accident?*

Ich habe von Tim gehört. [= Nachricht bekommen] Er hat gemailt. ● ● ● *I've **heard from** Tim. He's sent an email.*

heaven [ˈhevn] Himmel(reich) – hell Hölle   ▶ sky

■ **ohne** *the*

Heaven und *hell* werden ohne den bestimmten Artikel verwendet.

*be **in heaven** / **in hell** (~~in the heaven~~ / ~~in the hell~~)* ● ● ● im Himmel / in der Hölle sein

*go **to heaven** / **to hell** (~~to the heaven~~ / ~~(in)to the hell~~)* ● ● ● in den Himmel / in die Hölle kommen

*Do you believe in **heaven** / **hell**?* ● ● ● Glaubst du an den Himmel / die Hölle?

H

heavy

1 A I have only one suitcase, but a big difficult one.
  B I have only one suitcase, but a big grave one.
  C I have only one suitcase, but a big hard one.
  D I have only one suitcase, but a big heavy one.

2 A The suitcase is almost 30 kg heavy.
  B The suitcase is weighing almost 30 kg.
  C The suitcase weighs almost 30 kg.

3 I'm sorry, ...
  A but I find that really difficult to believe
  B but I find that really grave to believe
  C but I find that really hard to believe
  D but I find that really heavy to believe

4 I have bad news. ......
  A Tony has had a difficult accident.   B Tony has had a grave accident.
  C Tony has had a hard accident.   D Tony has had a heavy accident.
  E Tony has had a serious accident.   F Tony has had a severe accident.

5 ...... if you do that.
  A You'll be making a very difficult mistake   B You'll be making a very grave mistake
  C You'll be making a very hard mistake   D You'll be making a very heavy mistake
  E You'll be making a very serious mistake   F You'll be making a very severe mistake

6 ...... people in the region could remember.
  A It was one of the heaviest storms   B It was one of the hardest storms
  C It was one of the most serious storms   D It was one of the severest storms

7 A Some of the gravest fighting of the war took place in the area to the south of here.
  B Some of the heaviest fighting of the war took place in the area to the south of here.
  C Some of the severest fighting of the war took place in the area to the south of here.

8 A Your friend has been heavily injured in a fall down the north face of the mountain.
  B Your friend has been seriously injured in a fall down the north face of the mountain.

help

1 The task was not at all easy, ...
  A but they gave us one or two helps
  B but they gave us some help
  C but they gave us some helps

2 A Can you help pack these presents?   B Can you help to pack these presents?
  C Can you help me pack these presents?   D Can you help me to pack these presents?

hide

1 Where's the key? – ......
  A I've hid it.   B I've hidden it.   C I've hided it.

2 Don't try and .... They'll find out sooner or later anyway.
  A hide anything before your parents   B hide anything for your parents
  C hide anything from your parents

heavy ['hevi] schwer   ▶ strong

■ a **heavy** box ● ● ● eine schwere Kiste
Aber mit Gewichtsangabe:
   a box **weighing** [weɪɪŋ] 20 kg ● ● ● eine 20 kg schwere Kiste
   The box **weighs** 20 kg. ● ● ● Die Kiste ist 20 kg schwer.

Trouble Spot

■ **schwer**
1 „schwer zu ertragen"
   ein schwerer Schlag ● ● ● a **heavy** blow
   eine schwere Strafe ● ● ● a **heavy** punishment
   schwer bestrafen ● ● ● punish **heavily/severely** [sɪ'vɪəli]
2 „schwierig"
   eine schwere Aufgabe/Entscheidung ● ● ● a **difficult/hard** job/decision
   schwer zu glauben/zu verstehen ● ● ● **difficult/hard** to believe/to understand
   Schwer zu sagen. ● ● ● It's **hard** to say.
   Es fällt mir schwer, das zu glauben. ● ● ● I find it **difficult/hard** to believe that.
   Du bist schwer zu verstehen. ● ● ● It's **difficult** to hear what you're saying.
3 „ernst", „schlimm", „groß"
   ein schwerer Unfall ● ● ● a **major** ['meɪdʒə] / **serious** ['sɪəriəs] accident
   eine schwere Krankheit/Verletzung ● ● ● a **major/serious/severe** illness/injury
   schwer krank/verletzt/verwundet ● ● ● **seriously/severely** ill/injured/wounded
   schwere Schäden ● ● ● **serious/severe** damage
   schwer beschädigt ● ● ● **badly/seriously/severely** damaged
   ein schwerer Fehler ● ● ● a **serious/grave** mistake
   ein schweres Verbrechen ● ● ● a **serious** crime
   eine schwere Enttäuschung ● ● ● a **deep/great** disappointment
   schwer enttäuscht ● ● ● **deeply/greatly** disappointed
   ein schwerer Sturm ● ● ● a **severe/violent/heavy** storm
4 „intensiv", „zahlreich"
   schwere Kämpfe ● ● ● **heavy** fighting
   schwere Verluste ● ● ● **heavy** losses

help 1 Hilfe **2** helfen

■ **nicht zählbares Nomen**
Help hat keine Pluralform und kann nur in bestimmten Wendungen mit a verwendet werden.
   I'll give you **some help** (a help/some helps). ● ● ● Ich gebe euch etwas Hilfe/ein paar Hilfen.
Aber:
   be a (big/great) **help** (to sb.) ● ● ● (jmdm.) eine (große) Hilfe sein
■ **help (sb.) to do – help (sb.) do**
Nach help kann ein Objekt mit einem to-Infinitiv stehen.
   The bank **helped** her **to start** her own business. ● ● ● Die Bank half ihr, sich selbständig zu machen.
Vor allem im informellen gesprochenen Englisch wird to nach help (+ Objekt) häufig weggelassen.
   Can you **help** (me) **find** my glasses? ● ● ● Kannst du (mir) bitte helfen meine Brille (zu) suchen?

hide* (sich) verstecken

■ **hide – hid – hidden**
■ **in der Regel nicht reflexiv**
   I **hid** under the bed. ● ● ● Ich habe mich unter dem Bett versteckt.
■ **hide from sb.**
   They **hid** the thief **from** the police. ● ● ● Sie versteckten den Dieb vor der Polizei.
   Cathy is **hiding from** us. ● ● ● Cathy versteckt sich vor uns.

high – highly

1 We stopped and rested ....
  A high up on the mountainside   B highly up on the mountainside

2 ...... , but I enjoy it.
  A It's not a high paid job   B It's not a highly paid job

3 ...... and has several patents to her name.
  A Sarah is a high gifted engineer   B Sarah is a highly gifted engineer

4 It had snowed heavily in the night, and the snow was ....
  A at least a metre deep   B at least a metre high   C at least a metre tall

5 There's a lot of money in this box, ...
  A a really big amount   B a really high amount   C a really large amount

6 The police stopped me when I was doing 102 km/h. ......
  A I had to pay an expensive fine.   B I had to pay a heavy fine.   C I had to pay a high fine.

7 *[Im hohen Norden]*, days are very long in summer.
  A In the high north   B In the far north   C In the tall north

8 The business was a flop, ...
  A and we were heavy in debt   B and we were heavily in debt
  C and we were high in debt   D and we were highly in debt

hire – rent – let

1 A We hired a holiday flat from friends for two weeks.
  B We let a holiday flat from friends for two weeks.
  C We rented a holiday flat from friends for two weeks.

2 They have this apartment near Nice. ......
  A But they only hire it to people they know.   B But they only hire it out to people they know.
  C But they only rent it to people they know.   D But they only rent it out to people they know.

3 I found this place quite by chance. I saw a sign ...... in a shop window.
  A 'Flat to hire'   B 'Flat to let'   C 'Flat to rent'

historic – historical

1 A "Today," the headmaster said, "is a historic day."
  B "Today," the headmaster said, "is a historical day."

2 What happened in 1746, 1844, 1958? I don't know. ......
  A I've never been able to remember historic facts.
  B I've never been able to remember historical facts.

high – highly hoch

■ *high* als Adjektiv und Adverb

high mountains ● ● ● hohe Berge
a *high* temperature ● ● ● hohes Fieber
at *high* speed ● ● ● mit hoher Geschwindigkeit

Das zum Adjektiv *high* gehörige Adverb heißt im örtlichen Sinne ebenfalls *high*.

The balloon flew up *high* into the sky. ● ● ● Der Ballon flog hoch hinauf in den Himmel.

■ *highly* nur im übertragenen Sinn

Das Adverb *highly* bedeutet „äußerst", „höchst" oder „hoch" im übertragenen Sinn.

a *highly* interesting report ● ● ● ein höchst interessanter Bericht
a *highly* paid job ● ● ● eine hoch bezahlte Arbeit/Stelle
a *highly* gifted/educated/respected person ● ● ● eine hoch begabte/gebildete/geachtete Person

Trouble Spot

■ **hoch**

1 Adjektiv

hohes Gras ● ● ● *long*/*tall* grass
eine hohe Leiter ● ● ● a *long*/*tall* ladder
hoher Schnee ● ● ● *deep* snow
mit hoher Wahrscheinlichkeit … ● ● ● there's a *strong* possibility that …
ein hoher Betrag/eine hohe Summe ● ● ● a *large* amount/a *large* sum
ein hohes Alter ● ● ● a *great* age
Der Schaden ist hoch. ● ● ● The damage is *extensive*.
eine hohe Strafe ● ● ● a *heavy* punishment/penalty ['penəlti]
eine hohe Geldstrafe ● ● ● a *heavy* fine
der hohe Norden ● ● ● the *far* north

2 Adverb

hoch besteuert/verschuldet ● ● ● *heavily* taxed/in debt [det]
Hände hoch! ● ● ● *Hands up!*

hire mieten; vermieten – rent mieten; vermieten – let* vermieten

■ *Hire* verwendet man im BE, wenn es um das kurzzeitige Mieten (oder Vermieten) von Autos, Kleidung, Räumlichkeiten oder Gegenständen geht.

hire a car/a conference room/a boat/tables and chairs
hire sth. *(out)* to sb. ● ● ● jmdm. etwas vermieten, etwas an jmdn. vermieten

■ *Rent* verwendet man für das (Ver-)Mieten von Wohnraum oder Autos und generell im AE.

rent a flat/a car; (AE:) *rent* a boat/a tent/a video/…
rent sth. *(out)* to sb. ● ● ● jmdm. etwas vermieten, etwas an jmdn. vermieten

„Wohnraum vermieten" heißt im BE auch *let* sth. (out) to sb.

When they went round the world, they *let* their flat *to* a Japanese businessman for six months.

■ Die Wendung „zu vermieten" wird folgendermaßen ausgedrückt:

(BE:) Boats *for hire*/Boat *rental*/(AE:) Boats *for rent*
(BE:) Flat *to let*/(AE:) Apartment *for rent*

historic – historical historisch, geschichtlich

■ *Historic* bedeutet „historisch wichtig", „von geschichtlicher Bedeutung".

The signing of the peace treaty was a *historic* event. ● ● ● … war ein historisches Ereignis.
a *historic* building/a *historic* monument ● ● ● ein historisches Gebäude/ein historisches Denkmal
a *historic* day/a *historic* decision/a *historic* meeting ● ● ● ein historischer Tag/eine historische Entscheidung/ein historisches Treffen

■ *Historical* bedeutet „geschichtlich", „aus der Vergangenheit", „echt und nicht erfunden".

a *historical* document/a *historical* figure ● ● ● eine Geschichtsurkunde/eine geschichtliche Gestalt
Was Robin Hood a real **historical** *person, or is he just a legend?* ● ● ● Hat es Robin Hood tatsächlich gegeben …?

history

1 **A** Does history ever repeat itself?   **B** Does the history ever repeat itself?

2 ...... – Nothing!
  A What do you know about Canadian history?
  B What do you know about the Canadian history?

3 **A** History of Quebec is actually quite interesting, you know.
  B The history of Quebec is actually quite interesting, you know.

hold

1 How long can you ...... underwater?
  A hold your breath   **B** keep your breath   **C** stop your breath

2 The bus *[hält nicht]* unless you press the button.
  A doesn't call   **B** doesn't hold   **C** doesn't stop

3 ...... if I don't put it in the fridge?
  A How long will the fish hold   **B** How long will the fish keep   **C** How long will the fish last

4 Did you know that they expect you ...... ?
  A to give a short speech   **B** to hold a short speech
  C to keep a short speech   **D** to make a short speech

5 ...... , we'll see him when he comes back out.
  A If we all hold our eyes open   **B** If we all keep our eyes open

6 *[Ich hielt es für einen Witz]*, but she was deadly serious.
  A I held it for a joke   **B** I kept it for a joke   **C** I thought it was a joke   **D** I took it for a joke

holiday(s)

1 ...... , so we can have her car.
  A My mother is on holiday this week   **B** My mother is on holidays this week

2 When I was small, ...
  A we always went to the North Sea for holiday
  B we always went to the North Sea for our holiday
  C we always went to the North Sea for our holidays

3 I feel stressed out. ......
  A I need a holiday.   **B** I need holiday.   **C** I need holidays.

history Geschichte

■ **ohne *the* in Aussagen allgemeiner Art**

History gehört zu den abstrakten Nomen, die in Aussagen allgemeiner Art ohne den bestimmten Artikel verwendet werden.

   History can teach us a lot. ● ● ● Die Geschichte kann uns viel lehren.

Das gilt auch, wenn ein Adjektiv (z. B. *German*) vorausgeht.

   *1989 was a turning point in **German history**.* ● ● ● … ein Wendepunkt in der deutschen Geschichte.

Der Artikel ist jedoch zwingend, wenn auf *history* eine nähere Bestimmung folgt, z. B. ein Relativsatz oder eine *of*-Fügung.

   ***the history** we know* ● ● ● die Geschichte, die wir kennen / die uns bekannte Geschichte

   ***the history** of the Internet* ● ● ● die Geschichte des Internets

hold* halten

■ ***hold – held – held***

■ ***Hold** this while I open the door.* ● ● ● Halte das [in den Händen], während ich aufmache.

   Hold tight! ● ● ● Halt dich fest!

   *How long can you **hold your breath** (for)?* ● ● ● Wie lange kannst du den Atem / die Luft anhalten?

   *The rope didn't **hold**.* ● ● ● Das Seil hielt nicht [stand].

Trouble Spot

   ■ **halten**

1 In dieser Hitze hält sich die Milch nicht [frisch]. ● ● ● *In this heat the milk won't **keep**.*

   etwas trocken / geheim halten [= in einem bestimmten Zustand belassen] ● ● ● ***keep** sth. **dry** / **secret***

   Halt die Augen offen! ● ● ● ***Keep** your eyes **open**.*

   Können wir diese Geschwindigkeit halten [= aufrechterhalten]? ● ● ● *Can we **keep up** this **speed**?*

   den Kontakt / die Verbindung zu jmdm. halten [= aufrechterhalten] ● ● ● ***keep in touch** / **contact** with sb.*

2 ein Versprechen halten [= einhalten] ● ● ● ***keep** a **promise***

   Ordnung halten ● ● ● ***keep order***

3 Die Beziehung hielt nicht lange [an]. ● ● ● *The relationship didn't **last** (very) long.*

4 Der Zug hielt zwei Mal [an]. ● ● ● *The train **stopped** twice.*

5 Wer wird die Rede halten? ● ● ● *Who's going to **make** / **give** the **speech**?*

   einen Vortrag halten ● ● ● ***give** / **hold** a **lecture***

   eine Predigt halten ● ● ● ***give** / **preach** a **sermon*** ['sɜːmən]

6 Ich hielt ihn für Alis Bruder, aber es war … ● ● ● *I **took** him **for** Ali's brother, but he was …*

   Ich hielt ihn für einen ehrlichen Menschen. ● ● ● *I **thought (that) he was** an honest person.*

holiday(s) (BE) Urlaub, Ferien ▷ greet

■ *be **on holiday** (~~on holidays~~ / ~~in holidays~~)* ● ● ● im Urlaub sein, Urlaub machen / in den Ferien sein, Ferien haben

   *go **on holiday** (~~on holidays~~ / ~~in holidays~~)* ● ● ● in (den) Urlaub / in die Ferien fahren

   [Der Plural *on holidays* wird nur verwendet, wenn man von mehreren Urlaubsreisen spricht: *go **on holidays** to Japan, Chile and Greenland*]

   *go to Denmark **for one's holiday(s)*** ● ● ● nach Dänemark in (den) Urlaub / in die Ferien fahren

   *have / spend one week's / two weeks' **holiday** (~~holidays~~) in Ireland* ● ● ● eine Woche / zwei Wochen Urlaub in Irland machen / verbringen

   *I'm exhausted. I need **a holiday** (~~holidays~~).* ● ● ● … Ich brauche Urlaub / Ferien.

   *stay at home **in the Easter holidays** / **in the school holidays*** ● ● ● in den Osterferien / in den Schulferien zu Hause bleiben

„Die großen Ferien" [im Sommer] heißen auf Englisch ***the (long) summer holidays***.

homework – housework

1 ...... do we have for Monday?

  A How many bits of homework   B How many homeworks   C How much homework

2 In my family [muss jeder bei der Hausarbeit helfen].

  A everybody has to help with the homework   B everybody has to help with the homeworks

  C everybody has to help with the housework   D everybody has to help with the houseworks

hope

1 A There is no hope of finding any footprints after all the rain.

  B There is no hope to find any footprints after all the rain.

2 ...... What they've sent so far is minimal.

  A We're still hoping for more information.

  B We're still hoping on more information.

  C We're still hoping to more information.

3 Will the weather be better tomorrow? – ......

  A I hope it.   B I hope so.   C I hope yes.

hour

1 A The clock strikes four times a hour, at every quarter.

  B The clock strikes four times an hour, at every quarter.

  C The clock strikes four times the hour, at every quarter.

2 A We often work a 50- to 60-hour week in the high season.

  B We often work a 50- to 60-hours week in the high season.

house

1 We live [in einem Mietshaus].

  A in a rented house   B in an apartment house   C in a block of flats

2 A The hotel complex consisted of several houses.

  B The hotel complex consisted of several buildings.

household – housekeeping

1 In the past, ... , the cleaning and so on, was usually considered to be a woman's work.

  A doing the housekeeping   B doing the housework

  C making the housework   D making the housekeeping

2 Some people actually like ....

  A doing household chores   B doing household works   C doing jobs in the housekeeping

3 Do you have any idea [wie viel Haushaltsgeld] a family of four needs?

  A how much household money

  B how much housework cash

  C how much housekeeping money

homework Hausaufgabe(n) – **housework** Hausarbeit(en)   ▷ household

■ *homework* **[= nicht zählbares Nomen]**

Homework ist ein nicht zählbares Nomen. Man kann es nicht mit *a* oder im Plural verwenden.

*I've only got **one bit/piece of homework** (~~one homework~~) today.* ● ● ● … nur eine Hausaufgabe.

*I have **(some) difficult homework** (~~homeworks~~) today.* ● ● ● … schwierige Hausaufgaben.

■ *homework – housework*

Homework bezeichnet Hausaufgaben für die Schule usw.

*My mother often helped me with my **homework**.* ● ● ● … bei den Hausaufgaben.

Housework bezeichnet im Haushalt anfallende Arbeiten (wie Putzen, Waschen, Kochen).

*Do you help with the **housework**?* ● ● ● Hilfst du bei der Hausarbeit/im Haushalt?

*Who **does the housework** in your family?* ● ● ● Wer macht die Hausarbeit/den Haushalt …?

hope **1** Hoffnung **2** hoffen

■ *hope of doing – hope to do*

Das Nomen *hope* verbindet sich mit *of* + der *-ing*-Form des Verbs.

*I gave up **hope of catching** (~~hope to catch~~) the 7 o'clock train.* ● ● ● … die Hoffnung … zu kriegen.

Das Verb *hope* verbindet sich mit einem *to*-Infinitiv.

*We had **hoped to catch** the 7 o'clock train.* ● ● ● Wir hatten gehofft … zu kriegen

■ **Präpositionen**

*Is there any **hope of** survivors?* ● ● ● Gibt es/Besteht noch Hoffnung auf Überlebende?

*Is there any **hope for** the men?* ● ● ● Gibt es/Besteht noch Hoffnung für die Männer?

*We're **hoping for** good weather at the weekend.* ● ● ● Wir hoffen auf gutes Wetter …

■ **Sonstiges**

*Will Dave be there? – I **hope so**. (~~I hope it. / I hope yes.~~)* ● ● ● Ich hoffe es./Ich hoffe ja./Hoffentlich.

*Will Dave be there? – I **hope not**.* ● ● ● Ich hoffe nicht./Hoffentlich nicht.

*It **is to be hoped** (~~It is to hope~~) that a conflict can be avoided.* ● ● ● Es ist zu hoffen, dass …

hour [aʊə] [Zeit-]Stunde

■ *earn €10 **per/an** hour (~~€10 the hour~~)* ● ● ● 10 € pro Stunde/in der Stunde/die Stunde verdienen

*work **eight hours** a day = work **an eight-hour** day (~~an eight-hours day~~)* ● ● ● acht Stunden am Tag arbeiten = einen Achtstundentag haben

house Haus

Trouble Spot

■ **Haus**

Wir wohnen in einem [alleinstehenden Einfamilien-]Haus. ● ● ● *We live in a **(detached) house**.*

Im Stadtzentrum gibt es viele große Häuser [= Gebäude]. ● ● ● *There are a lot of tall **buildings** in the town centre.*

Ich wohne in einem Mietshaus. ● ● ● *I live in* (BE:) *a **block of flats**/an **apartment block**/* (AE:) *an **apartment house**/**building**.*

household – housekeeping Haushalt   ▷ homework

■ *Household* bezeichnet eine Lebensgemeinschaft.

*How many people live in this **household**?* ● ● ● Wie viele Personen leben in diesem Haushalt?

■ *Housekeeping* bezieht sich vor allem auf Aufgaben der Haushaltsorganisation, die mit Geld zusammenhängen, z. B. die Verwaltung des Haushaltsgeldes, das Einkaufen. (Vergleiche: „Putzarbeiten usw." = *housework*.)

*Mum is in charge of the **housekeeping**.* ● ● ● … hat die Verantwortung für die Haushaltsführung.

*How much **housekeeping money** does the family spend?* ● ● ● … Geld für die Haushaltsführung …

Aber:

household bills ● ● ● Rechnungen [für Strom, Wasser, Miete usw.]

household chores [tʃɔːz] ● ● ● [als lästig empfundene] Hausarbeit(en), Aufgaben im Haushalt

housemaster ≠ „Hausmeister"

1 A housemaster is ....
   A an architect   B a teacher in a boarding school   C the manager of an office block

2 I live in a very big building and we have a full-time *[Hausmeister]*.
   A caretaker   B organizer   C operator   D janitor

how? – what ... like?

1 I hear you have new neighbours. *[Wie sind sie?]* Are they nice?
   A How are they?   B What are they?   C What are they like?

2 ...... I must write it down.
   A How's the address of your hotel?
   B What's the address of your hotel?
   C What number is the address of your hotel?

3 We had to walk all the way home, over 20 kilometres. – *[Wie?!]*
   A How?!   B How much?!   C What?!

human – humane

1 Making mistakes, and making the same ones, ...
   A is a very human thing to do   B is a very humane thing to do

hurt – injured

1 Mr Venables won't be able to walk far, ...
   A he has a hurt foot   B he has an injured foot

2 The emergency services have the situation under control, ...
   A and all the hurt have now been taken to hospital
   B and all the injured have now been taken to hospital

idea

1 I've decided not to go to university, but to take a year out. ......
   A I like the idea of seeing a bit of the world first.   B I like the idea to see a bit of the world first.

2 A The idea of phoning his parents and asking them to send money made him feel sick.
   B The idea to phone his parents and ask them to send money made him feel sick.

3 A It was Julie's idea of asking Mary.   B It was Julie's idea to ask Mary.

housemaster Heimleiter, Internatsleiter

! **!** **!**
■ **False Friend!**
Housemaster (weibliche Entsprechung: *housemistress*) bedeutet nicht „~~Hausmeister~~", sondern „Internatsleiter" [der für die Schüler einer Wohngemeinschaft in einem Internat zuständig ist].
   a **housemaster** in a boarding school ● ● ● ein Heimleiter in einem Internat
Beachte die englischen Ensprechungen von „Hausmeister/-in":
   Der Hausmeister schließt immer ab. ● ● ● The (BE:) **caretaker** / (AE:) **janitor** always locks up.

how? – what ... like? wie?

■ *how?*
   How old are you? ● ● ● Wie alt bist du?
   How is Mrs Spears? ● ● ● Wie geht es Frau Spears?

■ *what ... like?*
Nicht mit *how?*, sondern mit *what ... like?* fragt man nach ständigen Eigenschaften oder Merkmalen einer Person oder Sache.
   What is Mrs Spears **like**? Is she a good teacher? ● ● ● Wie [= Was für ein Mensch?] ist Frau Spears?
   What is Berlin **like**? Is it a nice city? ● ● ● Wie [= Was für eine Stadt?] ist Berlin?

Trouble Spot
■ **wie?**
   Wie ist der Name / die Telefonnummer / die E-Mail-Adresse / die Temperatur? ● ● ●
      What's the name / the phone number / the email address / the temperature?
   Wie nennt man das auf Englisch? ● ● ● **What do you call** that in English?
   Wie lautet/heißt das auf Englisch? ● ● ● **What's that (called)** in English?
   Wie?! Sie haben euch nicht reingelassen? ● ● ● **What?!** They didn't let you in?

human [ˈhjuːmən] menschlich – humane [hjuːˈmeɪn] human

■ *Human* bedeutet „menschlich".
   the **human** body ● ● ● der menschliche Körper
   human error ● ● ● menschliches Versagen

■ *Humane* bedeutet „human", „nicht grausam", „menschenwürdig".
   the **humane** killing of animals ● ● ● das humane Töten von Tieren

hurt – injured [ˈɪndʒəd] verletzt

■ *Hurt* verwendet man eher bei leichteren Verletzungen.
   Are you **hurt**? – No, I'm quite all right. ● ● ● Sind Sie verletzt? / Haben Sie sich verletzt? – ...

■ *Injured* verwendet man eher bei ernsthaften Verletzungen, besonders nach einem Unfall.
   Ten people have died and at least fifty are **seriously injured**. ● ● ● ... sind schwer verletzt.
Vor einem Nomen kann nur *injured* stehen.
   She has an **injured** arm (~~a hurt arm~~). ● ● ● Sie hat einen verletzten Arm.
Nur *injured* kann als Nomen nach *the* verwendet werden.
   The injured (~~The hurt~~) were flown to hospital by helicopter. ● ● ● Die Verletzten ...

idea Idee, Gedanke, Plan

■ **the idea of doing**
   The idea of sharing a bed with him was awful. ● ● ● Die Vorstellung, ein Bett mit ihm zu teilen ...
   I like **the idea of spending** six months at an Australian school. ● ● ● Mir gefällt die Vorstellung,
      sechs Monate an einer australischen Schule zu verbringen.
   We've been **playing/toying with the idea of studying** in the USA. ● ● ● Wir haben mit dem
      Gedanken gespielt, in den USA zu studieren.

■ **it is/was ... idea to do**
   It was Tony's **idea** / a good **idea to ask** Mr Pim. ● ● ● Es war Tonys Idee / eine gute Idee ...

if – in case

1 ...... Cancel the meeting?

  A What will we do if Tracy says she can't come?

  B What will we do in case Tracy says she can't come?

2 I don't know what the traffic is like this evening, ... I don't want you to miss your train.

  A but we'd better leave now if there's a problem

  B but we'd better leave now in case there's a problem

ill – sick

1 ...... and won't be able to come.

  A I'm afraid Anette is ill today

  B I'm afraid Anette is sick today

  C I'm afraid Anette is being sick today

2 ...... did you see in the refugee camp? Can you tell us?

  A How many ill people   **B** How many sick people

3 **A** In church they often pray for the ill.   **B** In church they often pray for the sick.

imagine

1 **A** I can't imagine living in the USA, can you?   **B** I can't imagine to live in the USA, can you?

impossibly – can't possibly

1 The car wasn't going very fast, ...

  A but the driver could impossibly avoid hitting the child

  B but the driver couldn't possibly avoid hitting the child

2 **A** It was an impossible slow journey, and took hours!

  B It was an impossibly slow journey, and took hours!

include

1 The list has been updated ....

  A and is now including more information   **B** and now includes more information

2 There are seventeen families in this block, ...

  A included us   **B** including us   **C** us including   **D** us included

if – in case falls   ▷ unless   ▷ when

■ *If* verwendet man, um zu sagen, was man tun wird, nachdem etwas in der Zukunft geschieht.
If it rains, I'll put up my umbrella. ● ● ● Falls/Wenn [= im Falle dass] es regnet …

■ *In case* verwendet man, wenn man etwas vorsorglich tut.
I'm taking an umbrella in case it rains / should rain. ● ● ● … falls [= für den Fall, dass] es regnet.

ill – sick krank

■ **nach Verben: ill**
Tim was/felt ill all last week. ● ● ● Tim war/fühlte sich die ganze letzte Woche krank.
Nach Verben kann (besonders im AE) auch *sick* stehen.
Tim was/felt sick all last week.
Be sick wird meist in der Bedeutung „sich übergeben" verwendet. In der Verlaufsform hat es immer diese Bedeutung.
I was sick three times in the night. ● ● ● Ich musste mich in der Nacht drei Mal übergeben.
She's being sick in the back of the car. ● ● ● Sie muss sich gerade hinten im Auto übergeben.

■ **vor einem Nomen: sick**
They have a sick child to look after. ● ● ● Sie müssen sich um ein krankes Kind kümmern.
Nur wenn *ill* durch ein Adverb (z.B. *seriously*) näher bestimmt ist, kann es vor einem Nomen stehen.
These beds are reserved for seriously ill patients. ● ● ● … für schwer kranke Patienten reserviert.

■ **the sick**
Als Nomen wird *the sick* und – mit vorangehendem Adverb – auch *the ill* verwendet.
Mother Teresa cared for the sick / the seriously ill. ● ● ● … die Kranken / Kranke / Schwerkranke.

> ■ **Talking about illness**   ▷ fever   ▷ flu   ▷ healthy
> *Ann isn't feeling well.* ● ● ● Ann geht es nicht gut. / Ann fühlt sich nicht gut.
> *Tony's picked up a bug.* (infml) ● ● ● Tony hat sich etwas eingefangen.
> *David's caught (the) measles.* ● ● ● David hat die Masern.
> *Ms Carter's gone down with the flu.* (BE, infml) ● ● ● Frau Carter hat die Grippe erwischt.
> *Mr Singh's recovering slowly.* ● ● ● Herr Singh erholt sich langsam.
> *Bina's slowly getting over it.* ● ● ● Bina erholt sich langsam wieder davon.
> *Get well soon!* ● ● ● Gute Besserung! / Werde bald wieder gesund!

(Topic Box)

imagine [ɪ'mædʒɪn] sich (etwas) vorstellen

■ *imagine doing*
Auf *imagine* folgt die *-ing*-Form des Verbs, nicht der *to*-Infinitiv.
Can you imagine being (~~imagine to be~~) blind? ● ● ● Kannst du dir vorstellen, blind zu sein?

impossibly – can't possibly unmöglich

■ Mit *impossibly* kann man ein Adjektiv oder ein Adverb näher bestimmen.
He's asking an impossibly high price. ● ● ● … einen unglaublich/unmöglich hohen Preis.

■ In Verbindung mit einem Verb verwendet man *can't possibly*.
He can't possibly mean (~~can impossibly mean~~) that. ● ● ● Er kann das unmöglich ernst meinen.

include einschließen, enthalten

■ **nicht in der Verlaufsform**
Does the price include (~~Is the price including~~) tax? ● ● ● Ist die Steuer im Preis inbegriffen?

■ *including – included*
Including steht **vor** dem (Pro-)Nomen, auf das es sich bezieht, *included* jedoch **dahinter**.
There are six of us in the group including me. / There are six of us in the group, me included.
● ● ● Wir sind sechs in der Gruppe, mich eingeschlossen. / Mit mir sind wir sechs in der Gruppe.

increase

1 A We have seen only a small increase at the number of asylum seekers.

B We have seen only a small increase in the number of asylum seekers.

C We have seen only a small increase of the number of asylum seekers.

D We have seen only a small increase on the number of asylum seekers.

2 The number of people unemployed ....

A has increased at 6 %   **B** has increased by 6 %

C has increased for 6 %   **D** has increased with 6 %

independent – dependent

1 ...... In the 19th or in the 20th century?

A When did Canada become independent by Britain?

B When did Canada become independent from Britain?

C When did Canada become independent of Britain?

2 Winston is handicapped ...... for many things in his daily life.

A and is dependent by others   **B** and is dependent from others

C and is dependent of others   **D** and is dependent on others

inform

1 Hey, Joey. *[Bist du informiert?]* They're giving us a surprise test tomorrow.

A Are you informed?   **B** Have you heard?   **C** Has someone told you?   **D** Do you know?

information

1 ...... – No, sorry.

A Do you have all the information now?   **B** Do you have all the informations now?

2 ...... from the owner of the shop where they bought the powder.

A I picked up a very useful information   **B** I picked up a very useful piece of information

C I picked up some very useful information   **D** I picked up some very useful informations

insist on

1 ...... , even if it's just a handwritten scribble on a piece of paper.

A You must insist on get a receipt

B You must insist on getting a receipt

C You must insist to get a receipt

instead of

1 I'm going to send an email ....

A instead to wait for them to phone here

B instead of wait for them to phone here

C instead of waiting for them to phone here

intention

1 ...... , but he was not to be moved.

A I began with the intention of trying to get Wilkinson on our side

B I began with the intention to try to get Wilkinson on our side

increase 1 [ˈɪŋkriːs] Zunahme, Anstieg **2** [ɪnˈkriːs] ansteigen, erhöhen

■ *a big **increase in** the number of unemployed.* ● ● ● ein großer Anstieg der Arbeitslosenzahlen
*The price has **increased by** over 20%.* ● ● ● Der Preis ist um mehr als 20 % gestiegen.

independent unabhängig – **dependent** abhängig

■ ***independent of***
*an organization that is **independent of** the government* ● ● ● … unabhängig von der Regierung …
*At 18 he was completely **independent of** his parents.* ● ● ● … völlig unabhängig von seinen Eltern.
Statt *independent of* wird gelegentlich auch *independent from* verwendet (insbesondere wenn man von der Unabhängigkeit einer früheren Kolonie usw. spricht).
*India became **independent from/of** Britain in 1947.* ● ● ● Indien erlangte 1947 die Unabhängigkeit von Großbritannien.

■ ***dependent on***
*It's easy to become **dependent on** sleeping pills.* ● ● ● … von Schlaftabletten abhängig …

inform informieren

I

■ *Inform* gehört zur förmlichen Sprachebene.
*Please **inform** us **of** any change of address.* ● ● ● Bitte informieren Sie uns über eine Änderung der Anschrift.
In informellen Kontexten sollte *inform* nicht verwendet werden.
*I won't be here on time. Can you **tell** Dan, please?* ● ● ● … Kannst du bitte Dan informieren?
*We're doing an English test on Tuesday. Has someone **told** you? / Have you **heard**? / Do you **know**?*
● ● ● Hat dich jemand informiert? / Bist du darüber informiert?
*I'll **find out** about the latest developments.* ● ● ● Ich werde mich über die neuesten Entwicklungen informieren.

information Information(en)

■ **nicht zählbares Nomen**
Information ist ein nicht zählbares Nomen. Man kann es nicht mit *a/an* oder im Plural verwenden.
*find **(some)** interesting **information** (~~some interesting informations~~ / ~~an interesting information~~)*
● ● ● interessante Informationen / eine interessante Information finden
*find **an** interesting **piece of information*** ● ● ● eine interessante Information finden
*Have you got all the **information** (~~informations~~) together now?* ● ● ● … alle Informationen …?

■ *This is just **for (your) information**.* ● ● ● Das ist nur zur Information / zu Ihrer Kenntnis.

insist on bestehen auf

■ ***insist on doing***
*Dad **insisted on** coming (~~insisted to come~~) with me.* ● ● ● Papa bestand darauf, mitzugehen.

instead of (an)statt

■ ***instead of doing***
*Why don't you help, **instead of** sitting (~~instead of to sit~~) there?!* ● ● ● … anstatt da rumzusitzen?!

intention Absicht

■ ***intention to do***
*It was my **intention to tell** you later, sir.* ● ● ● Es war meine Absicht, es Ihnen später zu sagen, Sir.

■ ***intention of doing***
*I **have no intention of going** to Paris.* ● ● ● Ich habe nicht die Absicht, nach Paris zu fahren.
*I took notes **with the intention of writing** a full report later.* ● ● ● Ich habe mir Notizen gemacht mit/in der Absicht, später einen ausführlichen Bericht zu schreiben.
Aber:
*I did it **on purpose** [ˈpɜːpəs].* ● ● ● Ich habe es mit Absicht getan.

Internet

1 ...... , the phone line is unavailable for calls.

   A When I'm at the Internet   **B** When I'm in the Internet   **C** When I'm on the Internet

2 How many hours ...... on average?

   A do you surf in the internet   **B** do you surf on the internet   **C** do you surf the internet

into

1 **A** The man walked in the room without knocking.

   B The man walked in to the room without knocking.

   C The man walked into the room without knocking.

2 The other day a friend of my mother's asked me ....

   A to translate 'Frohe Weihnachten' in English for her

   B to translate 'Frohe Weihnachten' into English for her

3 ...... , till about two o'clock in the morning.

   A The party went on in the night   **B** The party went on into the night

introduce – introduction

1 **A** Let me introduce Marvin you.

   B Let me introduce you Marvin.

   C Let me introduce you to Marvin.

2 This two-day course offers ....

   A an introduction for modern astronomy   **B** an introduction in modern astronomy

   C an introduction into modern astronomy   **D** an introduction to modern astronomy

irritate ≠ „irritieren"

1 'Irritate' means ....

   A to annoy   **B** to disturb   **C** to worry

2 *[Ich bin irritiert.]* Two miles back it said Warborough was this way. Now it says it's that way.

   A I'm annyoyed.   **B** I'm bothered.   **C** I'm confused.   **D** I'm disturbed.

it's – its

1 People have been predicting for a long time that the Leaning Tower of Pisa is going to fall down,
....

   A but its not happened yet   **B** but it's not happened yet   **C** but its' not happened yet

2 Their car is nearly 20 years old, ...

   A but it doesn't look its age   **B** but it doesn't look it's age

3 **A** Rothenburg is famous for it's beautiful buildings.

   B Rothenburg is famous for its beautiful buildings.

4 **A** Its so easy to fall in love.   **B** It's so easy to fall in love.

5 **A** The school has its own tennis court.   **B** The school has it's own tennis court.

Internet Internet

■ **Groß- oder Kleinschreibung möglich**
the Internet/internet, the Net/net (infml)

> ■ *Talking about the Internet*
> *go on the Internet / be on the Internet* ● ● ● ins Internet gehen / im Internet sein
> *Do you surf the Internet/Net? / Do you browse the Web?* ● ● ● Surfst du im Internet?
> *Are you online* [ˌɒnˈlaɪn]? ● ● ● Bist du online? / Hast du Zugang zum Internet?
> *Do you have access to the Internet?* ● ● ● Hast du Zugang zum Internet?
> *Which search engine do you use?* ● ● ● Welche Suchmaschine verwendest du?
> *I'll send you the file as an attachment.* ● ● ● Ich schicke dir die Datei als Attachment/Anlage.
> *How long will it take to download this file?* ● ● ● Wie lange dauert es, diese Datei
> herunterzuladen?
> *Do you want to bookmark this (web)site?* ● ● ● Willst du diese Website zu deinen Favoriten/
> Lesezeichen hinzufügen?
> *I just want to check my email(s)/e-mail(s).* ● ● ● Ich will nur mal nach meinen E-Mails schauen.
> *I'll email/e-mail/mail it (over) to you.* ● ● ● Ich maile es dir (rüber).

Topic Box

into in (... hinein)

■ *fall/jump into the river* ● ● ● in den Fluss [hinein]fallen/[hinein]springen
throw/push sb. into the river ● ● ● jmdn. in den Fluss [hinein]werfen/[hinein]schubsen
walk into a room/building ● ● ● in einen Raum / ein Zimmer / ein Gebäude [hinein]gehen
speak into a microphone ● ● ● in ein Mikrofon sprechen
translate sth. into English ● ● ● etwas ins Englische übersetzen
continue into the night ● ● ● bis in die Nacht hinein andauern
develop into a problem ● ● ● sich zu einem Problem entwickeln
run into difficulties ● ● ● in Schwierigkeiten geraten

introduce [ˌɪntrəˈdjuːs] vorstellen; einführen – **introduction** [ˌɪntrəˈdʌkʃn] Vorstellung; Einführung

■ *introduce sb. to sb. else*
Can I introduce you to my father (introduce you my father)? ● ● ● ... dich meinem Vater vorstellen?

■ *introduction to*
As an introduction to (introduction into) her talk, she told a story about a woman in Nigeria. ● ● ●
Als Einführung in ihren Vortrag / Zur Einleitung ihres Vortrages ...

irritate [ˈɪrɪteɪt] ärgern

! ■ **False Friend!**
! *Irritate* bedeutet meist nicht „irritieren", sondern „ärgern".
! *It really irritates me when you don't help around the house.* ● ● ● Es ärgert mich wirklich ...
! Beachte die englischen Entsprechungen von „irritieren":
! Ich bin irritiert [= verwirrt]. Hier stehen andere Abfahrtszeiten. ● ● ● *I'm confused.*
! *The departure times given here are different.*
! Es irritiert [= beunruhigt] mich, dass Oma sich nicht meldet. ● ● ● *It bothers/disturbs/worries
me that grandma hasn't called.*

it's es (er/sie) ist; es (er/sie) hat – **its** sein, ihr

■ *It's* ist die Kurzform von *it is* oder *it has*.
It's a big dog. = *It is a big dog.*
It's got big ears. = *It has got big ears.*

■ *Its* wird als Possessivbegleiter vor einem Nomen verwendet. Deutsch: „sein(e)", „ihr(e)".
What's its name (it's name)? = *What's the dog's name?*

jealous

1 Why should I be ...... ?

  A jealous at you   B jealous to you   C jealous of you   D jealous on you   E jealous with you

jeans

1 A I bought this jeans on eBay.

  B I bought this pair of jeans on eBay.

  C I bought these jeans on eBay.

2 A They only had one jeans in my size.   B They only had one pair of jeans in my size.

job

1 A The job of cleaning up is the worst part of a party.

  B The job to clean up is the worst part of a party.

journey – trip – drive – ride – voyage – tour – travel

1 My parents have gone off ...... , so I have the place to myself.

  A on a weekend journey   B on a weekend ride

  C on a weekend travel   D on a weekend trip

2 [Es ist eine sechsstündige Autofahrt], but only four hours on the train.

  A It's a six-hour drive   B It's a six-hour car ride

  C It's a six-hour car tour   D It's a six-hour car travel

3 At the weekend we often get on our motorbikes ...... in the mountains.

  A and go for a drive   B and go for a journey   C and go for a ride   D and go for a tour

4 The flat is very handy for the university. ......

  A It's only a ten-minute drive on the underground.

  B It's only a ten-minute ride on the underground.

  C It's only a ten-minute tour on the underground.

  D It's only a ten-minute travel on the underground travel.

5 Cologne to Dresden is ....

  A a seven-hour train drive   B a seven-hour train journey

  C a seven-hour train tour   D a seven-hour train travel

6 The Titanic sank ....

  A on its maiden journey   B on its maiden ride   C on its maiden tour

  D on its maiden travel   E on its maiden trip   F on its maiden voyage

7 If you only have a little time, the best way to see the city is ....

  A to go on a bus drive   B to go on a bus journey   C to go on a bus ride

  D to go on a bus tour   E to go on a bus travel

8 High-speed trains have made the railways a competitive alternative to ....

  A air journey   B air tour   C air travel   D air trip

jealous ['dʒeləs] eifersüchtig

■ *jealous of sb.*
*Cathy had an admirer, and I was **jealous of** him.* ● ● ● *… und ich war eifersüchtig auf ihn.*

jeans Jeans

■ **Pluralnomen, keine Singularform**
Jeans gibt es nur als Pluralnomen (mit Verb im Plural).
These jeans were *very expensive.* ● ● ● Diese Jeans war(en) sehr teuer.
*You're wearing **some** new jeans.* ● ● ● Du hast neue Jeans an.
Um daraus ein zählbares Nomen zu machen, muss man *pair(s) of jeans* verwenden.
This pair of jeans (~~This jeans~~) **was** *expensive.* ● ● ● Dieses Paar Jeans war / Diese Jeans war(en) …
*You're wearing a new **pair of jeans** (~~a new jeans~~), aren't you?* ● ● ● … (ein Paar) neue Jeans …
How many pairs of jeans (~~How many jeans~~) *are you going to pack?* ● ● ● Wie viele (Paar) Jeans …?

job Aufgabe   ▶ work

■ *the job of doing*
*I was given **the job of informing** (~~the job to inform~~) the press.* ● ● ● Ich erhielt die Aufgabe,
die Presse zu informieren.

■ *it is/was … job to do*
*It was your **job** / an easy **job to inform** the press* ● ● ● Es war deine Aufgabe / eine leichte Aufgabe,
die Presse zu informieren.

J

journey – trip – drive – ride – voyage ['vɔɪɪdʒ] **– tour – travel** Reise, Fahrt

Trouble Spot

■ **Reise, Fahrt**
1 „Vorgang, von A nach B zu gelangen"
*How was the **journey** /* (BE auch, AE meist:) **trip**? *Are you tired?*
*How was your **journey** to school/work /* (BE auch, AE meist:) **trip** to school/work *today?*

2 „kürzere Urlaubs- oder Geschäftsreise"
*Have a good **trip**.*
*go away on a **weekend trip***
*How was your **trip** to Canada last year?*
*My mum's away in France on a **business trip**.*

3 „Autofahrt"
*If the motorway is clear, it's a two-hour **drive**.*
*The number of **car journeys** (~~drives~~) made by a single person has increased.*

4 „Zweiradfahrt"
*an exciting **motorbike ride** in the mountains*

5 „kurze Fahrt mit Bus oder (U-)Bahn"
*It's a short **bus ride** from here.*
*It's a short **ride** (BE:)* **on the underground/tube** / (AE:) **on the subway**.
*It's just a short **train ride**.*

6 „längere Fahrt mit (Reise-)Bus oder Bahn"
*It's at least a six-hour **coach journey**.*
*a **train journey** of at least three hours*

7 „längere Seereise/-fahrt"
*a **voyage** of several weeks in Columbus's day*

8 „Besichtigungsfahrt oder Rundreise zu verschiedenen Zielen"
*In the afternoon we went on a **tour of** the city.*
*a four-week **tour of** Canada*

9 „Luftfahrt"/„Raumfahrt"
*the age of **air travel** / **space travel***

just

1 Hi, Anna. This is Melinda. – Oh hi, Melinda. ......

  A It's funny, we just spoke about you.

  B It's funny, we were just speaking about you.

2 I'm sorry, Bernard, ... He won't be back till this evening.

  A but Julian has just left   **B** but Julian has left just

  C but Julian just left   **D** but Julian left just

3 When did this happen? – *[Gerade eben.]*

  A Just.   **B** Just ago.   **C** Just now.   **D** Just then.

keep

1 ...... You'll manage it eventually.

  A Just keep on trying.   **B** Just keep to try.   **C** Just keep trying.

kitchen – cuisine

1 Most people don't think much of ....

  A English cooking   **B** English cuisine   **C** English kitchen   **D** the English kitchen

2 London has no end of restaurants nowadays ....

  A with a really exciting cuisine   **B** with a really exciting kitchen

  C with really exciting cuisine   **D** with really exciting kitchen

3 The new restaurant needs *[mehr Küchenpersonal]*.

  A more cuisine staff   **B** more kitchen staff   **C** more kitchenroom staff

know

1 How many different sorts of mushroom ...... ?

  A are you now knowing   **B** do you now know

2 – Little Bernie has been at my chocolates again.

  – ......

  – Well, I was saving my favourite one till last, and now it's gone.

  A How are you knowing?   **B** How are you knowing it?

  C How do you know?   **D** How do you know it?

knowledge

1 She says she's an expert on the subject, ...

  A but I'm not sure how many knowledges she really has

  B but I'm not sure how much knowledge she really has

2 ...... , but I'm not really very good at it.

  A I have a basic knowledge in French   **B** I have a basic knowledge of French

  C I have basic knowledges in French   **D** I have basic knowledges of French

just gerade

■ *just* („jetzt gerade") + *present progressive*
What are you doing? – I'm just writing Max a mail. ● ● ● Ich schreibe gerade eine Mail an Max.

■ *just* („damals gerade") + *past progressive*
We were just going to bed, when the phone rang. ● ● ● Wir wollten gerade schlafen gehen …

■ *just* („gerade eben", „soeben") + *present perfect* oder *simple past*
I've just seen a fox. / (bes. AE:) *I just saw a fox.* ● ● ● Ich habe gerade/eben einen Fuchs gesehen.
It's just started to rain. / (bes. AE:) *It just started to rain.* ● ● ● Es hat gerade angefangen zu regnen.
Louis has just phoned. / (bes. AE:) *Louis just phoned.* ● ● ● Louis hat gerade angerufen.

■ *just now* + *simple past*
Just now bezieht sich meist auf die Vergangenheit („gerade eben", „gerade noch", „vor ein paar Minuten").
I saw a fox just now. ● ● ● Ich habe gerade eben einen Fuchs gesehen.
I saw her just now. ● ● ● Ich habe sie gerade noch gesehen.

keep* (immer) weiter-   ▶ hold

■ *keep (on) doing*
Keep (on) doing bedeutet „weiter(hin) tun".
Keep smiling. It won't keep on raining for ever. ● ● ● Immer nur lächeln! Es wird nicht ewig so weiterregnen.

K

kitchen – cuisine [kwɪˈziːn] Küche

■ *Kitchen* bezeichnet immer einen Raum.
He's in the kitchen.

■ Küche im Sinne von „Essen", „Kochkunst" heißt *cuisine*. *Cuisine* kann zählbar oder nicht zählbar sein.
That restaurant has excellent cuisine / an excellent cuisine. ● ● ● … eine ausgezeichnete Küche.
French cuisine/cooking ● ● ● die französische Küche

know* wissen; kennen

■ **nicht in der Verlaufsform**
I now know (I'm now knowing) over 2000 English words. ● ● ● Ich kenne jetzt …

■ *know – know it*
In folgendem Satz bezieht sich *it* auf etwas Konkretes:
I need the address. Do you know it [= the address]? ● ● ● … Kennst/Weißt du sie?
Im Rückbezug auf einen zuvor genannten Sachverhalt verwendet man *know* ohne *it*.
I hear you're leaving school. Sue told me, that's how I know (know it). ● ● ● … daher weiß ich's.
That was a stupid thing to do. You should know better (know it better). ● ● ● … Du müsstest es eigentlich besser wissen.
Beachte aber:
I knew it! They've booked the wrong flight again! ● ● ● Ich hab's doch gewusst! …

knowledge [ˈnɒlɪdʒ] Kenntnis, Kenntnisse; Wissen

■ **nicht zählbares Nomen**
Knowledge ist ein nicht zählbares Nomen, hat also keine Pluralform.
My knowledge of Iceland is slight. ● ● ● Ich weiß nur wenig über Island.
What knowledge of English does the man have? ● ● ● Was für Englischkenntnisse …?
Im Gegensatz zu anderen nicht zählbaren Nomen kann *knowledge*, wenn es durch ein Adjektiv näher bestimmt ist, manchmal mit *a/an* verwendet werden.
have a basic / a good / an extensive / a detailed knowledge of sth. ● ● ● Grund-/gute/umfangreiche/ detaillierte Kenntnisse von etwas haben

Which Word?

A   Choose the correct words.

1   Russian isn't an easy language to learn. **It's** grammar **Its** grammar is quite complicated.

2   The moment **passed** The moment **past**, and I said nothing.

3   I'll see you **sometime** I'll see you **sometimes** on Saturday afternoon then. Bye.

4   The Sahara **Desert** The Sahara **Dessert** is the largest on earth.

5   Think **hard** Think **hardly** now. What was the man doing with the hammer?

6   How much is the **fair** the **fare** to Newcastle, please? – Single or return?

7   Who does most of the **homework** most of the **housework** in your family?

8   Has anyone **laid** the table **lain** the table?

9   The **currant** rate of exchange The **current** rate of exchange is €1.25.

10   I was so tired, I **laid** down I **lay** down and fell asleep almost immediately.

11   I **first** met her I **firstly** met her at dance classes.

12   **At first**   **Firstly** I couldn't understand why he didn't react. Then I saw the blood.

13   You've **no doubt** heard You've **undoubtedly** heard Ann's news. – Yes, I'm so pleased for her.

14   People have begun to **raise** doubts to **rise** doubts. They're no longer sure about the idea.

15   The price hasn't **raised** The price hasn't **risen** since 2004.

16   The **principal** reason The **principle** reason for the change is lack of money.

17   The factory was closed down. It was no longer **economic** no longer **economical**.

18   I just can't remember basic **historic** facts basic **historical** facts.

19   In a dictatorship, a **human** life a **humane** life is often considered worthless.

20   Do you play a **music** instrument a **musical** instrument?

B   Are the expressions in bold correct? If not, replace them with the correct ones.

1   Shall I **bring** you to the station?

2   Afghanistan is **largely** mountainous.

3   Building workers found **rests** of old Roman baths.

4   This curry is very **sharp**.

5   It's **far** to the sea. You can't walk there.

6   The water is **cooking**. Shall I make the tea?

7   The sea was very **calm**.

8   We often **grill** on summer evenings.

9   What do you know about Julius Caesar and **old** Rome?

10   The cups **come** in the cupboard next to the fridge.

11   Quiet! I'm trying to **hear** the news.

12   In which part of the factory is the printing workshop? – In that **hall** there.

13 *I have been doing a lot of sport **in the last time**.*

14 *There are many tall **office** houses in that part of town.*

15 ***Leave** that! I hate it when you pat me on the head like that!*

16 *Dan has to help a lot at home because he has **an ill** mother to look after.*

17 *People often say that French **kitchen** is the best in the world.*

18 *This house is badly in need of repair. The **earlier** owner didn't look after it.*

19 *For the pizza can you buy a small **glass** of olives?*

20 *Mr Muscleman is one of those people who do **gymnastics** in bed before getting up.*

C   Complete the sentences with suitable words.

1 *Do the shoes … or are they too big?*

2 *Esperanto is very easy. … can learn it, even old people have no problems.*

3 *It doesn't matter where we put it. Just leave it …where.*

4 *How can you tell the sex of a fly? I mean is this one … or …?*

5 *I'd never have enough … to write a novel. I'm just not creative enough.*

6 *There were no … of mass destruction in Iraq, it seems.*

7 *I've always trusted her. I'm sure she'll … her promise.*

8 *How long can you … your breath underwater?*

9 *I'm sorry, I have to go now. I'd love to …, but the last train goes in 15 minutes.*

10 *May I … your camcorder this evening? Mine's broken.*

11 *He managed to escape from the country, using a … passport and a … name.*

12 *I had a very good driving … . Without her I'd never have passed my driving test.*

13 *It's not far to the French … from Karlsruhe.*

14 *The Nobel prizewinner's work has pushed back the … of science.*

15 *If you don't want to travel back with the group, you'll have to make other arrangements at your own … .*

16 *I tried to dig a hole, but the … was frozen and as hard as iron.*

17 *I only … my motorbike in the summer. In the winter it stays in the garage.*

18 *Oh no! I've … our passports and tickets at home!*

19 *… I already said, we won't wait for anyone who isn't at the coach on time.*

20 *This tooth is … . It's going to fall out soon.*

Checkpoint 1: Which Word?

D   **Translate the German parts into English.**

1   *Who won [den ersten Preis]?*
2   *[Du erinnerst mich] of your mother when you say that.*
3   *Look at that man! He's [betrunken].*
4   *Have the police found [den Mörder] yet?*
5   *It's 32° [im Schatten].*
6   *He [fiel] down the stairs and broke his right arm.*
7   *Do you help [bei der Hausarbeit]?*
8   *What's [der Name des Fotografen]?*
9   *I was [bewusstlos] for about 30 seconds, I suppose.*
10 *There are [die Wracks gesunkener Schiffe] all along this coastline.*
11 *One of the components was [defekt] and the system wasn't functioning properly.*
12 *My parents have gone on [eine Wochenendreise] to Bruges.*
13 *The government has announced [eine neue Politik].*
14 *[Wie viel Meter hoch] is this wall?*
15 *[Die moderne Technik] has made many things in everyday life easier.*
16 *If there are [keine weiteren Fragen], I'd like to [die Diskussion schließen].*
17 *I had [ein schnelles Mittagessen], then went to the beach.*
18 *[Die Verletzten] were taken to hospital.*
19 *Someone else can clear up. [Schließlich] I got everything ready.*
20 *Which party are you going to [wählen] at the next election?*
21 *If you have to leave school early, you'll need [eine Entschuldigung] from your parents.*
22 *I'll see you [so gegen vier Uhr].*
23 *[Jeder] parks here, even though it's not allowed.*

24 *Mrs Pillborough looked everywhere for the key, but it was [weg].*

E   Translate into English.

1   Die nächste Bank ist zehn Kilometer weit weg.

2   Hast du schon die neueste Nachricht gehört?

3   Eine Million – eins und sechs Nullen.

4   Wir haben einen schweren Fehler gemacht.

5   Was du sagst, ist schwer zu glauben.

6   Wir haben lange diskutiert – bis 10 Uhr abends.

7   Tony ist groß. Er ist 1,96 m groß.

8   Wir sind in großer Gefahr.

9   Wie komme ich zum Bahnhof?

10   Tina ist krank? Aber ich habe sie doch erst heute Morgen gesehen.

11   Was bedeuten die Buchstaben B.A. hinter einem Namen?

12   Es war Juli und das Gras war sehr hoch.

13   Hoher Schnee überall.

14   Ich habe einen anderen Vorschlag.

15   Könnten Sie dieses Buch bitte extra einpacken?

16   Paderborn ist eine mittelgroße Stadt.

17   Wir sind nicht direkt geflogen, sondern über London.

18   Es ist kalt geworden. Nimm einen Mantel mit.

19   Dieses Hemd ist sehr eng.

20   Wenn du bis Freitag nicht von mir hörst, informiere die Polizei.

21   Wir wohnen in einer Kleinstadt in der Nähe von Dresden.

22   Meine Schwester arbeitet bei einer Bank.

23   Frisches Obst ist gesund.

24   „Ist das dein großer Bruder?"

2 Collocations

A **Complete the sentences with the correct verbs (in the correct form).**

be   do   give   have   make   take

1. The two women ... the same age.
2. It's a difficult job. It will ... quite a long time.
3. Can you ... me an example of what you mean?
4. It was a beautiful day so we ... a picnic on the beach.
5. I ... a strange experience on my way here today. I must tell you about it.
6. What colour ... your mother's eyes?
7. We're ... a holiday next month.
8. Have you heard? Anette's sister has ... a baby.
9. In the afternoon we ... a tour of the city.
10. In the evening we ... a game of Pictionary.
11. What decision have they ...?
12. Who ... this photo?
13. When are you going to ... your driving test? – Next week.
14. I know there's a party organized for all of us, but who ... it?
15. At the school-leaving ceremony the head teacher decided against ... a long speech.

B *Do* or *make*?

1. I'm trying to ... this translation, but it isn't easy.
2. The climbers are going to ... another attempt tomorrow.
3. I can't promise anything, but I'll ... my best.

4. How much sport does young Perkins ...?

5 *I'm going to ... a course at a language school in England in the summer.*

6 *When do you ... your final exam?*

7 *I'll ... an exception, but only this once.*

8 *I ... breathing exercises before a test. It helps.*

9 *Please don't ... a habit of this, will you?*

10 *Amelia Earhart ... history as the first woman to fly the Atlantic.*

11 *Have you ... your French homework yet?*

12 *You've ... a good job.*

13 *How many mistakes did you ...?*

14 *I can earn extra money if I ... overtime.*

15 *Don't go away, we can ... room for you in the corner.*

16 *We have to ... the best of it. There's nothing else we can ... .*

C   **Complete the sentences with suitable adjectives or adverbs.**

1 *It rained ... all afternoon, and the road was flooded.*

2 *The development of a new drug costs a ... amount of money.*

3 *We only have a ... amount of money left. We'll have to be careful.*

4 *The car is ... damaged. They need at least a week to repair it.*

5 *It wasn't a ... crime so he didn't go to prison.*

6 *Please use only a ... quantity of salt, not a whole spoonful.*

7 *She lived to a ... age. She was 101 when she died.*

8 *The traffic was very ... . Everybody seemed to be going away for the weekend.*

9 *Father Christmas, children are told, lives in the ... north.*

10 *It wasn't just a bad accident, the drivers of both cars were very ... injured indeed.*

D   **Correct the mistakes.**

1 *Next week we're ~~writing~~ a maths test.*

2 *We had some very ~~strong~~ snow yesterday afternoon.*

3 *It's ~~well~~ possible that the flight will be late.*

4 *Sometimes I think she doesn't take me ~~serious~~.*

5 *I'm going to ~~cook~~ some fresh coffee.*

6 *Tina is ~~bringing~~ the children to bed.*

7 *I can't ~~recognize~~ the difference between the two. Can you?*

8 *Do fish sleep on the ~~seabottom~~?*

9 *Where did Tony Blair ~~visit~~ school as a child?*

10 *Can you pass me the salad ~~sauce~~.*

11 *Who is your skiing ~~teacher~~?*

12 *There was a sign on the door that said '~~Fresh~~ paint'.*

False Friends

A Which is the closest synonym or paraphrase in each case?

1 *overhear*
happen to hear   miss   misunderstand

2 *sensible*
easy to hurt   wise   sensitive

3 *blame sb.*
hit sb.   make a fool of sb.   say it's sb.'s fault

4 *irritate*
confuse   annoy   hesitate

5 *brave*
courageous   good   well-behaved

6 *notice*
memo   note   poster

7 *receipt*
piece of paper with the price that has been paid
piece of paper with instructions for cooking something
piece of paper with medicine you should have

8 *chef*
boss   cook   leader

9 *housemaster*
manager of a block of flats   caretaker   teacher in a boarding school

10 *gymnasium*
high school   grammar school   sports hall

11 *overtake*
take control of   take over   pass

12 *concept*
idea   plan   rough draft

13 *ordinary*
rude   not special   vulgar

14 *handy*
mobile   by hand   useful

15 *eventually*
possibly   in the end   perhaps

B   **Translate the German parts into English.**

1   *When was the organization [gegründet]?* ~~founded~~

2   *You can park [an der Rückseite] of the building.* ~~at the back~~

3   *[Was für eine Note] did you get in the last test?* ~~What mark~~

4   *Henry Ford was [einer der erfolgreichsten Unternehmer] of the 20th century.* ~~one of the most successful businessmen~~

5   *This timetable isn't [aktuell]. We'd better look on the Net.* ~~up to date~~

6   *When I was little, I always tried to [sparen] part of my pocket money.* ~~save~~

7   *Please fill in [das Formular].* ~~the form~~

8   *[Könnten Sie bitte kontrollieren] if I've filled in everything correctly?* ~~Could you please check~~

9   *It's become so expensive to eat out [in einem Gasthaus].* ~~in a restaurant~~

10   *I like Delia. She's really [sehr sympathisch].* ~~very nice~~

11   *Do you have [einen Prospekt] that I can take away with me?* ~~brochure~~

12   *[Das Publikum] thought the play was awful and booed at the end.* ~~the audience~~

13   *There are too many glasses to carry. I'll get [ein Tablett].* ~~tray~~

14   *"Be careful how you say it. You know how sensitive he is to [Kritik]."* ~~criticism~~

A Choose the correct prepositions.

1 We're going to meet again **at** a later date **on** a later date.

2 **As** answer to your question **In** answer to your question, I'd like to say this: …

3 How much money have you got **in** your account **on** your account?

4 I had tea with my great-grandmother **in** the afternoon of her 90th birthday **on** the afternoon of her 90th birthday.

5 From her flat **in** the 18th floor **on** the 18th floor, she had a fantastic view of the city.

6 How much do we spend **for** food spend **on** food **in** average **on** average each month?

7 She looks so happy, as though she's fallen in love **for** someone in love **with** someone.

8 How did you get here? – **By** my brother's bike. **On** my brother's bike.

9 Can I pay **by** credit card pay **with** credit card?

10 There's a big yellow object up **in** the sky up **on** the sky.

11 Stop talking **in** such a loud voice **with** such a loud voice.

12 The boys threw tomatoes **at** me **to** me, but luckily none of them hit me.

B Rewrite the sentences so that they mean the same. Use the words in brackets.

1 The number of unemployed has increased. (There has been an increase …)
There has been an increase in the number of unemployed.

2 I know you don't believe me, but I can clearly see that it's a fake. (I know you don't believe me, but it's obvious …)

3 William Wordsworth wrote the poem. (It's a poem …)

4 You fill me with pride. (I'm very proud …)

5 We visited Berlin. (We made a visit …)

6 We hope the weather will get better. (We … better weather.)

7 What does 'a very short time' mean to you? (What do you understand …?)

8 Young people like the café. (The café is popular …)

9 Ann asked me to come. (I'm here … request.)

10 "Our speed is now 180 km/h." ("We're now travelling …")

C   **Put in the correct prepositions.**

1   *Is there a cure … bird flu?*
2   *Freddie arrived, as usual, … the very last minute.*
3   *Have you heard … Julian recently? – Yes, I got an email last week.*
4   *I'm asking you to do this … two reasons.*
5   *What's the attitude of the local people … foreigners?*
6   *Can you name a novel … a Belgian author?*
7   *We were saved … almost certain death.*
8   *I've never heard … a place called "Wogmorton". Where is it supposed to be?*
9   *I'd love to live … the sea, rather than in the mountains.*
10   *This tastes … fish.*

D   **Are prepositions needed? If so, which ones?**

1   *We shouldn't waste any more time … this question.*
2   *I cannot comment … this matter until the official announcement has been made.*
3   *Terrorism is a threat … civilization as we know it.*
4   *I envy you … your freedom.*
5   *His mother was killed … a car accident.*
6   *I was very nervous as I approached … the door.*
7   *My father is always going on about "When I was … your age, I wasn't allowed to do that sort of thing".*
8   *Blacks are still being discriminated … .*
9   *I can't multiply 1734 … 47 without a calculator.*
10   *I discussed … my problem with my girlfriend.*

E   **Translate the sentences.**

1   Sheila ist mit einem Franzosen verlobt.
2   Tom ist gegen eine Mauer gefahren.
3   Warum lacht ihr mich aus?
4   Bitte nicht mit Bleistift schreiben.
5   Anns Bruder ist bei der Armee.
6   Was ist an dem Auto so besonders?
7   Was sollten wir deiner Meinung nach tun?
8   Bist du gut in Chemie?
9   Ich zahle den Scheck auf mein Konto ein.
10   Schrei mich nicht so an!

5

Articles

X

A   **Spot the mistakes and correct them. (Not all the sentences have a mistake!)**

Sel

1   *I got an interesting information from Ann this afternoon.*
2   *What are the most difficult things in the life?*
3   *He was in the prison for four years, but he's leading an honest life now.*
4   *This room is an absolute chaos!*
5   *I've often thought I'd like to go and live abroad for a year or two.*
6   *I was surprised. For a non-German, Mr Hendon speaks an excellent German.*
7   *A lot of young people aren't interested in the politics.*
8   *I don't know what to do. Can you give me an advice?*
9   *You seem to have a good knowledge of the subject.*
10   *There are some amazing things in the nature.*

B   **Rewrite the sentences using the words in brackets.**

gem

1   *The majority of Swiss people understand French. (most)*
    Most Swiss people understand French.
2   *I'll give you ten more minutes. (extra)*
3   *The bill was debated in the House of Commons and the House of Lords. (Parliament)*
4   *We're looking for a cheap hotel room. (accommodation)*
5   *Have you found a job? (work)*
6   *About 25 million people watch the show every week. (estimated)*
7   *Richard was ill last week. (flu)*
8   *I belong to a tennis club. (member)*

C   **Translate the sentences into English.**

Seb

1   Als Kind hatte ich Angst vor der Dunkelheit.
2   Ich rufe dich nach dem Abendessen an.
3   Der Sturm verursachte einen Riesenschaden.
4   Ich bin immer Optimist.
5   Wir fahren oft mit dem Reisebus in den Urlaub.
6   Mara wohnt in der Grove Road.
7   Selim ist einkaufen gegangen. Er ist in einer halben Stunde zurück.
8   Die europäische Geschichte ist eine Geschichte des Krieges.
9   Wie lange bleiben die Astronauten im Weltall?
10   Die Gesellschaft verändert sich.

6 Singular and Plural

A Complete the sentences with singular and plural forms (simple present) of the verb *be*.

1 The news ... excellent.
2 A number of questions ... still unanswered.
3 The United States ... a country of at least 270 million people.
4 The majority of people ... in favour of the changes.
5 The rest of the books ... still in the boxes.
6 Where ... my glasses? Do you know?
7 Veena's hair ... much shorter now.
8 The police ... everywhere.

B Replace the words in bold with the words in brackets. Make all necessary changes.

1 The **details** they've sent me are incomplete. (information)
The information they've sent me is incomplete.
2 This **pair** is a really cool colour: purple! (jeans)
3 **Tuesday or Wednesday** is OK for me. (Either day)
4 It was **very hot**, even in the shade. (32 degrees Celsius)
5 These **exercises** are for Tuesday, not for Monday. (homework)
6 A **mask** is useful when the sun is so low in the sky. (sunglasses)

C Translate the sentences into English.

1 Wo ist mein Schlafanzug?
2 Ein Erwachsener hat normalerweise 32 Zähne.
3 Ich brauche Ferien.
4 In Neuseeland gibt es mehr Schafe als Menschen.
5 Der Neubau *(new building)* wird zwei Millionen Euro kosten.
6 Wie groß sind deine Füße?
7 Deine Fortschritte sind beeindruckend!
8 Ich gebe euch ein paar Hilfen.
9 Niemand kennt dich, nicht wahr?
10 Wie viele Personen kommen zur Party?
11 Das Mittelalter ist der Zeitraum von etwa 1000 bis 1450 n. Chr.
12 Ich hatte wirklich schlimme Kopfschmerzen und konnte nicht zur Schule gehen.

Word Order

A   Where do the words in brackets go? Give all possible positions (A, B or C).

1   We   saw   him   .   (both)

2   My best friend lives in the   house   .   (opposite)

3   how long   did this happen   ?   (ago)

4   There were 12 in the group,   the leader   .   (included)

5   We   love   our English teacher   .   (all)

6   don't forget   your passports   .   (please)

7   I've done   the repairs   .   (all)

8   It was   a   difficult question.   (rather)

9   hospital doctors   work long hours.   (especially)

10   It's   12 degrees   outside this morning.   (minus)

11   The journey took   the   time   that it usually takes.   (double)

12   we   need   our own room. This one is too small for two.   (each)

B   Rewrite the sentences and include the word in brackets.

1   The students will have to resit the exam in January. (concerned = „betreffend")

2   Do you know the Evans? (family)

3   I don't think we'll need more than a day. (half)

4   It was an easy task for the students, and didn't really test them. (too = „zu")

5   We have eight lessons on Monday. (always)

6   What can this machine do? (else)

7   I've lost my contact lenses. (both)

8   The other parents were asked to leave the room. (present = „anwesend")

9   The party will be a disaster. (probably)

10   On Wednesday we had collected over €250. (already)

11   I've done four exams in the last week. (alone)

12   I think we've waited long enough. (a, time)

8

that-Clauses and Clauses with "dass"

1 Will there be enough time **that I can go home and change first?**

2 It was the first time **that I'd been away on my own**.

3 I feel **that he's too young for her**.

4 I don't trust Arnold **that he'll be there** when he said he would.

5 It worries me **that my sister isn't home yet**.

6 We can't allow **that people drink alcohol at school**.

7 The party was organized **without that he knew anything about it**.

8 Fatima will never forgive Daniel **that he lied to her**.

9 I wouldn't want **that you get the wrong impression**.

10 "I'm beginning to suspect **that this isn't the winter escape we booked on the Net**."

B Translate into English, using the verbs in brackets. You can't use a *that*-clause.

1 Damian entschuldigte sich, dass er zu spät kam. *(apologize)*

2 Ich möchte, dass du mitkommst. *(would like)*

3 Wir wollen nicht, dass du für uns bezahlst. *(want)*

4 Martin warf uns vor, dass wir unser Versprechen gebrochen hätten. *(accuse)*

5 Ann hat angeboten, dass sie uns zum Flughafen fährt. *(offer)*

Infinitive and *-ing* Form

A Complete the sentences with a suitable verb. Use a *to*-infinitive or an *-ing* form.

1. I practised … my way round the house with my eyes closed.
2. Ann denied … anywhere near the changing room at the time the money was stolen.
3. You must stop … about things that you can't change.
4. I suggest … a break for lunch soon.
5. I love … to parties, don't you?
6. Actually, I dislike … at parties. I prefer … with just one or two people.
7. I wouldn't advise … to cheat in the exam. They'll catch you.
8. Have you finished …? – No, we're still on our dessert.
9. Can you imagine … in the same class as that snob?
10. This room needs … . It's so dirty.
11. We'll need … quite early and leave the house by six.
12. I remember … on the beach and … the ship disappear over the horizon.
13. I can't understand people who say they enjoy … early in the morning.
14. I try to avoid … at the computer for more than 90 minutes without a break.
15. Would you like … with us?
16. Stay close. We don't want to risk … you in the crowd.
17. When I leave, I know I'll miss … all my friends.
18. I couldn't resist … through the keyhole.
19. People went on … to each other as though nothing had happened.
20. I advised them … an umbrella with them.
21. I can't ever forget … you kissing someone else.
22. Don't forget … a towel.
23. I'm sorry, but would you mind … a seat in the waiting room for a few minutes?
24. I regret … tell you that there's been an accident.

25. "Do you fancy … for a swim?"

B   Complete the sentences with prepositions and the *-ing* forms of the verbs in the box.

criticize   hack   live   look after   pay (2×)   persuade   steal   wait   win

1   Toby's capable … into the school computer to try and find out the exam questions.
2   What's the point … somebody to do something that we can just as well do ourselves?
3   Julia succeeded … Tom and Andrew to help her with the layout.
4   I insist … for the petrol.
5   The neighbours thanked me … their cat while they were away.
6   This won't prevent me … the decision when it is made public.
7   Is there any sense … any longer?
8   I'm fairly confident … the match.
9   Captain Ross punished the convict … food from the stores.
10 You'll soon get used … in the country.

C   Replace the infinitives with the correct *-ing* form structures – if necessary.

1   The fear **to get lost** made me turn back after about 200 metres.
2   What are the advantages **to use** a monolingual dictionary?
3   We had the intention **to get** a very early boat to Dover the next morning.
4   If we make people pay, it will of course have the effect **to reduce** the number of people who use the service.
5   Simon is very shy and has always had problems **to make** friends.
6   My dad used **to smoke**, but he gave up a couple of years ago.
7   Robbie ran home in the hope **to see** Tina before she left.
8   Is there a possibility **to take** the exam again if I fail first time?
9   Who had the idea **to have** the party by the river?
10 Did you have any difficulty **to find** somewhere to stay?
11 Whose idea was it **to reach** Paris just as the rush hour started?
12 I had no trouble **to find** the address.
13 David has a habit **to phone** very late at night.
14 The thought **to win** £20,000 electrified us all.
15 It was our intention **to stay** the night in Calais.

D   Translate into English, using the verbs in brackets.

1   Anna gestand, Jem „ganz süß" zu finden. *(confess)*
2   Wir freuen uns darauf, dich als unseren Gast hier zu haben. *(look forward)*
3   Ich bin es nicht gewohnt, so weit zu gehen. *(be used)*
4   David gab zu, von dem Problem gewusst zu haben. *(admit)*
5   Ich wehre mich dagegen, etwas zu bezahlen, das ich nicht brauche. *(object)*

Mixed Bag

A Correct the mistakes.

1. It's ~~far~~ to the centre on foot. I'd take a bus.
2. I've looked everywhere, but she's nowhere ~~to find~~.
3. In May Jeremy finally left home. He had made the decision several weeks ~~ago~~.
4. It isn't ~~allowed~~ to use a pocket calculator in this part of the exam.
5. I could see that Sheila was working ~~very concentratedly~~, so I didn't disturb her.
6. The plane leaves at ~~6 o'clock p.m.~~ exactly.
7. One room is 18 m^2, and the other is 17 m^2. They're almost ~~the same big~~.
8. Daniel always smiles ~~so friendlily~~ whenever I see him.
9. I'll give you the money back tomorrow, ~~promised~~.

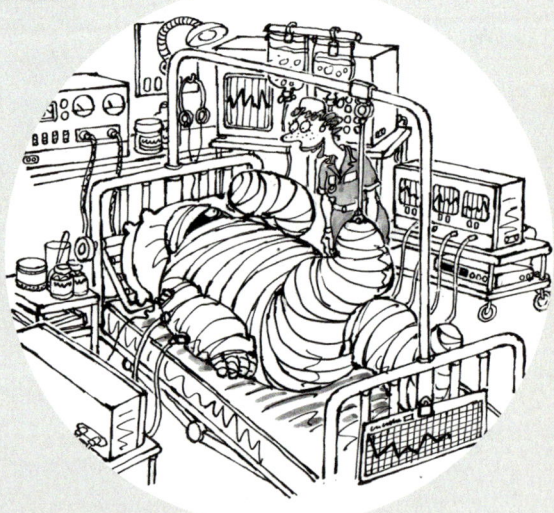

10. "How are we today, Mr Fairweather?"
    – "~~Very~~ fine, thanks, nurse."

B The sentences are incomplete as they stand. Add the missing words.

1. The last I did before going to bed was to feed the cat.
2. Fifty years ago many didn't have a TV or even a phone.
3. I don't know why he doesn't greet, I haven't done anything to him.
4. Last not least, can you tell me how much all this will cost?
5. Roger can Spanish very well. It's not surprising because his dad's Spanish.
6. I'm sorry, but the only I can advise you to do is to try and phone again tomorrow.
7. Too much cola and too much sugary food makes fat.
8. The atmosphere was fantastic – all people were in the streets singing and dancing.
9. I helped her downstairs, we shook hands, she thanked and then went out to her taxi.
10. I was afraid this would happen. That's why I warned you to buy it.

C In each sentence, the expression in bold is used once incorrectly. Correct the mistakes.

1. I left home two minutes **too late** and missed the bus, so was **too late** for school again.

2. The first few days with my host family were so embarrassing: I could remember **nothing** of my English and said practically **nothing**.

3. It's **fully** understandable that they made so many mistakes. They were **fully** exhausted.

4. I've spent **much** and don't have **much** money left now.

5. It's an **impossibly** difficult task. We can **impossibly** ask them to do it on their own.

6. We have **a lot of** time; it's still **a lot of** weeks before we have to make a decision.

7. Don't formulate your question **so**. It sounds **so** impolite, you know.

8. I wanted **nobody** of my friends to know, so I told **nobody**.

9. I'd like to have my **own** room. Unfortunately I've never had an **own** room.

10. You **seldom** see a leopard in the wild. It's a very **seldom** sight.

11. **Who** of you can tell me the answer? Come on, **who** knows?

12. We arrived **plenty** late because of the snow. But **plenty** of others did too.

D Add the words in brackets. Decide where they should go and whether you need *to* or *for*.

1. What time should I suggest? (them)

2. The whole plan seems completely crazy. (me)

3. Sorry, could you repeat that last number, please? (me)

4. David admitted his mistake. (his boss)

5. You can read this yourselves. I'm not going to dictate it. (you)

6. Can you describe the criminal. (us)

7. They bet that we couldn't do it. (us)

8. I apologized for my bad behaviour. (the teacher)

9. Before we start, I'd better explain the layout of the building. (you)

10. I asked his name. (the man)

11. This milk tastes sour. (me)

12. "We're terribly sorry. We didn't mean to spoil the evening." (you)

Checkpoint 10: Mixed Bag

E   **Make sentences that say almost the same, using the words in brackets.**

1   *Mrs Waters has been teaching here 30 years.*
Mrs Waters has been teaching here … . (long)

2   *This is my first game for the school team.*
This is the first time … for the school team. (play)

3   *Sheila went to Africa.*
Sheila went … . (abroad)

4   *I usually earn £7 an hour.*
I earn … . (average)

5   *We can't spend more than €400.*
We can spend … . (maximum)

6   *Germany isn't a big country, but it's not a small country either.*
Germany is … . (medium)

7   *Everybody thought this would happen.*
This was to … . (foresee)

F   **Put in *it*, *so* or *yes* – if one of these words is necessary.**

1   *There's a lovely little bistro just round the corner, Le Bol. – I don't know … .*

2   *Is Tony badly hurt? – Yes, I'm afraid … .*

3   *I still owe you 30p from last night. – Oh, forget … .*

4   *Should we ask for permission first, do you think? – I suppose … . Yes, we ought to.*

5   *How much money will we need? – I'm afraid I can't really say … .*

6   *I've tried six times, but I can't get a reply. – Let me try … .*

7   *What colour was the car? – I've forgotten … . Blue? No. Sorry, I just don't remember.*

8   *Is it going to rain? – I think … .*

9   *When will we hear from them, do you think? – I don't know … .*

10   *You were seen in a café near the school. – Who says …?*

11   *Philip can go with them and show them the way, if they want … .*

12   *"It looks as though it'll be a really nice day today."*
– "Yes, I hope … ."

G   **Correct the words in bold – if they are spelt incorrectly.**

1   I **payed** the hotel bill last night, so we can leave as soon as we're ready.

2   I'm afraid that your cat is **dieing**.

3   Two kilos of **potatoes**, please.

4   Regular **repeatition** is the only way to learn things like irregular verbs.

5   They **tryed** hard, that's the most important thing.

6   The countries in Europe are all **developped** countries, aren't they?

7   I think they're already **regretting** the decision.

8   The results won't be **pubicly** announced till next week.

9   I've always **envid** people with lots of money.

10   There were 17 of us **alltogether**.

11   That's £12.80. – Here you are, and I'd like a **receit**, please.

12   "What do you think the **pronounciation** of that might be?"

H   **Which letter is missing in the words in bold?**

a   c   e   i   s   y

1   Who gave you that **advi_e**?

2   Shall we go to the **be_ch** again this afternoon?

3   When did Kenya become an **independ_nt** country?

4   My grandmother **d_ed** last year.

5   I would **advi_e** you not to go in July.

6   There is a beautiful, 100-year-old **be_ch** tree in the back garden.

7   Do you wear **p_jamas** in bed?

8   Would you like some more orange **marm_lade**?

11 Topic Boxes

A Which is correct? Or are both correct?

1. Which **search engine** do you use? Which **search machine** do you use?
2. I'll send you **the dates** as an attachment. I'll send you **the file** as an attachment.
3. I'm **20 years**. I'm **20 years old**.
4. It was **nought** degrees. It was **zero** degrees.
5. Do you want to **bookmark** this website? Do you want to **put a reading sign** on this website?
6. It's Sunday tomorrow so I can **lie in**. It's Sunday tomorrow so I can **have a lie-in**.
7. **Three times two is** six. **Three twos are** six.
8. Today it's **the fourth of April**. Today it's **April the fourth**.
9. I don't want to decide now. I'll **sleep on it**. I don't want to decide now. I'll **sleep over it**.
10. When are you **doing** your exam? When are you **taking** your exam?
11. Come on, let's go home and **go to bed**. Come on, let's go home and **go to sleep**.
12. **The spring** is my favourite time of year. **Spring** is my favourite time of year.

B Complete the expressions with a suitable word.

1. I was so angry I just hung … . The phone rang again after a few moments, but I didn't … it again.
2. Perhaps he's gone … with the flu. Lots of people seem to have it.
3. I'm not hungry. I think I'll give supper a … .
4. Everybody else passed the exam, but Tony … . He was very unhappy.
5. All week it was in the … thirties, and on Saturday it got as high as 35.
6. … New Year! – And the same to you!
7. Jeremy isn't very well. He seems to have … up a bug.

8. "It's quite a long time since lunch. I think I could do with a … . What about you?"

C   **What do you say …**

1   … to someone who is ill? – You wish them "…"

2   … when you want someone to stay awake? – You say "Don't …!"

3   … when someone is going to take their driving test? – You wish them "… your driving test!"

4   … when someone has passed their driving test? – You say "… your driving test!"

5   … to someone on their birthday? – You wish them "… returns!"

6   … when you don't know the date? – You ask "…?"

7   … when you want to know how hot it is outside? – You say "What …?"

8   … when you tell someone it is plus one outside? – You say "… one degree …"

D   **Translate the text into English.**

1   Wir sind im Morgengrauen aufgestanden. Es war kurz nach vier.

2   Um Punkt fünf haben wir die Hütte (hut) verlassen und angefangen zu klettern.

3   So gegen elf haben wir den Gipfel (summit) erreicht. Es war heiß, an die 30 Grad. Ich war müde und fast am Verdursten.

4   Einer der anderen fragte mich, ob er mal eben mit meinem Handy telefonieren könne.

5   Es war Alfred, ein alter Schulfreund von mir. Wir sind gleich alt. Wir wurden zusammen eingeschult und sind zusammen von der Schule abgegangen.

6   Ich sagte: „O. K., hier. Ich mache ein kurzes Schläfchen."

7   Ich gab ihm mein Handy und legte mich hin. Ich bin sofort eingeschlafen und habe 30 Minuten geschlafen.

8   Als ich aufwachte, telefonierte Alfred immer noch mit seiner Freundin. Zum Schluss sagte er: „Und grüß deine Eltern ganz lieb von mir."

9   Ich war stinksauer (pissed off). Alfreds Freundin war über 1000 Kilometer weit weg – im Urlaub in Dänemark. Ich sagte: „30 mal 80 macht 2400. Du schuldest mir 24 Euro."

10   Es war kurz vor fünf, als wir wieder in der Hütte waren.

11   Ich hatte einen Bärenhunger. Ich war total am Verhungern. „Was gibt's zum Abendessen?", fragte ich.

12   „Nicht viel", war die Antwort. „Es sei denn, du willst einkaufen gehen." „Nein danke", sagte ich. Es waren zwei Stunden zu Fuß zum nächsten Supermarkt.

13   Ich habe versucht einzuschlafen. Nach zwanzig Minuten brachte mich das Plätschern des Baches (the burbling of the stream) draußen zum Einschlafen.

14   Dann klingelte mein Handy. Ich ging ran.

15   Es war Alfreds Freundin. Sie wollte Alfred sprechen. „Schöne Ferien", sagte sie zu mir. Ich konnte nicht wieder einschlafen.

16   Zum Abendessen gab es eine Dose Sardinen, Spiegelei und Himbeerjoghurt.

Correcting Texts

let

A   Correct the mistakes in this text.

The Rolls Royce was built in 1929, but ~~since~~ many years – ~~at last~~
twenty, maybe more – it had stood in a garage ~~making~~ nothing.

Then one day, ~~at~~ the late afternoon, a rich ~~undertaker~~ came and
~~buyed~~ it for a ~~big~~ amount of money and ~~brought~~ it away. He was
the owner of a ~~handy~~ factory. He decided that he didn't want to ~~let~~
the car at the ~~backside~~ of the factory, where ~~none~~ would see it
~~between~~ the ~~parking~~ cars of his 380 employees. But he didn't trust
~~that people~~ leave the car ~~in rest~~. So he ~~let~~ a glass box built ~~before~~
the factory building, ~~at~~ the main road, where everybody ~~were~~ able
to see the car. He wanted ~~that people~~ stop and admire it and
~~hold him for~~ a nice, old-fashioned person.

Only once in the years that followed ~~the car left~~ the box: when the
factory owner's daughter got married ~~with~~ a nice young man from
eastern Europe. The young ~~pair~~ went away in it on their honeymoon.
But the car was ~~robbed~~ from outside the first hotel they stayed at,
just outside London – and was never seen again.

B There are 36 mistakes in this text. Find them and write down a corrected version of the text.

For three weeks I made my driving exam. And now I have the driving licence and want to buy a car. But which one? People which have much money have no difficulty to decide for a model. But when you're still student, you can't spend a lot of money for a car. I asked all of my friends to say me what they mean. I wanted that they give me a good advice. I don't want to risk to buy the false model. But I mustn't fall a decision yet.

In the moment I can lend my mother's car the most time. But not my father's. He always warns me to drive too fast. When he sits besides me, he gets nervously when I do more as 60 miles the hour.

Last week I oversaw a traffic light. It can happen every, can't it? My father didn't tell anything, but he looked me as a murder. I thought: how can the own father be so mad at me? The morale of this story is: always let your father to drive.

36 mistakes!

last – lastly

1 Nobody ever tells me anything. ......
  A I'm always the last to know.   **B** I'm always the last knowing.

2 ...... , was that they were moving to Ireland.
  A The last what I heard   **B** The last which I heard   **C** The last thing I heard

3 I haven't seen Julia *[in letzter Zeit]*. – That's because she's been away on a course.
  A in last time   **B** in the last time   **c** recently   **D** lately

4 When I go away, ...
  A I always pack my washkit as last
  B I always pack my washkit last
  C I always pack my washkit lastly

5 **A** I last saw Julia over a month ago.
  B I lastly saw Julia over a month ago.
  C I the last time saw Julia over a month ago.

6 ...... for all the help she's given me.
  A As last, I'd like to thank Christine
  B As the last thing, I'd like to thank Christine
  C Lastly, I'd like to thank Christine
  D Finally, I'd like to thank Christine

last: at last – finally – eventually – in the end – after all

1 **A** It's at last a month since I saw her.   **B** It's at least a month since I saw her.

2 The wetsuit I bought on the Internet ......
  A has eventually arrived   **B** has finally arrived   **C** has in the end arrived

3 It's no surprise we lost the match. ......
  A The other team are after all professionals.   **B** The other team are eventually professionals.
  C The other team are finally professionals.   **D** The other team are lastly professionals.

4 **A** I've got an offer of a job in the end.
  B I've got an offer of a job at last.
  C I've finally got an offer of a job.

5 Discussions went on for months, ...
  A but an agreement was eventually reached
  B but an agreement was reached in the end
  C but an agreement was after all reached

last – take

1 The roads were bad ....
  A and the journey lasted ages   **B** and the journey took ages

2 ...... , and all the other programmes started a bit late.
  A The quiz show lasted about five minutes longer than usual
  B The quiz show took about five minutes longer than usual

last letzte(r/s); zuletzt – **lastly** zuletzt, schließlich

■ *the last to do – the last thing*

*Toby was **the last to pay**.* ● ● ● Toby war der Letzte, der bezahlte. / Toby hat als Letzter bezahlt.

***The last thing** I did (~~The last I did~~) was to switch the computer off.* ● ● ● Das Letzte, was ich getan habe, war, den Rechner auszuschalten. / Als Letztes habe ich den Rechner ausgeschaltet.

Die Wendung „in letzter Zeit" wird mit *recently* oder *lately* wiedergegeben.

*I've had a lot of headaches **recently**/**lately** (~~in the last time~~).* ● ● ● Ich habe in letzter Zeit / in der letzten Zeit oft Kopfschmerzen.

■ **Adverb** *last* **= „zuletzt", „als Letzte(r/s)"**

Das Adverb *last* bedeutet „zuletzt" im Sinne von „als Letzte(r/s)" oder „das letzte Mal".

When I eat a fried egg, I always eat the yolk [jəʊk] ***last**.* ● ● ● … esse ich das Eigelb immer zuletzt / als Letztes.

*We **last** met at a jazz concert.* ● ● ● Wir haben uns zuletzt / das letzte Mal bei einem Jazzkonzert getroffen.

■ **Adverb** *lastly* **= „zum Schluss", „als letzten Punkt"**

Mit dem Adverb *lastly* kündigt man an, dass man zum Schluss kommt.

***Lastly** (auch: **Finally**), I'd like to thank you all for being so patient. Thank you and goodbye.* ● ● ● Abschließend / Als Letztes möchte ich mich bei allen dafür bedanken …

last: at last – finally – eventually – in the end – after all schließlich, endlich

Trouble Spot

■ **endlich, schließlich**

1 „erfreulicherweise (nach längerer Zeit)"

Mein Visum ist endlich gekommen. ● ● ● *My visa has arrived **at last**.*

[Nicht verwechseln mit *at least* („mindestens" / „wenigstens"): *You'll have to wait **at least** four weeks for a visa.*]

2 „unerfreulicherweise viel später als erhofft / erwartet"

Um ein Uhr nachts sind wir schließlich angekommen. ● ● ● *We **finally** arrived at one o'clock in the morning.*

Ich habe endlich [nach langer Suche] eine Wohnung gefunden. ● ● ● *I've **finally** found a flat.*

Häufig kann man sowohl *finally* als auch *at last* verwenden – je nachdem, ob man das Geschehen eher negativ oder eher positiv bewertet:

*I've found a flat **at last**.* [Ich freue mich.]

3 „allmählich nach langer Zeit"; „irgendwann als Folge von etwas"

An dem Gebäude hat niemand etwas getan und schließlich ist es verfallen. ● ● ● *Nobody did anything to the building and **eventually** / **in the end** it fell into disrepair.*

Beachte: Um ein gegenwärtiges Ergebnis auszudrücken, werden *at last* oder *finally* und das *present perfect* verwendet.

Das Wetter ist endlich besser geworden. ● ● ● *The weather has improved **at last** / has **finally** improved. (~~The weather has eventually improved.~~ / ~~The weather has improved in the end.~~)*

4 „schließlich", „schließlich doch" ▶ after all

Ich kann keine 6000 € bezahlen. Ich bin schließlich nur Student. ● ● ● *I can't pay €6000. **After all**, I'm only a student.*

last – take* dauern

■ *Last* bedeutet „dauern" im Sinne von „andauern" „anhalten".

*The meeting **lasted** till half past seven.* ● ● ● Die Sitzung dauerte bis halb acht.

■ Man verwendet *take* im Sinne von „dauern", wenn man den Zeitaufwand beschreibt.

*The repair **took** over four hours.* ● ● ● Die Reparatur dauerte über vier Stunden.

*How much longer is this going to **take**?* ● ● ● Wie lange dauert das noch?

*It won't **take** long.* ● ● ● Es dauert nicht lange.

late – too late – lately

1 There was an accident on the underground, ... But then the interview went quite well.
   A so I was late for my interview   **B** so I was too late for my interview

2 ...... All the tickets were already sold.
   A I was late.   **B** I was too late.

3 ...... , after I'd gone to bed.
   A Mark phoned very late last night   **B** Mark phoned very lately last night

4 **A** I haven't been feeling very well late.   **B** I haven't been feeling very well lately.

laugh – smile

1 The audiences are different every night. ......
   A They never laugh at the same things.   **B** They never laugh over the same things.

2 The Westons' neighbours were very friendly ...... whenever they saw me.
   A and laughed at me   **B** and laughed to me   **C** and smiled at me

law

1 **A** It is forbidden after the law to take photographs in any part of this building.
   B It is forbidden by law to take photographs in any part of this building.
   C It is forbidden by the law to take photographs in any part of this building.
   D It is forbidden from the law to take photographs in any part of this building.

2 **A** After a new law, smoking in Ireland was made illegal in all public places.
   B By a new law, smoking in Ireland was made illegal in all public places.
   C Through a new law, smoking in Ireland was made illegal in all public places.
   D Under a new law, smoking in Ireland was made illegal in all public places.

learn – study

1 People always say ......, and it's true – sometimes!
   A that you learn from your mistakes   **B** that you learn out of your mistakes

2 I can't come this evening. ......
   A I'm learning for a French test tomorrow.   **B** I'm studying for a French test tomorrow.

least

1 **A** Last but not least you have to remember that it only cost €30 to get there.
   B Last not least you have to remember that it only cost €30 to get there.

left – right

1 My aunt is the person *[ganz links im Bild]*.
   A quite left in the picture   **B** on the extreme left of the picture
   C on the far left of the picture   **D** on the top left in the picture

2 Do you mean *[„rechts oben oder rechts unten"]*?
   A 'right up or right down'   **B** 'right top or right below'   **C** 'top right or bottom right'

late (zu) spät – too late zu spät – lately in letzter Zeit

■ *late – too late*
Late beinhaltet bereits die Bedeutung „zu spät", „nicht pünktlich".
 *I was **late** for school.* ● ● ● Ich kam zu spät / verspätet zur Schule.
Too late wird nur verwendet, wenn etwas tatsächlich verpasst wird.
 *I was **too late**. The train had already left.* ● ● ● Ich kam zu spät. Der Zug war schon abgefahren.

■ *late – lately*
Das zum Adjektiv *late* gehörende Adverb heißt ebenfalls *late*.
 *I got home **late** yesterday.* ● ● ● Ich bin gestern spät nach Hause gekommen.
Das Adverb *lately* bedeutet „in letzter Zeit". *Lately* wird mit dem *present perfect* verwendet.
 ***Have** you **heard** from Sue **lately**?* ● ● ● Hast du in letzter Zeit von Sue gehört?

laugh lachen – smile lächeln

■ *laugh at sth. / sb. – laugh about sth.*
 *Nobody **laughed at** the joke.* [= spontan loslachen] ● ● ● Niemand lachte über den Witz.
 *Other children **laughed at** me because I didn't have designer clothes.* [= sich über jmdn. lustig
 machen] ● ● ● Andere Kinder lachten mich aus / lachten über mich …
 *At the time I felt stupid, but now I can **laugh about** it.* [= es lustig finden] ● ● ● … aber jetzt kann
 ich darüber lachen.

■ *smile at sb.*
 *The little boy was so friendly, he **smiled at** me (~~laughed at me~~) the whole time.*
 [= jmdn. anlachen/anlächeln] ● ● ● … er lachte/lächelte mich die ganze Zeit an.

law Gesetz

■ *You must **by law** carry an identity card.* ● ● ● Nach dem Gesetz muss man immer einen Ausweis
 bei sich haben. [So ist die gesetzliche Vorschrift.]
 ***Under** this new **law**, smoking will become illegal.* ● ● ● Nach diesem neuen Gesetz [= nach den
 Bestimmungen dieses neuen Gesetzes] …
 ***In / Under** Chinese **law** …* ● ● ● Nach chinesischem Recht [= nach den Bestimmungen des
 chinesischen Rechtssystems] …

learn (*) – study lernen ▷ study

■ *I've started to **learn** Spanish.* ● ● ● Ich habe angefangen, Spanisch zu lernen.
 ***learn from** one's mistakes* ● ● ● aus seinen Fehlern lernen

■ „Für die Schule, eine Prüfung, einen Abschluss usw. lernen" drückt man mit *study* aus.
 *Kate is **studying** for her maths test / exam.* ● ● ● Kate lernt für ihre Mathearbeit /-prüfung.
 *What are you doing? – I'm **studying**.* ● ● ● Was machst du? – Ich lerne gerade (für die Schule).

least wenigste(r/s)

■ *last but not least*
Die Redewendung mit der Bedeutung „nicht zuletzt" heißt *last but not least* [wörtlich: „als Letztes,
aber nicht als Geringstes"], nicht *last not least*.
 ***Last but not least** I'd like to thank my father.* ● ● ● Nicht zuletzt möchte ich meinem Vater danken.

left linke(r/s); links; linke Seite – right rechte(r/s); rechts; rechte Seite

■ *my **left** foot and my **right** foot* ● ● ● mein linker Fuß und mein rechter Fuß
 *Turn **left**.* ● ● ● Biegen Sie (nach) links ab!
 ***Top left** or **bottom left**?* ● ● ● Links oben oder links unten?
 *Take the first road **on the left**.* ● ● ● Biegen Sie in die erste Straße links / auf der linken Seite!
 *Who is this **on the far left** / **on the extreme left**?* ● ● ● Wer ist das ganz links (außen)?
 ***To the left of** the café is the bank.* ● ● ● Links neben dem Café / Links vom Café ist die Bank.
 *Exercise 7 is on the **left-hand** page.* ● ● ● Übung 7 ist auf der linken Seite.

L

less – fewer

1 **A** There were fewer cars on the streets than on a weekday.
    B There were a fewer cars on the streets than on a weekday.
    C There were less cars on the streets than on a weekday.

2 I'm sorry I can't stop. .....
    A I have fewer time today.   **B** I have less time today.

let

1 **A** I can let you have a copy if you want.   **B** I can let you to have a copy if you want.

2 There's something wrong with the brakes. *[Ich lasse sie prüfen.]*
    A I'm having them checked.   **B** I have them checked.   **C** I let them be checked.

3 I know it isn't polite, but we're just going to have to ....
    A keep them waiting   **B** make them wait   **C** make them to wait

4 The shop assistant *[ließ die Geschäftführerin kommen]*.
    A let the manager come   **B** made the manager to come   **C** sent for the manager

5 **A** I think it'll be OK to leave the window open.   **B** I think it'll be OK to let the window open.

6 It's not a problem. *[Das lässt sich leicht machen.]*
    A That can easy be done.   **B** That can easily be done.   **C** That lets itself easily be done.

7 *[Frau Smithers lässt sagen]* that the meeting has been postponed half an hour.
    A Mrs Smithers asked me to say   **B** Mrs Smithers lets it be said   **C** Mrs Smithers has announced

8 I spoke to Susanne before I left. ......
    A She lets greet you.   **B** She wants to greet you.   **C** She sends her best wishes.

9 *[Lass das!]* You're getting on my nerves.
    A Leave that!   **B** Let that!   **C** Stop that!

lie – lie – lay

1 Jason is having a rest. ......
    A He's laying down on the sofa in the living room.
    B He's lieing down on the sofa in the living room.
    C He's lying down on the sofa in the living room.

2 The beach looked disgusting. ......
    A There was rubbish laying everywhere.
    B There was rubbish lieing everywhere.
    C There was rubbish lying everywhere.

3 ...... and fell asleep immediately.
    A I laid down on the bed   **B** I lay down on the bed   **C** I layed down on the bed

4 ...... when you wanted to meet someone in town?
    A How often have you laid to your parents   **B** How often have you lain to your parents
    C How often have you layed to your parents   **D** How often have you lied to your parents

5 ...... , but the dog came and sat on it.
    A I laid my sleeping bag straight down on the floor
    B I lay my sleeping bag straight down on the floor
    C I layed my sleeping bag straight down on the floor
    D I lied my sleeping bag straight down on the floor

less – fewer weniger   ▷ a little

■ **mit nicht zählbaren Nomen**

Less – nicht *fewer* – wird vor nicht zählbaren Nomen verwendet.

I earned **less money** (~~fewer money~~) in my last holiday job. ● ● ○ In meinem letzten Ferienjob habe ich weniger Geld verdient.

■ **mit zählbaren Nomen**

Less kann – anstelle von *fewer* – aber auch vor zählbaren Nomen im Plural verwendet werden.

I had **fewer/less friends** at my old school. ● ● ○ Auf meiner alten Schule hatte ich weniger Freunde.

let* (zu)lassen   ▷ hire

■ *let sb. do*

Auf *let* folgt ein Objekt + der Infinitiv ohne *to*.

My parents **let me stay** (= allowed me to stay) the night at my friend's house. ● ● ○ Meine Eltern ließen mich bei meinem Freund übernachten.

Trouble Spot

■ **lassen**

1 Ich lasse mir morgen die Haare schneiden. [= veranlassen, dass etwas getan wird; (sich) etwas machen lassen] ● ● ○ I'm going to **have** my hair **cut** tomorrow.

2 Wenn es nicht richtig ist, lasse ich dich alles nochmal machen! [= jmdn. zwingen, etwas zu tun] ● ● ○ If it's not right, I'll **make** you **do** it all again.
Lass dir das von Alexander machen/erklären. [= jmdn. veranlassen, etwas zu tun] ● ● ○ **Ask/Get** Alexander **to do** it / **to explain** it.
Er hat uns zwei Stunden warten lassen. ● ● ○ He **kept** us **waiting** / **made** us **wait** two hours.
Wir müssen den Arzt kommen lassen. ● ● ○ We must **send for** the doctor.

3 das Licht anlassen [= in einem bestimmten Zustand (zurück)lassen] ● ● ○ **leave the light(s) on**
etwas/jmdn. zu Hause lassen [= an einem Ort (zurück)lassen] ● ● ○ **leave** sth./sb. **at home**
etwas/jmdn. in Ruhe lassen ● ● ○ **leave** sth./sb. **alone**

4 Das lässt sich leicht machen. ● ● ○ That **can** easily **be done**.

5 Herr Barz lässt sagen/ausrichten, dass er etwas später kommt. ● ● ○ Mr Barz **asked me to say** / **wants you to know** that he'll be a little late.
Meine Eltern lassen euch grüßen. ● ● ○ My parents **send** their **best wishes**.

6 „Lass das!", habe ich gesagt. [= unterlassen, aufhören mit] ● ● ○ I said, **"Stop that!"**
Er kann das Fluchen nicht lassen. ● ● ○ He can't **stop** swearing.

lie* [laɪ] liegen – lie [leɪ] lügen – lay* [leɪ] legen

■ **lie (-*ing*-Form: *lying*) – *lay* – *lain* = „liegen"**

Lie wird ohne Objekt gebraucht.

Newspapers were **lying** all over the floor. ● ● ○ Überall auf dem Boden lagen Zeitungen.
For a few minutes she just **lay** there. ● ● ○ Ein paar Minuten lag sie einfach nur so da.

■ **lie down (-*ing*-Form: *lying down*) – *lay down* – *lain down* = „sich hinlegen"**

Lie down on the bed. ● ● ○ Leg dich aufs Bett.
I **lay down** and went to sleep. ● ● ○ Ich habe mich hingelegt und bin eingeschlafen.

■ **lie (-*ing*-Form: *lying*) – *lied* – *lied* = „lügen"**

Don't believe her. She's **lying**. ● ● ○ Glaube ihr nicht. Sie lügt.
You **lied to** me, you liar! ● ● ○ Du hast mich angelogen, du Lügner!

■ **lay (-*ing*-Form: *laying*) – *laid* – *laid* = „legen"**

Lay wird immer mit Objekt gebraucht.

Lay the baby on its side. ● ● ○ Leg das Baby auf die Seite.
He **laid** the papers on the desk. ● ● ○ Er legte die Papiere auf den Schreibtisch.

L

life – live [lɪv] – live [laɪv]

1 A Life on earth goes back millions of years. B The life on earth goes back millions of years.

2 A I wouldn't want to swap my life with life of someone 100 years ago.
   B I wouldn't want to swap my life with the life of someone 100 years ago.

3 A The old couple next door had never left Wales all life long.
   B The old couple next door had never left Wales all the life.
   C The old couple next door had never left Wales all their lives.
   D The old couple next door had never left Wales the whole life

4 A I don't think I could life in a hot country. B I don't think I could live in a hot country.

5 ...... It's just so much more exciting.
   A I still prefer to watch the matches life. B I still prefer to watch the matches live.

6 It's an exciting programme to watch ....
   A because it's a life show B because it's a live show

light – slight – easy

1 This bag is *[leicht]*. It's only got a couple of T-shirts in.
   A easy B light C slight

2 ...... , but no clouds.
   A There was a light westerly breeze B There was a slight westerly breeze

3 There has been some improvement, ...
   A but it's only a light improvement B but it's only a slight improvement

4 A Russian isn't easy to learn. B Russian isn't light to learn. C Russian isn't slight to learn.

like – would like

1 Now that they've taken away that ugly old shed, ...
   A I'm liking the view much better B I like the view much better

2 A I like meeting new people. B I like to meet new people. C I like the meeting new people.

3 ...... , so that I have the rest of the day free.
   A I like doing any jobs I have to do for my parents in the morning
   B I like to do any jobs I have to do for my parents in the morning

4 A We wouldn't like that you think we're unhelpful.
   B We wouldn't like you think we're unhelpful.
   C We wouldn't like you to think we're unhelpful.

5 A I'd like to tell you something. B I'd like telling you something.

L

life [laɪf] (das) Leben – **live** [lɪv] leben, wohnen – **live** [laɪv] lebendig; live

■ **kein *the* in Aussagen allgemeiner Art**

Life gehört zu den abstrakten Nomen, die in Aussagen allgemeiner Art ohne den bestimmten Artikel verwendet werden.

> ***Life** is so wonderful.* ● ● ● Das Leben ist so wunderbar.

Life wird jedoch **mit** dem bestimmten Artikel verwendet, wenn ein Relativsatz oder eine *of*-Fügung folgt.

> ***the life** we knew* ● ● ● das Leben, das wir kannten
> ***the life** of a teacher* ● ● ● das Leben einer Lehrerin

■ **Possessivbegleiter statt Artikel**

Das Leben wird als etwas eng zu einer Person Gehörendes angesehen, deshalb verwendet man im Englischen den Possessivbegleiter.

> *I've lived here **all my life**.* ● ● ● Ich habe mein ganzes Leben / das ganze Leben lang hier gewohnt.

Bei mehreren Personen verwendet man die Pluralform *li̱ves* [laɪvz].

> *Thousands lost **their lives** [laɪvz] in the floods.* ● ● ● … sind bei der Flut ums Leben gekommen.

■ **Verb *live***

Das Nomen *life* [laɪf] darf nicht mit dem Verb *live* [lɪv] („leben", „wohnen") verwechselt werden.

> *You **live** and learn.* ● ● ● Man lernt nie aus.
> *She **lives** [lɪvz] just across the street from me.* ● ● ● Sie wohnt mir direkt gegenüber.

■ **Adjektiv *live***

Das Nomen *life* [laɪf] darf nicht mit dem Adjektiv *live* [laɪv] („lebendig"; „nicht aufgezeichnet") verwechselt werden.

> *a real **live** tiger* ● ● ● ein echter, lebendiger Tiger
> *The interview was **live**.* ● ● ● Das Interview war live [„nicht aufgezeichnet"].

light – slight – easy leicht

■ **leicht**

1 Gegenteil von „schwer (von Gewicht)"

> Trag diese Tasche hier. Die ist am leichtesten. ● ● ● *Carrry this bag. It's the **lightest**.*

2 Gegenteil von „stark"

> eine leichte Brise, leichter Regen ● ● ● *a **light** breeze, **light** rain*

3 „geringfügig"

> eine leichte Verbesserung/Veränderung ● ● ● *a **slight** improvement/change*

4 Gegenteil von „schwierig"

> Die Prüfung war leicht. ● ● ● *The exam was **easy**.*

like mögen, gern haben/tun – **would like** wollen, würde gern, möchte

■ **nicht in der Verlaufsform**

In der Regel kann *like* nicht in der Verlaufsform stehen.

> *Can we stay here? I **like** it here.* ● ● ● Können wir hier bleiben? Es gefällt mir hier.

■ ***like doing – like to do***

Nach *like* kann meist ohne Unterschied eine *-ing*-Form oder ein *to*-Infinitiv stehen.

> *Do you **like going** / **like to go** to parties?* ● ● ● Gehst du gern auf Partys?

Wenn es jedoch um etwas geht, was eigentlich unangenehm ist, verwendet man nur den Infinitiv. *Like to do* bedeutet in diesem Fall „vorzugsweise tun", „es für richtig halten, zu tun".

> *I **like to go** to the dentist's at least twice a year.* ● ● ● Ich gehe möglichst/vorzugsweise mindestens zweimal jährlich zum Zahnarzt.

■ ***would like (sb.) to do***

Nach *would like (sb.)* verwendet man eine Infinitivkonstruktion, keinen *that*-Satz.

> *I'd **like her to go** (~~I'd like that she goes~~) to university.* ● ● ● Ich möchte, dass sie studiert.

a little – little – a few – few

1 Do you think ...... ?

  A you could lend me little money till Monday   B you could lend me a little money till Monday

  C you could lend me few money till Monday   D you could lend me a few money till Monday

2 A We get few complaints I'm pleased to say.   B We get a few complaints I'm pleased to say.

  C We get little complaints I'm pleased to say.   D We get a little complaints I'm pleased to say.

little – small

1 ...... I must have it.

  A I've never seen such a lovely little teapot.   B I've never seen such a lovely small teapot.

2 ...... I hope he hasn't fallen down the stairs again.

  A Where's little Timmy got to?   B Where's small Timmy got to?

3 A Westonzoyland is still quite a nice little place.

  B Westonzoyland is still quite a nice small place.

4 ...... They're bigger at Da Enzo's.

  A Your pizza is a bit little, isn't it?   B Your pizza is a bit small, isn't it?

5 A Which is the littlest animal in this zoo?   B Which is the smallest animal in this zoo?

6 It doesn't matter whether you write [in Kleinbuchstaben] or in capitals.

  A in little letters   B in small letters

7 I'm sorry, but I don't have any [Kleingeld].

  A little change   B little money   C small change   D small money

8 Always read [das Kleingedruckte].

  A the little print   B the little words   C the small print   D the small words

long – a long time

1 A I haven't been here long, only about ten minutes.

  B I haven't been here long time, only about ten minutes.

  C I haven't been here a long time, only about ten minutes.

2 ...... I don't know who it belongs to.

  A That car has been parked there long, several weeks.

  B That car has been parked there long time, several weeks.

  C That car has been parked there a long time, several weeks.

3 She hadn't eaten anything [drei Tage lang].

  A for three days   B three days   C three days long

4 For this trick you need [zwei gleich lange Schnüre].

  A two equally long pieces of string

  B two pieces of string the same length

  C two same long pieces of string

5 Every summer they go off [auf eine längere Reise] for at least eight weeks.

  A on a longer trip   B on quite a long trip

a little ein wenig, ein bisschen – **little** wenig – **a few** einige, ein paar – **few** wenige ▷ less

■ *(A) little* steht vor nicht zählbaren Nomen.
*Can you lend me **a little money**, please?* ● ● ● … ein wenig / ein bisschen / etwas Geld leihen?
*We have **a little time**.* ● ● ● Wir haben etwas Zeit [= immerhin etwas Zeit; mehr als nichts].
*We have **little time** to ourselves.* ● ● ● Wir haben (nur) wenig Zeit für uns.

■ *(A) few* steht vor zählbaren Nomen im Plural.
*I need **a few things** from the supermarket.* ● ● ● Ich brauche einige / ein paar Sachen …
*I know **a few people**.* ● ● ● Ich kenne ein paar Leute [= immerhin einige Leute; mehr als keine].
Few people *can say that they never lie.* ● ● ● (Nur) wenige Menschen können behaupten …

little – small klein

■ *little*: oft gefühlsbetont
*What lovely **little** children!* ● ● ● Was für niedliche kleine Kinder!
*I could never live in a tiny **little** flat like this.* ● ● ● … in so einer winzig kleinen Wohnung …

■ *small*: das sachlichere Wort
*Unsuitable for **small** children.* ● ● ● Für kleine Kinder ungeeignet.
*a **small** flat of 18 m²* ● ● ● eine kleine Wohnung von 18 m²

■ grammatische Unterschiede
Vor Namen von Personen wird nur *little* verwendet.
Little *Anna (Small Anna) is a very intelligent child.* ● ● ● Die kleine Anna …
Zusammen mit anderen Adjektiven wird ebenfalls in der Regel nur *little* verwendet.
*They live in a **little** old house (a small old house).* ● ● ● Sie wohnen in einem alten Häuschen.
Nach Verben wie *be, feel, seem* steht in der Regel nur *small*.
*The cake **is a bit small** (is a bit little) for 20 people.*
Nur *small* hat allgemein gebräuchliche Steigerungsformen.
*I think I need a **smaller** (littler) size. – Sorry, this is **the smallest** (the littlest) we have.*

■ feste Wendungen mit *little* und *small*
*my **little brother*** ● ● ● mein kleiner Bruder
*my **little finger/toe*** ● ● ● mein kleiner Finger/Zeh
***small letters**, not capitals / not capital letters* ● ● ● Kleinbuchstaben, nicht Großbuchstaben
*Do you have any **small change** [‚- '-]?* ● ● ● Hast du Kleingeld?
small ads *['- -] (BE, infml) in the newspaper* ● ● ● Kleinanzeigen in der Zeitung
*Don't sign before you've read **the small print** [‚- '-] (BE).* ● ● ● … das Kleingedruckte …

long – a long time lang(e); (eine) lange Zeit

■ In Fragen und verneinten Sätzen verwendet man meist *long*. *A long time* ist aber auch möglich.
*Have you been waiting **long**? – No, I haven't been waiting **long**.* ● ● ● Warten Sie schon lange? –
  Nein, ich warte noch nicht lange.

■ In bejahten Aussagesätzen kann *long* nur verwendet werden, wenn es näher bestimmt ist.
*We've waited **so long / too long / long enough**. He should have arrived **long ago**.* ● ● ● Wir warten
  schon so lange / zu lange / lange genug. Er hätte schon vor langer Zeit / längst ankommen sollen.
A long time kann auch ohne nähere Bestimmung stehen.
*We've been waiting **(for) a long time** (long), over two hours.* ● ● ● Wir warten schon lange (Zeit) …
Aber ohne *long*:
*We've been waiting **for two hours**.* ● ● ● Wir warten schon zwei Stunden lang.

■ Adjektiv „lang"
ein zehn Meter langer Teppich ● ● ● *a ten-metre **(long)** carpet / a carpet ten metres **long** /*
  *a carpet ten metres **in length***
zwei gleich lange Stangen ● ● ● *two poles **the same length***
schulterlanges Haar ● ● ● ***shoulder-length*** *(shoulder-long) hair*
eine längere [= ziemlich lange] Reise ● ● ● ***quite a long*** *journey*
Skilanglauf ● ● ● ***cross-country*** *skiing*

L

Trouble Spot

look – watch – see

1 ...... If the road is still clear, cross.
  A Look left, right, then left again.   **B** Look at left, right, then left again.
  C See left, right, then left again.   **D** Watch left, right, then left again.

2 Lots of people were lining the streets, ...
  A seeing the parade   **B** watching the parade

3 **A** Look carefully. Can you see anything unusual?
  B Look carefully. Can you watch anything unusual?
  C Look carefully. Can you look at anything unusual?

look forward to

1 **A** I look forward to hear from you again soon.
  B I look forward to hearing from you again soon.

lose – loose

1 I crashed into someone while playing basketball, ...
  A and now this tooth is lose   **B** and now this tooth is loose

2 ...... – Nothing.
  A What have you losed?   **B** What have you lost?   **C** What have you loosed?

loud – noisy

1 ...... , and we didn't sleep very well.
  A Our room was terribly loud   **B** Our room was terribly noisy

2 ...... , and then everything went black.
  A There was a loud explosion   **B** There was a noisy explosion

3 Sorry, I can't hear you. ......
  A Can you speak louder, please?   **B** Can you speak up, please?   **C** Can you speak more, please?

4 **A** The people in the next classroom were very loud all through the exam.
  B The people in the next classroom were very noisy all through the exam.

love

1 ...... It was someone he met on the bus!
  A Gareth fell in love for someone while he was away.
  B Gareth fell in love in someone while he was away.
  C Gareth fell in love to someone while he was away.
  D Gareth fell in love with someone while he was away.

2 If you know somebody well, you can finish a letter to them with ....
  A 'Love, Jenny'   **B** 'With loving greetings, Jenny'   **C** 'Lovely greetings, Jenny'

look – watch – see* schauen, sehen

■ *look* = „blicken", „schauen", „hinsehen", „bewusst anschauen"
*She's **looking** in this direction. Don't **look** now.* ● ● ● Sie schaut hierher. Sieh jetzt nicht hin.
*Don't **look** left or right, just **look** straight ahead.* ● ● ● Schau/Guck nicht nach links oder rechts …
*Can I help you? – No thanks. I'm **just looking**.* ● ● ● … – … Ich schaue/sehe mich nur um.

■ *look at* = „(sich etwas/jmdn.) ansehen/anschauen"
***Look at** the picture / the explanations / page 27, please.* ● ● ● Seht euch bitte das Bild / … an.

■ *watch* = „(sich etwas/jmdn.) ansehen/anschauen"; „zuschauen (bei)"; „beobachten"
Das Objekt von *watch* muss etwas Sich-Entwickelndes bzw. Sich-Bewegendes sein.
***watch** TV* ● ● ● fernsehen
***watch** a TV programme / a football match / a film* ● ● ● sich eine Fernsehsendung / ein Fußballspiel /
einen Film ansehen

■ *see* = „sehen", „wahrnehmen, ohne zu beachten"
*Have you **seen** my keys?* ● ● ● Hast du meine Schlüssel gesehen?
*I **saw** somebody, but didn't realize it was you.* ● ● ● Ich habe (zwar) jemanden gesehen, aber …
Man kann *see* auch mit Objekten verwenden, die sonst nach *watch* stehen. *See* drückt in diesen
Fällen aus, dass nicht der Vorgang, sondern das Ergebnis im Mittelpunkt steht.
*Did you **see** the news / the football match / that film you were interested in?* ● ● ● Hast du die
Nachrichten / das Fußballspiel / den Film, der dich interessiert hat, gesehen?

look forward to sich freuen auf

L

■ *look forward to doing*
In der Wendung *look forward to* ist *to* eine Präposition. Nach einer Präposition steht eine *-ing*-Form,
kein *to*-Infinitiv.
*We **look** / We're **looking forward to** seeing (~~to see~~) you.* ● ● ● Wir freuen uns darauf, dich zu sehen.

lose* [luːz] verlieren – loose [luːs] lose; locker

■ *lose – lost – lost* = „verlieren"
*Don't **lose** the money I gave you.* ● ● ● Verlier das Geld nicht, das ich dir gegeben habe.
*He's a bad **loser** (~~looser~~).* ● ● ● Er ist ein schlechter Verlierer.

■ *a **loose** screw* ● ● ● eine lose Schraube

loud – noisy laut

■ *Loud* („mit großer Lautstärke") wird mit Bezug auf Geräusche verwendet.
*a **loud** noise / sound / voice / doorbell / explosion*
***loud** music*
Loud kann auch als Adverb verwendet werden.
*Can you **speak louder**, please? (= Can you **speak up**, please?)* ● ● ● Kannst du bitte lauter sprechen?
*Can you **read** the poem **out loud**, please?* ● ● ● Kannst du das Gedicht bitte laut vorlesen?

■ *Noisy* („lärmend", „geräuschvoll", „unangenehmen Lärm verursachend") – nicht *loud* – wird mit
Bezug auf einen Ort oder eine Lärmquelle bzw. einen Lärmverursacher verwendet.
*a **noisy** street / hotel room / pub / classroom*
*It's very **noisy** here.*
*a **noisy** bulldozer / motorbike / group of tourists*
*The people who live next door are really **noisy**.* ● ● ● … sind sehr laut / machen viel Krach.

love Liebe

■ *His **love for** her didn't last.* [Liebe zu einer Person] ● ● ● Seine Liebe zu ihr war nicht von Dauer.
*his **love of** music* [Liebe zu einer Sache] ● ● ● seine Liebe zur Musik
*be / fall **in love (with** sb.)* ● ● ● (in jmdn.) verliebt sein / sich (in jmdn.) verlieben

■ ***Love**, Christine* [Briefschluss] ● ● ● Liebe / Herzliche Grüße – Christine

love – would love

1 **A** I love make people laugh.   **B** I love making people laugh.   **C** I love to make people laugh.

2 ...... before I go to university.
  A I'd love taking a year out and seeing a bit of the world
  B I'd love to take a year out and see a bit of the world

luck – be lucky

1 **A** Do you believe in luck?   **B** Do you believe in the luck?

2 We got to the airport late, ... because the plane was delayed.
  A but we had luck   **B** but we had the luck   **C** but we were lucky

lunch

1 Can you tell me ...... ?
  A what time lunch normally is in Spain   **B** what time the lunch normally is in Spain

2 ...... – A sandwich, or a salad.
  A What do you usually have at lunch?
  B What do you usually have for lunch?
  C What do you usually have to lunch?

machine – machinery

1 **A** When did they first introduce machine-readable passports?
  B When did they first introduce machines-readable passports?
  C When did they first introduce machinery-readable passports?

2 The motor industry has always invested heavily ....
  A in new machinery   **B** in new machineries

3 ...... for success in the competitive world of global business.
  A A modern machinery is essential   **B** Modern machinery is essential

4 The weather was awful, and *[unsere Maschine]* had to land in the middle of a thunderstorm.
  A our machine   **B** our plane

5 At the time, Google wasn't one of the most popular *[Suchmaschinen]*.
  A searching machines   **B** search machines   **C** searching engines   **D** search engines

majority – minority

1 **A** A small minority doesn't want to leave, but most are happy about being rehoused.
  B A small minority don't want to leave, but most are happy about being rehoused.
  C A large majority is happy about being rehoused, but a few don't want to leave.
  D A large majority are happy about being rehoused, but a few don't want to leave.

2 **A** A large majority of people in the country speak more than one language.
  B A large majority of people in the country speaks more than one language.

love lieben; sehr gern haben/tun **– would love** würde sehr gern, möchte sehr gern

■ *love doing – love to do*
Nach *love* kann man meist ohne Unterschied eine -*ing*-Form oder einen *to*-Infinitiv verwenden.
  I love going / love to go to parties. ● ● ● Ich gehe liebend / sehr gern auf Partys.

■ *would love (sb.) to do*
Nach *would love* verwendet man einen *to*-Infinitiv.
  I'd love to know why he did it. ● ● ● Ich wüsste zu gern / Ich würde sehr gern wissen, warum …

luck Glück **– be lucky** Glück haben   ▷ greet

■ *Luck (~~The luck~~) was with us.* ● ● ● Das Glück war mit uns.
  I hoped she would come, and I was lucky (~~had luck~~). She came. ● ● ● … und ich hatte Glück. …

lunch Mittagessen

■ **ohne** *the*
Lunch steht – ebenso wie *breakfast* und *dinner* – in der Regel ohne den bestimmten Artikel.
  Lunch is at 12.30. ● ● ● Das Mittagessen ist um 12.30 Uhr.

> **Topic Box**
>
> ■ *Talking about meals* ▷ appetite ▷ breakfast ▷ menu ▷ taste
> *Who's getting (the) breakfast?* ● ● ● Wer macht das Frühstück?
> *What's for lunch? / What are we having for lunch?* ● ● ● Was gibt's zum Mittagessen?
> *The main course is fish.* ● ● ● Das Hauptgericht ist Fisch.
> *There's a choice of desserts* [dɪ'zɜːts]. ● ● ● Es gibt verschiedene Desserts zur Auswahl.
> *I'm not really hungry.* ● ● ● Ich habe keinen richtigen Hunger / eigentlich keinen Hunger.
> *I think I'll give lunch a miss.* ● ● ● Ich glaube, ich lasse das Mittagessen ausfallen.
> *I could do with a bite (to eat). / I fancy a bite (to eat).* (infml) ● ● ● Ich könnte einen Happen /
>   Bissen vertragen.
> *I'm ravenous* ['rævənəs]. ● ● ● Ich habe einen Bärenhunger.
> *I'm absolutely starving.* (infml) ● ● ● Ich komme fast um vor Hunger.
> *I'm dying of thirst.* ● ● ● Ich verdurste.
> *I'm full (up). / I've had enough (to eat).* ● ● ● Ich bin satt.

L

machine [mə'ʃiːn] Maschine; Automat **– machinery** [mə'ʃiːnəri] Maschinen

■ *a washing machine* ● ● ● eine Waschmaschine
  machine-readable passports ● ● ● maschinenlesbare Pässe

■ Eine Gruppe von – insbesondere großen – Maschinen wird meist als *machinery* bezeichnet.
Machinery ist nicht zählbar.
  a factory equipped with state-of-the-art machinery ● ● ● eine mit hochmodernen Maschinen
    ausgestattete Fabrik

> **Trouble Spot**
>
> ■ **Maschine**
> Die Maschine [= das Flugzeug] war voll. ● ● ● *The plane was full.*
> Suchmaschine [im Internet] ● ● ● *search engine* ['endʒɪn]
> (Geschirr-)Spülmaschine ● ● ● *dishwasher*
> (elektrische) Bohrmaschine ● ● ● *(electric) drill*
> Maschinenbau ● ● ● *mechanical engineering*

majority [mə'dʒɒrəti] Mehrheit **– minority** [maɪ'nɒrəti] Minderheit

■ **mit Singular- oder Pluralverb**
Das zu den Nomen *majority* und *minority* gehörende Verb kann im Singular oder im Plural stehen.
  The majority was / (BE auch:) *were against the plan.* ● ● ● Die Mehrheit war gegen den Plan.
Die Wendungen „*majority/minority of* + Pluralnomen" stehen aber immer mit einem Verb im Plural.
  The majority of people were (~~was~~) against it. ● ● ● Die Mehrheit der Leute war / waren dagegen.

make – do

1 ...... – A revision schedule so that I'm ready for the exam when it comes.
   A What are you making?   B What are you doing?

2 ...... – Revising the tenses.
   A What are you making?   B What are you doing?

3 A If everyone makes their best, we'll be able to make the best of a bad situation.
   B If everyone makes their best, we'll be able to do the best of a bad situation.
   C If everyone does their best, we'll be able to make the best of a bad situation.
   D If everyone does their best, we'll be able to do the best of a bad situation.

4 ...... because she's going to Madrid to study for six months.
   A She's making an intensive Spanish course   B She's doing an intensive Spanish course

5 ...... before you start a match.
   A You should always make some warm-up exercises
   B You should always do some warm-up exercises

6 I really think his parents were just trying ....
   A to make difficulties for him   B to do difficulties for him

7 The boy scouts' ethic of ...... – do you think that's old-fashioned?
   A 'making good'   B 'doing good'

8 A The Soviet leader and the US president made history that day.
   B The Soviet leader and the US president did history that day.

9 A I've made a very stupid mistake.   B I've done a very stupid mistake.

10 A Have you made your homework yet?   B Have you done your homework yet?

11 In the first six months ....
   A the new magazine made a loss of €30,000   B the new magazine did a loss of €30,000

12 ...... Did you hear it?
   A I wonder what made that noise.   B I wonder what did that noise.

13 A The builders have made a really good job.   B The builders have done a really good job.

14 A Do you do any sport?   B Do you make any sport?

15 A When are you doing your exams?   B When are you making your exams?

make* – do* machen [siehe auch Trouble Spot auf Seite 173]

■ *make sb. do* ▶ let

■ *Make* bedeutet „anfertigen", „herstellen", „erzeugen", „bauen", „zubereiten", „schaffen".
make a cake / a noise / a new road / a plan
*What **are** you **making**? – A bookshelf.*

■ *Do* bedeutet „erledigen", „verrichten", „sich betätigen mit", „sich beschäftigen mit".
do work / a job / some shopping
*What **do** you **do**? – I'm a teacher.* ● ● ● Was machen Sie (beruflich)? – …
*What **are** you **doing**? – Some repairs.* ● ● ● Was machen Sie (gerade)? – …

■ **Wendungen mit *make***
make an attempt ● ● ● einen Versuch machen/unternehmen
make the beds ● ● ● die Betten machen [= die Betten beziehen oder nach dem Schlafen wieder
  herrichten]
make the best of sth. ● ● ● das Beste aus etwas machen
make a difference ● ● ● einen Unterschied machen, etwas ausmachen
make difficulties for sb. ● ● ● jmdm. Schwierigkeiten machen/bereiten
make a discovery ● ● ● eine Entdeckung machen
make an exception ● ● ● eine Ausnahme machen
make a fire ● ● ● (ein) Feuer machen
make a habit of (doing) sth. ● ● ● sich etwas zur Gewohnheit machen, etwas zur Gewohnheit
  werden lassen
make history ● ● ● Geschichte machen
make an impression ● ● ● (einen) Eindruck machen
make silly jokes ● ● ● dumme Witze machen
make a loss / profit ● ● ● (einen) Verlust/Gewinn machen
make a mistake ● ● ● einen Fehler machen
make a noise ● ● ● ein Geräusch machen, Krach machen
make notes ● ● ● sich Notizen machen
make an offer / a suggestion ● ● ● ein Angebot / einen Vorschlag machen
make a phone call ● ● ● einen Anruf machen / telefonieren
make progress ● ● ● Fortschritte machen
make room ● ● ● Platz machen
make trouble ● ● ● Ärger machen
make a visit ● ● ● einen Besuch machen

■ **Wendungen mit *do***
do the beds ● ● ● die Betten machen [= das Bettenmachen als Teil der Hausarbeit erledigen,
  „abhaken"]
do one's best ● ● ● sein Möglichstes tun, sein Bestes tun/geben
do business ● ● ● Geschäfte machen
do the cleaning ● ● ● sauber machen, putzen
do a course ● ● ● einen Kurs machen
do the dishes / (BE auch:) the washing-up ● ● ● den Abwasch machen
do one's duty ● ● ● seine Pflicht tun
do an exam / a test ● ● ● eine Prüfung / einen Test machen/schreiben
do exercises ● ● ● Übungen machen
do sb. a favour ● ● ● jmdm. einen Gefallen tun
do good ● ● ● Gutes tun
do one's hair ● ● ● sich die Haare machen/richten, sich frisieren
do one's homework ● ● ● die/seine Hausaufgaben machen
do the housework ● ● ● die Hausarbeit machen
do / work overtime ● ● ● Überstunden machen
do sport ● ● ● Sport machen/treiben
do a translation ● ● ● eine Übersetzung machen

M

make – do [Fortsetzung von Seite 170]

1 *[Ich mache Diät]* this week. I want to lose two kilos by the weekend.
  A I'm on a diet **B** I'm doing a diet **C** I'm making a diet

2 ...... I can't remember going there.
  A Who did this photo? **B** Who made this photo? **C** Who took this photo?

3 We've been going non-stop for four and a half hours. ......
  A We really must make break. **B** We really must make a break.
  C We really must take a break.

4 ...... and the difficult ones right.
  A I did the easy sentences wrong **B** I got the easy sentences wrong
  C I made the easy sentences wrong **D** I wrote the easy sentences wrong

5 **A** Sheep don't make 'miaow', they make 'baah'.
  B Sheep don't do 'miaow', they do 'baah'.
  C Sheep don't go 'miaow', they go 'baah'.

6 I'm sorry, I've forgotten to bring your disc back. – ......
  A That makes nothing. **B** That does nothing. **C** Never mind. **D** That doesn't matter.

male – masculine

1 ...... have a black body and a yellow beak *[= Schnabel]*.
  A Male blackbirds **B** Masculine blackbirds

2 The word 'person' can of course be used ....
  A with either a male or female pronoun **B** with either a masculine or feminine pronoun

many – a lot of – lots of

1 **A** I eat a lot of tomatoes at this time of year.
  B I eat lots of tomatoes at this time of year.
  C I eat many tomatoes at this time of year.

2 It was still early, ...
  A and of course a lot have a lie-in on Sunday mornings
  B and of course many have a lie-in on Sunday mornings
  C and of course many people have a lie-in on Sunday mornings

3 **A** Jamalia wasn't to see her home again for a lot of years.
  B Jamalia wasn't to see her home again for many years.

marmalade – jam

1 You can have ....
  A lemon jam or strawberry jam **B** lemon jam or strawberry marmalade
  C lemon marmalade or strawberry jam **D** lemon marmalade or strawberry marmalade

marry – get married

1 **A** Which famous person was he once married?
  B Which famous person was he once married to?
  C Which famous person was he once married with?
  D Which famous person was he once marryed with?

2 **A** The princess married the poor peasant. **B** The princess married to the poor peasant.
  C The princess got married the poor peasant. **D** The princess got married to the poor peasant.

make* – do* [Fortsetzung des Eintrags von Seite 171]

Trouble Spot

■ **machen**

(eine) Diät machen, Diät halten ● ● ● **go on** / **be on** *a diet* ['daɪət]

einen Spaziergang machen ● ● ● **go for** *a walk*

Katzen machen „Miau". ● ● ● *Cats* **go** *'miaow'.*

ein Foto machen ● ● ● **take** *a photo*

(eine) Pause machen ● ● ● **take** *a break*

ein Picknick machen ● ● ● **have** *a picnic*

eine unangenehme Erfahrung machen ● ● ● **have** *an unpleasant experience*

ein Spiel machen ● ● ● **have** / **play** *a game*

Urlaub machen ● ● ● **have** / **take** *a holiday*

Im Test habe ich drei Aufgaben falsch gemacht. ● ● ● *In the test I* **got** *three items wrong.*

Das macht nichts. ● ● ● *That* **doesn't matter.** / **Never mind.**

male – masculine ['mæskjəlɪn] männlich ▷ female

■ *Male* bedeutet „männlich" im Sinne von „männlichen Geschlechts".

Is the animal **male** *or female?* ● ● ● Ist das Tier männlich oder weiblich?

■ *Masculine* bezeichnet das sprachliche Genus.

'His' is **masculine***, 'her' is feminine.* ● ● ● „His" ist männlich, „her" ist weiblich.

Masculine bedeutet außerdem „männlich" im Sinne von „maskulin", „typisch für einen Mann".

His face is very **masculine***.* ● ● ● Sein Gesicht hat sehr männliche Züge.

many – a lot of – lots of viele ▷ much

■ *many – a lot of*

In bejahten Aussagesätzen werden meist *a lot of* bzw. *lots of* gegenüber *many* bevorzugt.

A lot of *people are coming to the party.* ● ● ● Es kommen viele Leute zu der Party.

Vor Angaben der Dauer wie *minutes, hours* usw. sind jedoch *a lot of* bzw. *lots of* nicht möglich.

It was **many minutes** / **hours** / **weeks** / **months** / **years** *(~~a lot of minutes~~ / ~~hours~~ / ~~...~~) before anything*

happened. ● ● ● Es dauerte viele Minuten/Stunden/Wochen/Monate/Jahre, ehe etwas passierte.

■ *many (people)* / *a lot (of people)* / *lots (of people)*

„Viele" im Sinne von „viele Menschen" kann man im Rückbezug auf bereits genannte Personen mit dem Pronomen *many* (ohne nachfolgendes Nomen) oder mit *a lot* / *lots* wiedergeben.

Twenty years ago people had less technology. **Many** / **A lot** / **Lots** *didn't have a computer.*

● ● ● … Viele hatten noch keinen Computer.

Wenn es keinen solchen Rückbezug gibt, muss nach *many* / *a lot of* / *lots of* das Nomen *people* stehen.

Twenty years ago there was less technology in our homes. **Many people** / **A lot of people** /

Lots of people *didn't have a computer.* ● ● ● … Viele (Leute) hatten noch keinen Computer.

marmalade ['mɑːməleɪd] **– jam** Marmelade

■ *Marmalade* (Schreibweise beachten!) wird nur bei Marmeladen aus Zitrusfrüchten (Orangen, Zitronen usw.) verwendet.

toast and orange / *lemon* **marmalade** ● ● ● Toast mit Orangen-/Zitronenmarmelade

■ Andere Marmeladen (Konfitüren) werden als *jam* bezeichnet.

toast and strawberry **jam** ● ● ● Toast mit Erdbeermarmelade/-konfitüre

marry – get married heiraten ▷ wedding day

■ *Kate* **married** *Tom. = Kate* **got married** *to Tom.* ● ● ● Kate hat Tom geheiratet.

Kate and Tom **got married.** ● ● ● Kate und Tom haben geheiratet.

Kate **is married** *to Tom (~~is married with Tom~~).* ● ● ● Kate ist mit Tom verheiratet.

M

maximum

1 Don't expect a lot of people to be there. *[Maximal 30 oder 40]*, I would think.

   A A maximum of 30 or 40   B Maximally 30 or 40

may (do)

1 Which question is more polite?

   A Can I bring a friend?   B May I bring a friend?

2 Which is the more usual form?

   A You can leave your bags with me, it's no problem really.

   B You may leave your bags with me, it's no problem really.

3 Which sentence means the same as 'It will perhaps rain'?

   A It can rain.   B It may rain.   C It maybe rain.

4 *[Wir dürfen nicht zu spät schlafen gehen]*, or we won't be able to get up in time.

   A We haven't to go to bed too late

   B We may not go to bed too late

   C We mustn't go to bed too late

5 *[Darf man dort arbeiten]*, or do you need a work permit first?

   A Are you allowed to work there   B May you work there

6 *[Wir durften nirgendwo hingehen]* without an official guide.

   A We mustn't go anywhere

   B We shouldn't go anywhere

   C We weren't allowed to go anywhere

7 I told you. *[Du hättest ihnen deine Adresse nicht geben dürfen.]*

   A You mustn't have given them your address.

   B You shouldn't have given them your address.

   C You may not have given them your address.

8 I refuse to believe it. *[Es darf einfach nicht wahr sein.]*

   A It can't be true.   B It may not be true.   C It mustn't be true.   D It shouldn't be true.

9 *[Es dürfte nicht allzu schwierig sein]* to find a taxi, even at that time of night.

   A It mustn't be too difficult   B It oughtn't be too difficult   C It oughtn't to be too difficult

   D It shouldn't be too difficult   E It shouldn't to be too difficult

mean

1 A What means the word 'set' in this context?

   B What does the word 'set' mean in this context?

   C What is the word 'set' meaning in this context?

2 A By 'fast', we mean 'within the next two days'.

   B Under 'fast', we mean 'within the next two days'.

   C With 'fast', we mean 'within the next two days'.

3 *[Was meinst du?]* Is it a good idea or not?

   A What are you thinking?   B What do you mean?   C What do you think?

4 *[Wie ist deine Meinung?]*

   A What's your meaning?   B How's your meaning?   C What's your opinion?

maximum [ˈmæksɪməm] 1 Maximum 2 Maximal-, Höchst-

■ *maximum*: **Nomen und Adjektiv**

Maximum kann ein Nomen oder ein Adjektiv sein. Es gibt kein Adverb ~~maximally~~.

*Each class has **a maximum of** 28 children.* ● ● ● … maximal 28 Kinder.
*The trip will cost **a maximum of** €80 per person.* ● ● ● … kostet maximal 80 € pro Person.
*The **maximum** amount of baggage is 28 kg per passenger.* ● ● ● Die Höchstmenge an Gepäck …

may (do) (tun) dürfen; vielleicht (tun)

■ **Bedeutungen von *may***

Mit *may* kann man höflich um Erlaubnis bitten. *May* ist höflicher als *can*.

***May** I make a phone call?* ● ● ● Darf/Dürfte ich mal telefonieren?

Um eine Erlaubnis zu geben, wird eher *can* verwendet. *May* zum Ausdruck einer Erlaubnis wirkt förmlich-steif.

*You **can** use my phone if you want.* ● ● ● Du kannst/darfst mein Telefon benutzen, wenn du willst.
*"You **may** kiss me," said the frog.* ● ● ● „Du darfst mich küssen", sagte der Frosch.

Mit *may (not)* kann man auch ausdrücken, dass etwas möglicherweise der Fall ist.

*I **may** be a little late.* ● ● ● Vielleicht komme ich etwas später.
*I **may not** come.* ● ● ● Vielleicht komme ich gar nicht.

Trouble Spot

■ **(nicht) dürfen**

1 ein Verbot (auch gegenüber sich selbst) aussprechen

Nein, du darfst nicht auf die Party. ● ● ● *No, you **can't** go to the party.* /
 [fml und sehr entschieden:] *No, you **may not** go to the party.*
Du darfst es niemandem sagen. ● ● ● *You **mustn't** tell anyone.*
Ich darf Theos Geburtstag nicht vergessen. ● ● ● *I **mustn't** forget Theo's birthday.*

2 über eine Erlaubnis oder ein Verbot berichten; Fragen, ob etwas erlaubt ist

Man kann/darf hier parken. ● ● ● *You **can** park / You're **allowed to** park here.*
Man kann/darf hier nicht parken. ● ● ● *You **can't** park / You **aren't allowed to** park here.*
Kann/Darf man hier parken? ● ● ● ***Can** you park / **Are** you **allowed to** park here?*

3 über eine Erlaubnis oder ein Verbot in der Vergangenheit sprechen

Wir durften ein Wörterbuch benutzen. ● ● ● *We **were allowed to** use a dictionary.*
Wir durften kein Wörterbuch benutzen. ● ● ● *We **weren't allowed to** use a dictionary.*

4 ausdrücken, dass man etwas für (un)möglich oder (un)wahrscheinlich hält

Das darf nicht wahr sein! ● ● ● *That **can't** be true.*
Das dürfte genügen. ● ● ● *That **should** be / **ought to** be enough.*
Die Mädchen dürften inzwischen angekommen sein. ● ● ● *The girls **should have** arrived / **ought to have** arrived by now.*

mean* bedeuten, meinen

■ **nicht in der Verlaufsform**

Mean zählt zu den Verben, die man normalerweise nicht in der Verlaufsform verwenden kann.

*"What **does** the word **mean** (~~What's the word meaning~~) in this context?" asked the teacher.* ● ● ●
 „Was bedeutet das Wort in diesem Kontext?" …

■ *What do you **mean by** (~~mean with~~) 'soon'?* ● ● ● Was meinst du mit / verstehst du unter „bald"?

Trouble Spot

■ **meinen**

Entschuldigung. Ich habe es nicht so gemeint. ● ● ● *Sorry. I didn't **mean** it like that.*
Du warst nicht gemeint. ● ● ● *I didn't **mean** you.*
Was meinst [= denkst] du? Sollen wir es riskieren? ● ● ● *What do you **think**? Shall we risk it?*
Ich meine [= bin der Ansicht], wir sollten es nicht tun. ● ● ● *I don't **think** we should do it.*

■ **Meinung** ▶ opinion

Was/Wie ist deine Meinung zu dieser Sache? ● ● ● *What's your **opinion** on the matter?*

medium

1 Would you say Paderborn was *[eine mittelgroße Stadt]*?
  A a medium town **B** a medium-sized town **C** a middle town

2 Could you describe the man? – ......
  A Well, he was medium tall. **B** Well, he was middle tall. **C** Well, he was of medium height.

3 The owner was *[ein Mann mittleren Alters]*.
  A a middle-aged man **B** a man of average age
  C a man of moderate age **D** a moderately aged man

member

1 **A** I'm a member in a computer club. **B** I'm a member of a computer club.
  C I'm member in a computer club. **D** I'm member of a computer club.

mention

1 ...... , but they took no action.
  A I did mention the fact the police at the time
  B I did mention the police the fact at the time
  C I did mention the fact to the police at the time

menu ≠ „Menü"

1 If we take *[das Menü]*, we'll get three courses for the same amount of money.
  A the menu **B** the set menu **C** the set meal **D** the special

metre/meter – meter

1 It's only a small pool, ...
  A 25 metre long **B** 25 metres long **C** 25 meter long **D** 25 meters long

Middle Ages

1 ...... when a lot of things changed.
  A The Middle Age was a time **B** The Middle Ages was a time **C** The Middle Ages were a time

million

1 The new building will cost ....
  A over ten million euros **B** over ten millions euros
  C over ten million of euros **D** over ten millions of euros

2 The photo is made up of ....
  A million of little dots **B** millions of little dots **C** millions little dots

mind

1 ...... just a few centimetres that way, please?
  A Would you mind moving your bag **B** Would you mind to move your bag

Trouble Spot

medium ['miːdiəm] mittel-, mittlere(r/s) [Größe, Menge usw.]

- *a medium-sized town* ● ● ● eine mittelgroße/mittlere Stadt
  a man of medium height/build ● ● ● ein mittelgroßer Mann/Mann mittlerer Größe
  medium-length hair ● ● ● mittellange Haare

  - **mittel-, mittlere(r/s)**
    1 das mittlere Haus [= in der Mitte befindlich] ● ● ● the **middle** house
    eine Frau mittleren Alters/im mittleren Alter ● ● ● a **middle-aged** woman
    das Mittelalter ● ● ● the **Middle** Ages ▶ Middle Ages
    eine Mittelklassefamilie ● ● ● a **middle-class** family
    2 mittlere Temperaturen [= durchschnittlich] ● ● ● **average** ['ævərɪdʒ] temperatures

member Mitglied

- *a member (of sth.)*
  Is Sue a member of (Is Sue member in) a sports club? ● ● ● Ist Sue Mitglied in einem Sportverein?

mention erwähnen

- *mention sth. to sb.*
  Nach *mention* wird die Person, der gegenüber man etwas erwähnt, mit *to* angeschlossen.
  mention sth. to your best friend ● ● ● etwas gegenüber der besten Freundin erwähnen

menu ['menjuː] Speisekarte; Menü [auf dem Computermonitor]

M

!
!
!

- **False Friend!**
  Menu bedeutet in der Computersprache „Menü", sonst aber „Speisekarte".
  The waiter brought the menu. ● ● ● Der Kellner brachte die Speisekarte.
  Beachte die englischen Entsprechungen von „Menü" im Sinne von „Speisenfolge":
  Das Mittagsmenü ist billig. ● ● ● *The set lunch is cheap. | The set meal at lunchtime is cheap. |*
  The set menu (The menu) at lunchtime is cheap. | The lunchtime special is cheap.

metre (BE)/**meter** (AE) Meter – **meter** Zähler, Messgerät

- Das Längenmaß „Meter" wird im BE *metre*, im AE *meter* geschrieben.
  six (BE:) *metres* / (AE:) *meters long* [Plural-s beachten!]
- *Meter* bezeichnet im BE und AE einen Zähler bzw. ein Messgerät.
  electricity meter, parking meter ● ● ● Stromzähler, Parkuhr

Middle Ages [ˌmɪdl ˈeɪdʒɪz] Mittelalter

- **Pluralnomen**
  The Middle Ages were a hard time for ordinary people. ● ● ● Das Mittelalter war …

million ['mɪljən] Million

- *two/three/four million* [ohne Plural-s]
  two million euros (two millions euros) ● ● ● zwei Millionen Euro
- *millions of* [mit Plural-s]
  Millions of people died. [ohne Zahl vor *millions*] ● ● ● Millionen (von) Menschen starben.

mind etwas dagegen haben

- *mind doing*
  Nach *mind* verwendet man die *-ing*-Form des Verbs, keinen *to*-Infinitiv.
  Would you mind closing (mind to close) the window? ● ● ● Würde es Ihnen etwas ausmachen, das
  Fenster zu schließen?/Würden Sie bitte das Fenster schließen?

minus

1 It's been a very cold night. ......

   A It's minus ten degrees out there now.   **B** It's ten degrees minus out there now.

minute

1 It was a real race against time, ...

   A but we just made it, at the last minute

   B but we just made it, in the last minute

   C but we just made it, on the last minute

miss

1 In Florida we lived very close to the ocean. ......

   A Now I miss being able to just go across the road onto the beach.

   B Now I miss that I can't just go across the road onto the beach.

   C Now I miss the fact that I can't just go across the road onto the beach.

mistake

1 **A** We did the mistake not to pack enough warm clothes.

   B We did the mistake of not packing enough warm clothes.

   C We made the mistake not to pack enough warm clothes.

   D We made the mistake of not packing enough warm clothes.

2 *[Wir haben alle unsere Fehler.]*

   A We all have defects.   **B** We all have faults.   **C** We all have mistakes.

3 I'd have got a better mark in the test *[wenn ich nicht so viele Flüchtigkeitsfehler gemacht hätte]*.

   A if I hadn't made so many careless mistakes

   B if I hadn't made so many little mistakes

   C if I hadn't made so many slips

4 *[Als die Fehlermeldung auf dem Bildschirm erschien]*, I realized there was something seriously wrong with the computer.

   A When the error message came up on the screen

   B When the fault message came up on the screen

   C When the mistake announcement came up on the screen

mob ≠ „mobben"

1 What is the meaning of 'mobbed' in the following newspaper headline?
Olympic Athletes Mobbed On Return Home

   A *von großer Menschenmenge belagert*   **B** *scharf kritisiert*   **C** *schikaniert*

2 There have been problems with *[Mobbing]* at the school, but the situation is under control.

   A bullying   **B** harrassment   **C** mobbing

3 The boss swore that there was *[kein Mobbing]*, but employees told a different story.

   A no bullying   **B** no harrassment   **C** no mobbing

minus ['maɪnəs] minus ▷ multiply

■ **minus vor Gradzahl**
In Temperaturangaben steht *minus* immer **vor** der Gradzahl.
*It's **minus twelve degrees** outside.* ● ● ● Draußen sind minus zwölf Grad / zwölf Grad minus.

minute ['mɪnɪt] Minute

■ *arrive **at the last minute*** ● ● ● in letzter Minute ankommen
*I'll be with you **in a minute**, Mike.* ● ● ● Ich komme gleich/sofort zu dir, Mike. / Ich kümmere mich gleich/sofort um dich, Mike.

miss vermissen ▷ overhear ▷ oversee

■ **miss the fact that … – miss doing**
Nach *miss* kann *the fact that* oder eine *-ing*-Form stehen. *Miss that* (ohne *the fact*) ist nicht möglich.
*Tony's got a motorbike now. I **miss the fact that** (~~miss that~~) we no longer meet on the bus.* ● ● ●
… Ich vermisse, dass wir uns nicht mehr im Bus treffen.
*I **miss meeting** him on the bus.* ● ● ● Es fehlt mir, dass ich ihn nicht mehr im Bus treffe.

mistake Fehler

■ **make the mistake of doing**
Nach *make the mistake* folgt *of* + die *-ing*-Form des Verbs, kein *to*-Infinitiv.
*Tony **made the mistake of asking** (~~made the mistake to ask~~) his mother for permission.* ● ● ●
Tony machte/beging den Fehler, seine Mutter um Erlaubnis zu bitten.

Trouble Spot

■ **Fehler**
1 allgemein
Jeder macht mal Fehler. ● ● ● *Anyone can **make a mistake**.*

2 „Fehler in der Schule"
Grammatikfehler ● ● ● **grammatical mistake** / (fml:) **grammatical error** ['erə]
Vokabel-/Wortschatzfehler ● ● ● **vocabulary mistake** / (fml:) **vocabulary error**
(Recht-)Schreib-/Tippfehler ● ● ● **spelling/typing mistake** / (fml:) **spelling/typing error**
Druckfehler ● ● ● **printing error** / **misprint** ['mɪsprɪnt]
Flüchtigkeitsfehler ● ● ● **careless mistake** / **slip**

3 „Charakterfehler", „Schuld"
Ed hat einen Fehler. Er ist ein schlechter Verlierer. ● ● ● *Ed has a **fault** [fɔːlt]. He's a bad loser.*

4 „technischer Fehler"
Das System hat einen Fehler. ● ● ● *There's a **defect** [ˈdiːfekt; dɪˈfekt] / **fault** in the system.*

5 „Computerfehler"
Aufgrund eines Computerfehlers wurde das Geld zweimal abgebucht. ● ● ● *The money was debited twice because of a **computer error**.*
eine Fehlermeldung auf dem Bildschirm ● ● ● *an **error message** on the screen*
Es ist ein Hardwarefehler. ● ● ● *It's a **hardware failure** [ˈfeɪljə].*

mob herfallen über, belagern

■ **False Friend!**
Mob bedeutet nicht „~~mobben~~", sondern „herfallen über", „belagern". Das Verb *mob* steht meist im Passiv: *be mobbed*.
*The star **was mobbed** by enthusiastic fans.* ● ● ● Der Star wurde von begeisterten Fans belagert.
Beachte die englische Entsprechung von „Mobbing":
Mobbing in der Schule ● ● ● ***bullying** at school*
Mobbing am Arbeitsplatz ● ● ● ***bullying/harassment** [ˈhærəsmənt; həˈræsmənt] at work*

moment

1 A What exactly are you doing at the moment?
  B What exactly are you doing in the moment?
  C What exactly are you doing on the moment?

2 Look at those clouds. ……
  A It could start raining any moment.
  B It could start raining every moment.
  C It could start raining at every moment.

moonlight

1 There was a full moon that night, and we could see everything quite clearly …… .
  A in the light from the moon **B** in the moonlight **C** in the moonshine

moral – morals – morale

1 …… , always teach us something.
  A I think a good story should always have some sort of moral
  B I think a good story should always have some sort of morals
  C I think a good story should always have some sort of morale

2 We're well prepared …… .
  A and our moral is high **B** and our morals are high **C** and our morale is high

3 A novel of manners [= *Sittenroman*] tells you about …… .
  A the moral of a particular society
  B the morals of a particular society
  C the morale of a particular society

more: no more – no longer

1 …… He lost his job and had to sell it.
  A He doesn't have a car any more. **B** He has a car no more. **C** He no longer has a car.
  D He no more has a car. **E** He doesn't have a car any longer.

morning – afternoon – evening

1 We'll discuss this …… .
  A in the morning **B** on the morning **C** tomorrow morning

2 The next meeting is …… .
  A at the afternoon of 18th November
  B in the afternoon of 18th November
  C on the afternoon of 18th November

3 It happened …… .
  A at Friday evening **B** in Friday evening **C** on Friday evening

4 School finishes …… .
  A at five in the afternoon **B** at five in the afternoons **C** at 5 p.m.

5 We have a meeting every Wednesday morning [*Punkt 10 Uhr*].
  A at point 10 o'clock **B** at ten o'clock on the point **C** at ten o'clock sharp

moment ['məʊmənt] Augenblick

■ *It's not raining **at the moment**.* ● ● ● … im Moment / im Augenblick / zurzeit.
*They could arrive **(at) any moment** (~~every moment~~).* ● ● ● … jeden Augenblick …

moonlight Mondlicht, Mondschein

■ *The moon was shining. We could see the mountains in the **moonlight** (~~moonshine~~).* ● ● ● Der Mond schien. Wir konnten die Berge im Mondschein sehen.

moral ['mɒrəl] – morals ['mɒrəlz] – morale [məˈrɑːl] Moral

■ *the **moral** of the story* ● ● ● die Moral [= Botschaft, Lehre] der Geschichte

■ *The book tells us a lot about the **morals** [Plural!] of that time.* ● ● ● Das Buch vermittelt viel über die Moral [= Moralvorstellungen, sittliche Werte] jener Zeit.

■ *After six defeats, the team's **morale** is very low.* ● ● ● Nach sechs Niederlagen ist die Moral [= Stimmung] der Mannschaft sehr schlecht.

more: no more – no longer nicht mehr, kein(e) … mehr

■ *No more* verwendet man im modernen Englisch nur in Bezug auf eine Menge oder einen Grad, nicht aber im zeitlichen Sinne.
*I have **no more** money.* ● ● ● Ich habe kein Geld mehr.
*He's **no more** an expert than I am.* ● ● ● Er ist ebenso wenig Experte wie ich.

■ Im zeitlichen Sinne verwendet man *no longer* (Stellung meist vor dem Verb) oder *not any more / not any longer.*
*We **no longer** (~~no more~~) have a dog. / We **don't** have a dog **any more** / **any longer**.* ● ● ● Wir haben keinen Hund mehr.
*I **can't** stand **any more** / **any longer**.* ● ● ● Ich kann nicht mehr stehen.

morning Morgen, Vormittag – afternoon Nachmittag – evening Abend

■ *in the (early) morning* [allgemeine Tageszeit] ● ● ● am (frühen) Morgen, (früh) morgens
in the (late) afternoon [allgemeine Tageszeit] ● ● ● am (späten) Nachmittag, (spät) nachmittags
in the evening [allgemeine Tageszeit] ● ● ● am Abend, abends

■ *on Tuesday morning / on Tuesday mornings* ● ● ● am Dienstagmorgen / jeden Dienstagmorgen
on the afternoon of 1st May ● ● ● am Nachmittag des 1. Mai
on a cold evening in early spring ● ● ● an einem kalten Abend zu Beginn des Frühlings

Topic Box

■ *Talking about times of the day* ▶ a.m. / p.m. ▶ today
*You can't phone now. It's **two o'clock in the morning** there.* ● ● ● Du kannst jetzt nicht anrufen. Dort ist es zwei Uhr nachts/morgens.
*I'm tired. I'll finish my homework **in the morning** / **tomorrow morning**.* ● ● ● Ich bin müde. Ich mache meine Hausaufgaben morgen früh fertig.
*The countryside looks beautiful **at dawn** / **at dusk** / **at sunrise** / **at sunset**.* ● ● ● Die Landschaft sieht im Morgengrauen / in der Abenddämmerung / bei Sonnenaufgang / bei Sonnenuntergang wunderschön aus.
*What are you doing **at lunchtime**?* ● ● ● Was machst du heute Mittag?
*What are you doing **tonight** / **this evening**?* ● ● ● Was machst du heute Abend?
*Excuse me, **do you have the time**?* ● ● ● Entschuldigen Sie, wissen Sie, wie spät es ist?
*It's **just after seven**. / It's **a little after seven**.* ● ● ● Es ist kurz nach sieben.
*It's **just before six**. / It's **nearly six**. / It's **coming up for six**.* ● ● ● Es ist kurz vor sechs.
*I'll be back **(at) about** / **around seven**.* ● ● ● Ich bin gegen sieben zurück.
*Is late afternoon OK, **about** / **around five(ish)**?* ● ● ● Passt dir der späte Nachmittag, so gegen fünf?
*The meeting starts **at eight o'clock sharp**.* ● ● ● Die Sitzung beginnt (um) Punkt acht Uhr.

M

most

1 ...... , but gourmets ['gʊəmeɪz] live to eat.
  A Most people eat to live   **B** The most people eat to live

2 **A** Which shop has most special offers?
  B Which shop has the most of special offers?
  C Which shop has the most special offers?

3 **A** We spent most of our holiday just lazing around.
  B We spent the most of our holiday just lazing around.

motor – engine

1 We had to stop on the motorway. ......
  A There was something wrong with the engine.
  B There was something wrong with the machine.
  C There was something wrong with the motor.

2 Electric toothbrushes are driven ....
  A by very small electric engines   **B** by very small electric motors

much – many – a lot of – plenty of

1 ...... , and did a two-day sand-yachting course.
  A We swam a lot   **B** We swam a plenty   **C** We swam much

2 ...... – the train doesn't leave for another 50 minutes.
  A We have a lot of time   **B** We have much time   **C** We have plenty of time

3 **A** How many times have you been here?   **B** How much times have you been here?

4 **A** Did you eat quite a lot of fish?
  B Did you eat quite much fish?
  C Did you eat quite plenty of fish?

5 ...... The winters are generally very mild.
  A We don't have a lot of snow here.
  B We don't have much snow here.
  C We don't have lots of snow here.

multiply

1 ...... , we'll know how much drinking water we'll need to carry.
  A If we multiply three litres by the number of people and the number of days
  B If we multiply three litres and the number of people and the number of days
  C If we multiply three litres with the number of people and the number of days

2 How do you say this sum? $4 \times 6 = 24$
  A Four six is twenty-four.   **B** Four sixes are twenty-four.
  C Four times six is twenty-four.   **D** Four times six are twenty-four.

3 How do you say this sum? $24 \div 6 = 4$
  A Twenty-four divided by six is four.
  B Twenty-four through six is four.
  C Six into twenty-four is four.

most (der/die/das) meiste

■ **ohne** *the*

Most steht in aller Regel ohne den bestimmten Artikel.

> *Most people like sunny weather.* ● ● ● Die meisten Menschen [= die Mehrheit der Menschen] …
>
> *I've already spent **most of my money** (~~the most money~~/~~the most of my money~~).* ● ● ● … das meiste Geld [= den größten Teil meines Geldes] …

■ **(the) most**

Nur in (ausgesprochenen oder unausgesprochenen) Vergleichen kann *most* mit *the* stehen.

> *Nora got **(the) most points** in the test.* ● ● ● Nora bekam im Test die meisten Punkte.
> [im Vergleich zu den anderen Schülern/Schülerinnen]
>
> *Who had the job with **(the) most money**?* ● ● ● Wer hatte die Stelle mit dem meisten Geld?
> [im Vergleich zu den anderen Personen, an die man denkt]

motor [ˈməʊtə] – engine [ˈendʒɪn] Motor

■ Mit *motor* bezeichnet man meist den Elektromotor eines kleineren Gerätes.

> *an electric **motor*** ● ● ● ein Elektromotor

■ Den Motor in einem Kraftfahrzeug, Flugzeug, Boot oder Schiff bezeichnet man nicht als *motor*, sondern als *engine*.

> *We couldn't start the **engine**, so we had to push the car.* ● ● ● Wir konnten den Motor nicht starten/anlassen …
>
> *The pilot started the **engines**.* ● ● ● Die Pilotin startete die Triebwerke.

much viel – many viele – a lot of/lots of viel(e) – plenty of viel(e) ▶ many ▶ plenty

■ *Much* und *many* verwendet man vorwiegend in Fragen und verneinten Sätzen.

> *How much money/How many euros do you have?* ● ● ● Wie viel Geld/Wie viel(e) Euros …?
>
> *I **don't** have **much** free time/**many** free evenings.* ● ● ● … nicht viel Freizeit/nicht viele freie Tage.

■ In bejahten Sätzen benutzt man meist *a lot (of)*, *lots (of)* oder *plenty (of)*. Der Gebrauch von *much* als Objekt (oder Teil des Objekts) wirkt bisweilen so steif, dass er nicht akzeptabel ist.

> *What are your hobbies? – I read **a lot** (~~read much~~).* ● ● ● … – Ich lese viel.
>
> *We'll need **a lot of**/**lots of**/**plenty of** money (~~need much money~~). I don't think we have enough.* ● ● ● Wir werden viel Geld brauchen. …

Nach *quite* kann nur *a lot of* stehen.

> *We had **quite a lot of** time (~~quite much time~~).* ● ● ● … ziemlich viel Zeit.
>
> *We met **quite a lot of** people (~~quite many people~~).* ● ● ● … ziemlich/recht viele Leute …

■ **one … too many**

In der Konstruktion Zahlwort + Nomen + *too* steht *many*, nicht *much*.

> *You've had **one drink too many** (~~one drink too much~~).* ● ● ● Du hast einen Drink zu viel getrunken.

multiply [ˈmʌltɪplaɪ] multiplizieren, malnehmen

■ *What's 40 **multiplied by** (~~multiplied with~~) 25?* ● ● ● Wie viel ist 40 mal 25/40 multipliziert mit 25?

	■ **Numerical operations** ▶ nil	
Topic Box	$3 + 9 = 12$	Three **plus** nine is/equals twelve. / Three **and** nine is/are/make(s) twelve.
	$12 - 3 = 9$	Twelve **minus** three is/equals nine. / Twelve **take away** three is/leaves nine. / Three **from** twelve is/leaves nine.
	$3 \times 2 = 6$	Three **multiplied by** two is/equals six. / Three **times** two is six. / Three twos are six.
	$12 \div 4 = 3$	Twelve **divided by** four is/equals three. / Four **into** twelve is three.
	$3^2 = 9$	Three **squared** is nine.
	$8^3 = 512$	Eight **cubed** is 512.
	$6^4 = 1296$	Six **to the power of** four is 1296.

murder – murderer

1 It's a classic party game in which you have to find out ....
   A who is the murder   B who is the murdered   C who is the murderer

2 A When did the murder take place?   B When did the murderer take place?

music – musical

1 Don't you know it? ......
   A It's a piece of music by one of our most famous modern composers.
   B It's a piece of music from one of our most famous modern composers.

2 A They say that learning to play a music instrument makes you more intelligent.
   B They say that learning to play a musical instrument makes you more intelligent.

must – have to

1 Which sentence is more likely?
   A We must hand in our homework tomorrow.   B We have to hand in our homework tomorrow.

2 In this house, ...
   A if there's anything you don't like, you don't have to eat it
   B if there's anything you don't like, you don't need to eat it
   C if there's anything you don't like, you mustn't eat it

3 Which sentence is more likely?
   A I really have to remember to go to the bank.   B I really must remember to go to the bank.

narrow

1 These shoes are *[so eng]*! I really can't wear them for any length of time.
   A so close   B so limited   C so narrow   D so tight

2 She was *[eine sehr enge Freundin]*, and I'm so sorry to lose her.
   A a very close friend   B a very narrow friend   C a very tight friend

3 It was *[eine schmale Straße]* and there was nowhere where you could overtake.
   A a close road   B a limited road   C a narrow road   D a thin road   E a tight road

4 She has a very delicate, *[ein sehr schmales Gesicht]*.
   A a very small face   B a very narrow face   C a very thin face

nature

1 When you see an animal tear another to death, you think ....
   A nature can be very cruel   B the nature can be very cruel

2 ...... , that's why you hardly ever see one in the wild.
   A Leopards are very shy after nature   B Leopards are very shy by nature
   C Leopards are very shy from nature   D Leopards are very shy through nature

3 The air is so much better *[hier draußen in der Natur]*.
   A out here in nature   B out here in the nature   C out here in the countryside

near – nearby

1 A There's a river near, and you can hire boats from a near pub.
   B There's a river nearby, and you can hire boats from a nearby pub.
   C There's a river in the near, and you can hire boats from a nearby pub.

murder Mord, Ermordung – **murderer** Mörder/-in

■ The **murderer** had committed ten **murders**. ● ● ● Der Mörder hatte zehn Morde begangen.

music Musik – **musical** Musik-

■ a piece of **music by** Mozart (~~music from Mozart~~) ● ● ● ein Musikstück von Mozart
a **music** lesson ● ● ● eine Musikstunde

■ a **musical** instrument (~~music instrument~~) ● ● ● ein Musikinstrument

must – have* to müssen

■ Must drückt in der Regel einen vom Sprecher ausgehenden Befehl oder eine innere Überzeugung aus.
Passengers **must** show their passports. ● ● ● Passagiere sind verpflichtet, ihren Pass vorzuzeigen.
We **must** meet more often. ● ● ● Wir müssen uns wirklich öfter treffen.

■ Have to drückt in der Regel aus, was von anderen angeordnet oder durch Umstände erzwungen wird/wurde.
We **have to** park here. The road is closed to traffic from here on. ● ● ● Wir müssen hier parken. …
I **have to** go now, or I'll miss my bus. ● ● ● Ich muss [gezwungenermaßen] jetzt gehen …

Trouble Spot

■ **nicht müssen** ▷ need
Du musst Sue nichts von der Party sagen. Sie weiß Bescheid. ● ● ● You **needn't** tell Sue/
don't have to tell Sue/**don't need to** tell Sue about the party. She knows.
Beachte: Dem englischen Verb mustn't entspricht das deutsche Verb „nicht dürfen".
You **mustn't** tell Sue about the party. It's a secret. ● ● ● Du darfst Sue nichts … erzählen. …

N

narrow eng, schmal

■ a **narrow** road ● ● ● eine enge/schmale [= nicht breite] Straße
have a **narrow/limited** outlook on life things ● ● ● einen engen [= begrenzten] Horizont haben

Trouble Spot

■ **eng, schmal**
1 eine enge [= eng anliegende] Hose ● ● ● a **tight** pair of trousers
ein enger [= naher vertrauter] Freund ● ● ● a **close** [kləʊs] friend
ein enger [= beengter beschränkter] Raum ● ● ● a **cramped/constricted** space/room
eng [= dicht gedrängt] beieinander sitzen/stehen ● ● ● sit/stand **close together**
2 ein schmales [= dünnes] Buch ● ● ● a **thin** book
ein schmales [= dünnes/schlankes] Gesicht ● ● ● a **thin/narrow** face

nature ['neɪtʃə] Natur

■ **ohne** the
Nature wird in Aussagen allgemeiner Art ohne den bestimmten Artikel verwendet.
the wonders/laws of **nature** (~~of the nature~~) ● ● ● die Wunder/Gesetze der Natur

■ aggressive/shy **by nature** ● ● ● von Natur (aus) aggressiv/schüchtern

Trouble Spot

■ **die Natur**
Am Wochenende muss ich raus in die (freie) Natur [Gegensatz zu „Stadt"]. ● ● ● At the weekend I have to get out into **the open air/the countryside**.
Im Herbst sieht die Natur [Landschaft] so schön aus. ● ● ● In autumn **the countryside** looks so beautiful.

near in der Nähe (von) – **nearby** nahe (gelegen); in der Nähe ▷ by ▷ next

■ I live **near (to)** the station. [Präposition] ● ● ● … nahe am/beim Bahnhof/in der Nähe des Bahnhofs.
We swam at a **nearby** beach. [Adjektiv] ● ● ● … an einem nahe gelegenen Strand.
Do you live **near/nearby**? [Adverb] ● ● ● … in der Nähe?

need

1   **A**   There wasn't a queue and we didn't need wait.
  B   There wasn't a queue and we didn't need to wait.
  C   There wasn't a queue and we needn't wait.
  D   There wasn't a queue and we needn't to wait.

2   Thank you for the present, ...
  A   but you really didn't need to buy me anything
  B   but you really needn't have bought me anything
  C   but you really needn't to have bought me anything

3   ...... So I went straight up to my hotel room.
  A   I didn't need check in, because my parents had already done it for me.
  B   I didn't need to check in, because my parents had already done it for me.
  C   I needn't have checked in, because my parents had already done it for me.

4   These shoes are soaking wet ....
  A   and will need dry   **B**   and will need drying   **C**   and will need to be dried

5   **A**   There was an accident and I needed over an hour.
  B   There was an accident and it took me over an hour.
  C   There was an accident and the journey took me over an hour.

neither – none – no

1   **A**   Neither place had a hotel.
  B   None of both places had a hotel.
  C   No place of the two had a hotel.

2   **A**   There are said to be leopards in the park, but we saw neither.
  B   There are said to be leopards in the park, but we saw no.
  C   There are said to be leopards in the park, but we saw none.

3   ...... Just tell me how it happened.
  A   I want neither of all your usual excuses.
  B   I want no of all your usual excuses.
  C   I want none of all your usual excuses.

4   **A**   I'm sorry, but I really have no time at all.   **B**   I'm sorry, but I really have none time at all.

5   **A**   I wanted to ask one of the neighbours, but no was at home.
  B   I wanted to ask one of the neighbours, but no were at home.
  C   I wanted to ask one of the neighbours, but none was at home.
  D   I wanted to ask one of the neighbours, but none were at home.

need brauchen, (tun) müssen   ▷ must

■ *need* als Vollverb

Need kann immer als Vollverb (mit nachfolgendem *to*-Infinitiv und mit *do*-Umschreibung in verneinten Sätzen und Fragen) verwendet werden.

He **needs to see** a doctor. ● ● ● Er muss zum Arzt gehen.

You **don't need to come** if you don't want to. ● ● ● Du brauchst nicht (zu) kommen …

■ *need* als Modalverb

Need als Modalverb (ohne *do*-Umschreibung und mit nachfolgendem Infinitiv ohne *to*) steht hauptsächlich in verneinten Sätzen im BE.

You **needn't come** if you don't want to. ● ● ● Du brauchst nicht (zu) kommen …

■ *didn't need to* und *needn't have done*

Mit *didn't need to do* und *needn't have done* (hauptsächlich BE) spricht man über die Vergangenheit. Beachte den unterschiedlichen Gebrauch.

John had lots of time, so he **didn't need to hurry**. [John hat sich nicht beeilt.] ● ● ● John hatte viel Zeit. Deshalb brauchte er sich nicht (zu) beeilen / musste er sich nicht beeilen.

John got there much too early. As it turned out, (BE:) he **needn't have hurried** / (AE:) he **didn't need to hurry**. [John hat sich umsonst beeilt.] ● ● ● John war viel zu früh dort. Wie sich herausstellte, hätte er sich nicht so (zu) beeilen brauchen / hätte er sich nicht so beeilen müssen.

■ *need doing*

Anstelle des Infinitivs Passiv verwendet man nach dem Vollverb *need* oft die *-ing*-Form.

The whole house **needs painting** [= **needs to be painted**]. ● ● ● … muss gestrichen werden.

Trouble Spot

■ **brauchen**

1 Ich brauche eine Pause. [= nötig haben, benötigen] ● ● ● I **need** a break.

2 Ich habe eine Stunde für die Übungen gebraucht. [= Zeit brauchen, in Anspruch nehmen] ● ● ● The exercises **took me** an hour. / It **took me** an hour **to do** the exercises.

Ich brauche eine halbe Stunde zur Schule. ● ● ● It **takes me** half an hour **to get** to school.

N

neither [ˈnaɪðə, ˈniːðə] keine(r/s) – **none** [nʌn] keine(r/s) – **no** kein(e)   ▷ both

■ *neither*   ▷ also

Neither bedeutet „keine(r/s) von beiden", „beide nicht". *Neither* wird als Begleiter **oder** Pronomen verwendet.

Neither team played well. [Begleiter] ● ● ● Keines der beiden Teams spielte gut. / Beide Teams spielten nicht gut.

They had tea and coffee, but I drink **neither (of them)**. [Pronomen] ● ● ● … aber ich trinke beides nicht / keines von beiden.

■ *none*   ▷ nobody   ▷ nothing

None bedeutet „keine(r/s) von mehreren". *None* wird nur als Pronomen verwendet.

Did you know any of the people at the party? – No, I knew **none of them**. ● ● ● … keinen.

We've got all the Harry Potter books, but I've read **none (of them)**. ● ● ● … keines (davon) …

■ *no*

No („kein", „keine") wird im Gegensatz zu *none* nur als Begleiter verwendet.

There were **no tickets** left. ● ● ● … keine Karten mehr da.

■ **Verb im Singular oder Plural**

Ein Verb nach *neither* oder *none* kann – je nach Bezugswort – im Singular oder im Plural stehen.

Neither answer is correct. [Bezugswort: *answer*, Singular] ● ● ● Keine der beiden Antworten ist …

Neither of the answers **is/are** correct. [Bezugswort: *neither* (= not one), Singular, oder *answers*, Plural] ● ● ● Keine der beiden Antworten stimmt. / Die Antworten sind beide falsch.

None of this **is** true. [Bezugswort: *this*, Singular] ● ● ● Nichts davon stimmt.

None of these pens **works/work**. [Bezugswort: *none* (= not one), Singular, oder *pens*, Plural] ● ● ● Keiner dieser Füller funktioniert.

newest – latest

1 The phrase 'it's all the rage' means ....

   A 'it's the latest fashion'   **B** 'it's the newest fashion'

2 I've been on eBay. There are six boats on offer. ......

   A The latest is just six months old and has never been sailed.

   B The newest is just six months old and has never been sailed.

news

1 **A** I've heard a very sad news.

   B I've heard a very sad piece of news.

   C I've heard some very sad news.

2 **A** The news from Iraq aren't good.

   B The news from Iraq isn't good.

next – nearest

1 We broke down in the middle of nowhere. ......

   A The nearest towns to where it happened were both over 20 miles away.

   B The next towns to where it happened were both over 20 miles away.

2 ...... , is dry your wet clothes.

   A The next we must do   **B** The next thing we must do   **C** The next what we must do

3 You won't be seeing much of me *[in nächster Zeit]*. I've found a part-time job.

   A in next time   **B** in the next time   **C** in the next few weeks

nil – zero – nought – oh – love

1 ...... It's minus 12, isn't it?

   A Minus 6 minus 6 isn't nil.   **B** Minus 6 minus 6 isn't nought.

   C Minus 6 minus 6 isn't oh.   **D** Minus 6 minus 6 isn't zero.

2 **A** The exact figure is six point nil three (6.03).

   B The exact figure is six point nought three (6.03).

   C The exact figure is six point zero three (6.03).

3 **A** How many noughts are there in a billion?   **B** How many ohs are there in a billion?

   C How many zeros are there in a billion?   **D** How many zeroes are there in a billion?

4 In the winter the temperature can drop to as low as ....

   A 40 below nought   **B** 40 below zero   **C** 40 under nought   **D** 40 under zero

5 **A** My mobile number is nil one six four, then ... Sorry, I've forgotten.

   B My mobile number is nought one six four, then ... Sorry, I've forgotten.

   C My mobile number is oh one six four, then ... Sorry, I've forgotten.

   D My mobile number is zero one six four, then ... Sorry, I've forgotten.

6 **A** We lost two to nil.   **B** We lost by two goals to nil.   **C** We lost two nil.

newest – latest neueste(r/s)

■ *Newest* ist das Gegenteil von *oldest*.
*The oldest car in the car park is a 1957 Buick, the **newest** a brand new Toyota.*

■ „Neueste(r/s)" im Sinne von „(bisher) letzte(r/s)", „aktuellste(r/s)" drückt man meist mit *latest* aus.
*the **latest** news / report / information / fashion trend / model*
*Have you heard the **latest**?* ● ● ● Weißt du schon das Neueste?

news Nachricht(en)

■ **nicht zählbares Nomen**
News ist nicht zählbar; man kann es also nicht mit *a* verwenden.
*I have **some** interesting **news** / an interesting **piece of news** (~~an interesting news~~).* ● ● ● Ich habe
interessante Nachrichten / eine interessante Nachricht.
Das zu *news* gehörende Verb steht im Singular.
*The **news is** good.* ● ● ● Die Nachricht ist / Die Nachrichten sind gut.

next – nearest nächste(r/s)

■ **nächste(r/s)**
1 „(räumlich/zeitlich) nächstfolgend"
Nimm die nächste Straße rechts. ● ● ● *Take the **next** street on the right.*
Die nächste Tür, die ich probierte, war abgesperrt. ● ● ● *The **next** door I tried was locked.*
(am) nächsten Freitag ● ● ● ***next** Friday*
Ich habe in der nächsten Zeit / in nächster Zeit ziemlich viel zu tun. ● ● ● *I have quite a lot
to do **in the next few days** / **weeks** / **months** (~~in the next time~~).*
Das Nächste, was du machen musst, ist … ● ● ● ***The next thing** you have to do is …*

2 „nächstgelegen", „räumlich am nächsten"
Die nächsten Nachbarn waren einen Kilometer entfernt. ● ● ● *The **nearest** neighbours
were one kilometre away.*

N

nil – zero – nought [nɔːt] – oh – love null

■ **null**
1 „die Ziffer 0" [z. B. beim Rechnen]
Eine Million ist eine Eins mit sechs Nullen. ● ● ● *A million is a one and six **zeros** /
(BE auch:) a one and six **noughts**.*
6,08 = sechs Komma null acht ● ● ● *6.08 = six point **zero** eight / (BE auch:) six point **nought**
eight*
Fünf minus fünf ist null. ● ● ● *Five minus five is (BE:) **nought** / (AE:) **zero**.*

2 „Nullpunkt"
Wir haben zehn Grad unter null. ● ● ● *It's ten (degrees) below **zero**.*
Die Inflationsrate ist null. ● ● ● *The inflation rate is **zero**.*
von null auf 100 beschleunigen ● ● ● *accelerate from (BE:) **nought** / (AE:) **zero** to 100*

3 „null" in Telefon- und Kontonummern
Die Telefon-/Kontonummer lautet sechs null … ● ● ● *The phone / account number is
(BE:) six **oh** … / (meist AE:) six **zero** …*

4 „null" in Spielstandangaben beim Sport
Das Spiel endete null zu null. ● ● ● *The match ended (BE:) **nil-nil** / (AE:) **zero to zero**.*
Unsere Mannschaft hat drei zu null gewonnen. ● ● ● *Our team won three **nil**. / Our team won
by three goals to **nil**.*
Es / Das Spiel steht zwei zu null. ● ● ● *The score is two **love**.* [bei Tennis, Tischtennis, Squash,
Badminton]

Trouble Spot

nobody / no one – somebody/someone

1 A Nobody will ever find out, will he?
  B Nobody will ever find out, will one?
  C Nobody will ever find out, will they?

2 A Somebody can bring a dictionary with him, can't he?
  B Somebody can bring a dictionary with them, can't they?

3 A One of his relatives has a skiing lodge in the Rockies.
  B Somebody of his relatives has a skiing lodge in the Rockies.

4 A Somebody from the other team has offered to give me a lift.
  B Somebody of the other team has offered to give me a lift.

note ≠ „Note"

1 A note can be ....
  A a piece of paper you have written on   B a sound in music
  C some paper money   D something you write down

2 [Was für eine Note] did you get? – 'B', I was really pleased.
  A What grade   B What mark   C What note

nothing

1 Rats are clever. ......
  A None of the poison had been touched.   B Nothing of the poison had been touched.

2 I tried lots of websites, ...
  A but I didn't find anything interesting
  B but I found nought interesting
  C but I found nothing interesting

notice ≠ „Notiz"

1 What is the nearest synonym for 'notice'?
  A letter sent by post   B poster   C Post-it sticker

2 I took [so viele Notizen], it's going to take me half a day to write them up!
  A so many notes   B so many notices

3 What time did you say? 6.30? ......
  A I'll make a notice so I don't forget.
  B I'll make a note so I don't forget.
  C I'll take a notice so I don't forget.
  D I'll take a note so I don't forget.

nobody / no one niemand – somebody / someone jemand

■ **Rückbezug mit** *they, them, their*

Zum Rückbezug auf *nobody / no one* bzw. *somebody/someone* verwendet man die Pluralformen *they, them, their*.

Nobody *seems to care, do* **they**? ● ● ● Niemand scheint sich zu kümmern, nicht wahr?

Somebody *always forgets to bring* **their** *passport with* **them**. ● ● ● Irgendjemand vergisst immer seinen Pass.

■ *none/one of – somebody/nobody from* ▶ **neither**

Um zu sagen, dass niemand/jemand aus einer Gruppe etwas tut, verwendet man nicht *nobody of / somebody of*, sondern *none of* bzw. *one of.*

None of my friends (Nobody of my friends) *was/were at the party.* ● ● ● Niemand/Keiner von meinen Freunden war auf der Party.

One of us (Somebody of us) *should warn him.* ● ● ● Jemand/Einer von uns sollte ihn warnen.

Möglich sind aber *somebody from / nobody from* + eine Sammelbezeichnung (für eine Gruppe).

Somebody from the palace guard *took him to the king.* ● ● ● Jemand/Einer von der Palastwache brachte ihn zum König.

note Notiz, Zettel; Geldschein ▶ **notice** *(noun)* ▶ **notice** *(verb)* ▶ **excuse** *(noun)*

■ **False Friend!**

Note bedeutet nicht „Note" (außer in der Musik: *sing a high note*), sondern „Notiz", „Zettel", „Geldschein".

I **made a note** *so that I wouldn't forget.* ● ● ● Ich habe mir eine Notiz gemacht …

Did you **take** *any* **notes** *during the last lesson?* ● ● ● Hast du … mitgeschrieben?

I left a **note** *for my mum on the kitchen table.* ● ● ● Ich habe auf dem Küchentisch einen Zettel für meine Mutter hinterlassen.

I'm sorry, I only have a €50 **note** (meist BE). ● ● ● Ich habe nur einen 50-Euro-Schein.

Beachte die englischen Entsprechungen von „(Schul-/Zeugnis-)Note", „Zensur":

eine gute/schlechte Note in Französisch bekommen ● ● ● *get a good/poor* (BE:) **mark** / (meist AE:) **grade** *in French*

nothing nichts

■ **Nothing** *has been eaten.* ● ● ● Es ist nichts gegessen worden.

Mrs Cox does **nothing but** *grumble.* ● ● ● Frau Cox macht nichts anderes, als sich zu beschweren. / Frau Cox beschwert sich andauernd.

Wenn „nichts" als Objekt verwendet wird, wird es häufig mit *not anything* wiedergegeben.

I **didn't** *say* **anything**. = *I said* **nothing**. ● ● ● Ich habe nichts gesagt.

■ *none of* ▶ **neither**

Vor *of* + Nomen verwendet man nicht *nothing*, sondern *none*, wenn „kein Teil einer Menge" gemeint ist.

None of the bread (Nothing of the bread) *has been eaten.* ● ● ● Nichts von dem Brot ist gegessen worden.

notice ['nəʊtɪs] Bekanntmachung, Mitteilung, Aushang ▶ **note**

■ **False Friend!**

Notice bedeutet nicht „Notiz" (außer in der Wendung *take (no) notice of sb./sth.*), sondern „Bekanntmachung", „Mitteilung", „Aushang", „Schild".

a **notice** *on the door* ● ● ● eine Mitteilung / ein Aushang / ein Schild an der Tür

Beachte die englische Entsprechung von „Notiz(en)":

sich schnell ein paar Notizen machen ● ● ● *make a few quick* **notes**

sich Notizen machen [= mitschreiben, protokollieren] ● ● ● *take* **notes**

ein Notizblock ● ● ● *a* **notepad**

N

notice – realize/realise – remember – note

1 The building must have been there all the time, ...

  A but I'd never noted it   **B** but I'd never noticed it

  C but I'd never realized it   **D** but I'd never remembered it

2 *[Schließlich und endlich merkte ich]* what my mistake had been. What a fool I had been!

  A At long last I noted   **B** At long last I noticed

  C At long last I realized   **D** At long last I remembered

3 Some people are good at it, ...

  A but I just can't note jokes   **B** but I just can't remember jokes   **C** but I just can't keep jokes

4 **A** Please note that this office will be closed on Monday afternoon.

  B Please realize that this office will be closed on Monday afternoon.

number

1 **A** The number of deaths from lung cancer has gone down.

  B The number of deaths from lung cancer have gone down.

2 **A** A number of people has been arrested.

  B A number of people have been arrested.

3 **A** You'll only need a little number of nails to fix it.

  B You'll only need a small number of nails to fix it.

4 **A** We've had a big number of applications.

  B We've had a large number of applications.

object

1 ...... I just don't like being treated like an idiot!

  A I don't object to be asked questions.   **B** I don't object to being asked questions.

2 ...... , but there was nothing he could do about it.

  A Tom objected that he was made to wait

  B Tom objected to that he was made to wait

  C Tom objected to the fact that he was made to wait

obvious

1 ...... , but no one said anything.

  A It was obvious for everyone who had made the mistake

  B It was obvious to everyone who had made the mistake

  C It was obvious with everyone who had made the mistake

offer

1 ...... , but I didn't take it.

  A They offered me €8000   **B** They offered €8000 to me

  C I was offered €8000   **D** Me was offered €8000

2 Jilly is nice. ......

  A She's offered us that she'll take us to the airport.

  B She's offered to take us to the airport.

Trouble Spot

■ **(be)merken, sich merken**

1 „mit den Sinnen wahrnehmen"

Wo warst du? Ich habe dich nicht bemerkt. ● ● ● *Where were you? I didn't **notice** you.*

2 „sich einer Sache bewusst werden", „erkennen" ▷ realize

Ich (be)merkte plötzlich, dass ich die Adresse vergessen hatte. ● ● ● *I suddenly **realized** that I had forgotten the address.*

3 „im Gedächtnis behalten" ▷ remember

Ich kann mir keine Namen merken. ● ● ● *I have trouble **remembering** names.*

4 „besonders beachten und danach handeln"

Bitte merken: Morgen fällt die letzte Stunde aus. ● ● ● *Please **note**: the last lesson is cancelled tomorrow.*

number Zahl, Nummer; Anzahl

■ *the* **number of** + Singularverb

Nach *the number of* steht das Verb im Singular.

***The number of** cars **has** decreased.* ● ● ● Die Zahl der Autos ist zurückgegangen.

■ *a* **number of** + Pluralverb

A number of hat die gleiche Bedeutung wie *some*. Danach folgt das Verb im Plural.

***A number of** questions **were** asked.* ● ● ● Es wurde eine Reihe von Fragen gestellt. / Es wurden mehrere/einige Fragen gestellt.

■ *a **large**/**small** number of insects (a big/little number of ...)* ● ● ● eine große/kleine Anzahl Insekten

■ *You can reach me **at**/**on** this number.* ● ● ● Du kannst mich unter dieser (Telefon-)Nummer erreichen.

O

object [əb'dʒekt] etwas dagegen haben, dagegen sein

■ *object to doing*

In *object to* ist *to* eine Präposition. Da ein Verb nach einer Präposition in der *-ing*-Form steht, folgt auf *object to* eine *-ing*-Form und kein Infinitiv.

*Stella **objected to being** (objected to be) paid less than a man.* ● ● ● Stella hatte etwas dagegen / war nicht damit einverstanden, weniger Geld als ein Mann zu bekommen.

■ *object to the fact that ...*

Ein *that*-Satz kann nicht direkt an *object to* angeschlossen werden, sondern nur in Verbindung mit einem Ausdruck wie *the fact that*.

*Stella **objected to the fact that** (objected that) she was paid less than a man.* ● ● ● Stella hatte etwas dagegen / war nicht damit einverstanden, dass sie weniger Geld als ein Mann bekam.

obvious ['ɒbviəs] offensichtlich

■ *It was **obvious to** (obvious for) everyone what had happened.* ● ● ● Es war jedem / für jeden klar ...

offer anbieten

■ *offer sb. sth. / offer sth. to sb.*

*They **offered** me the job. / They **offered** the job **to** me.* ● ● ● Sie boten mir die Stelle an.

*I was **offered** the job. (Me was offered the job.)* ● ● ● Mir wurde die Stelle angeboten. / Man bot mir die Stelle an.

■ *offer to do*

*Julia **offered to feed** her neighbours' cat.* ● ● ● Julia bot an, die Katze ihrer Nachbarn zu füttern.

Nicht möglich sind *offer sb. to do* und *offer (sb.) + that*-Satz.

Julia offered her neighbours to feed their cat.

Julia offered (her neighbours) that she would feed their cat.

old – ancient – antique

1 Life as a slave ...... was a miserable existence.

  A in ancient Egypt **B** in old Egypt **C** in antique Egypt

once

1 ...... It wasn't as bad as I thought it would be.

  A I've eaten haggis once. **B** I've eaten haggis onetime. **C** I've eaten haggis one time.

2 *[Meine Mutter hat früher einmal geraucht]*, but that was years ago before she knew better!

  A My mother has smoked earlier **B** My mother has smoked once

  C My mother once smoked **D** My mother used to smoke

3 ...... and live there for a couple of months.

  A Once, when I have enough money, I'd like to visit Japan

  B One day, when I have enough money, I'd like to visit Japan

  C One time, when I have enough money, I'd like to visit Japan

  D Sometime, when I have enough money, I'd like to visit Japan

4 If I hear you say that *[noch einmal]*, I'll explode!

  A once **B** once more **C** again

5 They gave me two copies anyway. *[Ich musste nicht einmal fragen.]*

  A I didn't once have to ask. **B** I didn't even have to ask.

one – you – they – people

1 Choose the best translation:

The exam's dead easy. *[Man muss fünf Multiplechoicefragen beantworten.]* That's all.

  A One has to answer fifty multiple-choice questions.

  B People have to answer fifty multiple-choice questions.

  C They have to answer fifty multiple-choice questions.

  D You have to answer fifty multiple-choice questions.

2 *[Man sagt]* the house is haunted, but I don't believe nonsense like that.

  A One says **B** People say **C** They say **D** You say

3 **A** How do you spell 'rhythm'? – R H Y T H M.

  B How do people spell 'rhythm'? – R H Y T H M.

  C How is 'rhythm' spelt? – R H Y T H M.

only

1 I'd heard the name before, ...

  A but only then did I realize who she was

  B but only then I did realize who she was

  C but only then I realized who she was

2 *[Das Einzige, was ich sicher weiß]* is that it's going to be hellishly expensive.

  A The one that I know for certain **B** The only that I know for certain

  C The only thing that I know for certain **D** The single that I know for certain

3 *[Diana ist die Einzige, die weiß]* how to work the lighting equipment.

  A Diana is the only who knows **B** Diana is the only person who knows

  C Diana is the only one who knows **D** Diana is the single who knows

old – ancient ['eɪnʃənt] **– antique** [ænˈtiːk] **alt** ▷ age

Trouble Spot

■ **alt**
eine alte Frau [bei Lebewesen] ● ● ● *an old woman*
ein altes Auto [= nicht mehr neu] ● ● ● *an old car*
alte Geschichte/Kulturen [= das Altertum betreffend] ● ● ● ***ancient*** *history/civilizations*
das alte Rom ● ● ● ***ancient*** *Rome (the ancient Rome)*
wunderschöne alte Möbel [= von antiquarischem Wert] ● ● ● *beautiful **antique** furniture*

once [wʌns] **einmal**

■ *I've only been to Scotland **once** (one time).* ● ● ● Ich war erst einmal in Schottland.
***Once** one is one.* ● ● ● Einmal eins ist eins.
***once** a week* ● ● ● einmal in der Woche

Trouble Spot

■ **(ein)mal**
1 „irgendwann einmal in der Vergangenheit" ▷ used to
Er war (ein)mal ein berühmter Schauspieler. ● ● ● *He **once** was a famous actor. / He was
a famous actor **at one time**. / He **used to** be a famous actor.*
Wir waren schon (ein)mal in Polen. ● ● ● *We've been to Poland **before**.*
Seid ihr schon (ein)mal in Polen gewesen? ● ● ● *Have you **ever** been to Poland?*
Es war einmal … [im Märchen] ● ● ● ***Once upon a time** there was …*

2 „irgendwann einmal in der Zukunft"
Ich möchte einmal fliegen lernen. ● ● ● *I'd like to learn to fly **one day** / **sometime**.*

3 „noch einmal"
Ich sage es noch (ein)mal. ● ● ● *I'll say it **again** / **once more**.*

4 „nicht einmal"
Er hat mich nicht (ein)mal angesehen. ● ● ● *He did**n't even** look at me.*

O

one – you – they – people man

■ Dem deutschen Wort „man" entsprechen im Englischen *one* und *you*. *One* ist sehr förmlich.
***One** can never be too careful.* (fml) ● ● ● Man kann nicht vorsichtig genug sein.
Im Alltagsenglisch verwendet man *you*.
*Today he might say 'yes', tomorrow 'no'. **You** never know what he'll say.* ● ● ● … Man weiß nie …
***You** have to drive on the left in Britain.* ● ● ● Man muss in Großbritannien links fahren.
*How do **you** spell that?* ● ● ● Wie schreibt man das?

■ Oft wird das deutsche „man" im Englischen durch eine Passivform ausgedrückt.
*Nothing could **be done**.* ● ● ● Man konnte nichts machen.

■ *They* und *people* entsprechen „man" im Sinne von „die Leute".
***They** / **People** say the old man is a millionaire.* ● ● ● Man sagt …

only 1 nur, erst 2 einzige(r/s) ▷ first

■ *only am Satzanfang + Hilfsverb + Subjekt (= „Inversion")*
Only ist oft Teil einer adverbialen Bestimmung (z. B. *only slowly, only later*). Steht eine adverbiale
Bestimmung mit *only* am Satzanfang, verwendet man dieselbe Wortstellung wie in einer Frage.
***Only slowly did I** realize (Only slowly I realized) what happened.* ● ● ● Nur langsam begriff ich …
***Only later was I** told (Only later I was told) what happened.* ● ● ● Erst später wurde mir gesagt …

■ *the only person / thing*
„Der/Die/Das Einzige" drückt man im Englischen mit *the only person / one* bzw. *the only thing* aus.
***The only person / one** who knows where we're going is our teacher.* ● ● ● Der Einzige, der weiß …
***The only thing** he told us is that we'll need a passport.* ● ● ● Das Einzige, was er uns gesagt hat …

opinion

1 ...... it was a complete waste of time.

  A According to my opinion   **B** After my opinion   **C** In my opinion

opposite

1 I know who owns the building next door, but not who owns ....

  A the house opposite   **B** the house opposite the street   **C** the opposite house

2 The pharmacy is next to a hairdresser's, ...

  A opposite the Shoprite supermarket

  B opposite from the Shoprite supermarket

  C the Shoprite supermarket opposite

opposition

1 **A** We don't expect a lot of opposition against the idea.

  B We don't expect a lot of opposition at the idea.

  C We don't expect a lot of opposition to the idea.

2 **A** There has been some unexpected opposition against changing the system.

  B There has been some unexpected opposition at changing the system.

  C There has been some unexpected opposition to change the system.

  D There has been some unexpected opposition to changing the system.

optimist – pessimist

1 ...... I'm sure everything will work out OK.

  A I've always been an optimist.   **B** I've always been optimist.

ordinary ≠ „ordinär"

1 Which is the best synonym for 'ordinary'?

  A impolite   **B** normal   **C** rude   **D** uneducated

2 I can't stand him. He always makes *[so ordinäre Witze]*.

  A such crude jokes   **B** such orderly jokes   **C** such vulgar jokes

other – different

1 **A** I have other ideas. Yes, my ideas are other.

  B I have different ideas. Yes, my ideas are other.

  C I have other ideas. Yes, my ideas are different.

2 **A** My keys must be in an other jacket.   **B** My keys must be in another jacket.

3 I don't know why they do it, ...

  A but they seem to leave the keys in an other place every time

  B but they seem to leave the keys in a different place every time

opinion Meinung ▶ according to

■ *In my opinion* dogs should not be allowed in city parks. ● ● ● Meiner Meinung/Ansicht nach …

opposite [ˈɒpəzɪt; ˈɒpəsɪt] gegenüber(liegend)

■ *the building opposite* = „das gegenüberliegende Gebäude"
Das Adjektiv *opposite* mit der Bedeutung „gegenüberliegend" stellt man **hinter** das Nomen, auf das es sich bezieht.
a flat in the building **opposite** ● ● ● eine Wohnung in dem gegenüberliegenden Gebäude/
in dem Gebäude gegenüber

■ *opposite the buiding* = „gegenüber (von) dem Gebäude"
In folgendem Satz ist *opposite* eine Präposition und steht **vor** dem Nomen:
The post office is (right) **opposite** *the station.* ● ● ● … liegt (direkt) gegenüber (von) dem Bahnhof.

opposition [ˌɒpəˈzɪʃn] Widerstand; Opposition

■ *opposition to (doing) sth.*
There is a lot of **opposition to** (~~opposition against~~) *the plan.* ● ● ● … Widerstand gegen den Plan.
There is a lot of **opposition to building** (~~opposition to build~~) *a new road.* ● ● ● … Widerstand
gegen den Bau einer neuen Straße.

optimist [ˈɒptɪmɪst] Optimist/-in – **pessimist** [ˈpesɪmɪst] Pessimist/-in

■ **mit** *a/an*
Optimist und *pessimist* stehen mit dem unbestimmten Artikel.
Are you **an optimist** *or* **a pessimist**? ● ● ● Bist du (ein) Optimist oder (ein) Pessimist?

ordinary [(BE:) ˈɔːdnri; (AE:) ˈɔːrdneri] gewöhnlich, normal, üblich

!
!
!
!
■ **False Friend!**
Ordinary bedeutet nicht „~~ordinär~~", sondern „gewöhnlich", „normal".
It was just an **ordinary** *day like any other.* ● ● ● … nur ein ganz normaler Tag wie jeder andere.
ordinary *people like you and me* ● ● ● einfache/ganz normale Leute so wie du und ich
Beachte die englischen Entsprechungen von „ordinär" im Sinne von „unfein", „unanständig",
„vulgär":
Sei nicht so ordinär! ● ● ● *Don't be so* **vulgar** [ˈvʌlgə]/**crude**.

O

other andere(r/s) – **different** anders; verschieden, unterschiedlich ▶ different

■ *I have* **other** *memories of that day.* ● ● ● Ich habe andere Erinnerungen an diesen Tag./Ich habe
diesen Tag anders in Erinnerung.
among other things ● ● ● unter anderem

■ *Other* kann nicht nach *be* gebraucht werden. Stattdessen verwendet man *different*.
My memories are **different** (~~are other~~). ● ● ● Meine Erinnerungen sind anders.
Other kann auch nicht nach einem Adverb wie *very* oder *quite* stehen.
I have **quite different** *memories* (~~quite other memories~~). ● ● ● Ich habe ganz andere Erinnerungen
daran./Ich habe das ganz anders in Erinnerung.

■ **andere(r/s)**
1 „unterschiedlich"
Er trägt jeden Tag ein anderes T-Shirt. ● ● ● *He wears a* **different** *T-shirt every day.*

2 „nicht diese(r/s), sondern ein/e andere(r/s)"
Nicht heute, sondern an einem anderen Tag. ● ● ● *Not today, but* **another** *day.*

3 feste Wendung
Einem schüchternen Menschen fällt es schwer, mit dem anderen Geschlecht in Kontakt
zu treten. ● ● ● *A shy person finds it difficult to get into contact with* **the opposite sex**.

Trouble Spot

over

1 A Are you above 18? I can't let you in if you're not.

  B Are you over 18? I can't let you in if you're not.

2 A We were away across the weekend.

  B We were away over the weekend.

  C We were away during the weekend.

3 It was late May, ...

  A but the temperature was only a few degrees above zero

  B but the temperature was only a few degrees over zero

4 The railway line runs along the mountainside, ...

  A high above the valley   **B** high over the valley

5 A Results this year were above average.   **B** Results this year were above the average.

  C Results this year were over average.   **D** Results this year were over the average.

6 A Jane was always two classes above me at school.

  B Jane was always two classes over me at school.

7 ...... , because it was quicker.

  A We chose the longer route above Oxford   **B** We chose the longer route across Oxford

  C We chose the longer route over Oxford   **D** We chose the longer route via Oxford

8 A I was really shocked about how thin he was.

  B I was really shocked at how thin he was.

  C I was really shocked over how thin he was.

overhear ≠ „überhören"

1 Which is the best synonym for 'overheard' in this sentence?

I overheard you say that Jilly wasn't coming tonight. Why is that?

  A heard   **B** didn't hear   **C** happened to hear

2 Why didn't you answer the phone? – *[Ich habe es wohl überhört.]*

  A I think I missed it.   **B** I think I overheard it.   **C** I don't think I heard it.

oversee ≠ „übersehen"

1 Which are synonyms for 'oversee' in the following sentence?

Who is going to oversee the project?

  A be in charge of   **B** control   **C** finish   **D** summarize

2 ...... , but don't do it again.

  A I'm prepared to oversee it this time   **B** I'm prepared to overlook it this time

3 A You were driving so fast, it's not surprising you oversaw me.

  B You were driving so fast, it's not surprising you missed me.

  C You were driving so fast, it's not surprising you didn't see me.

over über

■ **Bedeutungen von** *over*

1 *Fog hung **over** the fields.* [= bedeckend] ● ● ● Der Nebel hing über den Feldern.

*We have a roof **over** our heads, we're warm and dry, so why complain?* [= „höher als" – siehe aber auch den folgenden Trouble Spot] ● ● ● Wir haben ein Dach über dem Kopf …

*a bridge **over**/**across** the river* [= über etwas Langgestrecktes hinweg] ● ● ● eine Brücke über den Fluss

*walk **over** the bridge* ● ● ● über die Brücke gehen

*the restaurant **over**/**across** the road* [= auf der anderen Seite von etwas Langgestrecktem] ● ● ● das Restaurant auf der anderen/gegenüberliegenden Straßenseite

*jump **over** a fence* [= über ein Hindernis hinweg] ● ● ● über einen Zaun [hinüber]springen

2 *be **over** 90* [= mehr als] ● ● ● über 90 sein

3 *be away **over** Christmas* [= während] ● ● ● über Weihnachten verreist sein

■ **über**

1 „höher als"

das Bild an der Wand über dem Bett ● ● ● *the picture on the wall **over**/**above** the bed*

Wenn etwas hoch über etwas anderem ist, verwendet man nur *above*.

hoch über den Wolken fliegen ● ● ● *fly high **above** the clouds*

eine Burg auf einem Hügel über der Stadt ● ● ● *a castle on a hill **above** the town*

Wenn etwas über einem Nullpunkt liegt, verwendet man ebenfalls nur *above*.

über dem Meeresspiegel/null/dem Gefrierpunkt ● ● ● ***above** sea level/zero/freezing*

über dem Durchschnitt ● ● ● ***above** average*

2 „höher als" [in einem Text, einer Rangfolge oder Liste]

die Zeile über dem Bild ● ● ● *the line **above** the picture*

ein Schüler in der Klasse über mir ● ● ● *a student in the class **above** me*

3 „auf dem Weg über"

nach Dublin über Amsterdam fliegen ● ● ● *fly to Dublin **via** ['vaɪə; 'viːə] Amsterdam*

4 „wegen" + Auslöser einer Reaktion

über einen Witz lachen ● ● ● *laugh **at** a joke*

über etwas schockiert sein ● ● ● *be shocked **at** sth.*

Trouble Spot

O

---

overhear* mitbekommen, zufällig mit anhören

! ! ! !

■ **False Friend!**

Overhear bedeutet nicht „~~überhören~~", sondern „(zufällig) mitbekommen".

*I **overheard** them arguing.* ● ● ● Ich habe zufällig mitbekommen, wie sie sich stritten.

Beachte die englischen Entsprechungen von „überhören":

Sie nannte das Datum, aber ich habe es offenbar überhört. ● ● ● *She said the date, but I obviously **missed**/**didn't hear** it.*

Das will ich überhört haben! ● ● ● *I **didn't hear** that.*

---

oversee* [Arbeiten, Beschäftigte usw.] beaufsichtigen, überwachen

! ! ! !

■ **False Friend!**

Oversee bedeutet nicht „~~übersehen~~", sondern „beaufsichtigen", „überwachen".

*An architect is **overseeing** the renovation work.* ● ● ● … überwacht die Renovierungsarbeiten.

Beachte die englischen Entsprechungen von „übersehen":

Ich war müde und habe den Fehler übersehen. [= versehentlich nicht sehen] ● ● ● *I was tired and **missed**/**didn't see**/**overlooked** the mistake.*

Mein Chef sagte, er könne einen so schweren Fehler nicht einfach übersehen. [= bewusst ignorieren] ● ● ● *My boss said he couldn't simply **overlook** such a serious mistake.*

overtake ≠ „übernehmen"

1 Which are synonyms for 'overtake' in the following sentence?
China will soon overtake the USA.
  A attack and take possession of B get ahead of C pass D replace

2 You've driven for over three hours. Come on, *[lass mich mal eine Weile übernehmen]*.
  A let me take on for a while B let me take over for a while C let me take care for a while

3 A If you overtake the shopping, I'll do the cleaning.
  B If you take care of the shopping, I'll do the cleaning.

own

1 Are you on ISDN? ....
  A Do you have an own phone number at home?
  B Do you have your own phone number at home?

2 One reason old people don't like to travel so much is ....
  A that they like to sleep in the own bed B that they like to sleep in their own bed

3 A I'd really like a place of my own, but I can't afford it.
  B I'd really like an own place, but I can't afford it.
  C I'd really like my own place, but I can't afford it.

packet ≠ „Paket"

1 Which of the following collocations are possible?
  A a parcel of books B a package of measures designed to halt inflation C a packet of biscuits

2 At Christmas there always used to be *[ein großes Paket]* from my aunt in Switzerland.
  A a big package B a big packet C a big parcel

pair – couple – a few

1 A lot of hotels in Niagara Falls specialize in ....
  A holidays for honeymoon couples B holidays for honeymoon pairs

2 Our neighbours have .... , and they're so noisy!
  A a pair of parrots B a parrot pair C a parrot couple

3 Can you bring *[ein paar Coladosen]*, too, please?
  A a pair cans of cola B a pair of cans of cola
  C a couple cans of cola D a couple of cans of cola
  E a few cans of cola F a few of cans of cola

overtake* überholen [im Auto usw.]

!
!
!
!

■ **False Friend!**
Overtake bedeutet nicht „~~übernehmen~~", sondern „überholen".
  *A red Ferrari **overtook** us at 200 km/h.* ● ● ● Ein roter Ferrari überholte uns mit 200 km/h.
Beachte die englischen Entsprechungen von „übernehmen":
  Mach mal eine Pause. Ich übernehme eine Weile. ● ● ● *Take a break. I'll **take over** for a while.*
  Ich kann keine weitere Arbeit übernehmen. ● ● ● *I can't **take on** any extra work.*
  Könntest du das übernehmen? [= erledigen] ● ● ● *Could you **do** that / **take care of** that?*

own [əʊn] eigene(r/s) ▶ alone

■ *my / your / his / her / its / our / their **own***
Own verwendet man in Verbindung mit einem Possessivbegleiter (*my, your* usw.). Es gibt zwei
Konstruktionen: „*my own / your own /* … + Nomen" oder „Nomen + *of + my own / your own /* …".
Verbindungen aus Artikel + *own* (~~an own, the own~~) bzw. Mengenbezeichnung + *own* (~~no own,~~
~~a lot of own~~) sind nicht möglich.
  *I have **my own** TV. / I have **a** TV **of my own**.* ● ● ● … einen eigenen Fernseher.
  *I don't have **my own** TV. / I have **no** TV **of my own**.* ● ● ● … keinen eigenen Fernseher.
  *People never find **their own** life strange.* ● ● ● … das eigene / ihr eigenes Leben …
  *I can give **a lot of** examples **of my own**.* ● ● ● … viele eigene Beispiele …

packet ['pækɪt] Päckchen, Packung

!
!
!
!

■ **False Friend!**
Packet bedeutet nicht „~~Paket~~", sondern „Päckchen" oder „Packung".
  *a **packet** of tea* ● ● ● ein Päckchen Tee
  *a **packet** of chewing gum / biscuits* ● ● ● eine Packung Kaugummis/Kekse
  *a **packet** of cigarettes* ● ● ● eine Packung/Schachtel Zigaretten
Beachte die englischen Entsprechungen von „Paket":
  ein Paket [zum Verschicken] zur Post bringen ● ● ● *take a **parcel** / **package*** ['pækɪdʒ]
    to the post office
  ein großes Paket mit 30 Büchern ● ● ● *a big **parcel** / **package** of 30 books*
  ein Softwarepaket ● ● ● *a software **package***
  ein Maßnahmenpaket ● ● ● *a **package** of measures*

P

pair – couple ['kʌpl] Paar – a few ein paar

Trouble Spot

■ **Paar**
1 „Ehepaar", „Liebespaar", „Mann und Frau"
  ein Ehepaar ● ● ● *a married **couple***
  ein junges (Liebes-)Paar ● ● ● *a young **couple***
  Das Paar nebenan war sehr laut. ● ● ● *The **couple** next door were / was very noisy.*

2 „zwei zusammengehörende Menschen, Tiere oder Dinge"
  das Paar, das das Restaurant betreibt [= die zwei, die das Restaurant betreiben] ● ● ●
    *the **pair** that run / runs the restaurant*
  ein Wellensittichpaar ● ● ● *a **pair** of budgerigars* ['bʌdʒərigɑːz]
  ein Paar Schuhe ● ● ● *a **pair of** shoes*

3 „paarweise"
  in Paaren arbeiten / gehen ● ● ● *work / walk **in pairs***

■ **ein paar**
  ein paar Regentropfen ● ● ● *a **couple of** raindrops / a **few** raindrops (= some raindrops)*

pants

1 When we changed for the PE lesson, ...

  A I saw that Karel was wearing a yellow pant

  B I saw that Karel was wearing a yellow pants

  C I saw that Karel was wearing a yellow pair of pants

  D I saw that Karel was wearing some yellow pants

park

1 .... , but the right-hand side is no parking.

  A There's always a row of parked cars on the left

  B There's always a row of parking cars on the left

parliament

1 Our Westminster correspondent says that the Prime Minister is to ....

  A make an announcement in parliament this afternoon

  B make an announcement in Parliament this afternoon

  C make an announcement in the parliament this afternoon

  D make an announcement in the Parliament this afternoon

part

1 Which is more common?

  A We spent a part of the day on the beach.   **B** We spent part of the day on the beach.

2 I've already sent out *[einen Teil der Einladungen]*.

  A a number of the invitations   **B** a part of the invitations   **C** some of the invitations

party

1 Beth takes any opportunity ....

  A to celebrate a party   **B** to hold a party   **C** to throw a party   **D** to have a party

2 ...... I didn't see you.

  A Were you at the Christmas party?

  B Were you by the Christmas party?

  C Were you on the Christmas party?

pass – past

1 **A** We've passed the church, and now we've just driven passed a pub called 'The Holy Grail'.

  B We've passed the church, and now we've just driven past a pub called 'The Holy Grail'.

  C We've past the church, and now we've just driven passed a pub called 'The Holy Grail'.

  D We've past the church, and now we've just driven past a pub called 'The Holy Grail'.

2 ...... , with about 20 cars crawling along behind it.

  A A tractor has just gone passed   **B** A tractor has just gone past

3 ...... , but not in many parts of Asia.

  A The time when large numbers of people cycled to work may be passed here

  B The time when large numbers of people cycled to work may be past here

pants (BE:) Unterhose; (AE/BE:) Hose ▷ shorts ▷ trousers

■ **Pluralnomen, keine Singularform**

Pants bezeichnet im BE eine Unterhose, im AE (und informell im BE) eine Hose. Wie *trousers* gibt es *pants* nur als Pluralnomen (mit Verb im Plural). Um daraus eine Singularform zu machen, muss man *a pair of* verwenden.

*After my shower I put on **some** clean **pants** / a clean **pair of pants** (a clean pants).* ● ● ● Nach dem Duschen habe ich eine neue (Unter-)Hose / neue (Unter-)Hosen angezogen.

Im AE und teilweise auch im BE wird eine Unterhose als *underpants* bezeichnet.

park parken, abstellen [Auto]

■ *The street was full of **parked** cars (parking cars).* ● ● ● Die Straße war voller parkender Autos.

parliament ['pɑːləmənt] Parlament

■ **ohne Artikel**

Das britische Parlament wird im BE großgeschrieben (wie ein Eigenname) und – wenn es nicht näher bestimmt ist – ohne Artikel verwendet.

*When does **Parliament** break for Easter?* ● ● ● Wann beginnt für das Parlament die Osterpause?

Aber:

*The German **parliament** is called 'Bundestag'.* ● ● ● Das deutsche Parlament heißt „Bundestag".

part Teil

■ **ohne *a* vor Nomen im Singular**

Vor einem Nomen im Singular wird *part of* meist ohne *a* verwendet.

*He lives in Australia for **part of** the year.* ● ● ● Er lebt einen Teil des Jahres in Australien.

Aber wenn vor *part* ein Adjektiv steht, verwendet man *a*.

*He lives in Australia for **a large part of** the year.* ● ● ● Er lebt einen großen Teil des Jahres in Australien.

■ **nicht vor Nomen im Plural**

Vor einem Nomen im Plural verwendet man nicht *part*, sondern z. B. *some* oder *a number of*.

***Some** (of the) glasses were broken.* ● ● ● Einige (der) Gläser waren kaputt.

***A number of** (the) glasses were broken.* ● ● ● Ein Teil der Gläser war / Ein Teil Gläser waren kaputt.

party Party, Feier

■ ***give* / *have* / *hold* (celebrate) *a party*** ● ● ● eine Party geben / machen / feiern

throw a party (infml) ● ● ● eine Party schmeißen

*be **at a party*** ● ● ● auf einer Party sein

*go **to a party*** ● ● ● zu einer Party / auf eine Party gehen

pass bestehen [Prüfung]; geben; vorbeigehen an – past 1 vorbei (an); nach 2 Vergangenheit

■ *passed*: **Form des Verbs *pass***

*I've **passed** my exam.* ● ● ● Ich habe meine Prüfung bestanden.

*I **passed** you the salt already.* ● ● ● Ich habe dir das Salz schon gereicht / gegeben.

*We had **passed** a church.* ● ● ● Wir waren an einer Kirche vorbeigegangen / -gefahren.

*The moment **passed**.* ● ● ● Der Augenblick ging vorüber / ist vorübergegangen.

■ *past*: **Präposition, Adverb, Adjektiv oder Nomen**

*A big black car has just driven **past** the house.* [Präposition] ● ● ● … an dem Haus vorbei.

*ten (minutes) **past** three* [Präposition] ● ● ● zehn (Minuten) nach drei

*A big black car has just driven **past**.* [Adverb] ● ● ● … ist gerade vorbeigefahren.

*Those days are **past**.* [Adjektiv] ● ● ● Jene Tage sind vorbei / vorüber. / Die Zeit ist vorbei.

*What has happened in the **past** 24 hours?* [Adjektiv] ● ● ● … in den vergangenen 24 Stunden …?

*In the **past** people wrote more letters.* [Nomen] ● ● ● In der Vergangenheit / Früher …

***past** tense, **past** perfect, **past** participle* ● ● ● Präteritum, Plusquamperfekt, Partizip Perfekt

P

patience

1 **A** A big patience is certainly an asset if you want to become a teacher.

B A great patience is certainly an asset if you want to become a teacher.

C Great patience is certainly an asset if you want to become a teacher.

2 **A** I kept saying to myself, 'I mustn't lose my patience'.

B I kept saying to myself, 'I mustn't lose the patience'.

pause – break – interval/intermission

1 **A** Quite a lot of people nowadays don't take a lunch break at all.

B Quite a lot of people nowadays don't take a pause for lunch at all.

C Quite a lot of people nowadays don't take a lunch pause at all.

2 The door opened and the speaker stopped for a moment. ...... , all heads turned towards the door.

A In the break that followed   **B** In the pause that followed

3 **A** The concert consisted of two pieces with a 15-minute pause between them.

B The concert consisted of two pieces with a 15-minute interval between them.

C The concert consisted of two pieces with a 15-minute intermission between them.

pay

1 ...... Can we go?

A Have you paid?   **B** Have you payed?   **C** Have you paid for?

2 There are some restaurants ....

A where you can't pay by credit card

B where you can't pay through credit card

C where you can't pay with credit card

3 **A** The family was so poor that often they couldn't pay the rent.

B The family was so poor that often they couldn't pay for the rent.

4 ...... , if we buy the drinks.

A Jenny said she'd pay the food   **B** Jenny said she'd pay for the food

pencil

1 ...... in case I have to go back and correct something later on.

A I always write by pencil   **B** I always write in pencil

C I always write with pencil   **D** I always write with a pencil

people

1 **A** Why do people always make the same mistakes, generation after generation?

B Why do the people always make the same mistakes, generation after generation?

2 **A** Do you know any of people from the building next door?

B Do you know any of the people from the building next door?

3 In a democracy, a country's parliament is supposed to be ...... , isn't it?

A 'the voice of people'   **B** 'the voice of the people'

4 Don't do it! ......

A All people think you're mad enough already.

B All the people think you're mad enough already.

C Everybody think you're mad enough already.

D Everybody thinks you're mad enough already.

patience ['peɪʃns] Geduld

■ **ohne** *the/a*

Patience ist ein abstraktes Nomen. Daher steht es in Aussagen allgemeiner Art ohne den Artikel *the*.
  Patience (~~The patience~~) is a virtue ['vɜːtʃuː]. ● ● ● (Die) Geduld ist eine Tugend.

Patience ist nicht zählbar und steht daher grundsätzlich ohne den unbestimmten Artikel *a(n)*.
  She had such great patience (~~such a big patience~~)! ● ● ● Sie hatte (eine) solch große Geduld!

Beachte auch:
  Don't lose your patience (~~the patience~~). ● ● ● Verlier nicht die Geduld!

pause [pɔːz] – break [breɪk] – (BE:) interval ['ɪntəvl] / (AE:) intermission Pause

■ *Pause* bezeichnet eine kurze Unterbrechung von wenigen Augenblicken, z. B. eine Sprechpause.
  a four-second pause ● ● ● eine Pause von vier Sekunden
  After a moment's pause, he answered. ● ● ● Nach einer kurzen Pause antwortete er.

■ *Break* bezeichnet eine Erholungspause bzw. Arbeitspause.
  Break (BE) *is after the third lesson.* ● ● ● Die [Schul-]Pause ist nach der dritten Unterrichtsstunde.
  a coffee break / a lunch break ● ● ● eine Kaffeepause / eine Mittagspause

■ *Interval* und *intermission* bezeichnen die Pause bei einer Theateraufführung oder einem Konzert.
  There'll be a 20-minute (BE:) *interval / (AE:) intermission after the second act.* ● ● ● Nach dem
  zweiten Akt ist eine zwanzigminütige Pause.

pay* (be)zahlen

■ *pay (-ing-Form: paying) – paid – paid (~~payed~~)*

■ *pay by cheque* ● ● ● mit Scheck bezahlen
  pay by credit card ● ● ● mit Kreditkarte bezahlen
  pay (in) cash ● ● ● bar (be)zahlen

■ *pay sb./sth.* = „jmdn. / eine Summe / eine Rechnung bezahlen"
  I paid the taxi driver. ● ● ● Ich habe den Taxifahrer bezahlt.
  I paid the bill / the rent / €120. ● ● ● Ich habe die Rechnung / die Miete / 120 € bezahlt.

■ *pay for sth.* = „eine Ware / Dienstleistung bezahlen"
  Who paid for the taxi / the coffee / the advertisement / the repair? ● ● ● Wer hat das Taxi /
  den Kaffee / die Anzeige / die Reparatur bezahlt?

pencil Bleistift

■ *Please don't do your homework in pencil / with a pencil again.* ● ● ● … mit Bleistift …

people Leute ▶ one

■ **Gebrauch von** *the*

People verwendet man ohne *the*, wenn man die Menschen/Leute ganz allgemein meint.
  People (~~The people~~) will never believe me when I tell them I've seen a ghost. ● ● ● Die Leute
  werden mir niemals glauben / Man wird mir niemals glauben …

Man verwendet *the people*, wenn eine nähere Bestimmung folgt (z. B. ein Relativsatz wie *I met*).
  The people I met were all very helpful. ● ● ● Die Menschen, denen ich begegnet bin, waren alle
  sehr hilfsbereit.

The people bedeutet auch „die Bevölkerung", „das Volk". Vergleiche:
  This government is out of touch with people. ● ● ● Diese Regierung hat den Kontakt zu den
  Menschen verloren.
  This government is out of touch with the people. ● ● ● Diese Regierung hat den Kontakt zur
  Bevölkerung / zum Volk verloren.

■ „**alle Leute**" = *everyone / everybody*

„Alle Leute" gibt man mit *everyone / everybody* wieder. Danach steht das Verb im Singular.
  Everyone / Everybody knows you. ● ● ● Alle Leute kennen dich.

P

perhaps

1 A Perhaps we find out some more at the meeting this evening.

B Perhaps we'll find out some more at the meeting this evening.

person

1 It's only a small party. ......

A We've only invited 12 persons.   B We've only invited 12 people.

personal ≠ „Personal"

1 At the end of the summer when the season ended, ...

A a lot of the personal had to leave

B a lot of the personality had to leave

C a lot of the staff had to leave

phone

1 Where's Julie? – ...... I think she's talking to her mum.

A She's at the phone.   B She's to the phone.   C She's on the phone.

2 ...... , but he isn't there either.

A I've phoned with the hotel   B I've phoned to the hotel   C I've phoned the hotel

3 I was having a shower, ...

A so I couldn't answer the phone

B so I couldn't go on the phone

C so I couldn't reply to the phone

4 I'm sorry, I was in a meeting ....

A and couldn't take your call

B and couldn't take in your call

C and couldn't take on your call

5 You can go in now, ...

A she's hung up   B she's laid up

C she's laid the phone down   D she's put the phone down

photo(graph) – photographer – photography

1 It was a fantastic festival. ......

A I did lots of photos.   B I made lots of photos.

C I took lots of photos.   D I took lots of pictures.

2 A Did you make a photo of the prize-giving ceremony?

B Did you take a photo of the prize-giving ceremony?

C Did you take a photo from the prize-giving ceremony?

3 ...... – whose is it?

A This car at the photo   B This car in the photo   C This car on the photo

4 A She was one of the most famous female photographs of the 20th century.

B She was one of the most famous female photographers of the 20th century.

5 A My main hobby is photographing.

B My main hobby is photographies.

C My main hobby is photography.

perhaps vielleicht

■ **bei Zukunftsbezug:** *perhaps* meist mit *will-future* oder *present progressive*

Perhaps verwendet man meist mit dem *will-future* oder dem *present progressive*, wenn man über die Zukunft spricht.

> *I'll perhaps see (I perhaps see) you tomorrow.* ● ● ● Vielleicht sehe ich dich morgen.
> *I'm perhaps coming by car, but I haven't decided yet.* ● ● ● Ich komme vielleicht mit dem Auto …

person ['pɜːsn] Person, Mensch

■ **Pluralform normalerweise** *people*

Nur in förmlichen Zusammenhängen verwendet man die Pluralform *persons*.

> [Schild im Aufzug:] *Maximum: 15 persons*

Aber: *There were 30 people (persons) in the room.* ● ● ● Es waren 30 Leute/Menschen/Personen …

personal ['pɜːsənl] persönlich

!
!
!

  ■ **False Friend!**

Personal bedeutet nicht „Personal", sondern ist ein Adjektiv mit der Bedeutung „persönlich".

> *personal problems* ● ● ● persönliche Probleme
> *personal pronoun* ● ● ● persönliches Fürwort, Personalpronomen

Beachte die englische Entsprechung von „Personal":

> Ein Teil des Personals wurde entlassen. ● ● ● *Some of the **staff** were dismissed.*

phone 1 Telefon 2 telefonieren, anrufen

Topic Box

> ■ *Telephoning*
> *Can I make a quick phone call?* ● ● ● Kann ich mal eben (schnell) telefonieren?
> *I'd better phone for an ambulance.* ● ● ● Ich rufe lieber einen Krankenwagen.
> *Hello, this is Sue. / Hello, Max Busch speaking.* ● ● ● Hallo, hier ist Sue / hier spricht Max Busch.
> *Could I speak to (AE auch: speak with) Doris, please?* ● ● ● Kann ich bitte mit Doris sprechen?
> *Hold on, I'll get her. / I'm afraid she's not in. Can I give her a message?* ● ● ● Augenblick, bitte.
>   Ich hole sie. / Sie ist leider nicht da. Kann ich ihr etwas ausrichten?
> *I'll give you a call / (BE infml auch:) give you a ring later.* ● ● ● Ich rufe dich später an.
> *I'll send you a text (message). / I'll text you.* ● ● ● Ich schicke dir eine SMS. / Ich simse dir.
> *It's engaged/busy.* ● ● ● Es/Da ist besetzt.
> *answer the phone / take a call* ● ● ● ans Telefon gehen / einen Anruf entgegennehmen
> *pick up the phone* ● ● ● (den Hörer) abheben/abnehmen
> *put the phone down / hang up* ● ● ● (den Hörer) auflegen
> *be on the phone (to sb.)* ● ● ● am Telefon sein, gerade (mit jmdm.) telefonieren
> *speak to sb. on the phone / over the phone / by phone* ● ● ● mit jmdm. am Telefon sprechen
> *phone the school (phone in the school / with the school).* ● ● ● in/bei der Schule anrufen

P

photo(graph) ['fəʊtəgrɑːf] Foto(grafie) – photographer Fotograf/-in – photography Fotografie

■ *I discovered six old photographs.* ● ● ● Ich habe sechs alte Fotografien entdeckt.
  Whose is the dog in the photo (on the photo)? ● ● ● Wem gehört der Hund auf dem Foto?

■ *Who was the photographer [fəˈtɒgrəfə]?* ● ● ● Wer war der Fotograf / die Fotografin?

■ *Are you interested in photography [fəˈtɒgrəfi]?* ● ● ● Interessierst du dich für Fotografie / das
  Fotografieren [als Kunstform, Hobby usw.]?

Trouble Spot

> ■ **fotografieren**
>   fotografieren [= Fotos machen] ● ● ● *take photos/pictures (make photos/pictures)*
>   jmdn./etwas fotografieren ● ● ● *take a photo/picture of sb./sth.*
>   sich fotografieren lassen ● ● ● *have one's photo/picture taken*
>   Fotografieren verboten ● ● ● *No photographs*

picnic

1 It was a lovely day, ...

   A so we did a picnic by the river   **B** so we had a picnic by the river

   C so we made a picnic by the river   **D** so we went on a picnic by the river

picture

1 For years nobody realized ....

   A that the picture was by one of the most famous artists of the era

   B that the picture was from one of the most famous artists of the era

2 A The building at the picture still exists, but it's no longer a hotel.

   B The building in the picture still exists, but it's no longer a hotel.

   C The building on the picture still exists, but it's no longer a hotel.

place

1 Next to the cathedral is [ein großer Platz] with a fountain in the middle.

   A a large place   **B** a large square

2 There are [zwei Plätze] in the third row from the back, but that's all. They cost £8.50.

   A two places   **B** two spaces   **C** two seats

3 The flat is quite noisy in summer, because there's [ein Spielplatz] next door.

   A a playground   **B** a playfield   **C** a playspace   **D** a playplace

4 A There's place in the car for five.   **B** There's room in the car for five.

play

1 The Shakespeare Company [spielt Macbeth] this autumn.

   A is acting Macbeth   **B** is performing Macbeth

   C is playing Macbeth   **D** is putting on Macbeth

2 A I used to hate playing dialogues in Years 5 and 6. I can't act.

   B I used to hate acting out dialogues in Years 5 and 6. I can't act.

   C I used to hate acting dialogues in Years 5 and 6. I can't play theatre.

please

1 ...... There's plenty of room there.

   A Park please at the end of the road, opposite the church.

   B Please park at the end of the road, opposite the church.

2 A Yes, madam. What would you like? – Please some more bread.

   B Yes, madam. What would you like? – Some more bread, please.

3 A Thank you very much. That's really very kind of you. – It's a pleasure.

   B Thank you very much. That's really very kind of you. – Please.

   C Thank you very much. That's really very kind of you. – That's all right.

   D Thank you very much. That's really very kind of you. – You're welcome.

4 [Wie bitte?] I'm afraid I didn't understand.

   A How?   **B** Pardon?   **C** Sorry?   **D** What, please?

5 ...... The big one is the key to the front door, the other is the key to the back door.

   A Can I have the keys, please? – [handing them over] Here you are.

   B Can I have the keys, please? – [handing them over] Please.

   C Can I have the keys, please? – [handing them over] You're welcome.

picnic Picknick

- *Let's **have a picnic** / **go on a picnic** / **go for a picnic** (~~make a picnic~~) this afternoon.* ● ● ● Machen wir heute Nachmittag ein Picknick.
  *Can you help me **make the picnic**?* ● ● ● … helfen, das Picknick vorzubereiten/zuzubereiten?

picture Bild   ▷ photo(graph)

- *What is the building **in the picture** (~~on the picture~~)?* ● ● ● … auf dem Bild/Foto?
  *It's a **picture by** Picasso (~~picture from Picasso~~).* ● ● ● … ein Bild von Picasso. [Picasso hat es gemalt.]

place Platz, Stelle, Ort; Zuhause

- *The campsite was **in a nice place**.* ● ● ● … an einer schönen Stelle / einem schönen Ort.
  *Let's meet **at my place**.* ● ● ● Treffen wir uns bei mir zu Hause.

■ **Platz**
ein großer Platz in der Stadtmitte ● ● ● *a big **square** in the town centre*
Sportplatz ● ● ● ***sports ground** / **sports field***
Tennisplatz ● ● ● ***tennis court***
Fußballplatz ● ● ● ***football pitch** [Spielfeld] / **football ground** [Anlage]*
Parkplatz [für viele Autos] ● ● ● *(BE:) **car park** / (AE:) **parking lot***
Parkplatz [= Parklücke für ein Auto] ● ● ● ***parking space***
Kinder auf dem Spielplatz ● ● ● *children in the **playground***
Ist dieser (Sitz-)Platz noch frei? ● ● ● *Is this **seat** taken?*
Es ist nicht genug Platz [= freier Raum] da. ● ● ● *There's not enough **space** / **room**.*

play spielen   ▷ game

- *I can't **play (the) guitar**.* ● ● ● Ich kann nicht Gitarre spielen.

■ **spielen**
Die Theater-AG spielt ein Stück von Miller. ● ● ● *The drama group is **performing** a play / **putting on** a play by Miller.*
Tina spielt sehr gut [Theater]. / Tina ist eine sehr gute Schauspielerin. ● ● ● *Tina **acts** very well.*
Wer spielt den Romeo [= Romeos Rolle]? ● ● ● *Who is **playing** / **acting** (the **part** / **role** of) Romeo?*
Das Stück spielt in Verona. ● ● ● *The play **is set** in Verona.*
Spielt die Szene / das Gespräch bitte vor. ● ● ● *Please **act out** the scene / the conversation.*

please bitte

■ **Stellung**
Please stellt man in der Regel **vor** das Verb (nicht hinter das Verb) oder an das Satzende.
***Please phone** (~~Phone please~~) this afternoon. She'll be home then.* ● ● ● Ruf bitte … an! …

■ **bitte**
1 Reaktion auf Dank
Vielen Dank. – Bitte (schön). ● ● ● *Thank you. – **That's all right.** / **It's a pleasure.** / **You're welcome.*** („Keine Ursache." / „Gern geschehen.")

2 Zustimmung zu einer Bitte
Darf ich mich setzen? – Bitte. ● ● ● *May I sit down? – **Of course.** / **Certainly.** / **Please do.***

3 Rückfrage bei Nichtverstehen
Er heißt Fitzherbert. – Wie bitte? ● ● ● *His name is Fitzherbert. – **Sorry?** / **Pardon (me)?***

4 Entrüstung
Sie Idiot! – Wie bitte!? ● ● ● *You idiot! – **I beg your pardon!** (meist BE)*

5 beim Überreichen
Bitte schön, Ihre Suppe. Vorsicht, sie ist heiß. ● ● ● ***Here you are**, your soup. Careful, it's hot.*

plenty

1 **A** Glenn has plenty time.   **B** Glenn has plenty of time.

2 What kept you? *[Du bist reichlich spät dran.]*
  A You're plenty late.   **B** You're pretty late.   **C** You're quite late.   **D** You're very late.

poem

1 **A** Can you name one poem by a Dutch poet? I can't.
  B Can you name one poem from a Dutch poet? I can't.
  C Can you name one poem of a Dutch poet? I can't.

point *(verb)*

1 **A** Don't point your finger at me. It's not my fault!
  B Don't point your finger on me. It's not my fault!
  C Don't point your finger to me. It's not my fault!

2 ...... , even if these things have nothing to do with them.
  A Before an election politicians always point at things that have improved in our lives
  B Before an election politicians always point on things that have improved in our lives
  C Before an election politicians always point to things that have improved in our lives

point *(noun)*

1 **A** We reached a dot where we couldn't agree on anything any more.
  B We reached a point where we couldn't agree on anything any more.

2 ...... , or is it more modern without?
  A Is it still normal to spell 'Mr' with a dot   **B** Is it still normal to spell 'Mr' with a full stop
  C Is it still normal to spell 'Mr' with a period   **D** Is it still normal to spell 'Mr' with a point

3 My email address is now ...... , not 'Weaverlights' in one word.
  A 'Weaver dot lights'   **B** 'Weaver full stop lights'   **C** 'Weaver point lights'

4 ...... he grumbled, and went to bed.
  A "What's the point of staying up?"   **B** "What's the point to stay up?"

5 **A** There's no point waiting any longer.
  B There's no point to wait any longer.
  C There's no point in waiting any longer.

police

1 **A** The police are changing their way of tracking criminals.
  B The police is changing its way of tracking criminals.

policy – politics

1 **A** The government is changing its policy on education.
  B The government is changing its politics on education.

2 ...... Are you a Democrat or a Republican?
  A What's your policy?   **B** What's your politics?   **C** What are your politics?

3 **A** Fewer and fewer young people are taking an active interest in politic.
  B Fewer and fewer young people are taking an active interest in politics.
  C Fewer and fewer young people are taking an active interest in the politics.

plenty viel(e), reichlich   ▷ much

■ **Begleiter, aber nicht Adverb**
Die Mengenbezeichnung *plenty of* steht vor nicht zählbaren und vor zählbaren Nomen.
*She has **plenty of** money / **plenty of** friends.* ● ● ● Sie hat viel Geld / viele Freunde.
Plenty kann in der Hochsprache nicht als Adverb vor einem Adjektiv stehen.
*They arrived **pretty/rather/quite/very** tired (~~plenty tired~~).* ● ● ● Sie kamen reichlich müde an.

poem ['pəʊɪm] Gedicht

■ *a **poem by** Shakespeare (~~poem from Shakespeare~~)* ● ● ● ein Gedicht von Shakespeare [= ein Gedicht, das Shakespeare verfasst hat]

point zeigen

■ *Point at sb./sth.* bedeutet „mit dem Finger oder einem Gegenstand auf jemanden oder etwas zeigen", „einen Gegenstand auf jemanden oder etwas richten".
*point (a finger) **at** sb./sth.* ● ● ● (mit dem Finger) auf jmdn. / etwas zeigen
*point a gun **at** sb./sth.* ● ● ● eine Waffe auf jmdn. / etwas richten
■ *Point to sth.* bedeutet „die Aufmerksamkeit auf etwas lenken", „auf etwas hinweisen".
*point **to** a wet patch on the wall* ● ● ● auf einen nassen Fleck an der Wand hinweisen
*point **to** improvements in the new system* ● ● ● auf Verbesserungen im neuen System hinweisen

point Punkt; Zweck

■ *at a **point** in my childhood* ● ● ● an einem Punkt (in) meiner Kindheit

■ **Punkt**
  Hier am Satzende fehlt der Punkt [als Satzzeichen]. ● ● ● *The (BE:) **full stop** / (AE:) **period** is missing here at the end of the sentence.*
  www.bbc.co.uk [Punkt in Internetadressen] ● ● ● [gesprochen:] *www **dot**, bbc **dot**, co **dot**, uk*
  Über dem kleinen „i" steht ein Punkt [= Pünktchen]. ● ● ● *There's a **dot** above the small 'i'.*

Trouble Spot

■ *the **point of** doing – no **point in** doing*
  *What's **the point of** crying (~~the point to cry~~)?* ● ● ● Welchen Zweck hat es, zu heulen?
  *There's **no point (in)** crying (~~no point to cry~~).* ● ● ● Es hat keinen Zweck zu heulen.

police Polizei

■ **Pluralnomen mit Pluralverb**
Das Nomen *police* wird im Englischen als Plural konstruiert.
*The **police are** interviewing (~~The police is interviewing~~) the man **they** arrested yesterday.* ● ● ●
  Die Polizei verhört den Mann, den sie gestern verhaftet hat.

policy ['pɒləsi] – **politics** ['pɒlətɪks] Politik

■ *Policy* bezeichnet eine politische Maßnahme oder Linie, eine Verfahrensweise.
  *the government's new economic **policy*** ● ● ● die neue Wirtschaftspolitik der Regierung
  *What **policy** should we adopt on this issue?* ● ● ● Welche Politik sollen wir bei dieser Frage verfolgen? / Wie sollen wir bei dieser Frage verfahren?
■ *Politics* bezieht sich auf die Welt der Politik oder das Fach Politik und wird in der Regel als Singular (ohne *the*!) konstruiert.
  *I'm not interested in **politics** (~~the politics~~). **Politics is** boring.* ● ● ● Ich interessiere mich nicht für (die) Politik [allgemein]. (Die) Politik ist langweilig.
  ***Politics** (~~The politics~~) **takes** up more and more of my time.* ● ● ● Die Politik [= politische Aktivitäten] beansprucht mich immer mehr.
  *I'm studying **politics**. It's a very interesting subject.* ● ● ● Ich studiere Politikwissenschaft. ...
Politics kann auch „politische Einstellung(en)" bedeuten und wird dann als Plural konstruiert.
  *His **politics are** extreme.* ● ● ● Seine politischen Ansichten / politische Einstellung ...

P

poor

1 ...... living next door in this part of town.
   A You won't find a poor and a rich   **B** You won't find a poor person and a rich person

2 Glenn has broken a finger playing tennis, ...
   A the poor   **B** the poor thing

3 **A** The poor in this country are very poor.   **B** The poors in this country are very poor.

popular

1 I don't want to meet Sonia. After what I said last night ....
   A I don't think I'm very popular by her
   B I don't think I'm very popular for her
   C I don't think I'm very popular with her

possibility – chance – opportunity – way

1 ...... before the conflict was resolved.
   A The possibility of war hung in the air for several weeks
   B The opportunity of war hung in the air for several weeks
   C The way of war hung in the air for several weeks

2 I don't know ...... with everybody concerned.
   A when we'll have the chance to discuss this again
   B when we'll have the opportunity to discuss this again
   C when we'll have the possibility to discuss this again

3 ...... without getting soaking wet ourselves.
   A There must be a chance to wash the dog
   B There must be a possibility to wash the dog
   C There must be a way to wash the dog

4 ...... , do you think?
   A Is there any possibility of getting Ralph's permission beforehand
   B Is there any possibility to get Ralph's permission beforehand

possible

1 **A** It's possible of course that Harry forgets to bring his digital camera tonight, isn't it?
   B It's possible of course that Harry will forget to bring his digital camera tonight, isn't it?

2 **A** Yes, that's good possible.   **B** Yes, that's quite possible.   **C** Yes, that's well possible.

post – mail – post office

1 ...... , in the regular mail.
   A The money came by normal post
   B The money came per normal post
   C The money came with normal post

potato

1 **A** How many potatoes would you like?
   B How many potatos would you like?
   C How many potatoe's would you like?

poor arm ▶ bad

■ **als Nomen nur zur Bezeichnung einer Gruppe**

The poor (ohne Plural-*s*) bezeichnet eine Gruppe von Armen (oft im Sinne von „alle Armen").

pray for **the poor** ● ● ● für die Armen beten

Aber:

A poor person *can't afford luxuries.* ● ● ● Ein Armer / Eine Arme kann sich keinen Luxus leisten.

Poor people *can't afford luxuries.* ● ● ● Arme (Leute) können sich keinen Luxus leisten.

The poor man *was very surprised to see the king at his door.* ● ● ● Der Arme / Der arme Mann …

You **poor thing**! *What's happened to you?* ● ● ● Du Arme(r) / Ärmste(r)! …

popular [ˈpɒpjələ] beliebt

■ *popular with*

This car is very **popular with** (~~popular by~~) *women.* ● ● ● Dieses Auto ist bei Frauen sehr beliebt.

possibility – chance – opportunity – way Möglichkeit

■ *possibility – chance – opportunity*

Mit *possibility* und *chance* drückt man aus, dass etwas eintreten könnte.

the **possibility / chance** *of a price reduction* ● ● ● die Möglichkeit / Chance einer Preissenkung

Mit *chance* und *opportunity* drückt man aus, dass eine Gelegenheit für etwas besteht.

the **chance / opportunity** *to buy souvenirs* ● ● ● die Möglichkeit / Chance / Gelegenheit, Souvenirs zu kaufen

Normalerweise verwendet man nach *have* nicht *possibility*, sondern *chance* oder *opportunity*.

Mohammed **had the chance / opportunity** *to study* (~~had the possibility to study~~) *abroad.* ● ● ● Mohammed hatte die Möglichkeit, im Ausland zu studieren.

■ *way*

Mit *way* spricht man von einem möglichen Weg oder einer möglichen Methode.

find a **way** *to speed up the process* ● ● ● eine Möglichkeit finden, das Verfahren zu beschleunigen

■ *possibility of doing – possibility that …*

Possibility kann man nicht mit einem *to*-Infinitiv verbinden. Nach *possibility* verwendet man *of* + die -*ing*-Form oder einen *that*-Satz.

I see no **possibility of winning** *the match.* ● ● ● Ich sehe keine Möglichkeit, das Spiel zu gewinnen.

There's a **possibility (that) the election will be postponed**. ● ● ● Es besteht die Möglichkeit, dass die Wahl verschoben wird.

possible möglich

■ **bei Zukunftsbezug:** *possible* **mit** *will-future* **oder** *present progressive*

It's possible verwendet man meist mit dem *will-future* oder dem *present progressive*, wenn man über die Zukunft spricht.

It's possible that **I'll see** (~~I see~~) *you tomorrow.* ● ● ● Es kann sein, dass ich dich morgen sehe.

It's possible that they **'re coming** (~~they come~~) *later.* ● ● ● Es kann sein, dass sie später kommen.

■ *It's* **quite possible** (~~good / well possible~~) *that it will snow.* ● ● ● Es ist gut möglich, dass es schneit.

post – mail – post office Post

■ *They sent it by courier* [ˈkʊriə], *not* **by** *normal* **post / mail** / *not* **in the** *normal* **post / mail**. ● ● ● Sie haben es per Kurier geschickt, nicht mit der normalen Post.

Is there any **post / mail** *for me?* ● ● ● Ist Post für mich da?

I'm just going through my **post / mail** / *my* **email(s)**. ● ● ● Ich lese gerade meine Post / meine E-Mails.

■ *go to the* **post office** (~~go to the post~~) ● ● ● zur Post [= zum Postamt] gehen

potato Kartoffel

■ **Schreibung**

one **potato**, *two* **potatoes**

P

practise/practice – practice

1 ...... before I can take part in a competition.
   A I think I need some more practice   B I think I need some more practise

2 Your written English is very good ....
   A but you need to practice to speak it   B but you need to practise to speak it
   C but you need to practise speaking it   D but you need to practise how to speak it

prefer – would prefer

1 We used to drink a lot of coffee, ...
   A but now we're prefering tea   B but now we're preferring tea   C but now we prefer tea

2 ...... where this suggestion came from. It's disgusting.
   A I'd prefer not knowing   B I'd prefer not to know

3 ...... made of paper, not electronic ones.
   A I prefer reading real books   B I prefer to read real books   C I prefer to reading real books

prepare

1 Is there anything sensible I can do ...... ?
   A to prepare for the oral part of the test   B to prepare on the oral part of the test
   C to prepare to the oral part of the test

present

1 A May I ask the parents present to leave the room for a few minutes, please?
   B May I ask the present parents to leave the room for a few minutes, please?

prevent

1 ...... , so why not tell them?
   A You can't prevent people from finding out the true facts for themselves on the Internet
   B You can't prevent people to find out the true facts for themselves on the Internet
   C You can't prevent people finding out the true facts for themselves on the Internet

price – prize – cost

1 A Tina is so happy she won one of the prices.   B Tina is so happy she won one of the prizes.

2 ...... Last week it only cost €3.60.
   A The price has gone up again.   B The prize has gone up again.

3 Stop the press finding out, please, *[um jeden Preis]*.
   A at every price   B at all prizes   C at all costs

principal – principally – principle

1 A What's the principal behind this?   B What's the principle behind this?

2 A That was my principal reason for moving.   B That was my principle reason for moving.

3 Of course ......, but I still have to disagree on certain details.
   A you're right in principle   B you're right in the principle   C you're right on principle

4 A I don't eat meat from principle.
   B I don't eat meat on principle.
   C I don't eat meat out of principle.

practise (BE) / **practice** (AE) ['præktɪs] üben, trainieren – **practice** Übung, Training

- **Schreibung**
  [Verb:] (BE:) *You have to **practise** for the test.* / (AE:) *You have to **practice** for the test.*
  [Nomen:] (BE und AE:) *You need some **practice**.*

- *practise doing – practise how/what/when/... to do*
Nach *practise* steht eine *-ing*-Form oder ein Fragewort + *to*-Infinitiv, nicht aber direkt der *to*-Infinitiv.
  practise speaking (~~practise to speak~~) *into the microphone* ● ● ● üben, ins Mikrofon zu sprechen
  practise how to speak *into the microphone* ● ● ● üben, wie man ins Mikrofon spricht

prefer lieber haben, lieber tun – **would prefer** würde lieber haben, würde lieber tun

- **Schreibung**
  prefer, prefe<u>rr</u>ing, prefe<u>rr</u>ed

- **nicht in der Verlaufsform**
Prefer zählt zu den Verben, die man normalerweise nicht in der Verlaufsform verwenden kann.
  *I used to like coffee, but now I **prefer** (~~I'm preferring~~) tea.* ● ● ● ... aber jetzt trinke ich lieber Tee.

- *prefer doing – prefer to do*
Nach *prefer* kann man entweder eine *-ing*-Form oder einen *to*-Infinitiv anschließen.
  *I **prefer cooking** / **prefer to cook** my own meals.* ● ● ● Ich koche am liebsten selbst.

- *would prefer (sb.) to do*
Nach *would prefer* verwendet man einen *to*-Infinitiv.
  *I'd **prefer to stay** at home.* ● ● ● Ich würde gern / am liebsten zu Hause bleiben.

prepare (sich) vorbereiten; zubereiten

- ***prepare for*** *guests* ● ● ● sich auf Gäste vorbereiten

present ['preznt] gegenwärtig, jetzig, derzeitig; anwesend

- *The **present** rate of inflation is 1.9%.* ● ● ● Die derzeitige/aktuelle Inflationsrate beträgt 1,9 %.
- **in der Bedeutung „anwesend" hinter dem Nomen**
  *The people **present** agreed with me.* ● ● ● Die anwesenden Personen stimmten mir zu.
Aber:
  present company *excepted* ● ● ● die Anwesenden ausgenommen

prevent (ver)hindern

- *prevent sb. (from) doing*
  *He tried to **prevent** her **(from) leaving**.* ● ● ● Er versuchte sie daran zu hindern, zu gehen.

price [praɪs] – **prize** [praɪz] – **cost** [kɒst] Preis

Trouble Spot

- **Preis**
  64 €. Ist das der normale [zu zahlende] Preis? ● ● ● *€64. Is that the normal **price**?*
  Ich habe die Hose zum halben Preis bekommen. ● ● ● *I got the trousers **half-price**.*
  Wer hat den ersten Preis [in dem Wettbewerb] gewonnen? ● ● ● *Who won (the) first **prize**?*
  Das müssen wir um jeden Preis verhindern. ● ● ● *We must prevent that **at all costs**.*

principal ['prɪnsəpl] **1** (AE) Rektor/-in **2** Haupt- – **principally** hauptsächlich – **principle** Prinzip

- *the **principal** of a school* [Nomen] ● ● ● der Leiter/Rektor / die Leiterin/Rektorin einer Schule
- *the **principal** reason* [Adjektiv] ● ● ● der Hauptgrund / der hauptsächliche Grund
  *aimed **principally** at teenagers* [Adverb] ● ● ● hauptsächlich für Teenager (bestimmt)
- *the **principle** of 'one person, one vote'* [Nomen] ● ● ● das Prinzip „pro Person eine Stimme"
  *In **principle** (~~In the principle~~) I am for the idea.* ● ● ● Im Prinzip / An sich bin ich für die Idee.
  *Tony is against it **on principle**.* ● ● ● Tony ist aus Prinzip / prinzipiell dagegen.

P

prison

1 ...... changes a person for ever.
   A Being at prison   B Being in prison   C Being in the prison

2 He was found guilty ...... for seven years.
   A and went into the prison   B and went to the prison
   C and went to prison   D and came to prison

probably

1 A They probably run out of money sometime in the next ten days.
   B They run probably out of money sometime in the next ten days.
   C They'll probably run out of money sometime in the next ten days.

2 ...... We'd better not phone now.
   A Probably they are in the middle of dinner.   B They are probably in the middle of dinner.

problem

1 A I always have problems remembering the name of the place.
   B I always have problems to remember the name of the place.

program – programme

1 In a recent article in the London *Times*, Lord Norton wrote: ......
   A "I think our BBC still produces some of the best TV programmes in the world,"
   B "I think our BBC still produces some of the best TV programs in the world,"

2 A Install the program on your hard disk.   B Install the programme on your hard disk.

progress

1 A We've been making good progress in the last few weeks.
   B We've been making good progresses in the last few weeks.

promise

1 A I promise it doesn't happen again.   B I promise it won't happen again.

2 If I hear anything, ...
   A I'll let you know straightaway, I promise
   B I'll let you know straightaway, promised
   C I'll let you know straightaway, I promise you
   D I'll let you know straightaway, I promise it you

pronounce – pronunciation

1 Grammar mistakes often cause fewer problems in communication than ....
   A mistakes in pronouncing   B mistakes in pronounciation   C mistakes in pronunciation

prospect ≠ „Prospekt"

1 What does 'the prospects' mean in the following sentence?
   The prospects aren't good.
   A the adverts   B the chances of future success   C the reports

2 Perhaps we should have some flyers or *[Prospekte]* printed.
   A brochures   B prospects

prison Gefängnis

■ *Prison* im Sinne von „Haft" steht ohne den bestimmten Artikel.
What effect does **prison** *(the prison) have on young offenders?* ● ● ● Welche Auswirkungen hat das Gefängnis auf junge Straftäter/-innen?
go **to prison**/ *be* **in prison** ● ● ● ins Gefängnis kommen/ im Gefängnis sein

probably ['prɒbəbli] wahrscheinlich

■ **bei Zukunftsbezug: *probably* meist mit *will-future* oder *present progressive***
Wenn man über die Zukunft spricht, verwendet man *probably* meist mit dem *will-future* oder dem *present progressive*,
I'll **probably see** *(I probably see) you tomorrow.* ● ● ● Ich sehe dich wahrscheinlich morgen.
Dirk's not here, but he's **probably coming** *(he probably comes) later.* ● ● ● … aber er kommt wahrscheinlich später.

■ **Stellung in der Satzmitte**
Probably steht in der Regel in der Satzmitte (vor dem Vollverb), nicht am Satzanfang.
It'll **probably** *rain again at the weekend.* ● ● ● Wahrscheinlich regnet es am Wochenende wieder.

problem Problem

■ *have a problem*/ *problems doing*
Auf *have a problem*/ *have problems* folgt ein Verb als *-ing*-Form, nicht als *to*-Infinitiv.
I had a problem/ *had problems finding (had a problem*/ *problems to find) the house.* ● ● ● Ich hatte Probleme, das Haus zu finden.

program – programme ['prəʊɡræm] Programm

■ *computer program* ● ● ● Computerprogramm
(BE:) *TV programme*/ (AE:) *TV program* ● ● ● Fernsehsendung
(BE:) *a programme*/ (AE:) *a program of reform* ● ● ● ein Reformprogramm [= Plan für Reformen]

progress [(BE:) 'prəʊɡres, (AE:) 'prɑːɡres] Fortschritt(e)

■ **nicht zählbares Nomen**
Progress ist ein nicht zählbares Nomen und kann daher nicht im Plural oder mit *a* verwendet werden.
make (some) **progress** *(progresses)* ● ● ● Fortschritte machen
That's **progress** *(a progress).* ● ● ● Das ist (schon mal) ein Fortschritt.

promise versprechen

■ **bei Zukunftsbezug: *promise* meist mit *will-future***
I promise I'll pay (I pay) you back tomorrow. ● ● ● Ich verspreche, dass ich das Geld morgen zurückzahle.

■ *I'll do it tomorrow.* **I promise.** *(Promised.)*/ **I promise you**. *(I promise you it.)* ● ● ● Ich mache es morgen. Versprochen./ Ich verspreche es dir.

pronounce [prə'naʊns] aussprechen – pronunciation [prə,nʌnsi'eɪʃn] Aussprache

■ *How do you* **pronounce** *this?* ● ● ● Wie spricht man das aus?
■ *English* **pronunciation** *can be difficult.* ● ● ● Die englische Aussprache kann schwierig sein.

prospect ['prɒspekt] (Zukunfts-)Aussicht

■ **False Friend!**
Prospect bedeutet nicht „Prospekt", sondern „(Zukunfts-)Aussicht".
Are the **prospects** *of success better this time?* ● ● ● Sind die Erfolgsaussichten diesmal besser?
Beachte die englische Entsprechung von „Prospekt":
Reise-/Werbeprospekt ● ● ● *travel*/ *advertising* **brochure** [(BE:) 'brəʊʃə; (AE:) brəʊ'ʃʊr]

P

protect

1 **A** When cycling, wear glasses to protect yourself against eye injury.
B When cycling, wear glasses to protect yourself for eye injury.
C When cycling, wear glasses to protect yourself from eye injury.

proud

1 .... You did a great job.
A I'm really proud at you.   **B** I'm really proud of you.   **C** I'm really proud on you.

public ≠ „Publikum"

1 What is the best synonym for 'the public' in the following sentence?
This question is completely irrelevant to the public.
A ordinary people in general
B people in public places
C the people who support a sports team

2 It isn't something that people like to ....
A talk about publically   **B** talk about publicly
C talk about in public   **D** talk about in the public

3 [Das Publikum] booed and hissed and threw eggs onto the stage.
A The audience   **B** The public   **C** The watchers

punish

1 ...... that wasn't really his fault at all.
A His dad punished him about something   **B** His dad punished him because of something
C His dad punished him for something

puzzle

1 **A** We spent all evening doing a 1000-piece jigsaw.
B We spent all evening making a 1000-piece jigsaw.

2 ...... I don't know what can have happened to it. It's just completely disappeared!
A It's a complete jigsaw to me.   **B** It's a complete puzzle to me.

pyjamas/pajamas

1 **A** I don't normally wear a pyjama, but this one is silk. My aunt bought it in Thailand.
B I don't normally wear pyjamas, but these ones are silk. My aunt bought them in Thailand.

2 **A** How much does a silk pajama cost?   **B** How much does a pair of silk pajamas cost?
C How much do silk pajamas cost?

qualify

1 **A** None of the German swimmers have qualifyed themselves for the final.
B None of the German swimmers have qualified themselves for the final.
C None of the German swimmers have qualified for the final.

quantity

1 **A** You only need a little quantity water.   **B** You only need a little quantity of water.
C You only need a small quantity water.   **D** You only need a small quantity of water.

protect (be)schützen

■ *Put cream on to **protect** yourself **from**/**against** the sun.* ● ● ● Schmier dich ein, um dich vor der Sonne / gegen die Sonne zu schützen.

proud stolz

■ *"I'm very **proud of** you (~~proud on you~~)," he said.* ● ● ● „Ich bin sehr stolz auf dich", sagte er.

public ['pʌblɪk] **1** öffentlich **2** Öffentlichkeit

!
!
!
!
!
!

■ **False Friend!**
Public bedeutet nicht „~~Publikum~~", sondern „öffentlich" bzw. „Öffentlichkeit".
*There were **public** protests against the regime.* ● ● ● Es gab öffentliche Proteste …
*People don't talk about it **publicly** (~~publically~~) / **in public** (~~in the public~~).* ● ● ● Die Leute reden nicht öffentlich / in der/aller Öffentlichkeit darüber.
***The public** is/are against the new law.* ● ● ● Die Bevölkerung/Öffentlichkeit ist …
Beachte die englischen Entsprechungen von „Publikum":
Das Publikum lacht immer bei dieser Szene. ● ● ● *The **audience** ['ɔːdɪəns] always laugh/laughs in this scene.*
Das Publikum [bei einer Sportveranstaltung] erlebte ein spannendes Spiel. ● ● ● *The **crowd**/ **spectators** saw an exciting match.*

punish bestrafen

■ **punish sb. for doing**
*She was **punished for stealing**.* ● ● ● Sie wurde wegen Stehlens bestraft. / Sie wurde bestraft, weil sie gestohlen hatte.

puzzle ['pʌzl] Rätsel; Puzzle

■ **meist „Rätsel", nicht „Puzzle"**
Puzzle kann dem deutschen „Puzzle" entsprechen.
*do a **puzzle** / (BE auch:) **jigsaw (puzzle)** with 500 pieces* ● ● ● ein Puzzle mit 500 Teilen machen/ zusammensetzen
Meist bedeutet *puzzle* jedoch „Rätsel(spiel)".
*crossword **puzzle*** ● ● ● Kreuzworträtsel
*I bought a book of **puzzles** for the long train journey.* ● ● ● … ein Rätselheft …
*solve a **puzzle*** ● ● ● ein Rätsel raten/lösen

P

pyjamas (BE) [pə'dʒɑːməs] / **pajamas** (AE) Schlafanzug, Pyjama

■ **Pluralnomen, keine Singularform**
Wie *trousers* gibt es *pyjamas* nur als Pluralnomen (mit Verb im Plural). Um daraus eine Singularform zu machen, muss man *a pair of* verwenden.
*The nights are cold, so pack **some** warm **pyjamas** / a warm **pair of pyjamas** / a **pair of** warm pyjamas.* ● ● ● … also pack einen warmen Schlafanzug ein.
***These pyjamas are** warm enough.* ● ● ● Dieser Schlafanzug ist warm genug.

qualify ['kwɒlɪfaɪ] sich qualifizieren

■ **nicht reflexiv**
*Which teams have **qualified** (~~qualified themselves~~) for the final?* ● ● ● Welche Mannschaften haben sich für das Finale qualifiziert?

quantity ['kwɒntəti] Menge ▷ amount

■ *The police found a **large**/**great**/**small quantity** (~~a big / little quantity~~) of cocaine.* ● ● ● Die Polizei fand eine große/beträchtliche/kleine Menge Kokain.

quiet – silent – calm – smooth – still

1 Where can we do the recording? Perhaps the cellar is *[der ruhigste Ort]*.
   A the calmest place   **B** the quietest place   **C** the most silent place
   D the smoothest place   **E** the stillest place

2 Ann is *[sehr ruhig]* this evening, she's hardly said a word. Is anything the matter?
   A very calm   **B** very quiet   **C** very silent   **D** very smooth   **E** very still

3 Don't panic, please. *[Wenn alle ruhig bleiben]*, we'll be able to evacuate you all faster.
   A If everyone stays calm   **B** If everyone stays quiet   **C** If everyone stays silent
   D If everyone stays smooth   **E** If everyone stays still

4 We were expecting autumn storms, but the sea was *[ganz ruhig]*.
   A quite calm   **B** quite quiet   **C** quite silent

5 How was the ferry? How was the crossing? – *[Sehr ruhig]*, thanks.
   A Very still   **B** Very quiet   **C** Very silent   **D** Very smooth

6 **A** If you sit still, this won't hurt.   **B** If you sit calm, this won't hurt.

quite – pretty – fairly – rather

1 **A** I know a quite nice campsite a few miles inland from the coast.
   B I know quite a nice campsite a few miles inland from the coast.
   C I know a rather nice campsite a few miles inland from the coast.
   D I know fairly a nice campsite a few miles inland from the coast.
   E I know a pretty nice campsite a few miles inland from the coast.

2 ...... We got lost twice.
   A It was a quite problem finding you actually.   **B** It was quite a problem finding you actually.

rain

1 **A** It rained hard all morning.
   B It rained heavily all morning.
   C It rained strongly all morning.
   D It poured with rain all morning.

2 We don't hear much *[über sauren Regen]* these days.
   A about acid rain   **B** about bitter rain   **C** about sour rain

raise – rise

1 **A** The price of oil has raised again.
   B The price of oil has risen again.
   C The price of oil has rised again.

2 Prices are going up all the time, ...
   A but they haven't raised my wages
   B but they haven't rised my wages
   C but they haven't risen my wages

3 ...... , and another hot Sahara day began.
   A The sun raised over the horizon
   B The sun rised over the horizon
   C The sun rose over the horizon

quiet – silent – calm – smooth [smuːð] **– still** ruhig, leise, still

Trouble Spot

■ **ruhig**

1 „ohne Lärm"

Das Schlafzimmer ist schön ruhig. ● ● ● *The bedroom is nice and* **quiet**.

2 „ereignisarm"

ein ganz ruhiges Leben führen ● ● ● *lead a very* **quiet** *life*

ganz ruhige Ferien zu Hause verbringen ● ● ● *spend a very* **quiet** *holiday at home*

3 „schweigsam", „still"

Du bist so ruhig. Was ist los? ● ● ● *You're so* **quiet/silent**. *What's wrong?*

4 „gelassen", „reglos"

Er sagte mit ganz ruhiger Stimme … ● ● ● *In a very* **calm** *voice he said …*

Sie wartete ganz ruhig. ● ● ● *She waited quite* **calmly**.

5 „nicht aufgewühlt", „glatt", „windstill" [Meer, Wetter]

Das Meer/Wetter war ruhig. ● ● ● *The sea/weather was* **calm**.

eine ruhige Überfahrt nach Dover [bei glattem Meer] ● ● ● *a* **smooth** *crossing to Dover*

6 „ohne sich zu bewegen", „reglos"

Das Kind kann nicht ruhig/still sitzen. ● ● ● *The child can't* **sit still**.

Aber:

Das Kind saß ruhig [= still, schweigsam] auf seinem Stuhl. ● ● ● *The child sat* **quietly** *in its chair.*

---

quite – pretty – fairly – rather ['rɑːðə] ziemlich, recht

■ **Schreibung und Aussprache beachten:** *quite – quiet*

It's **quite quiet** [ˌkwaɪt ˈkwaɪət] *here today.* ● ● ● Heute ist es ziemlich ruhig hier.

■ **Stellung von** *a/an*

Quite und *rather* können vor **oder** nach dem unbestimmten Artikel stehen. *Quite a(n)* ist jedoch üblicher als *a quite*.

Today is **quite a** *hectic day* / [seltener:] **a quite** *hectic day*. ● ● ● … ein ziemlich hektischer Tag.

Today is **rather a** *hectic day* / **a rather** *hectic day*. ● ● ● … ein ziemlich hektischer Tag.

Bei einem allein (d. h. ohne Adjektiv) stehenden Nomen heißt es immer *quite a/rather a*.

It was **quite a** *surprise*. ● ● ● … eine ziemliche Überraschung.

It was **rather a** *shock*. ● ● ● … ein ziemlicher Schock.

Pretty und *fairly* stehen nur hinter *a*.

We had **a pretty** *good journey*. ● ● ● … eine ziemlich gute Reise.

We had **a fairly** *good journey*. ● ● ● … eine ziemlich gute Reise.

---

rain 1 regnen **2** Regen

■ *It's* **raining** *hard/heavily (~~strongly~~)*. ● ● ● Es regnet stark/heftig.

The **rain** *is very heavy (~~strong/hard~~)*. ● ● ● Der Regen ist sehr stark/heftig.

It's pouring (with **rain***)*. ● ● ● Es gießt (in Strömen).

I set off in pouring **rain**. ● ● ● Ich bin bei strömendem Regen aufgebrochen.

Acid rain [ˌæsɪd ˈreɪn] *(~~Sour rain~~) rain is a big problem in Scandinavia.* ● ● ● Saurer Regen …

---

raise [reɪz] (an)heben, erhöhen **– rise*** [raɪz] (an)steigen; sich erheben; aufgehen [Sonne]

■ *raise – raised – raised*

They have **raised** *the price*. [*raise* + Objekt] ● ● ● Sie haben den Preis erhöht/angehoben.

Over 20 people **raised** *their hands*. [*raise* + Objekt] ● ● ● Über 20 Leute hoben die Hand.

■ *rise – rose – risen* ['rɪzn]

The price has **risen**. ● ● ● Der Preis hat sich erhöht/ist gestiegen.

One person **rose** *and left the room*. ● ● ● Einer erhob sich und verließ den Raum.

What time does the sun **rise***?* ● ● ● Wann geht die Sonne auf?

Q

rather: would rather

1 The tennis star said ....

  A she'd rather lose than win because of an umpire's mistake

  B she'd rather to lose than win because of an umpire's mistake

2 A I'd rather that you didn't say anything about all this to my parents.

  B I'd rather that you wouldn't say anything about all this to my parents.

react – reaction

1 .... , because it must have been quite a surprise?

  A How did people react at the announcement

  B How did people react on the announcement

  C How did people react to the announcement

ready – finish

1 A We're just getting ready to leave.

  B We're just making ourselves ready to leave.

  C We're just finishing to leave.

2 .... We need another ten minutes or quarter of an hour.

  A We aren't quite ready with packing.   **B** We haven't quite finished packing.

realize/realise – recognize/recognise

1 A How did you realize me among all those people?

  B How did you recognize me among all those people?

2 It wasn't till much later ....

  A that I realized how much I missed the old place

  B that I recognized how much I missed the old place

reason

1 A Was there a reason for not inviting Samantha?

  B Was there a reason why you didn't invite Samantha?

  C Was there a reason that you didn't invite Samantha?

2 A Because of some reason he didn't seem to understand my question.

  B For some reason he didn't seem to understand my question.

  C From some reason he didn't seem to understand my question.

receipt ≠ „Rezept"

1 A receipt is ....

  A a piece of paper that says how much you have paid

  B a piece of paper that says how to cook a meal

  C a piece of paper that says what medicine you should take

2 .... , but she always seems to win.

  A I don't know what Sarah's prescription for success is

  B I don't know what Sarah's recipe for success is

3 A This medicine is available on prescription only.

  B This medicine is available on recipe only.

rather [ˈrɑːðə]: **would rather** möchte/würde lieber   ▶ quite

■ **would rather do**

I'd rather do it / I would rather do it bedeutet „ich würde es lieber tun", „mir wäre es lieber, es zu tun". Nach *would rather* steht ein Infinitiv ohne *to*.

   He'd rather stay (He'd rather to stay) at home today. ● ● ● Er würde heute lieber zu Hause bleiben.

■ **would rather that ...**

Nach *would rather* kann auch ein *that*-Satz stehen. Im *that*-Satz steht das *past tense*, aber kein *would* (also wie in *if*-Sätzen).

   I'd rather (that) you asked (I'd rather you would ask) my parents. ● ● ● Mir wäre es lieber, du würdest meine Eltern fragen.

   I'd rather (that) you didn't come (I'd rather you wouldn't come) today. I don't feel too good. ● ● ● Mir wäre es lieber, du würdest heute nicht kommen. ...

react reagieren – **reaction** Reaktion

■ *How did Ms Cook **react to** the suggestion?* ● ● ● Wie hat Frau Cook auf den Vorschlag reagiert?

   *the government's **reaction to** the oil crisis* ● ● ● die Reaktion der Regierung auf die Ölkrise

ready fertig, bereit – **finish** fertig machen, beenden

■ *Ready* entspricht „fertig" im Sinne von „bereit".

   ***Are** you **ready** (to begin)? Can we start?* ● ● ● Bist du fertig/bereit? Können wir anfangen?

   *Ann is **getting ready**.* ● ● ● Ann macht sich fertig.

■ *Finished* entspricht „fertig" im Sinne von „erledigt", „abgeschlossen", „beendet".

   *My homework **is finished**.* ● ● ● Meine Hausaufgaben sind fertig.

   *I've **finished** (doing) my homework.* ● ● ● Ich bin mit den Hausaufgaben fertig.

   *I'm **finished**.* ● ● ● Ich bin fertig.

realize / (BE auch:) realise [ˈriːəlaɪz] – **recognize / (BE auch:) recognise** [ˈrekəgnaɪz] erkennen

■ *Realize* bedeutet „erkennen" im Sinne von „bemerken", „begreifen", „einsehen". ▶ **notice** *(verb)*

   *I suddenly **realized** that I'd made a mistake.* ● ● ● Plötzlich erkannte ich / wurde mir klar, dass ich einen Fehler gemacht hatte.

■ *Recognize* bedeutet „erkennen" im Sinne von „wiedererkennen", „identifizieren".

   *Her hair was short, and I almost didn't **recognize** her.* ● ● ● ... ich hätte sie fast nicht erkannt.

■ **nicht in der Verlaufsform**

In den angegebenen Bedeutungen kann weder *realize* noch *recognize* in der Verlaufsform stehen.

   *I **realize** now (I'm now realizing) why she didn't talk to me.* ● ● ● Jetzt ist mir klar, warum ...

   *Now that you've taken your hat off, I **recognize** (I'm recognizing) you.* ● ● ● ... erkenne ich dich.

R

reason [Beweg-]Grund

■ *What was his **reason for** phoning? / What was the **reason why** / that he phoned?* ● ● ● Aus welchem Grund hat er angerufen? / Was war der Grund für seinen Anruf?

   *I'm against the idea **for** several **reasons**.* ● ● ● Ich bin aus mehreren Gründen gegen die Idee.

receipt [rɪˈsiːt] Quittung

■ **False Friend!**

Receipt bedeutet nicht „Rezept", sondern „Quittung", „Kassenbon", „Empfangsbestätigung".

   *get a **receipt** from the taxi driver* ● ● ● eine Quittung/Rechnung vom Taxifahrer bekommen

Beachte die englischen Entsprechungen von „Rezept":

   ein neues [Koch-]Rezept ausprobieren ● ● ● *try out a new **recipe*** [ˈresəpi]

   ein Erfolgsrezept ● ● ● *a **recipe** for success*

   das Rezept vom Arzt zur Apotheke bringen ● ● ● *take the doctor's **prescription*** [prɪˈskrɪpʃn] *to the chemist's* [ˈkemɪsts]

recently

1 The train used to be very crowded, ...

   A but recently it's been a bit emptier   **B** but recently it was a bit emptier

refuse – reject

1 I tried hard, ...

   A but I'm afraid the suggestion was refused   **B** but I'm afraid the suggestion was rejected

2 ...... It's the chance of a lifetime!

   A They've made me an offer I can't refuse.   **B** They've made me an offer I can't reject.

regret

1 My father once told me ....

   A that he always regreted not going to university

   B that he always regretted not going to university

   C that he always regretted not to go to university

2 A We regret announcing that flight KJ 3758 has been cancelled.

   B We regret to announce that flight KJ 3758 has been cancelled.

related

1 Your name's Beckham? ......

   A Are you related from David Beckham?

   B Are you related to David Beckham?

   C Are you related with David Beckham?

relevant

1 You can skip the next page, ...

   A it isn't relevant for people like us   **B** it isn't relevant to people like us

remember – remind

1 Oh, yes. ...... That was the day after he came to school in a kilt, wasn't it?

   A I'm remembering now.   **B** I remember now.

2 A Do you remember the name of the pub near there?

   B Do you remember yourself the name of the pub near there?

   C Do you remember to the name of the pub near there?

   D Do you remember yourself to the name of the pub near there?

3 It's a very long time ago now, ... My mother carried me into the house straight into bed.

   A but I can remember to arrive very late at night

   B but I can remember to have arrived very late at night

   C but I can remember arriving very late at night

4 A Please remember bringing two copies.

   B Please remember to bring two copies.

5 A Can you remember me to buy some bread on the way home?

   B Can you remind me to buy some bread on the way home?

6 A I must remind Jeremy about that money he owes me.

   B I must remind Jeremy of that money he owes me.

recently in letzter Zeit; vor kurzem

■ **mit** *present perfect* **oder** *past tense*
Recently in der Bedeutung „in letzter Zeit" steht mit dem *present perfect*.
   *We **haven't seen** much of David **recently**.* ● ● ● Wir haben David in letzter Zeit nicht oft gesehen.
Recently in der Bedeutung „vor kurzem" steht mit dem *past tense*.
   *David **passed** his driving test **recently**.* ● ● ● David hat vor kurzem die Fahrprüfung bestanden.

refuse – reject ablehnen

■ **refuse** *an invitation / an offer / a request* ● ● ● eine Einladung / ein Angebot / eine Bitte ablehnen
   *It's an offer you can't **refuse**.* ● ● ● Dieses Angebot kann man nicht ausschlagen.

■ **reject** *a suggestion / a plan / an idea / a bill / a (financial) offer* ● ● ● einen Vorschlag / einen Plan / eine Idee / einen Gesetzentwurf / ein (finanzielles) Angebot ablehnen

regret bedauern

■ **Schreibung**
   *regret, regre**tt**ing, regre**tt**ed*

■ **regret doing = „etwas Vergangenes bedauern"**
   *I **regret giving** away (= I regret that I gave away) that old tent. I could use it now.* ● ● ●
      Ich bedauere, dass ich das alte Zelt weggegeben habe. …

■ **regret to do = „etwas bedauern, was man gleich tun wird"**
   *I **regret to tell** you that you have only 43 points and have failed the exam.* ● ● ● Ich muss Ihnen
      leider mitteilen, dass … / Ich bedaure, Ihnen mitteilen zu müssen, dass …

related verwandt

■ **related to sb. / sth.**
   *Sid is **related to** (~~related with~~) my piano teacher.* ● ● ● Sid ist mit meinem Klavierlehrer verwandt.

relevant ['reləvənt] relevant, bedeutsam, wichtig

■ **relevant to sb. / sth.**
   *How is this **relevant to** the discussion?* ● ● ● Inwiefern ist das für die Diskussion relevant / wichtig /
      von Bedeutung?

remember (sich) erinnern – remind erinnern ▶ notice *(verb)*

■ **remember (sth. / sb.): nicht in der Verlaufsform; nicht reflexiv**
Remember (nicht reflexiv!) gehört zu den Verben, die man normalerweise nicht in der Verlaufsform
verwenden kann.
   *I **remember** (~~I'm remembering~~) now. He broke his arm, didn't he?* ● ● ● Jetzt erinnere ich mich. …
Ein Objekt wird ohne Präposition an *remember* angeschlossen.
   *Can you **remember** Renate (~~remember to Renate~~)?* ● ● ● Kannst du dich noch an Renate erinnern?

■ **remember doing = „sich an etwas Vergangenes erinnern"**
   *I **remember visiting** my great-grandmother.* ● ● ● Ich weiß noch / erinnere mich, wie ich meine
      Urgroßmutter besucht habe.

■ **remember to do = „sich etwas für die Zukunft vormerken"**
   *I must **remember to buy** Janice a birthday present.* ● ● ● Ich muss daran denken, ein Geburtstags-
      geschenk für Janice zu kaufen.

■ **remind sb. about / of – remind sb. to do**
   ***Remind** Alexander **about** his homework, please. He still hasn't done it.* ● ● ● Erinnere Alexander
      bitte an seine Hausaufgaben! Er hat sie immer noch nicht gemacht.
   *You **remind** me **of** someone I knew where I used to live.* ● ● ● Du erinnerst mich an jemanden, den
      ich an dem Ort kannte, wo ich früher gewohnt habe.
   *Please **remind** me **to phone** Mr Wright.* ● ● ● Bitte erinnere mich daran, Herrn Wright anzurufen.

repeat – repetition

1 ...... I think someone has been downloading stuff off the Internet.
  A Three repeatings of exactly the same sentence in three different essays?
  B Three repeatitions of exactly the same sentence in three different essays?
  C Three repetitions of exactly the same sentence in three different essays?

2 ...... , then throw this piece of paper away.
  A Repeat me the password again   B Repeat the password to me again

report

1 ...... , from the moment you left the classroom.
  A I'd like you to report the inspector everything that happened
  B I'd like you to report everything that happened to the inspector

reputation

1 A Mrs Courtney has a reputation for being rather difficult.
  B Mrs Courtney has the reputation to be rather difficult.

request

1 ...... that I stayed on another two days.
  A It was at Martha's request   B It was on Martha's request

2 A Names and addresses will only be made available at request.
  B Names and addresses will only be made available on request.

resist

1 ...... that would tie me to one provider for over 12 months.
  A Up till now I've always resisted from signing a contract
  B Up till now I've always resisted signing a contract
  C Up till now I've always resisted to sign a contract

responsible

1 ...... They seem to have done a wonderful job.
  A Who was responsible for organizing the publicity?
  B Who was responsible to organize the publicity?

rest

1 ...... , in other words with a private bathroom.
  A The rest of the rooms was all en suite   B The rest of the rooms were all en suite

2 At Pompeii you can see ....
  A the remains of two-thousand-year-old buildings
  B the remainders of two-thousand-year-old buildings
  C the rests of two-thousand-year-old buildings

repeat wiederholen – repetition [ˌrepəˈtɪʃn] Wiederholung

■ **Schreibung**
rep<u>ea</u>t – rep<u>e</u>tition

■ *repeat sth. to/for sb.*
Nach *repeat* muss die Person, der gegenüber man etwas wiederholt, mit *to* oder *for* stehen.
*Can you **repeat** the last two numbers **to/for** me (~~repeat me the last two numbers~~), please?* ● ● ●
Kannst du mir bitte die letzten beiden Zahlen wiederholen?

report berichten, melden

■ *report (sth.) to sb.*
Nach *report* steht die Person oder Gruppe, der man etwas berichtet, mit *to.*
***report** back **to** the class* ● ● ● der Klasse einen Bericht erstatten/berichten
***report** the theft **to** the police (~~report the police the theft~~)* ● ● ● der Polizei den Diebstahl melden
*I **reported** what I saw **to** my parents.* ● ● ● Ich habe meinen Eltern berichtet, was ich gesehen habe.

reputation [ˌrepjuˈteɪʃn] Ruf

■ *reputation for doing*
*have **a reputation for being** (~~the reputation to be~~) late* ● ● ● den Ruf haben, immer zu spät zu
kommen/dafür bekannt sein, dass man immer zu spät kommt

request Bitte, Anfrage

■ *do sth. **at** sb.'s **request*** ● ● ● etwas auf jmds. Bitte hin tun
*do sth. **at the request of** sb.* ● ● ● etwas auf Bitte von jmdm. tun

■ *do sth. **on request*** ● ● ● etwas auf Anfrage/Wunsch tun

resist [rɪˈzɪst] widerstehen, sich wehren gegen

■ *resist doing*
*I couldn't **resist asking** (~~resist to ask~~) what he had paid for it.* ● ● ● Ich musste einfach fragen/Ich
konnte mir nicht verkneifen zu fragen, was er dafür bezahlt hatte.

responsible verantwortlich

■ *responsible for doing*
*When we have a concert, I'm **responsible for informing** (~~responsible to inform~~) the press in time.*
● ● ● … bin ich dafür verantwortlich, die Presse rechtzeitig zu informieren.

rest Rest

■ **rest + Singular- oder Pluralverb**
Je nach Bezug kann *rest* mit einem Verb im Singular oder Plural stehen.
*The **rest** of the exam **was** easy.* [exam = Singular] ● ● ● Der Rest der Prüfung war leicht.
*The **rest** of the questions **were** easy.* [questions = Plural] ● ● ● Der Rest der Fragen war einfach./
Die restlichen Fragen waren einfach.

Trouble Spot

■ **Rest(e)**
1 „der verbleibende Teil einer Menge"
der Rest der Klasse/Bücher ● ● ● *the rest/remainder of the class/books*

2 „die Überreste von etwas, das früher einmal eine Einheit war"
die Reste eines alten Gebäudes ● ● ● *the remains of an old building*

3 „ein letzter Rest"
Es ist noch ein Rest Kuchen da. ● ● ● *There's still a bit of cake left.*

4 „Essensreste"
die Reste an die Schweine verfüttern ● ● ● *feed the leftovers to the pigs*

return

1 ...... , but now we need to focus our attention on something else.

  A We'll return back to this question later on   **B** We'll return to this question later on

---

rich

1 **A** Only a rich could afford a car like that.   **B** Only a rich person could afford a car like that.

  C Only rich people could afford a car like that.   **D** Only the rich could afford a car like that.

2 **A** In the story, the rich dies all alone.   **B** In the story, the rich woman dies all alone.

---

right: be right

1 ...... He's really not to be trusted.

  A You were right about Julian all along.   **B** You were right with Julian all along.

  C You were right for Julian all along.

---

risk

1 Leave your camera at home. ......

  A The risk of having it stolen is too great.   **B** The risk to have it stolen is too great.

2 If you do that, ... who might otherwise support us.

  A you risk making an enemy of someone   **B** you risk of making an enemy of someone

  C you risk to make an enemy of someone

---

rob – mug – steal – burgle

1 What's the matter? – ...... It happened on the way home. She's talking to the police now.

  A Kathy's been burgled.   **B** Kathy's been mugged.

  C Kathy's been robbed.   **D** Kathy's been stolen.

2 **A** A priceless painting has been burgled in a daring raid on a major museum.

  B A priceless painting has been robbed in a daring raid on a major museum.

  C A priceless painting has been stolen in a daring raid on a major museum.

3 ...... But now it's happened here too.

  A We moved from Windsor because our house was burgled three times.

  B We moved from Windsor because our house was robbed three times.

  C We moved from Windsor because our house was stolen three times.

---

rubbish/garbage

1 **A** Our rubbish are destroying the planet.   **B** Our rubbish is destroying the planet.

---

rule – govern – reign

1 **A** How long have the Labour Party governed the country overall?

  B How long have the Labour Party ruled the country overall?

  C How long have the Labour Party reigned the country overall?

2 You could say .... He was certainly successful, but he was a terrible despot ['despɒt].

  A that he 'governed' the company he built up   **B** that he 'reigned' the company he built up

  C that he 'ruled' the company he built up

3 ...... – Over 60 years, I think.

  A How long did Queen Victoria govern?   **B** How long did Queen Victoria reign?

  C How long did Queen Victoria rule?

return zurückkehren, zurückgehen, zurückkommen

■ *We **returned** (~~returned back~~) to the same café the next day. = We went back to the same café the next day.* ● ● ● Wir gingen am nächsten Tag wieder in dasselbe Restaurant.

rich reich

■ **als Nomen nur zur Bezeichnung einer Gruppe**
The rich (ohne Plural-*s*) bezeichnet eine Gruppe von Reichen (oft im Sinne von „alle Reichen").
   ***The rich** (= **Rich people**) don't care what happens to the poor.* ● ● ● Den Reichen ist es egal …
Aber:
   *Only **a rich person** can afford to live here.* ● ● ● Nur ein Reicher / eine Reiche kann es sich leisten …
   ***The rich man** gave the beggar five dollars.* ● ● ● Der Reiche / Der reiche Mann …

right: be* right Recht haben

■ *I **was right about** (~~right with~~) the price. It's gone up now.* ● ● ● Ich hatte Recht mit dem Preis. …

risk **1** Risiko **2** riskieren

■ **risk of doing**
   ***The risk of meeting** (~~The risk to meet~~) your dad is small.* ● ● ● Das Risiko, deinen Vater zu treffen …
   ***At the risk of seeming** stupid, I have to ask …* ● ● ● Auch auf die Gefahr hin, doof zu erscheinen …
   *If you don't revise, you **run the risk of failing**.* ● ● ● … läufst du Gefahr durchzufallen.

■ **risk doing**
   *I don't want to **risk getting** (~~risk to get~~) wet.* ● ● ● Ich will nicht riskieren, nass zu werden.

rob (aus)rauben – **mug** überfallen und ausrauben – **steal*** stehlen – **burgle** einbrechen in

Trouble Spot

■ **(aus)rauben**
1 „eine Bank überfallen / eine Person berauben"
   ***rob** a bank / a person*

2 „eine Person auf offener Straße überfallen (und ausrauben)"
   ***mug** a person in the street*

3 „Sachen stehlen"
   ***steal** money / jewels / computers (from sb.)*

4 „in ein Gebäude einbrechen (und etwas stehlen)"
   (BE:) **burgle** / (AE:) **burglarize** *a house / building*
   We've been (BE:) **burgled** / (AE:) **burglarized**. ● ● ● Bei uns ist eingebrochen worden.

R

rubbish (BE) / garbage [ˈgɑːrbɪdʒ] (AE) Abfall, Abfälle, Müll

■ **nicht zählbare Nomen**
Rubbish und *garbage* sind nicht zählbar. Man kann sie also nicht im Plural verwenden.
   *There **was rubbish** everywhere.* ● ● ● Überall lag Abfall / lagen Abfälle.

rule – govern [ˈgʌvn] – **reign** [reɪn] regieren

Trouble Spot

■ **regieren**
1 „allein herrschen (über)", „beherrschen"
   Der Diktator regierte mit eiserner Hand. ● ● ● *The dictator **ruled** with an iron* [ˈaɪən] *hand.*

2 „die Regierungsgewalt haben (über)"
   Das Land wird von einer Koalition regiert. ● ● ● *The country is **governed / ruled** by a coalition.*

3 „als Monarch/-in herrschen"
   Königin Elisabeth I. regierte über 40 Jahre. ● ● ● *Queen Elizabeth I **reigned / ruled** for over 40 years.*

salad – lettuce

1 I've started ...... on the balcony.
   A to grow lettuce   **B** to grow salad

2 A pizza salami, ... , please.
   A and a small lettuce   **B** and a small salad

sale

1 ...... from 1st October.
   A The new model will be for sale
   B The new model will be in sale
   C The new model will be on sale

2 I'm very sorry, but that's part of our window display. ......
   A It's not to buy.   **B** It's not to sell.   **C** It's not for sale.   **D** It's not on sale.

the same

1 **A** My best friend and I are equal aged.
   B My best friend and I are the same age.
   C My best friend and I are the same old.

sauce – gravy – dressing

1 When the meat is cooked, ...
   A use the juices from the meat to make the dressing
   B use the juices from the meat to make the gravy
   C use the juices from the meat to make the sauce

2 I think ...... if you put a little sugar in it.
   A the salad dressing always tastes better   **B** the salad gravy always tastes better
   C the salad sauce always tastes better

save

1 I think Juliana deserves a medal. ......
   A She saved us all against disaster.   **B** She saved us all for disaster.
   C She saved us all from disaster.

2 If you book now, ...
   A you can save up to 30% by the price   **B** you can save up to 30% from the price
   C you can save up to 30% on the price

say – tell

1 **A** What did the manager say you?   **B** What did the manager tell you?

2 I can't decide .... I don't know whether to believe all this or not.
   A if he's saying the truth or not   **B** if he's telling the truth or not

3 You were the last to leave the building. – ......
   A Who says?   **B** Who says it?   **C** Who says so?

4 What are they going to do next? – ......
   A They didn't say.   **B** They didn't say it.   **C** They didn't say so.

5 I don't know what time the meeting starts, ... as soon as I find out.
   A but I'll say it to you   **B** but I'll say you   **C** but I'll tell it to you   **D** but I'll tell you

salad [ˈsæləd] – **lettuce** [ˈletɪs] Salat

- **salad** = „angemachter Salat als Gericht"
  eat a **salad** for lunch; a tomato/potato/fruit/chicken/mixed **salad**

- **lettuce** = „Salatpflanze/-kopf", „Kopfsalat"
  buy a **lettuce**; wash the **lettuce**; plant **lettuce** in the garden

sale Verkauf

- Is it **for sale**? Has it got a price label? ● ● ● Ist es zu verkaufen? Hat es ein Preisschild?
  When will the next Harry Potter book be **on sale**? ● ● ● Wann wird der nächste Harry-Potter-Band
  verkauft? / Wann ist der nächste Harry-Potter-Band erhältlich? / Wann gibt's den nächsten …?

same: the same der-/die-/dasselbe, der/die/das gleiche; der/die/das Gleiche

- **the same** + Nomen
  The same verwendet man nur vor Nomen, nicht vor Adjektiven oder Adverbien.
  The rooms are **the same** size (~~the same big~~). ● ● ● Die Zimmer sind gleich groß.
  be **the same** age/weight/price ● ● ● gleich alt/schwer/teuer sein
  We drove at **the same** speed. ● ● ● Wir fuhren gleich schnell.

- My train is always late. – It's **the same with** (~~the same by~~) me. ● ● ● … – Bei mir ist es genauso.

sauce [sɔːs] – **gravy** [ˈgreɪvi] – **dressing** Soße

<table>
<tr><td rowspan="4" style="writing-mode: vertical-rl">**Trouble Spot**</td><td>

- Soße
  Tomaten-/Soja-/Schokoladensoße ● ● ● tomato/soy/chocolate **sauce** [Betonung auf sauce]
  Bratensoße über die Kartoffeln gießen ● ● ● pour **gravy** over the potatoes
  Salatsoße ● ● ● (salad) **dressing**
</td></tr>
</table>

save retten; sparen; [Daten] (ab)speichern, sichern

- **save** sb. **from** drowning ● ● ● jmdn. vor dem Ertrinken retten/bewahren

- **save** €50 **on** your flight by travelling on Monday ● ● ● 50 € beim Flug [ein]sparen …

- **save** the files **onto** your hard disk ● ● ● die Dateien auf der Festplatte speichern/sichern

S

say* – **tell*** sagen

- Faustregel: Wird die Person genannt, der etwas gesagt wird, so verwendet man *tell*, sonst *say*.
  Come on, **tell us**. What did she **say**? ● ● ● Los, sag schon! Was hat sie gesagt?
  She **told me** (~~said me~~) to park at the end of the street. ● ● ● Sie sagte mir, ich solle … parken.
  I **said** (~~told~~) that we would be coming later. ● ● ● Ich habe gesagt, dass wir später kommen würden.

- feste Wendungen mit *tell*
  tell the truth ● ● ● die Wahrheit sagen
  tell lies/jokes/a story ● ● ● Lügen/Witze/eine Geschichte erzählen

<table>
<tr><td rowspan="4" style="writing-mode: vertical-rl">**Trouble Spot**</td><td>

- es/das sagen
  1 Hör gut zu, weil ich es [= eine konkrete Information] nur einmal sage. ● ● ● Listen carefully
  because I'm only going to **say it** once.
  Du hast das Geld gestohlen. – Wer sagt das [= dass es so ist]? ● ● ● … – Who **says (so)**?
  Ich lösche alles, wenn du es sagst [= dass ich es soll]. ● ● ● I'll delete everything if you **say so**.
  Was kommt in der Arbeit dran? – Der Lehrer hat es nicht gesagt [= mitgeteilt]. ● ● ● What's
  going to be in the test? – The teacher didn't **say**.

  2 Was ist passiert? – Ich sage [= erzähle] es dir später. ● ● ● What happened? – I'll **tell you** later.
  Wer hat es getan? Jetzt sag es (endlich)! ● ● ● Who did it? Now **tell me/us**!
  Ich habe es dir ja gleich gesagt. ● ● ● I **told you so**.
</td></tr>
</table>

school

1 When you think about afternoons, weekends and holidays, ... , does it?

  A school doesn't really take up an awfully large part of your life

  B the school doesn't really take up an awfully large part of your life

2 ...... Is it the same as on the other days?

  A What time does school finish on a Friday?   **B** What time does the school finish on a Friday?

3 What's the earliest age ...... in this country? – 16.

  A people can finish the school   **B** people can go from school   **C** people can leave school

4 You passed the exam, didn't you? Why are you not saying? ......

  A You didn't fail, did you?   **B** You didn't fall through, did you?   **C** You didn't miss, did you?

sea – seaside

1 The novel is about a boy who survives a shipwreck ...... with a live tiger.

  A and is then at sea for over 130 days in a lifeboat

  B and is then on sea for over 130 days in a lifeboat

  C and is then on the sea for over 130 days in a lifeboat

2 If you live ...... all the time, you don't see it as anything unusual.

  A in a town at sea   **B** in a town at the sea   **C** in a town by sea   **D** in a town by the sea

3 The traditional holiday for families with young kids is still ....

  A a sea holiday   **B** a seaside holiday   **C** a holiday at the seaside   **D** a holiday by the seaside

search (for) – look for – seek

1 ...... Is there anywhere you could recommend?

  A We're looking for somewhere to stay.

  B We're seeking somewhere to stay.

  C We're searching somewhere to stay.

2 It's a race against time. It's a really big operation: everybody is involved, including the police and the army. ......

  A We're all looking frantically.

  B We're all seeking frantically.

  C We're all searching frantically.

3 **A** Whose advice have you searched?   **B** Whose advice have you searched for?

  C Whose advice have you seeked?   **D** Whose advice have you sought?

see

1 ...... Is there anything you want me to ask her?

  A I'm probably seeing Kim this evening.   **B** I probably see Kim this evening.

2 It's much better with the microscope. ......

  A I'm seeing what a beautiful pattern it is now.

  B I can see what a beautiful pattern it is now.

  C I see what a beautiful pattern it is now.

3 No more, thanks. I'm on a diet. – ......

  A Oh, I'm seeing.   **B** Oh, I can see.   **C** Oh, I see.

school (die) Schule

■ **ohne the, wenn der Schulunterricht gemeint ist**

School steht ohne den bestimmten Artikel, wenn die Institution oder der Unterrichtsbetrieb, nicht das Schulgebäude gemeint ist.

Do you like school (~~the school~~)? ● ● ● Gefällt dir die Schule? / Macht dir die Schule Spaß?

> **Topic Box**
>
> ■ *Talking about school and qualifications* ▶ exam ▶ gymnasium ▶ study ▶ test
> *go to school* ● ● ● in die Schule / zur Schule gehen
> *Children start school at six.* ● ● ● Kinder werden mit sechs Jahren eingeschult / kommen
> mit sechs Jahren in die Schule.
> *They leave school at about 19.* ● ● ● Sie gehen mit ungefähr 19 Jahren von der Schule ab.
> *School starts at 9.00 / finishes at 4.00.* ● ● ● Die Schule beginnt um 9 Uhr / ist um 16 Uhr aus.
> *I'm doing / taking my final exam(s) soon.* ● ● ● Ich mache bald meine Abschlussprüfung /
> (auch:) das Abitur.
> *I('ve) passed.* ● ● ● Ich habe bestanden.
> *I('ve) failed.* ● ● ● Ich bin durchgefallen / habe nicht bestanden.
> *I('ve) got a (grade) 2 in French.* ● ● ● Ich habe in Französisch eine 2 bekommen.
> *A good grade in one subject can cancel out a bad one in another / can make up for a bad*
> *one in another.* ● ● ● Eine gute Note in einem Fach kann eine schlechte in einem anderen
> ausgleichen.

sea – seaside Meer, (die) See

■ *A swimmer drowned in the sea last night.* ● ● ● Ein Schwimmer ist … im Meer ertrunken.
live by the sea ● ● ● am Meer leben
The ship was at sea for 12 days. ● ● ● Das Schiff war 12 Tage auf See.
far out to sea ● ● ● weit draußen im Meer / weit draußen auf dem Meer / weit aufs Meer hinaus

■ Wenn vom Meer als einem Urlaubs- oder Vergnügungsort gesprochen wird, verwendet man besonders im BE oft *the seaside*.
go to the seaside for the day / for a holiday ● ● ● für einen Tag / in den Urlaub ans Meer fahren
have a seaside holiday / a holiday at / by the seaside ● ● ● Urlaub am Meer / an der See verbringen

search (for) [sɜːtʃ] – look for – seek* suchen (nach)

■ Mit *search* ist eine besonders intensive Suche gemeint.
The police searched everywhere. ● ● ● Die Polizei hat überall gesucht.
They're still searching for the missing child. ● ● ● Sie sucht noch immer nach dem vermissten Kind.
Arab passengers were searched. ● ● ● Arabische Fluggäste wurden durchsucht.

■ Die übliche Entsprechung für „suchen" lautet *look (for)*.
I've looked everywhere. ● ● ● Ich habe überall gesucht / geschaut.
Where were you? We've been looking for you. ● ● ● … Wir haben dich / nach dir gesucht.

■ *Seek* („versuchen zu bekommen", „benötigen") ist ein unregelmäßiges Verb *(seek – sought – sought)* und wird in folgenden Wortkombinationen verwendet:
seek advice / help / employment ● ● ● Rat / Hilfe / Arbeit suchen

S

see* sehen; verstehen ▶ look ▶ oversee

■ **einfache Form und Verlaufsform**

In den Bedeutungen „mit den Augen wahrnehmen" und „verstehen" ist die Verlaufsform nicht möglich.

I (can) see (~~I'm seeing~~) him now. He's just come out of the house. ● ● ● Ich kann ihn jetzt sehen. …
I missed the train, that's why I didn't come. – Oh, I see (~~I'm seeing~~). ● ● ● … – Ach so (, ich verstehe).
In der Bedeutung „(sich) treffen (mit)" ist die Verlaufsform jedoch möglich.
I'm seeing Peter again next Wednesday. ● ● ● Ich sehe / treffe Peter am nächsten Mittwoch wieder.

seem

1 ...... than she was before she went to Canada.

  A My daughter seems me to be so much more independent

  B My daughter seems to me to be so much more independent

2 ...... What's the matter?

  A You seem very nervous.   **B** You seem very nervously.

3 **A** The situation is now seeming to be largely under control.

  B The situation now seems to be largely under control.

seldom – rare(ly)

1 ...... now that he has his own flat.

  A We rarely see him   **B** We seldom see him   **C** We seldomly see him

2 A solar eclipse like this is .... The next won't be for another 83 years.

  A a very rare event   **B** a very seldom event

self-conscious ≠ „selbstbewusst"

1 **A** A self-conscious person is sure of himself or herself.

  B A self-conscious person is unsure of himself or herself.

2 Ann was always [ein sehr selbstbewusster Mensch], even as a young child.

  A a very self-conscious person   **B** a very self-confident person   **C** a very self-sure person

sense

1 [Es hat keinen Sinn, länger zu warten.] They're not going to come, and that's that.

  A It has no sense to wait any longer.

  B There is no sense in waiting any longer.

  C There is no sense to wait any longer.

sensible ≠ „sensibel"

1 'Sensible' means ....

  A 'based on emotions and feelings'

  B 'based on good thinking'

  C 'based on what you can see, hear, smell and taste'

2 Be careful what you say to her. She's [sehr sensibel].

  A very sensible   **B** very sensitive   **C** very sensitized

serious

1 He's so self-centred. ...... , apart from himself.

  A He takes nobody serious   **B** He takes nobody seriously

shade – shadow

1 As the sun set, ...

  A our shades grew longer and longer   **B** our shadows grew longer and longer

2 It was a scorching hot day. ...... the temperature was well over 30.

  A Even in the shade   **B** Even in the shadow

seem scheinen [= den Anschein haben] ▷ appear

- **nicht in der Verlaufsform**
  *He now **seems** (He's now seeming) (to be) a lot happier.* ● ● ● Er scheint jetzt viel glücklicher zu sein.
- **mit Adjektiv, nicht Adverb**
  *She **seemed** (to be) very **angry** (seemed [to be] very angrily).* ● ● ● Sie schien sehr böse zu sein.
- ***seem to sb.***
  *It **seems to** me (It seems me) very unusual.* ● ● ● Es scheint mir sehr ungewöhnlich zu sein.

seldom ['seldəm] – rare(ly) selten

- ***seldom/rarely:* Adverbien**
  *They live in Africa and I **seldom/rarely** see them.* ● ● ● … und ich sehe sie selten.
- ***rare:* Adjektiv**
  Anders als das deutsche Wort „selten" kann *seldom* nicht als Adjektiv verwendet werden.
  *a **rare** plant (a seldom plant)* [Adjektiv] ● ● ● eine seltene Pflanze

self-conscious [ˌselfˈkɒnʃəs] unsicher, befangen, gehemmt

! **False Friend!**
! *Self-conscious* bedeutet nicht „selbstbewusst", sondern genau das Gegenteil, nämlich
! „unsicher".
 *I was on stage for the first time and felt very **self-conscious.*** ● ● ● Ich stand zum ersten Mal
  auf der Bühne und fühlte mich sehr unsicher.
! Beachte die englische Entsprechung von „selbstbewusst":
  eine selbstbewusste junge Frau ● ● ● a **self-confident** young woman

sense Sinn, Zweck ▷ point

- ***sense in doing***
  Nach *sense in* steht die *-ing*-Form des Verbs, kein *to*-Infinitiv.
  ***There's no sense in going** (no sense to go) now. He'll be at work.* ● ● ● Es hat keinen Sinn, jetzt
  zu gehen. …

sensible ['sensəbl] vernünftig

! **False Friend!**
 Sensible bedeutet nicht „sensibel", sondern „vernünftig".
  ***sensible** advice* ● ● ● (ein) vernünftiger Rat
! Beachte die englische Entsprechung von „sensibel" [= „empfindsam", „empfindlich"]:
  ein sensibles Kind ● ● ● a **sensitive** ['sensətɪv] child

S

serious ['sɪəriəs] ernst ▷ heavy

- ***take sb./sth. seriously***
  *You don't **take** that old fool **seriously** (take that old fool serious), do you?* ● ● ● Du nimmst diesen
  alten Spinner doch nicht ernst, oder?

shade – shadow ['ʃædəʊ] Schatten

- ***shade* = „schattige Stelle", „vor Sonnenstrahlen geschützte Stelle"**
  *sit in the **shade** (of a tree)* ● ● ● im Schatten (eines Baumes) sitzen
  *light and **shade*** ● ● ● Licht und Schatten
- ***shadow* = „Schattenumriss", „Schattenbild"**
  *see a **shadow** on the wall* ● ● ● einen Schatten an der Wand sehen
  *The **shadows** get longer in the evening.* ● ● ● Abends werden die Schatten länger.

sharp – hot/spicy – in focus/clear

1 **A** How hot are a shark's teeth?
  B How spicy are a shark's teeth?
  C How sharp are a shark's teeth?

2 ......, with chillies for example.
  A I love eating hot things **B** I love eating spicy things **C** I love eating sharp things

3 I can't read the sign in the foreground. ......
  A The photo is out of focus. **B** The photo isn't sharp.

4 What she says and what she does ....
  A are in strong contrast to one another **B** are in sharp contrast to one another

sheep

1 ...... – I can't remember, I fell asleep.
  A How many sheep did you count? **B** How many sheeps did you count?

2 ......, but I still couldn't get to sleep.
  A I counted a whole flock of sheep **B** I counted a whole flock of sheeps
  C I counted a whole herd of sheep **D** I counted a whole herd of sheeps

shine

1 It was a terrible holiday. ...... for a total of exactly five and a half hours.
  A The sun shined **B** The sun shon **C** The sun shone

ship – boat

1 There is a regular service across the lake. ......
  A The boats are part of the local public transport system.
  B The ships are part of the local public transport system.

2 ...... were waiting to get into the harbour.
  A Two big ferries **B** Two big ferry boats **C** Two big ferry ships

3 I've only been through the Channel Tunnel once. ......
  A I still prefer to cross by boat. **B** I still prefer to cross by ship.

shopping

1 Can you help me ...... ? It's full.
  A get the shopping out of the car **B** get the shoppings out of the car

shorts

1 ...... It's so embarrassing.
  A The shorts my father wears are so uncool. **B** The shorts my father wears is so uncool.

2 I need to buy ....
  A a new pair of shorts **B** a new shorts **C** some new shorts

sharp – hot/spicy – in focus / clear scharf

■ **scharf**

1 „gut schneidend"
ein scharfes Messer ● ● ● a **sharp** knife

2 Wortkombinationen mit *sharp*
ein scharfer [= deutlich erkennbarer] Kontrast ● ● ● a **sharp** contrast
scharfe [= deutliche] Kritik ● ● ● **sharp** criticism
scharfe [= genau wahrnehmende] Augen ● ● ● **sharp** eyes

3 „scharf gewürzt"
Das Gericht war richtig scharf. ● ● ● The dish was really **hot**/**spicy**.

4 „nicht verschwommen", „klar erkennbar" [Foto, Bild usw.]
Das Auto im Vordergrund ist nicht scharf (= ist unscharf). ● ● ● The car in the foreground
isn't **in focus** / isn't **clear** (= is **out of focus**).

sheep Schaf

■ one **sheep** – two **sheep** (~~sheeps~~)

■ a **flock of sheep** (~~herd of sheep~~) ● ● ● eine Herde Schafe / eine Schafherde

shine* scheinen [Sonne, Mond] ▷ appear ▷ seem

■ **shine – shone** [(BE:) ʃɒn, (AE:) ʃəʊn] – **shone**
The sun **shone** all afternoon. ● ● ● Die Sonne schien den ganzen Nachmittag.

ship – boat Schiff

■ **Schiff**

1 „großes, für das offene Meer gebautes Schiff"
ein großes Schiff auf dem Meer ● ● ● a big **ship** on the sea

Aber bei Fährverkehr (z. B. über den Ärmelkanal): *boat*
mit dem Schiff nach England fahren ● ● ● travel to England **by boat**

2 „auf Binnengewässern verkehrendes Schiff"
Schiffe auf dem Bodensee / der Themse ● ● ● **boats** on Lake Constance / the Thames
eine Schifffahrt auf dem Rhein machen ● ● ● take a **boat** trip on the Rhine

3 feste Wortkombination
Fährschiff/Fähre ● ● ● **ferry (boat)**

shopping Einkauf, Einkäufe

■ **nicht zählbares Nomen**
Shopping ist ein nicht zählbares Nomen. Man kann es also nicht mit *a* oder im Plural verwenden.
do the shopping (~~shoppings~~) (BE) ● ● ● die Einkäufe machen/erledigen, einkaufen
unpack the **shopping** (~~shoppings~~) (meist BE) ● ● ● die Einkäufe [= eingekauften Sachen] auspacken

shorts Shorts, kurze Hose(n) ▷ pants ▷ trousers

■ **Pluralnomen, keine Singularform**
Das Wort *shorts* gibt es, wie *trousers*, nur als Pluralnomen (mit Verb im Plural).
These shorts were very expensive. ● ● ● Diese Shorts waren / Diese kurze Hose war sehr teuer.
Um daraus eine Singularform zu machen, muss man *pair of* voranstellen.
This pair of shorts was very expensive. ● ● ● Dieses Paar Shorts war sehr teuer.
buy a **new pair of shorts** / **some new shorts** (~~a new shorts~~) ● ● ● (ein Paar) neue Shorts kaufen

S

should – ought to

1 ...... than ask a person like that for advice.

  A You ought to know better   **B** You ought know better

  C You should to know better   **D** You should know better

2 **A** If you ought to hear anything else, could you let me know?

  B If you should hear anything else, could you let me know?

3 *[Was sollen wir heute Abend machen?]* Is there anything special you'd like to do?

  A What shall we do this evening?

  B What should we do this evening?

  C What will we do this evening?

4 No promises on our part. Is that absolutely clear, Williams? – I know. Mrs Taylor told me.

  [Ich soll nichts versprechen.]

  A I'm not to make any promises.

  B I oughtn't to make any promises.

  C I shan't make any promises.

5 *[Raymond soll wohl später kommen]*, but I shan't believe it till I see him come through that door.

  A Raymond is to be coming later

  B Raymond is supposed to be coming later

  C Raymond shall be coming later

6 The renovation work *[soll über sechs Millionen Euro gekostet haben]*.

  A is to have cost over six million euros

  B is said to have cost over six million euros

  C shall have cost over six million euros

7 There must have been over 1000 people in the hall. ......

  A How should we have found you?   **B** How were we to find you?

  C How were we supposed to find you?

8 She didn't know at the time. But only six months later ....

  A that same prison guard should become her most loyal follower

  B that same prison guard was to become her most loyal follower

  C that same prison guard was supposed to become her most loyal follower

shout

1 ...... How dare you?!

  A Don't shout at me like that!   **B** Don't shout to me like that!

2 **A** Can you just shout at Giles upstairs and tell him that dinner is nearly ready?

  B Can you just shout Giles upstairs and tell him that dinner is nearly ready?

  C Can you just shout to Giles upstairs and tell him that dinner is nearly ready?

side

1 ...... East or west?

  A Which side of the Wall did you live at?   **B** Which side of the Wall did you live on?

2 It's better to place any photos or illustrative elements *[auf die Vorderseite, nicht auf die Rückseite]*.

  A on the former side, not on the rear side   **B** on the front side, not on the back side

  C on the front, not on the back

3 **A** On the one side I'd love to meet Julie, but on the other, I've got so much work to do.

  B On the one hand I'd love to meet Julie, but on the other, I've got so much work to do.

should – ought to sollte(n)

■ **Bedeutungen von** *should* **und** *ought to*

1 *We **should** go / **ought to** go now. It's late.* [sagen, was ratsam/richtig/notwendig wäre] ● ● ●
  Wir sollten jetzt gehen. Es ist schon spät.
  *They **should** build / **ought to** build more hospitals.* ● ● ● Man sollte mehr Krankenhäuser bauen.

2 *The money **should** be / **ought to** be enough.* [eine Vermutung äußern; sagen, was der Fall sein
  müsste] ● ● ● Das Geld sollte/müsste reichen.
  *It **shouldn't** be / **oughtn't to** be difficult to find somewhere to park on Sunday morning.* ● ● ●
  Sonntags morgens sollte/dürfte es nicht schwierig sein, einen Parkplatz zu finden.

3 *If it **should** rain, I have an umbrella. / I have an umbrella in case it **should** rain.* [sagen, dass man
  etwas für wenig wahrscheinlich hält] ● ● ● Wenn es regnen sollte, habe ich einen Schirm. /
  Ich habe einen Schirm für den Fall, dass es regnen sollte.
  *Why **should** anyone want to break in here?* ● ● ● Warum sollte jemand hier einbrechen wollen?

Trouble Spot

■ **sollen**

1 fragen, was gewünscht/erwartet wird
  Soll ich/Sollen wir auf dich warten? ● ● ● *Shall I / Shall we wait for you?*

2 etwas befehlen/anordnen
  Du sollst sofort nach Hause kommen. ● ● ● *You're to come home at once.*

3 sagen, was vorgesehen/geplant ist und so gut wie sicher eintreten wird
  Der Bundeskanzler soll morgen eine Erklärung abgeben. ● ● ● *The Chancellor is to make
  a statement tomorrow.*

4 sagen, was vorgesehen/geplant ist, aber vielleicht nicht eingehalten wird
  Das neue Sofa soll morgen kommen. ● ● ● *The new sofa is supposed to come tomorrow.*

5 sagen, was die Leute behaupten
  Er soll (angeblich) Millionär sein. ● ● ● *He is said to be a millionaire.*

6 Hilflosigkeit/Ratlosigkeit/Unverständnis ausdrücken
  Wo soll ich einen grünen Papagei auftreiben? ● ● ● *Where am I (supposed) to get hold
  of a green parrot?*
  Woher sollte ich wissen, dass er bewaffnet war? ● ● ● *How was I (supposed) to know
  that he was armed?*
  Was soll dieses Wort bedeuten? ● ● ● *What is this word supposed to mean?*

7 ein Schicksal oder eine Bestimmung vorausschauend beschreiben
  Fünf Jahre später sollte sich alles, was die alte Frau sagte, bewahrheiten. ● ● ● *Five years
  later everything the old woman said was to come true.*

S

shout rufen, schreien

■ *I **shouted to** a police officer across the street.* [= jmdm. etwas zurufen, um dessen Aufmerksamkeit
  zu erlangen] ● ● ● Ich rief einen Polizisten auf der anderen Straßenseite.

■ *The colonel* ['kɜːnl] ***shouted at** the man who had lost his gun.* [= jmdn. wütend anschreien und mit
  lauter Stimme zurechtweisen] ● ● ● Der Oberst schrie den Mann … an.

side Seite

■ *the **sides** of a triangle* ● ● ● die Seiten eines Dreiecks
  *Don't cross over. It's on this **side** of the street.* ● ● ● … Es ist auf dieser Straßenseite.

Trouble Spot

■ **Seite**
  die Vorderseite des Umschlags ● ● ● *the **front** (~~front side~~) of the envelope*
  die Rückseite des Gebäudes ● ● ● *the **back** (~~back side~~) of the building* [*backside* = „Hintern"!]
  der Text auf [Buch-]Seite 99 ● ● ● *the text on **page** 99*
  auf der einen/anderen Seite [= einerseits/andererseits] ● ● ● *on the one / other hand*

since – for

1 .... , but he's already a great friend.

  A I know David for only two weeks   **B** I know David since only two weeks

  C I've known David for only two weeks   **D** I've known David since only two weeks

2 .... But we don't see them often.

  A We know the Smiths for sometime last year.

  B We know the Smiths since sometime last year.

  C We've known the Smiths since sometime last year.

  D We've known the Smiths for sometime last year.

3 Where were you?! ......

  A I'm waiting for over half an hour.   **B** I'm waiting since over half an hour.

  C I've been waiting for over half an hour.   **D** I've been waiting since over half an hour.

size

1 *[Welche Größe haben Sie?]* – 38 usually, but these boots are actually 39.

  A What size are you?   **B** What size do you have?   **C** What size do you take?

sky

1 ...... the moon shone brightly.

  A Up at the sky   **B** Up in the sky

sleep – be asleep

1 **A** I sleeped right through the storm.

  B I slept right through the storm.

  C I slept right through the storm.

2 I'm sorry I woke you. I didn't know ....

  A you were asleep   **B** you were sleeping

3 The fever was less ...... than the previous night.

  A and she was asleep more peacefully   **B** and she was sleeping more peacefully

4 My brother has a job now and has to get up at 6.30 every day. He always gets mad at me when I say ....

  A I can have a sleep-in   **B** I can have a lie-in   **C** I can sleep long

  D I can sleep for a long time   **E** I can sleep late

5 Please turn the music down. ......

  A Your grandfather is trying to have a nap.   **B** Your grandfather is trying to take a nap.

  C Your grandfather is trying to have a snooze.   **D** Your grandfather is trying to make a snooze.

6 **A** Boring old programmes like this always bring me in sleep.

  B Boring old programmes like this always send me to sleep.

  C Boring old programmes like this always take me into sleep.

7 ...... because it was so light.

  A I woke at five o'clock and couldn't get back to sleep

  B I woke at five o'clock and couldn't fall asleep again

8 Never make an important decision ...... , that's what I say.

  A without sleeping at it   **B** without sleeping on it   **C** without sleeping over it

since – for seit

Trouble Spot

- ■ seit
1 „seit" + Zeitpunkt
   Ich spiele seit 2001 Tennis. ● ● ● *I've been playing tennis **since 2001**.* [*present perfect!*]
2 „seit" + Zeitspanne
   Wir wohnen seit fünf Jahren hier. ● ● ● *We've lived here **for five years**.* [*present perfect!*]

size Größe

- ■ *What **size** are you? / What **size** do you take? (~~What size do you have?~~)* ● ● ● Welche [Kleidungs-/
  Schuh-]Größe hast du / haben Sie?

sky Himmel ▷ heaven

- ■ *stars **in the sky** (~~at the sky~~)* ● ● ● Sterne am Himmel

sleep* – be* asleep schlafen

- ■ *sleep – slept – slept*

- ■ Um auszudrücken, dass jemand sich im Zustand des Schlafs befindet, verwendet man normaler-
  weise nicht *sleep*, sondern *be asleep*.
  *Have I woken you? **Were** you **asleep**? (~~Did you sleep / Have you slept?~~)* ● ● ● … Hast du geschlafen?
  *I didn't hear you. I must **have been asleep**. (~~I must have slept.~~)* ● ● ● … Ich muss geschlafen haben.
  *Everybody **is** still **fast asleep** (~~is still sleeping fast~~). It's only 4 a.m. here in New York.* ● ● ●
  Alle schlafen noch fest. …

Topic Box

- ■ *Talking about sleep*
  *I usually **sleep** very **well**.* [Beschreibung, wie jemand schläft] ● ● ● Ich schlafe meistens
    sehr gut.
  *The child was **sleeping peacefully**.* ● ● ● Das Kind schlief friedlich.
  *Did you **sleep well** / **sleep all right** / **have a good night('s sleep)**?* ● ● ● Haben Sie gut
    geschlafen? / Sind Sie ausgeschlafen?
  *I **slept** really **well**. / I **had** a really **good night('s sleep)**.* ● ● ● Ich habe richtig gut geschlafen.
  *I **slept badly**. / I **didn't sleep well**. / I **had a bad night**.* ● ● ● Ich habe schlecht / nicht gut
    geschlafen.
  *I **slept eight hours** last night.* [Angabe der Schlafdauer] ● ● ● Ich habe letzte Nacht acht
    Stunden geschlafen.
  *Who is going to **sleep in the bunk beds**?* [Schlafplatzregelung] ● ● ● Wer schläft in den
    Etagenbetten?
  *Let's **sleep on it**.* ● ● ● Lasst uns eine Nacht darüber schlafen / das Ganze überschlafen.

  *Jill is **having a nap** / **taking a nap** / **having a snooze**.* ● ● ● Jill macht ein kleines Schläfchen.
  *I turned out the light and **went to sleep**.* ● ● ● Ich habe das Licht ausgemacht und bin
    eingeschlafen.
  *I **fell asleep** at once / in the middle of the film.* ● ● ● Ich bin sofort / mitten im Film
    eingeschlafen.
  *Quiet! I'm trying to **get** / **go to sleep**.* ● ● ● Ruhe! Ich versuche einzuschlafen.
  *Some noise woke me, and I couldn't **get** / **go back to sleep**.* ● ● ● Irgendein Geräusch hat
    mich geweckt und ich konnte nicht wieder einschlafen.
  *Long train journeys always **send** me **to sleep**.* ● ● ● Lange Zugfahrten bringen mich immer
    zum Einschlafen.
  *Come on, let's **go to bed** (~~go to sleep~~).* ● ● ● Komm, lasst uns schlafen gehen / zu Bett gehen.
  *There's no school tomorrow. I can **sleep late** / (BE, infml:) **lie in** [- '-] / **have a lie-in** ['- -].* ● ● ●
    Morgen ist keine Schule. Ich kann ausschlafen / lange schlafen / später aufstehen.

S

smell

1 What are you cooking? ......
  A It's smelling deliciously. **B** It smells delicious. **C** It smells deliciously.

2 It's difficult to identify. ......
  A It smells of wood for me. **B** It smells of wood to me.
  C It smells me of wood. **D** It smells me like wood.

so – such – like this/that

1 It was a fabulous trip. ......
  A We had a so great time. **B** We had a such great time.
  C We had so a great time. **D** We had such a great time.

2 ...... getting the beamer to work.
  A It was so a problem **B** It was such a problem

3 Addressing 960 envelopes was ....
  A so a work **B** such a work **C** such work

4 In Chinese you would ....
  A write your name like this **B** write your name so

5 **A** I feel so sorry for him. **B** I feel such sorry for him.

social – social-minded

1 Truman has problems fitting into a group. ......
  A He has few social skills. **B** He has few society skills.

2 Glenn is involved in lots of voluntary work. ......
  A He's very social. **B** He's very social-minded. **C** He's very socially-minded.

society

1 ...... without being didactic.
  A His novels are critical of the Victorian society **B** His novels are critical of Victorian society

sometimes – sometime / some time

1 ...... that they announced the changes.
  A It was some time last year **B** It was sometime last year **C** It was sometimes last year

2 ...... It's quite a complicated job, you know.
  A This will take some time. **B** This will take sometime. **C** This will take sometimes.

sound

1 I don't know much about this sort of thing, but the way they want to do it ....
  A is sounding strange **B** is sounding strangely **C** sounds strange **D** sounds strangely

2 ...... , but Kevin didn't seem to like them.
  A The choir from Spain sounded great for me **B** The choir from Spain sounded great to me

smell (*) riechen

■ **normalerweise nicht in der Verlaufsform**
It smells (It's smelling) in here. ● ● ● Hier drinnen riecht es.

■ **mit Adjektiv, nicht Adverb**
These roses smell beautiful (smell beautifully). ● ● ● Diese Rosen riechen wunderbar.

■ *smell ... to sb.*
The milk smells funny to me. ● ● ● Ich finde, die Milch riecht komisch.

■ *smell of sth.*
Her breath smelled/smelt of garlic (smelled/smelt after garlic). ● ● ● Ihr Atem roch nach Knoblauch.

so – such – like this/that so

■ *so + Adjektiv/Adverb*
The morning was so beautiful. ● ● ● Der Morgen war so schön.
She sings so beautifully. ● ● ● Sie singt so schön.

■ *such + Nomen*
Vor Nomen (mit oder ohne Adjektiv) verwendet man nicht *so*, sondern *such* („solch", „derart").
It was such a beautiful morning (so a beautiful morning). ● ● ● Es war so ein schöner Morgen.
The whole concert was such a disaster (so a disaster). ● ● ● Das ganze Konzert war so ein Reinfall.
Vor einem nicht zählbaren Nomen steht *such* ohne *a/an*.
We had such beautiful weather (such a beautiful weather). ● ● ● Wir hatten so schönes Wetter.
The man talked such rubbish (such a rubbish). ● ● ● Der Mann redete so einen Blödsinn.

■ *like this/that = „dieser Art"; „auf diese Art und Weise"*
One day I'd like to drive a car like this/that. ● ● ● Irgendwann würde ich gern so ein Auto fahren.
Fold the tent like this. (Fold the tent so.) ● ● ● Lege das Zelt so zusammen.

social ['səʊʃl] – social-minded sozial

■ *The slum area is a place with a lot of social problems.* ● ● ● ... mit vielen sozialen Problemen.
The social life of the village focusses round the village pub. ● ● ● Das gesellschaftliche Leben ...

■ *Tina is very social-minded (social). She's always helping people.* ● ● ● ... sozial (eingestellt). ...

society [sə'saɪəti] Gesellschaft

■ **ohne *the* in Aussagen allgemeiner Art**
Society gehört zu den abstrakten Nomen, die in Aussagen allgemeiner Art ohne den bestimmten Artikel verwendet werden.
the ills of modern society (the modern society) ● ● ● die Übel der modernen Gesellschaft

S

sometimes manchmal – sometime/some time irgendwann ▷ once

■ *I sometimes think he's mad.* ● ● ● Ich denke manchmal, dass er verrückt ist.

■ *I'm going to move sometime/some time next year.* ● ● ● Ich ziehe irgendwann nächstes Jahr um.
Aber nur getrennt geschrieben:
I need some time to think about this. ● ● ● Ich brauche etwas Zeit/ein bisschen Zeit ...

sound sich anhören, klingen

■ **normalerweise nicht in der Verlaufsform**
It now sounds (It's now sounding) as though the Americans are changing their policy. ● ● ● Es hört sich jetzt so an, als ob die Amerikaner ihre Politik ändern.

■ **mit Adjektiv, nicht Adverb**
Your idea sounds good (sounds well). ● ● ● Deine Idee klingt gut/hört sich gut an.

■ *sound ... to sb.*
The idea sounds really good to me. ● ● ● Ich finde, die Idee hört sich wirklich gut an.

space

1 **A** The astronauts will be in space for over six weeks.

  B The astronauts will be in the space for over six weeks.

spaghetti

1 **A** Are the spaghetti cooked? – No, they need another two to three minutes.

  B Is the spaghetti cooked? – No, it needs another two to three minutes.

spare ≠ „sparen"

1 The adjective 'spare' means ....

  A 'additional', 'extra' **B** 'mean, not generous' **C** 'rare', 'unusual'

2 *[Sie können 20 Euro sparen]* if you buy before 15th October.

  A You can keep 20 euros **B** You can save 20 euros

  C You can save up 20 euros **D** You can spare 20 euros

speak – talk

1 Omar, I think we need to sit down together ...... , don't you?

  A and speak this through in detail **B** and talk this through in detail

2 ...... Is she there?

  A I'd like to speak Mrs Willis, please.

  B I'd like to speak to Mrs Willis, please.

  C I'd like to speak with Mrs Willis, please.

special

1 I love coming here. ......

  A There's something very special about this place for me.

  B There's something very special on this place for me.

  C There's something very special with this place for me.

specialist

1 His mum is a university lecturer. ....

  A She's a specialist for Chinese history. **B** She's a specialist in Chinese history.

  C She's specialist for Chinese history. **D** She's specialist in Chinese history.

specialize/specialise

1 Mark is studying law. ......

  A He's specializing himself on commercial law.

  B He's specializing himself in commercial law.

  C He's specializing in commercial law.

speech

1 ...... – Yes, Julia's father, after the main course.

  A Is anybody going to give a speech?

  B Is anybody going to hold a speech?

  C Is anybody going to make a speech?

space Weltraum ▸ place

■ **ohne** *the*
> *Is **space** (~~the space~~) infinite* ['ɪnfɪnət]*?* ● ● ● Ist der Weltraum unendlich?
> *a satellite **in space** (~~in the space~~)* ● ● ● ein Satellit im Weltall

spaghetti Spaghetti

■ **nicht zählbares Nomen**
Spaghetti ist ein nicht zählbares Nomen. Es hat keine Pluralform.
> ***This spaghetti is** (~~These spaghettis are~~) wonderful!* ● ● ● Diese Spaghetti sind toll!

spare 1 [Zeit, Geld usw.] erübrigen, übrig haben 2 übrig; Ersatz-

■ **False Friend!**

Das Verb *spare* bedeutet nicht „~~sparen~~", sondern „erübrigen".
> *I'd love to help you, but I can't **spare** the time.* ● ● ● … aber ich kann die Zeit nicht erübrigen/ aber ich habe nicht die Zeit (dafür).

Oft ist *spare* ein Adjektiv mit der Grundbedeutung „übrig", d. h. „zusätzlich zum Bedarf".
> *Do you have any **spare** cash?* ● ● ● Hast du etwas Geld übrig?
> *What do you do in your **spare** time?* ● ● ● … in deiner Freizeit?
> *We have a **spare** room in the cellar.* ● ● ● … einen zusätzlichen Raum/ein Gästezimmer …
> ***spare** parts for a car; a **spare** wheel* ● ● ● Ersatzteile für ein Auto; ein Ersatzrad/Reservereifen

Beachte die englischen Entsprechungen von „sparen":
> Zeit/Geld sparen ● ● ● *save time/money*
> Ich spare für ein neues Fahrrad. ● ● ● *I'm **saving up** for a new bike.*

speak* – talk sprechen

■ *speak*
> *Jane didn't **speak** a single word.* ● ● ● Jane hat kein einziges Wort gesprochen/gesagt.
> *Can I **speak to**/* (AE:) ***speak with** Jane, please?* (~~Can I speak Jane, please?~~) ● ● ● Kann ich bitte (mit) Jane sprechen?

■ *talk*
Faustregel: Man verwendet *talk*, nicht *speak*, wenn nicht nur eine Aussage gemacht wird, sondern ein Informationsaustausch in Form eines Gesprächs stattfindet.
> *What were you and Phil **talking about**?* ● ● ● Worüber hast du mit Phil gesprochen?
> *We need to **talk about** what we're going to do tomorrow.* ● ● ● Wir müssen darüber sprechen …

special ['speʃl] besondere(r/s)

■ *What's **special about** this writer?* ● ● ● Was ist das Besondere/besonders an dieser Schriftstellerin?

specialist ['speʃəlɪst] Spezialist/-in, Fachmann/-frau

■ **mit** *a*
Specialist (in sth.) steht nach *be* und ähnlichen Verben mit dem unbestimmten Artikel.
> *She's **a specialist in** (~~She's specialist for~~) forensic science.* ● ● ● Sie ist Spezialistin für Kriminalistik.

specialize ['speʃəlaɪz]/(BE auch:) **specialise** sich spezialisieren

■ *specialize in sth.*
Specialize ist kein reflexives Verb. Auf *specialize* folgt die Präposition *in*.
> *This firm **specializes in** (~~specializes itself on~~) web design.* ● ● ● Diese Firma hat sich auf Webdesign spezialisiert/ist auf Webdesign spezialisiert.

speech Rede

■ *make/give/* (fml:) *deliver a speech* (~~hold a speech~~) ● ● ● eine Rede halten

S

speed

1 This new computer is so fast, you'll think ....
   A everything's happening at the speed of light
   B everything's happening with the speed of light

spend ≠ „spenden"

1 You can ....
   A spend money for a new graphics card   B spend money on a new graphics card
   C spend money to charity   D spend somebody an ice-cream

2 Once costs have been covered, ...
   A all surplus will be donated to charity   B all surplus will be sponsored to charity
   C all surplus will be spent to charity

3 ...... before we found the right flat.
   A We spent several months looking for somewhere to live
   B We spent several months to look for somewhere to live

spoil

1 A The news really spoilt the evening for us.   B The news really spoilt us the evening.

sport

1 ...... , that's why you're so unfit.
   A You don't do enough sport   B You don't make enough sport

stadium ≠ „Stadium"

1 A stadium is ....
   A an ancient theatre   B a place where sporting events take place
   C part of a sequence of events

2 I'm afraid it's too late to make changes [in diesem Stadium].
   A at this stage   B in this stage

stand

1 A On the sign it said 'No smoking'.   B On the sign it stood 'No smoking'.
   C On the sign stood 'No smoking'.   D On the sign there stood 'No smoking'.

2 You're not allowed to pass a school bus [wenn er vor einer Schule steht].
   A when it's stopped outside a school   B when it stands outside a school

3 A The bus was full and I had to stand all the way.
   B The bus was full and I had to stay all the way.
   C The bus was full and I had to stop all the way.

stationary – stationery

1 ...... , you know, pens and notebooks etc., as well as food and drink.
   A The school shop sells stationary   B The school shop sells stationery
   C The school shop sells stationeries

2 ...... And this other car just ran straight into the back of us.
   A We were stationary because the traffic lights were red.
   B We were stationery because the traffic lights were red.

speed Geschwindigkeit, Tempo

■ *at (a speed of)* 150 km/h ● ● ● mit (einer Geschwindigkeit von) 150 Stundenkilometern

spend* [Zeit] verbringen; [Geld] ausgeben

! ■ **False Friend!**
Spend bedeutet nicht „~~spenden~~"/„~~Spende~~", sondern „[Zeit] verbringen", „[Geld] ausgeben".
  spend the weekend with friends ● ● ● das Wochenende mit Freunden verbringen
  spend over $400 **on** new furniture ● ● ● über 400 $ für neue Möbel ausgeben
Beachte die englischen Entsprechungen von „spenden" und „Spende":
  Die meisten Leute sind bereit zu spenden. ● ● ● *Most people are willing to **give to charity**.*
  Zelte für die Erdbebenopfer spenden ● ● ● ***donate*** *tents for the earthquake victims*
  eine Spende an UNICEF ● ● ● *a **donation*** [dəʊˈneɪʃn] *to UNICEF*

■ *spend time doing* ▷ waste
Auf „spend + Zeitausdruck" folgt eine *-ing*-Form, kein *to*-Infinitiv.
  *I **spent hours looking** (~~spent hours to look~~) for information on the Internet.* ● ● ● Ich habe Stunden
    damit verbracht, Informationen im Internet zu suchen.

spoil(*) verderben

■ *spoil sth. for sb.*
Die Person, der etwas verdorben wird, muss man mit *for* anschließen.
  *You've **spoiled**/**spoilt** the whole weekend **for** me.* (~~You've spoiled/spoilt me the whole weekend.~~)
  ● ● ● Du hast mir das ganze Wochenende verdorben.

sport Sport

■ *Do you **do** a lot of **sport*** (~~make a lot of sport~~)? ● ● ● Machst/Treibst du viel Sport?

stadium [ˈsteɪdiəm] Stadion

! ■ **False Friend!**
Stadium bedeutet nicht „~~Stadium~~", sondern „Stadion".
  *the famous Wembley **Stadium*** ● ● ● das berühmte Wembley-Stadion
Beachte die englische Entsprechung von „Stadium":
  In diesem Stadium kann ich nichts versprechen. ● ● ● *I can't promise anything **at this stage**.*
  Wir befinden uns noch im Anfangsstadium. ● ● ● *We're still **in the early stages**.*

S

stand* stehen

■ *Susanne is **standing** in the last row.* ● ● ● Susanne steht [= sitzt nicht] in der letzten Reihe.

<table>
<tr><td rowspan="6">**Trouble Spot**</td><td>

■ **stehen**
Der Fernseher steht [= befindet sich/ist] im Wohnzimmer. ● ● ● *The TV **is** in the living room.*
Erst aussteigen, wenn der Zug steht [= zum Stillstand gekommen ist]. ● ● ● *Don't get out*
  *till the train **has stopped**/**has come to a stop**.*
In der Zeitung steht [geschrieben], dass … ● ● ● ***It says*** *in the paper that …*
Wie steht es? [= Wie ist der Spielstand?] ● ● ● *What's the score?*
Schwarz steht dir gut. ● ● ● *Black **suits** you.*
</td></tr>
</table>

stationary [(BE:) ˈsteɪʃənri, (AE:) -neri] stehend – stationery [(BE:) ˈsteɪʃənri, (AE:) -neri] Schreibwaren

■ *a **stationary** car* ● ● ● ein stehendes Auto [*station**a**ry* = „station**ä**r"]
  *The bus **was stationary**.* ● ● ● Der Bus stand.

■ ***Station**ery* [nicht zählbar!] *is pens, pencils, paper, etc.* ● ● ● Schreibwaren sind …

stay – remain

1 ...... I really have to go now.
   A I'm afraid I can't remain.   **B** I'm afraid I can't stay.

2 ...... You're making me really nervous.
   A Keep away from the edge of the cliff, will you?
   B Remain away from the edge of the cliff, will you?
   C Stay away from the edge of the cliff, will you?

3 ...... till the teacher says that you may sit.
   A You have to remain stand   **B** You have to remain standing
   C You have to remain stood   **D** You have to stay stood

4 ...... whether the two sides will manage to reach an agreement that will last.
   A It remains to be seen   **B** It remains to see   **C** It remains seeing

still

1 You can still change your mind, if you want to. ......
   A Still you have time.   **B** You still have time.   **C** You have still time.

2 I've checked everything, ...
   A but it doesn't still work   **B** but it still doesn't work

stop

1 We can go now, ...
   A it's stopped raining   **B** it's stopped to rain

2 It was a steep climb, ...
   A and I stopped getting my breath back
   B and I stopped to get my breath back
   C and I stopped in order to get my breath back

3 **A** Stop talking and listen to me!   **B** Stop to talk and listen to me!

4 **A** On the way to work I stopped buying a newspaper, *The Times*.
   B On the way to work I stopped to buy a newspaper, *The Times*.

storey – story

1 Our offices take up ....
   A the three top storeys of a building on Fifth Avenue
   B the three top stories of a building on Fifth Avenue
   C the three top storys of a building on Fifth Avenue

2 **A** I wish I could tell storeys as well as you can.   **B** I wish I could tell stories as well as you can.

stay – remain bleiben

Trouble Spot

■ **bleiben**

1 „im gleichen Zustand bleiben"
Ich blieb während des ganzen Fluges ängstlich. ● ● ● I **stayed** / (fml:) **remained** anxious for the whole flight.

2 „am gleichen Ort bleiben", „nicht weggehen"
Meine Mutter blieb im Auto. ● ● ● My mother **stayed** / (fml:) **remained** in the car.
Heute Abend bleiben wir zu Hause. ● ● ● We'll **stay** at home tonight / **stay in** tonight.
Bleib doch ein bisschen länger! Bleib zum Essen! ● ● ● Do **stay** a little longer. **Stay** for dinner.

3 „[abends] aufbleiben", „wach bleiben"
Ich blieb lange / bis ein Uhr auf. ● ● ● I **stayed up** late / till one o'clock.

4 „wegbleiben von", „sich fern halten von"
Bleiben Sie weg von meiner Tochter! / Halten Sie sich von meiner Tochter fern! ● ● ●
Stay / **Keep away from** my daughter!

5 „stehen/sitzen bleiben"
Sie blieb die ganze Zeit stehen. ● ● ● She **remained standing** the whole time.
[Aber: Meine Uhr ist stehen geblieben. ● ● ● My watch has **stopped**.]
Bitte bleiben Sie doch sitzen! ● ● ● Please **don't get up** / **stay seated** / (fml:) **remain seated**.

6 „[als Rest] übrig bleiben"; „[für die Zukunft] zu tun übrig bleiben"
Es bleibt sehr wenig Zeit. ● ● ● **There remains** very little time.
Es bleibt abzuwarten, ob er sein Versprechen hält. ● ● ● **It remains to be seen** if he'll keep his promise.

still (immer) noch ▶ quiet

■ **Stellung in der Satzmitte**
Still steht in der Regel in der Satzmitte.
Up north it's **still** light – at 11.30 p.m. [hinter *be*] ● ● ● Oben im Norden ist es noch hell – um 23 Uhr 30.
It's **still** not dark. ● ● ● Es ist immer noch nicht dunkel.
Does Jane **still** drive her Mini? [vor einem Vollverb außer *be*] ● ● ● Fährt Jane immer noch ihren Mini?
I **still** don't know the answer. [vor einem verneinten Hilfsverb] ● ● ● Ich weiß die Antwort immer noch nicht.
Still kann nicht am Satzanfang stehen.
We **still** have time. (~~Still we have time.~~) ● ● ● Noch haben wir Zeit.

stop aufhören, anhalten

■ **Schreibung**
stop, stopping, stopped

■ **stop doing**
Stop + die *-ing*-Form des Verbs bedeutet „aufhören etwas zu tun", „mit etwas aufhören".
My mum has **stopped smoking**. ● ● ● Meine Mutter hat aufgehört zu rauchen.

■ **stop to do**
Stop + *to*-Infinitiv bedeutet „anhalten / mit etwas aufhören, um etwas anderes zu tun".
We **stopped (in order) to look** at the map. ● ● ● Wir hielten an, um auf die Karte zu schauen.

storey ['stɔːri] / (AE meist:) story Stockwerk – story Geschichte ▶ floor

■ The building has 10 (BE:) **storeys** / (AE:) **stories**. The top (BE:) **storey** / (AE:) **story** is a restaurant.
● ● ● Das Haus hat zehn Stockwerke. Im obersten Stockwerk befindet sich ein Restaurant.

■ read the children **a story** / **stories** ● ● ● den Kindern eine Geschichte / Geschichten vorlesen

S

street – road

1 ...... , that's a good place to learn to drive.
   A   A country road with no traffic   B   A country street with no traffic

2 The mayor said .... And look what's happened: the crime rate has gone up yet again.
   A   he would make the roads safer in this part of town
   B   he would make the streets safer in this part of town

3 In some hilly regions there are problems for drivers this morning ....
   A   because of icy roads   B   because of icy streets

4 The first thing we need to do when we get to Sydney is ....
   A   to buy a road plan   B   to buy a street plan   C   to buy a street map

5 A   Wait for me at the road corner.   B   Wait for me at the street corner.

6 A   Your girlfriend lives somewhere in Silver Street, doesn't she?
   B   Your girlfriend lives somewhere in the Silver Street, doesn't she?

7 ...... I don't want to come in.
   A   I'll wait for you outside at the street.
   B   I'll wait for you outside in the street.
   C   I'll wait for you outside on the street.

8 The Walton Hotel? ......
   A   That's at the road to Aylesbury, isn't it?
   B   That's in the road to Aylesbury, isn't it?
   C   That's on the road to Aylesbury, isn't it?

strong

1 In a job like this ....
   A   you have to have great nerves   B   you have to have heavy nerves
   C   you have to have strong nerves   D   you have to have severe nerves

2 ...... and it took us ages to get to the airport.
   A   There was very great traffic   B   There was very heavy traffic
   C   There was very strong traffic   D   There was very severe traffic

3 Sandhya doesn't feel too good. ......
   A   She has a bad cold.   B   She has a heavy cold.   C   She has a strong cold.

4 The walls in this part of the castle are up to ....
   A   six metres great   B   six metres heavy   C   six metres strong   D   six metres thick

5 A 500% increase? Oh, come on! ......
   A   That really is a great exaggeration.   B   That really is a heavy exaggeration.
   C   That really is a strong exaggeration.   D   That really is a thick exaggeration.

6 ...... in many areas of northern Britain.
   A   Tonight there will again be a great frost   B   Tonight there will again be a hard frost
   C   Tonight there will again be a heavy frost   D   Tonight there will again be a strong frost
   E   Tonight there will again be a severe frost

7 Thousands of homes have been destroyed ...... in one of the worst hurricanes in living memory.
   A   or badly damaged   B   or severely damaged   C   or strongly damaged

8 A   The father's comments were followed by loud applause.
   B   The father's comments were followed by strong applause.

street – road Straße

■ *street* = „Straße in der Stadt"

Mit *street* bezeichnet man eine Straße innerhalb einer Ortschaft – mit Häusern, Geschäftsgebäuden und Gehwegen. Man denkt dabei an das Straßenleben.

*We live in a busy **street** with lots of shops.* ● ● ● … in einer belebten Straße …
*The **streets** aren't safe. There is a lot of crime.* ● ● ● Die Straßen sind nicht sicher. …
*go shopping in **Oxford Street*** [Straßennamen ohne *the*!] ● ● ● in der Oxford Street einkaufen
***street** plan/map* ● ● ● Stadtplan
***street** corner* (~~road corner~~) ● ● ● Straßenecke
***street** light* / (BE auch:) ***street** lamp* (~~road light/lamp~~) ● ● ● Straßenlaterne

■ *road* = „Fahrbahn bzw. Straße als Verbindungsweg"

Mit *road* bezeichnet man eine Verkehrsverbindung innerhalb oder außerhalb von Ortschaften. Man denkt dabei an den Verkehr auf der Straße, das Fahren, die Straßenverhältnisse usw.

*cross the **road** at a zebra crossing* ● ● ● die Straße an einem Zebrastreifen überqueren
*Is this the **road** to Wendover?* ● ● ● Ist das die Straße nach Wendover?
*a country **road*** ● ● ● eine Landstraße
*go shopping in **Essex Road*** [Straßennamen ohne *the*!] ● ● ● in der Essex Road einkaufen
*There are icy **roads** this morning.* ● ● ● Heute Morgen gibt es Glatteis auf den Straßen.
*The **roads** aren't safe. There are a lot of accidents.* ● ● ● Die Straßen sind nicht sicher. …
***road** map/atlas* ● ● ● Straßenkarte/-atlas

■ Präpositionen

The children were playing (BE:) ***in the street*** / (AE:) ***on the street**.* ● ● ● … spielten auf der Straße.
live (BE:) ***in Kings Street/Road*** / (AE:) ***on Kings Street/Road*** ● ● ● in der Kings Street/Road wohnen
*live **at 26 Kings Street/Road*** ● ● ● in der Kings Street/Road (Nr.) 26 wohnen
*an accident **on the road** to Burton* ● ● ● ein Unfall auf der Straße nach Burton
*be **on the road** to London* ● ● ● (mit dem Auto) unterwegs nach London sein

strong stark, kräftig ▷ heavy

■ *a **strong** man with **strong** arms* ● ● ● ein starker Mann mit kräftigen Armen
*a **strong** wind* ● ● ● ein starker/kräftiger Wind
*You need **strong** nerves.* ● ● ● Man braucht starke Nerven.
*a **strong** personality* ● ● ● eine starke Persönlichkeit
*The coffee is very **strong**.* ● ● ● Der Kaffee ist sehr stark.

S

■ **stark**

1 mit Bezug auf Regen/Schnee, Rauchen, Verkehr, Druck, Erkältung, Zunahme: *heavy*
starker Regen/Schnee; stark regnen/schneien ● ● ● ***heavy** rain/snow; rain/snow **heavily***
ein starker Raucher; stark rauchen ● ● ● *a **heavy** smoker; smoke **heavily***
starker Verkehr auf der Autobahn ● ● ● ***heavy** traffic on the motorway*
auf jmdn. starken Druck ausüben ● ● ● *exert* [ɪɡˈzɜːt] ***heavy** pressure on sb.*
eine starke Erkältung ● ● ● *a **heavy**/bad cold*

2 sonstige Wortkombinationen
5 mm starker Karton ● ● ● *cardboard 5 mm **thick***
Das Buch ist 600 Seiten stark. ● ● ● *The book is 600 pages **long**.*
eine starke Übertreibung ● ● ● *a **great** exaggeration* [ɪɡˌzædʒəˈreɪʃn]
etwas stark übertreiben ● ● ● ***greatly** exaggerate* [ɪɡˈzædʒəreɪt] *sth.*
starke Schmerzen haben ● ● ● *be in **great**/intense/severe* [sɪˈvɪə] *pain*
(eine) starke Hitze ● ● ● ***great**/intense/severe heat*
(ein) starker Frost ● ● ● *a **hard**/heavy/severe frost*
starker Applaus ● ● ● ***loud**/enthusiastic* [ɪnˌθjuːziˈæstɪk] *applause*
Das Auto ist stark beschädigt. ● ● ● *The car is **badly**/seriously/severely damaged.*
Das hat er gesagt?! Das ist wirklich stark [= unerhört]. ● ● ● *He said that?! That really is **a bit much**.*

Trouble Spot

251

study

1 I'm not sure I really want to go back to Germany just yet. But I suppose it's time ....
  A to begin my study   B to begin my studies   C to start university

2 *[Ein Studium]* in Germany still takes much longer than in many other developed countries.
  A A course of study   B A study course   C A study   D A studying   E A university course

3 The reason it took me so long to get my degree is that I had to work to earn money ....
  A during my study period   B while I was at university   C while I was a student

4 ...... , the other works in an advertising agency as a designer.
  A One brother is at university   B One brother is studying   C One brother studies

stuff ≠ „Stoff"

1 Which expression means almost the same as 'stuff' in the following sentence?
  "You've got so much furniture, it's unbelievable. What are you going to do with all this stuff when you move?"
  A all this material   B all these things

2 Nylon was *[einer der ersten synthetischen Stoffe]*.
  A one of the first synthetic fabrics
  B one of the first synthetic staffs
  C one of the first synthetic stuffs

succeed

1 ...... What did you promise him?
  A How did you succeed at getting old Williams on our side?
  B How did you succeed in getting old Williams on our side?
  C How did you succeed to get old Williams on our side?

suffer

1 A Sue suffers at low blood pressure.   B Sue suffers by low blood pressure.
  C Sue suffers from low blood pressure.   D Sue suffers under low blood pressure.

suggest

1 ...... You probably won't find a space nearer the centre.
  A I suggest parking here.   B I suggest that we park here.   C I suggest to park here.

2 ...... I'm open to any option that will make things easier for us all.
  A Can you suggest any alternative to me?   B Can you suggest me any alternative?

summary

1 For homework, I'd like you ....
  A to make a summary for Wilkinson's long speech on page 55
  B to make a summary from Wilkinson's long speech on page 55
  C to make a summary of Wilkinson's long speech on page 55

study **1** Studium; Studie, (wissenschaftliche) Untersuchung **2** studieren ▷ learn ▷ university

- *Cosmology* [kɒzˈmɒlədʒi] *is the study of the universe.* ● ● ● … ist das Studium des Kosmos.

Trouble Spot

- **Studium; Studien-**
  einen Studienplatz erhalten zum Studium zugelassen werden ● ● ● *get a place at university*
  das Studium beginnen ● ● ● *start/begin university/* (fml:) *start/begin one's studies*
  das Studium beenden ● ● ● *finish university/* (fml:) *finish/complete one's studies*
  den Studienabschluss erreichen ● ● ● *get one's degree*
  Welches Studienfach hast du gewählt? ● ● ● *Which subject have you chosen?*
  Jura ist ein langes Studium. ● ● ● *Law is a long (university) course/* (fml:) *course of study.*
  Während des Studiums habe ich gejobbt. ● ● ● *When/While (I was) a student/*
   When/While (I was) at university/ When/While (I was) studying, I had part-time jobs.

- **studieren**
  Jenny studiert Betriebswirtschaft. ● ● ● *Jenny is studying business administration.*
  Paul studiert in Potsdam. ● ● ● *Paul is studying in Potsdam.*
  Paul studiert an der Universität Potsdam. ● ● ● *Paul is studying/is at Potsdam University.*
  Meine Schwester studiert. ● ● ● *My sister is at university.*
  Haben deine Eltern studiert? ● ● ● *Did your parents go to university?*

stuff Zeug, Sachen

- **False Friend!**
  Stuff bedeutet nicht „~~Stoff~~", sondern „Zeug" oder „Sachen".
   What's all this stuff doing on my desk? ● ● ● … dieses ganze Zeug/diese ganzen Sachen …?
  Beachte die englischen Entsprechungen von „Stoff":
  ein Kleid aus einem schönen Stoff ● ● ● *a dress made of beautiful material* [məˈtɪəriəl] /
   fabric [ˈfæbrɪk] / *cloth* [klɒθ]
  chemische Stoffe ● ● ● *chemical substances* [ˈsʌbstənsɪz]
  ein Stofftier ● ● ● (BE:) *a soft toy/* (AE:) *a stuffed animal*

succeed [səkˈsiːd] es schaffen; gelingen

- *succeed in doing*
Nach *succeed* verwendet man *in* + die *-ing*-Form des Verbs, keinen *to*-Infinitiv.
   She succeeded in selling (~~succeeded to sell~~) her designs to an agency. ● ● ● Sie hat es geschafft
    Es ist ihr gelungen, ihre Entwürfe an eine Agentur zu verkaufen.

suffer leiden

- *suffer from a rare disease* ● ● ● an einer seltenen Krankheit leiden

suggest [səˈdʒest] vorschlagen

- *suggest doing*
Nach *suggest* verwendet man die *-ing*-Form des Verbs, keinen *to*-Infinitiv.
   I suggest asking (~~suggest to ask~~) Tina. ● ● ● Ich schlage vor, Tina zu fragen.
Ein *that*-Satz ist auch möglich.
   I suggest (that) we/you ask Tina. ● ● ● Ich schlage vor, dass wir Tina fragen/dass du Tina fragst.

- *suggest sth. to sb.*
Die Person, der man etwas vorschlägt, muss mit *to* angeschlossen werden.
   I've suggested the idea to Sid (~~suggested Sid the idea~~). ● ● ● Ich habe die Idee Sid vorgeschlagen.

summary [ˈsʌməri] Zusammenfassung

- *make a summary of (~~summary from~~) a text* ● ● ● eine Zusammenfassung eines Textes machen/
    eine Zusammenfassung von einem Text machen/einen Text zusammenfassen

S

sunk – sunken

1 The waters round this part of the coast are dangerous, ...
   A   and there are quite a number of sunk wrecks
   B   and there are quite a number of sunken wrecks

2 A   Two ships have sunk so far this year.   B   Two ships have sunken so far this year.

suppose

1 ...... when you leave school in the summer and start your training.
   A   I suppose you take a room or a flat   B   I suppose you'll take a room or a flat

2 Will it be very expensive, do you think? – ......
   A   I suppose it.   B   I suppose so.   C   I suppose yes.

3 Do you think they'll pay us? – ......
   A   I don't suppose it.   B   I don't suppose so.   C   I suppose it not.

surprised

1 ...... He took the news very well.
   A   We were all surprised about his reaction.   B   We were all surprised at his reaction.
   C   We were all surprised from his reaction.   D   We were all surprised over his reaction.

suspect – suspicious

1 A   The police have identified a suspect package.
   B   The police have identified a suspicious package.
   C   The police have identified a package that looks suspect.
   D   The police have identified a package that looks suspicious.

2 They say they're expecting over 1000 visitors a day, and an income of £5000. ......
   A   I think these figues are very suspect.
   B   I think these figures are very suspicious.

3 ...... They promised the same amount last time, but didn't give a penny.
   A   I'm suspect.   B   I'm suspicious.

suspect (verb)

1 ...... who planned the break-in.
   A   The police suspect him to be the brains of the gang
   B   The police suspect him of being the brains of the gang

symbol

1 A   Black is a symbol for evil, white a symbol for good.
   B   Black is a symbol of evil, white a symbol of good.

sunk – sunken gesunken, versunken

■ *Sunk* ist das Partizip Perfekt von *sink (sink – sank – sunk)*.
  Many ships **have sunk** *in these waters.* ● ● ● In diesen Gewässern sind schon viele Schiffe gesunken.

■ Vor einem Nomen verwendet man jedoch das Adjektiv *sunken*.
  a **sunken** *ship* ● ● ● ein gesunkenes Schiff

suppose annehmen, vermuten

■ **suppose + will-future**
Wenn sich der auf *suppose* folgende Nebensatz auf die Zukunft bezieht, verwendet man darin eine Zukunftsform des Verbs, nicht das *simple present*.
  I **suppose** *we'll* **find out** *(~~we find out~~) sooner or later.* ● ● ● Ich nehme an, dass wir es früher oder später herausfinden (werden).

■ **I suppose so/not**
Wenn man *suppose* in einer kurzen Antwort verwendet, steht *so/not* dahinter, nicht *it/yes/no*.
  Will Philip be there? – I **suppose so**. *(~~I suppose it/yes.~~)* ● ● ● … – Ich nehme es an./Ich glaube schon.
  We won't need our passports, will we? – I **don't suppose so**./*I* **suppose not**. ● ● ● … – Ich nehme es nicht an./Ich glaube nicht.

surprised überrascht, verwundert

■ **surprised at sth./sb.**
  I was **surprised at** *the large number of people who were there.* ● ● ● Ich war überrascht über/habe mich gewundert über die vielen Leute, die da waren.
  I'm **surprised at** *you.* ● ● ● Ich muss mich doch (über dich) wundern./Du überraschst mich.

suspect 1 Verdächtige(r) 2 verdächtig; zweifelhaft – suspicious verdächtig; misstrauisch

■ **Nomen: *suspect* [ˈsʌspekt]**
  The police have arrested four **suspects**. ● ● ● Die Polizei hat vier Verdächtige festgenommen.

■ **die Adjektive *suspect* [ˈsʌspekt] und *suspicious* [səˈspɪʃəs]**
Sowohl *suspect* als auch *suspicious* bedeuten „verdächtig". Beachte die Unterschiede:
  a **suspect**/**suspicious** *package* [= Verdacht erregender, eventuell gefährlicher Gegenstand] ● ● ● ein verdächtiges Paket
  suspicious *behaviour* [= Verdacht erregendes Verhalten] ● ● ● verdächtiges Verhalten
Nach Verben kann nur *suspicious* stehen, um zu sagen, dass etwas oder jemand verdächtig ist, aussieht usw.
  This package/behaviour is highly **suspicious**. ● ● ● Dieses Paket/Verhalten ist höchst verdächtig.
Suspect bedeutet auch „zweifelhaft", „fragwürdig", „nicht glaubwürdig", „suspekt". In dieser Bedeutung steht es sowohl vor Nomen als auch nach Verben.
  suspect *evidence* ● ● ● zweifelhafte Beweise
  The evidence was highly **suspect**. ● ● ● Die Beweise waren höchst zweifelhaft/fragwürdig.
Suspicious bedeutet auch „misstrauisch".
  I'm **suspicious**. *I don't trust them.* ● ● ● Ich bin misstrauisch. Ich traue ihnen nicht.

suspect [səˈspekt] verdächtigen; vermuten

■ *Who do the police* **suspect**? ● ● ● Wen verdächtigt die Polizei?
  He is **suspected of having** *(~~suspected to have~~) contacts to terrorist groups.* ● ● ● Er wird verdächtigt, Kontakte zu Terroristengruppen zu unterhalten.

■ *I* **suspect** *that the price will be too high.* ● ● ● Ich vermute, der Preis wird zu hoch sein.

symbol [ˈsɪmbl] Symbol

■ *The dove* [dʌv] *is a* **symbol of** *peace.* ● ● ● Die Taube ist ein Symbol [Sinnbild] für den Frieden.
  "€" is the **symbol for** *"euro".* ● ● ● „€" ist das Symbol [Zeichen/Abkürzung] für „Euro".

S

sympathetic ≠ „sympathisch"

1 If you say someone is sympathetic, you mean they are ....
A friendly   B nice   C understanding

2 Pete is the best of my colleagues. *[Er ist mir sehr sympathisch.]*
A He's very sympathetic towards me.
B He's to me very understanding.
C I like him very much.

3 Most of the staff at the hotel where I did my work placement were very nice. ......
A But a few were really unpleasant.   B But a few were really unsympathetic.

4 When my grandmother died, ...
A all my friends were very feeling with me
B all my friends were very sympathetic towards me
C all my friends were very understanding of me

tablet ≠ „Tablett"

1 *[Wenn du alles auf ein Tablett stellst]*, it'll be easier to carry.
A If you put everything on a tablet
B If you put everything on a tablett
C If you put everything on a tray

2 ...... , but they're often so difficult to swallow.
A Pills are small   B Tablets are small   C Tabletts are small

task

1 We need to find someone reliable ......
A who will take on the task of looking after the finances.
B who will take on the task looking after the finances.
C who will take on the task to look after the finances.

taste

1 I haven't eaten chocolate like this ever! ......
A It tastes!   B It tastes and how!   C It tastes wonderful!

2 Seaweed is a local speciality. ......
A Does it taste?   B Does it taste good?   C Does it taste well?   D Do you like it?

3 It's funny ...... than it did this morning.
A how things taste different at different times of the day. This cheese is tasting different now
B how things are tasting different at different times of the day. This cheese tastes different now
C how things taste different at different times of the day. This cheese tastes different now

4 You must try this. It's Arabian. Ali's sister made it. ......
A It tastes wonderful.   B It tastes wonderfully.

5 ...... How strange!
A This cheese tastes after chocolate!
B This cheese tastes of chocolate!

sympathetic [ˌsɪmpəˈθetɪk] mitfühlend, verständnisvoll

■ False Friend!
Sympathetic bedeutet nicht „~~sympathisch~~", sondern „mitfühlend" bzw. „verständnisvoll".
*I have **sympathetic** parents who support me.* ● ● ● Ich habe verständnisvolle Eltern, die mich unterstützen.
*be **sympathetic** to/towards sb.* ● ● ● mit jmdm. mitfühlen, Verständnis für jmdn. haben
*She's **sympathetic** towards the idea.* ● ● ● Ihr gefällt die Idee. / Sie steht der Idee wohlwollend gegenüber.
Beachte die englischen Entsprechungen von „sympathisch/unsympathisch":
Frau Kuhnert ist eine sympathische Lehrerin mit viel Humor. ● ● ● *Mrs Kuhnert is a **nice** teacher with a good sense of humour.*
Sie sieht sehr sympathisch aus. ● ● ● *She looks very **nice**.*
Sie ist mir (sehr) sympathisch. ● ● ● *I **like** her (a lot).*
Der Taxifahrer war sehr unsympathisch. ● ● ● *The taxi driver was very **unpleasant**.*

tablet [ˈtæblət] Tablette

■ False Friend!
Tablet bedeutet nicht „~~Tablett~~", sondern – wie *pill* – „Tablette".
*Take two **tablets**/pills with a little water.* ● ● ● Nehmen Sie zwei Tabletten/Pillen mit etwas Wasser.
Beachte die englische Entsprechung von „Tablett":
das Tablett mit den Teetassen fallen lassen ● ● ● *drop the **tray** with the teacups*

task Aufgabe ▷ work

■ the task of doing
Auf *the task* folgt *of* + die *-ing*-Form des Verbs, kein *to*-Infinitiv.
*the difficult **task of clearing up** after the floods* ● ● ● die schwere Aufgabe, nach den Überschwemmungen aufzuräumen

taste schmecken

■ „gut schmecken"
Das Verb *taste* bedeutet nicht schon an sich „gut schmecken"; man muss eine entsprechende Ergänzung oder eine andere Ausdrucksweise verwenden.
*Try that. That **tastes good**/great/wonderful/nice! (~~That tastes!~~)* ● ● ● Probier mal. Das schmeckt!
*The soup **is delicious**!* ● ● ● Die Suppe schmeckt – und wie! / Die Suppe ist einfach köstlich!
Die Frage „Schmeckt's (dir)?" und die Aussage „Es hat mir (gut) geschmeckt" lauten auf Englisch:
*Do you **like** it? / Does it **taste good**? / **Is** it **nice**? / Are you **enjoying** it?*
*I really **enjoyed** the meal / that.*

■ nicht in der Verlaufsform
*The coffee **tastes** (~~is tasting~~) very strange today.* ● ● ● Der Kaffee schmeckt heute sehr seltsam.

■ mit Adjektiv, nicht Adverb
taste good/bad/wonderful/sweet (~~taste well/badly/wonderfully/sweetly~~) ● ● ● gut/schlecht/wunderbar/süß schmecken

■ taste ... to sb.
*The milk **tastes** funny **to** me.* ● ● ● Ich finde, die Milch schmeckt komisch.

■ taste of sth.
*The yoghurt **tastes of** (~~tastes after~~) alcohol.* ● ● ● Der Joghurt schmeckt nach Alkohol.
*The bread **tastes of** (~~tastes after~~) onions.* ● ● ● Das Brot schmeckt nach Zwiebeln.
Aber:
*This coffee **tastes like** dishwater!* ● ● ● Dieser Kaffee schmeckt wie Abwaschwasser!

T

teacher – instructor – lecturer

1 ...... isn't very pleased with me when I don't practise.
   A My piano instructor   B My piano lecturer   C My piano teacher

2 I nearly hit a queue of people at a bus stop, and ...... nearly had a heart attack.
   A my car instructor   B my driving instructor   C my driving teacher

3 Too many people hope to stay on after they've got their degree ....
   A and become a lecturer
   B and become a university lecturer
   C and become a university teacher

technique – technology

1 A If it weren't for technique, we would have no cars, no computers and no coffee machines.
   B If it weren't for technology, we would have no cars, no computers and no coffee machines.

2 ...... in this picture? Do you know the word for it?
   A Which technique did the painter use   B Which technology did the painter use

teenage

1 It's a silly programme. It's supposed to appeal to ......, but it feels as if it's made for 12-year-olds.
   A interests of teenagers   B teenage interests   C teenager interests

temperature

1 ...... today, that's a bit warmer than yesterday.
   A We have 15 degrees   B There are 15 degrees   C It's 15 degree   D It's 15 degrees

2 Was it colder yesterday? ......
   A How many degrees did we have?   B How many degrees were there?
   C What was the temperature?

3 You'll need your coat this morning. ......
   A It's just over nil degree.   B It's just above zero.   C It's just above zero degree.

4 ...... for the rest of the week.
   A The temperature will remain at about the thirty degrees
   B The temperature will remain in the upper twenties
   C The temperature will remain in the lower thirties

5 ...... does milk freeze? Is it the same as water?
   A At what temperature   B By what temperature   C In what temperature

terrible – terrific

1 You should try it, ...
   A it's a terrible once-in-a-lifetime experience   B it's a terrific once-in-a-lifetime experience

2 Just look at the fog! ......
   A What a terrible morning.   B What a terrific morning.

test

1 I've got to work. On Wednesday ....
   A we're doing a test   B we're making a test   C we're writing a test

2 I hear .... Good luck!
   A you're making your driving test today   B you're taking your driving test today

teacher – instructor [ɪnˈstrʌktə] – lecturer [ˈlektʃərə] Lehrer/-in

Trouble Spot

■ **Lehrer/-in**
1 „Schul- oder Musiklehrer/-in"
mein Englischlehrer / meine Englischlehrerin ● ● ● *my English **teacher***
ein guter Klavierlehrer / eine gute Klavierlehrerin ● ● ● *a good piano **teacher***
Lehrerzimmer ● ● ● ***staff** room*

2 „Lehrer/-in für praktische Fertigkeiten"
Fahr-/Ski-/Tauchlehrer/-in ● ● ● *driving/skiing/diving **instructor***

3 „Hochschullehrer/-in", „Dozent/-in"
Hochschullehrer/-in ● ● ● ***university teacher** / (university) **lecturer***

technique [tekˈniːk] – technology [tekˈnɒlədʒi] Technik

■ *Technique* entspricht „Technik" im Sinne von „Verfahren", „Methode", „Vorgehensweise".
*There are various **techniques** you can use to help you learn vocabulary more effectively.* ● ● ●
Es gibt verschiedene Techniken, die du anwenden kannst, um Vokabeln effizienter zu lernen.

■ *Technology* entspricht „Technik" im Sinne von „(angewandte) Technologie".
*Information **technology** has changed the world in the last 20 years.* ● ● ● Die Informations-
technik/-technologie hat die Welt in den letzten 20 Jahren verändert.

teenage Teenager-, für Teenager; im Teenageralter

■ **Adjektiv: *teenage*, nicht *teenager***
***teenage** girls/boys* ● ● ● Mädchen/Jungen im Teenageralter
***teenage** problems* ● ● ● Probleme von Teenagern/Teenagerprobleme

temperature [ˈtemprətʃə] Temperatur ▷ fever

Topic Box

■ ***Talking about temperature*** ▷ degree ▷ minus ▷ warm
What's the temperature? ● ● ● Wie viel Grad / Wie warm ist es? / Wie viel Grad haben wir?
It's one degree. ● ● ● Es ist ein Grad. / Wir haben ein Grad.
It's six degrees. ● ● ● Es sind sechs Grad. / Wir haben sechs Grad.
It's nought/zero degrees. It's freezing. ● ● ● Es ist null Grad. Es friert.
It's three degrees above/below zero. ● ● ● Es sind drei Grad über/unter null.
It's plus/minus three. ● ● ● Es sind plus/minus drei Grad.
It's been / The temperature has been in the thirties every day this week. ● ● ● Es waren
diese Woche jeden Tag über 30 Grad. / Wir hatten diese Woche jeden Tag über 30 Grad.
It was in the lower thirties. / It was over 30 degrees. ● ● ● Es waren (etwas) über 30 Grad.
It was in the upper thirties. / It was nearly 40 degrees. ● ● ● Es waren fast 40 Grad.
Water freezes at a temperature of nought/zero degrees Celsius/Centigrade. ● ● ● Wasser
gefriert bei einer Temperatur von null Grad Celsius.

T

terrible schrecklich, furchtbar – terrific [təˈrɪfɪk] toll, großartig

■ *It was a **terrible** exam. I'm sure I failed.* ● ● ● Es war eine schreckliche Prüfung. …
*I'm **terribly** sorry.* ● ● ● Es tut mir furchtbar leid.

■ *We had a **terrific** party. It was fantastic.* ● ● ● Wir hatten eine super Party. …

test Test, Klassenarbeit, Prüfung ▷ exam

■ *We're **doing** / We've got a **test** (We're writing a test) tomorrow.* ● ● ● Wir schreiben morgen
einen Test / eine (Klassen-)Arbeit / eine Klausur.
*When are you going to **take**/**do** your driving **test** (make your driving exam)?* ● ● ● Wann machst du
deine Fahrprüfung / deinen Führerschein?

thank – thank you / thanks

1 ...... I was so afraid that someone might have stolen it.
   A I'd like to thank you for rescuing my camera.
   B I'd like to thank you that you rescued my camera.

2 It was a very short farewell. He took off his hat, shook my hand, ... and then got on the train.
   A thanked   B thanked me   C said thank you

3 A bit more wine, anyone? – ......, no more for me.
   A No, thank you   B Thank you

thick – fat

1 I don't know how much he weighs, ... It must be ages since he last saw his feet.
   A but he's so fat   B but he's so thick

2 It has over 1500 pages. ...... and weighs a ton!
   A It's a great big fat book   B It's a great big thick book   C It's a great big wide book

3 It tastes wonderful, but don't eat too much of it. ......
   A It makes fat.   B It will make you fat.

think

1 At first it seemed ridiculous, ...
   A but now I'm thinking it's actually quite a clever idea
   B but now I think it's actually quite a clever idea

2 ...... Do you think it would be a good idea to ask Roger?
   A I've been thinking.   B I've thought.

3 Try this. ...... It's better than her first book.
   A I think you find it quite interesting.   B I think you'll find it quite interesting.

4 Have we got enough money? – ...... At least, I hope we have.
   A I think it.   B I think yes.   C I think so.

5 ...... – That's very kind of you. I'd love to.
   A I thought if you might like to come with me.
   B I was thinking if you might like to come with me.
   C I was wondering if you might like to come with me.

thought

1 It was ...... that made him work harder and harder.
   A the thought of making lots of money   B the thought to make lots of money

thank danken, sich bedanken bei – thank you / thanks danke

■ *thank* + Objekt
Nach *thank* muss ein Personenobjekt stehen.
> He **thanked us** (~~He thanked~~) and left. ● ● ● Er dankte (uns) / bedankte sich (bei uns) und ging.
> = He **said thank you** and left. ● ● ● Er bedankte sich / sagte danke und ging.

■ *thank sb. for doing*
Im Anschluss an das Verb *thank* oder an *thank you / thanks* verwendet man *for* + die *-ing*-Form des Verbs, um zu sagen, wofür man sich bedankt. Ein *that*-Satz ist nicht möglich.
> I **thank you / Thank you / Thanks (a lot) for being** so patient (~~thank you that you were so patient~~).
> ● ● ● Ich danke Ihnen / Danke / Vielen Dank, dass Sie so geduldig waren.

■ „danke (nein)" = *no, thank you / no, thanks*
Thank you / Thanks ist eine zustimmende Reaktion.
> Would you like some more tea? – **Thank you. / Thanks.** ● ● ● … – (Ja gern,) danke. / Ja, bitte.

Wenn man etwas ablehnen will, muss man *no* voranstellen.
> Would you like some more tea? – **No, thank you. / No, thanks.** ● ● ● … – Danke (nein). / Nein, danke.

thick – fat dick

■ *thick* bei Sachen
Thick bezieht sich auf den Durchmesser von Dingen.
> a **thick** wall / carpet / coat / piece of bread

Mit Bezug auf Bücher ist neben *thick* auch *fat* möglich.
> a **thick/fat** book

■ *fat* bei Menschen
Fat bezieht sich auf das Gewicht von Menschen und Tieren.
> a **fat** man / woman / dog
> Fast food **makes you fat** (~~makes fat~~). ● ● ● Fastfood macht dick.

think* (nach)denken, glauben

■ wann in der Verlaufsform?
In der Bedeutung „(nach)denken", „überlegen" kann *think* in der Verlaufsform verwendet werden.
> Shut up! I'**m thinking**. ● ● ● Halt die Klappe! Ich denke nach / überlege.

In der Bedeutung „glauben", „finden", „der Meinung sein" ist die Verlaufsform nicht möglich.
> I used to hate getting up early. Now I **think** (~~Now I'm thinking~~) it's sometimes quite nice. ● ● ●
> Früher fand ich frühes Aufstehen schrecklich. Jetzt finde ich es manchmal ganz schön.

■ *think + will-future*
Wenn sich der auf *think* („glauben") folgende Nebensatz auf die Zukunft bezieht, verwendet man darin eine Zukunftsform des Verbs, kein *simple present*.
> I **think** Simon **will get** (~~Simon gets~~) the job. ● ● ● Ich glaube, Simon bekommt die Stelle.

■ I (don't) think so
Wenn man *think* in einer kurzen Antwort verwendet, steht *so* dahinter, nicht *it / yes / no*.
> Will Philip be there? – I **think so**. (~~I think it / yes.~~) ● ● ● Wird Philip da sein? – Ich glaube ja.
> Will Philip be there? – I **don't think so**. (~~I think no. / I don't think it.~~) ● ● ● … – Ich glaube nicht / nein.

■ höfliche Bitten und Einladungen mit *wonder* [ˈwʌndə]
Eine vorsichtige Bitte oder Einladung spricht man mit *wonder* aus, nicht mit *think*.
> I **was wondering** (~~I was thinking~~) if you could help me. ● ● ● Ich dachte, ob du mir vielleicht helfen könntest.

thought Gedanke

■ the thought of doing
Auf *the thought* folgt *of* + die *-ing*-Form des Verbs, kein *to*-Infinitiv.
> **The thought of losing** (~~The thought to lose~~) her is terrible. ● ● ● Der Gedanke, sie zu verlieren …

T

threat

1 The team is so strong, ...

   A only the Australians are a real threat of them

   B only the Australians are a real threat to them

throw

1 ...... It isn't my fault that you lost.

   A Don't throw your towel against me!

   B Don't throw your towel at me!

   C Don't throw your towel to me!

2 A Throw that pack of tissues over at me, can you, please?

   B Throw that pack of tissues over to me, can you, please?

3 If you don't shut up, ...

   A we'll get threwn off the train

   B we'll get throwed off the train

   C we'll get thrown off the train

time („Zeit")

1 ...... my granny said to him.

   A "It's time that you're learning some manners, young man,"

   B "It's time that you learn some manners, young man,"

   C "It's time that you learnt some manners, young man,"

2 ...... They've started to invade the kitchen now.

   A It's high time we're doing something about the mice in the house.

   B It's high time we do something about the mice in the house.

   C It's high time we did something about the mice in the house.

3 We were ten minutes late leaving Berlin, ...

   A but still landed in Cologne in time, at exactly 11.25

   B but still landed in Cologne on time, at exactly 11.25

4 ...... out of the back door.

   A I was just in time to see Hanno disappearing

   B I was just on time to see Hanno disappearing

5 [In der ersten Zeit] there were quite a few problems, but everything is OK now.

   A In the beginning   **B** In the first few weeks   **C** In the first time   **D** In the first times

6 There haven't been many overseas visitors [in der letzten Zeit].

   A in the last time   **B** in the last times   **C** in the latest time   **D** lately   **E** recently

7 There is going to be a lot of work to do [in der nächsten Zeit].

   A in the near future   **B** in the near time   **C** in the next times   **D** soon

time („Mal")

1 ...... It's a lovely country.

   A It's the first time I'm in Ireland.   **B** It's the first time I've been to Ireland.

2 They addressed the letter to 'Peter Schmidt' instead of 'Petra Schmidt'. ......

   A This is the second time this happens to me.

   B This is the second time this has happened to me.

threat [θret] Bedrohung, Gefahr

■ a **threat to** world peace ● ● ● eine Bedrohung Gefahr für den Weltfrieden, eine Bedrohung des Weltfriedens

throw* werfen

■ **throw – threw – thrown**

■ **throw sth. at sb.**
Throw at verwendet man, wenn der Wurfgegenstand jemanden treffen soll.
   Protesters **threw** bottles **at** the police. ● ● ● Demonstranten bewarfen die Polizei mit Flaschen /
   warfen mit Flaschen nach der Polizei.

■ **throw sth. to sb.**
Throw to verwendet man, wenn jemand den Wurfgegenstand auffangen soll.
   throw the ball **to** a teammate ● ● ● den Ball einer Mitspielerin zuwerfen

time Zeit

■ **it's (high) time + to-Infinitiv oder past tense**
Nach it's (high) time kann man – wie im Deutschen – einen Infinitiv verwenden.
   It's time (for us) **to leave**. It's getting late. ● ● ● Es wird Zeit zu gehen / dass wir gehen. …
   The problem is getting worse. **It's high time to do** something about it. ● ● ● ● … Es ist höchste Zeit,
   etwas in dieser Sache zu unternehmen.
Wird ein Nebensatz (mit oder ohne that) angeschlossen, so steht das Verb im simple past.
   It's time (that) **we left** (we leave). ● ● ● Es wird Zeit, dass wir gehen.
   It's high time (that) **the government did** (the government does) something about it. ● ● ● Es ist
   höchste Zeit, dass die Regierung etwas in dieser Sache unternimmt.

■ **on time**
On time bedeutet „pünktlich".
   The plane was (right) **on time**. ● ● ● Die Maschine war pünktlich (auf die Minute).

■ **in time (to do / for sth.)**
In time bedeutet „rechtzeitig".
   We arrived **in time** to see the magician. ● ● ● Wir kamen rechtzeitig, um den Zauberer zu sehen.
   Will I be **in time** for the bus? ● ● ● Werde ich den Bus noch kriegen?

Trouble Spot

■ **Zeit**
In der ersten Zeit musste ich sehr viele Fragen beantworten. ● ● ● **In the beginning /
In the first few days / weeks / months** I had to answer quite a lot of questions.
Hast du deinen Heimtrainer in letzter Zeit / in der letzten Zeit benutzt? ● ● ● Have you used
your exercise bike **recently / lately**?
Wir treffen uns in nächster Zeit / in der nächsten Zeit wieder. ● ● ● We're meeting again
in the near future / soon.
Herr Ferguson ist zurzeit in Urlaub. ● ● ● Mr Ferguson is on holiday **at the moment**.
zur Zeit Shakespeares ● ● ● **in Shakespeare's day**
In welcher Zeit(form) steht dieser Satz? ● ● ● What **tense** is this sentence in?

time Mal

■ **it's the first time (that) … („es ist das erste Mal, dass …") + present perfect**
Nach … is the first / second / last / only time (that) folgt das present perfect, keine Gegenwartsform.
   Today is **the first time** (that) **I've eaten** (the first time that I eat) sushi ['suːʃi]. ● ● ● Heute ist das
   erste Mal, dass ich Sushi esse. / Heute esse ich zum ersten Mal Sushi.
   This is **the second time** (that) **I've been** here (the second time that I'm here). ● ● ● Dies ist das
   zweite Mal, dass ich hier bin. / Ich bin zum zweiten Mal hier.
   It's **the third time** (that) she **has won** silver (the third time that she wins silver). ● ● ● Es ist das dritte
   Mal, dass sie Silber gewinnt. / Sie hat zum dritten Mal Silber gewonnen.

T

toast

1 ......, and a cup of tea, that's my usual breakfast.
A Two pieces of toast with marmalade
B Two toast breads with marmalade
C Two toasts with marmalade

today – tomorrow

1 ...... I'll be in Ecuador.
A A week today   B One week from this day   C Today in a week

2 ...... with Charlie Fish of the London Weather Centre.
A And now the weather from today
B And now the weather of today
C And now today's weather

3 A There was a terrible storm last night.
B There was a terrible storm tonight.
C There was a terrible storm this night.

too

1 ......, so we decided to play safe.
A It was a too big risk   B It was too big a risk

tooth

1 ...... does a human being have? Is it 32? Or 34?
A How many teeth   B How many teeths   C How many tooths

tour

1 We're planning ...... this year, by motorhome.
A to do a tour of Canada   B to do a tour through Canada
C to go on a tour of Canada   D to go on a tour through Canada
E to make a tour of Canada   F to make a tour through Canada

traffic

1 ...... on this road before. It's a nightmare!
A I've never seen such a traffic   B I've never seen such traffic

2 ......, it took us three times as long as usual.
A The traffic was so heavy   B The traffic was so strong

trouble

1 ...... at the beginning because of my trumpet, but we get on fine now.
A I had a trouble with the neighbours
B I had trouble with the neighbours
C I had troubles with the neighbours

2 A Have you had any trouble contacting the server recently?
B Have you had any trouble to contact the server recently?
C Have you had any troubles to contact the server recently?

toast Toast

■ **nicht zählbares Nomen**

Toast ist nicht zählbar, kann also nicht mit *a* oder im Plural verwendet werden.

> have *a slice*/*piece of toast*/*some toast* (~~a toast~~) *for breakfast* ● ● ● (eine Scheibe/einen) Toast zum Frühstück essen
>
> eat *two slices*/*pieces of toast* (~~two toasts~~) ● ● ● zwei Scheiben Toast/zwei Toasts essen

today heute – tomorrow morgen

Trouble Spot

■ **heute; morgen**

> heute/morgen in einer Woche ● ● ● *a week today*/*tomorrow*
>
> heute in zehn Tagen ● ● ● *ten days from today*/*in ten days*/*in ten days' time*
>
> heute/morgen vor drei Wochen ● ● ● *three weeks ago today*/*tomorrow*
>
> heute/morgen Abend ● ● ● *this*/*tomorrow evening*
>
> heute Nacht ● ● ● *tonight* [= kommende Nacht]/*last night* [= vergangene Nacht]
>
> morgen um diese Zeit ● ● ● *this time tomorrow*
>
> die Zeitung von heute/morgen ● ● ● *today's*/*tomorrow's paper*

too (all)zu ▶ also ▶ much

■ **Stellung**

Fügt man *too* zu der Wendung „*a*/*an* + Adjektiv + Nomen" hinzu, gilt die folgende Reihenfolge: „*too* + Adjektiv + *a*/*an*".

> *too long a time* (~~a too long time~~) ● ● ● eine zu lange Zeit

tooth Zahn

■ *one **tooth**, two **teeth***

tour [tʊə, tɔː] Rundreise, Rundfahrt ▶ journey

■ *go on*/*do a tour of* (~~make a tour through~~) *Italy* ● ● ● eine Rundreise durch Italien unternehmen

> *go on*/*do a tour of the old part of the town* ● ● ● eine Rundfahrt durch die Altstadt machen

traffic Verkehr

■ **nicht zählbares Nomen**

Traffic ist nicht zählbar, kann also nicht mit *a* verwendet werden.

> *What **traffic**!* (~~What a traffic!~~) *I've never seen this road so busy.* ● ● ● Was für ein Verkehr! …

■ *light*/*heavy traffic* ● ● ● wenig/dichter Verkehr

trouble Problem, Ärger, Schwierigkeit

■ **nicht mit *a***

Trouble wird nie mit *a* verwendet.

> *I had **trouble** (~~a trouble~~/~~troubles~~) with my computer.* ● ● ● Ich hatte ein Problem/Probleme/Ärger mit meinem Computer.
>
> *be **in trouble*** ● ● ● in Schwierigkeiten sein
>
> *get **into trouble*** ● ● ● in Schwierigkeiten geraten

Die selten verwendete Pluralform *troubles* bedeutet „politische Unruhen" oder „eine anhaltende Serie von Problemen".

> *the **Troubles** in Northern Ireland* ● ● ● die Unruhen in Nordirland
>
> *We've had endless **trouble(s)** with the new washing machine.* ● ● ● … unendliche Probleme …

■ *have trouble doing*

Auf *have trouble* folgt die *-ing*-Form (wie bei *have difficulty*/*problems*), nicht der *to*-Infinitiv.

> *I had **trouble** finding (~~had trouble to find~~) the house.* ● ● ● Ich hatte Probleme, das Haus zu finden.

T

trousers

1 Where did your buy your new trousers? ......
   A They're really cool.   B It's really cool.

2 I need to buy ....
   A a new pair of trousers   B a new trousers   C some new trousers

true – truth

1 Gone are the days when I thought ....
   A all my dreams would become true
   B all my dreams would come true

2 I don't know whether to believe her or not. Do you think ...... ?
   A she's saying the truth   B she's telling the truth

trust

1 ...... Stay away from him.
   A Julian Hammerforth is not to be trusted.   B Julian Hammerforth is not to trust.

2 ...... without having to be reminded again?
   A Can we trust them that they'll pay   B Can we trust them to pay

try – attempt

1 Freddy ...... but couldn't get it to work. Now Marion ....
   A tried ... is trieing   B tried ... is trying   C tryed ... is trieing   D tryed ... is trying

2 I wonder how we can contact them. ......
   A I'll try finding out the address on the Internet.
   B I'll try to find out the address on the Internet.

3 ...... , but the traffic is just as bad.
   A I've tried leaving a quarter of an hour later in the mornings
   B I've tried to leave a quarter of an hour later in the mornings

4 ...... , just for a change you know, to see how I like it.
   A I've decided to try drinking green tea for breakfast for a while
   B I've decided to try to drink green tea for breakfast for a while

5 Do you think you could get here by 6.30? – ......
   A I'll try it, but I can't promise.   B I'll try so, but I can't promise.   C I'll try, but I can't promise.

6 I went round and round, and finally found somewhere to park ....
   A at the fourth attempt   B by the fourth attempt   C by the fourth try

typical

1 ...... that he had an exam the next day.
   A It was typical of Sonny to forget
   B It was typical for Sonny to forget
   C It was typical for Sonny that he forgot

2 A I wish my accent didn't sound so typical German.
   B I wish my accent didn't sound so typically German.

trousers (BE) Hose(n)   ▶ pants ▶ shorts

■ **Pluralnomen, keine Singularform**
Trousers gibt es nur als Pluralnomen (mit einem Verb im Plural).
   ***These trousers are** (~~This trouser is~~) cool.* ● ● ● Diese Hose ist / Diese Hosen sind cool.
Um daraus eine Singularform zu machen, muss man *pair of* voranstellen.
   ***This pair of trousers is** cool.* ● ● ● Diese Hose / Dieses Paar Hosen ist cool.
   *buy **a new pair of trousers** / **some new trousers** (~~a new trousers~~)* ● ● ● (ein Paar) neue Hosen kaufen

true wahr – **truth** Wahrheit

■ **Schreibung**
   true – truth (~~trueth~~)

■ *All your dreams will **come true** (~~become true~~).* ● ● ● … werden wahr / werden in Erfüllung gehen.
   *Yes, **that's true**.* ● ● ● Ja, das stimmt.

■ ***tell the truth** (~~say the truth~~)* ● ● ● die Wahrheit sagen

trust (ver)trauen

■ **Infinitiv Passiv**
   *That man **is not to be trusted** (~~is not to trust~~).* ● ● ● Diesem Mann ist nicht zu trauen.

■ ***trust** sb. **to do***
Nach *trust* verwendet man ein Objekt + einen *to*-Infinitiv, keinen *that*-Satz.
   *I **trust him to help** me (~~trust him that he helps me~~).* ● ● ● Ich verlassse mich darauf, dass er mir hilft.

try versuchen – **attempt** Versuch

■ **Schreibung**
   *try, tr**ies**, trying, tr**ied***

■ ***try to do*** = „versuchen / sich bemühen, etwas zu tun"
Mit *try* + dem *to*-Infinitiv drückt man aus, dass man versucht etwas zu tun, was schwierig ist oder bei dem nicht sicher ist, ob es klappt.
   *I **tried to lift** the piano, but it was too heavy.* ● ● ● Ich habe versucht, das Klavier anzuheben …
   *I **tried to phone** Damian, but I only got his mailbox.* ● ● ● Ich habe versucht, Damian anzurufen …

■ ***try doing*** = „etwas versuchsweise tun", „etwas ausprobieren"
Mit *try* + der *-ing*-Form des Verbs drückt man aus, dass man etwas ausprobiert, um zu sehen, ob es hilft, ein Problem löst oder Spaß macht.
   *I **tried closing** my eyes, but I still felt giddy* ['gɪdi]. ● ● ● Ich habe (es damit) probiert, die Augen zu
      schließen … [= Ich habe ausprobiert, ob ich mich besser fühle, wenn ich die Augen schließe …]
   *I'd like to **try gliding**.* ● ● ● Ich würde gern mal Segelfliegen probieren.

■ **in kurzen Antworten: ohne** *it*
   *Can you translate this for me? – **I'll try**. (~~I'll try it.~~)* ● ● ● … – Ich werd's versuchen.
   *I can't see what to do. – Let me **try**. (~~Let me try it.~~)* ● ● ● … – Lass (es) mich mal versuchen.

■ **Verb:** *try* – **Nomen:** *attempt*
Das zu *try* gehörige Nomen heißt in der Regel *attempt*.
   *It was their third **attempt to climb** / **attempt at climbing** Everest.* ● ● ● Es war ihr dritter Versuch,
      den Everest zu besteigen.
   *It only worked **at the** third **attempt**.* ● ● ● Es klappte erst beim dritten Versuch.

typical ['tɪpɪkl] typisch

■ ***typical of***
   *a wine **typical of** the region* ● ● ● ein für die Gegend typischer Wein
   *It's **typical of** Dave **to be** late.* ● ● ● Es ist typisch für Dave, dass er zu spät kommt.

■ ***typically** + Adjektiv/Adverb*
   *Don't do that. It's so **typically German** (~~typical German~~).* ● ● ● … Das ist so typisch deutsch.

T

unable – incompetent – able – competent

1 If you ask me, the person who designed this building was ....
   A a very incompetent architect   B a very unable architect

2 ...... She can speak four languages.
   A Li Wenwen is a very able linguist.
   B Li Wenwen is a very competent linguist.
   C Li Wenwen is a very incompetent linguist.

unconscious – subconscious

1 The bottle hit him on the head ....
   A and knocked him subconscious
   B and knocked him unconscious
   C and knocked him consciousless

2 She told me that I make a funny movement with my left hand when I'm nervous. ......
   A I was completely subconscious of this.
   B I was completely unconscious of this.
   C I was completely unconscious to this.

3 The report seems to say that there is new scientific evidence ....
   A supporting Freud's theory of the subconscious
   B supporting Freud's theory of the unconscious

under – below

1 My brother was .... I was in year ten and he was in year nine.
   A in the year below me at school
   B in the year down of me at school
   C in the year under me at school

2 The whole trip should cost ....
   A below €70   B under €70

3 Temperatures in January were ....
   A two degrees below average   B two degrees under average

4 It's a very low-lying area. Some parts are actually ....
   A below sea level   B under sea level

5 There was ....
   A quite a lot of noise from the street below
   B quite a lot of noise from the street down under
   C quite a lot of noise from the street under

6 All you have to do is ....
   A walk below and ring the bell   B walk downstairs and ring the bell

7 The police found a revolver ....
   A at the bottom of his suitcase, under all his clothes
   B below in his suitcase, under all his clothes

8 In an emergency, ...
   A you can always reach us at this number
   B you can always reach us on this number
   C you can always reach us under this number

unable – incompetent [ɪnˈkɒmpɪtənt] unfähig – able – competent fähig

■ *Unable* kann nur prädikativ, also nach einem Verb wie *be*, verwendet werden. Vor einem Nomen verwendet man *incompetent*.
> *Frank **was unable to** motivate his students. He was a very **incompetent** teacher (~~unable teacher~~).*
> ● ● ● Frank war nicht in der Lage, seine Schüler zu motivieren. Er war ein sehr unfähiger Lehrer.

■ Im Gegensatz zu *unable* kann *able* sowohl nach *be* als auch vor einem Nomen verwendet werden.
> *Neil **was able to** motivate his students. He was a very **able/competent** teacher.* ● ● ● Neil schaffte es, seine Schüler zu motivieren. Er war ein sehr fähiger Lehrer.

unconscious [ʌnˈkɒnʃəs] bewusstlos; unbewusst – subconscious [ˌsʌbˈkɒnʃəs] unterbewusst

■ Wenn ein Mensch *unconscious* ist, ist er „bewusstlos", d. h. nicht bei Bewusstsein.
> *After the accident Liz was **unconscious** for several minutes.* ● ● ● … mehrere Minuten bewusstlos.

Mit *unconscious* bezeichnet man außerdem Gefühle und Abläufe, die „unbewusst", d. h. nicht willentlich gesteuert sind.
> *I didn't plan to hit him. It was an **unconscious** reaction.* ● ● ● … eine unbewusste Reaktion.
> *I was **unconscious** (= unaware) of Debbie's secret plans.* ● ● ● Ich wusste nichts von Debbies geheimen Plänen./Debbies geheime Wünsche waren mir nicht bewusst.

■ Mit *subconscious* bezeichnet man etwas, was aus dem Unterbewusstsein stammt.
> *Psychologists [saɪˈkɒlədʒɪsts] say we're full of **subconscious** fears and desires.* ● ● ● … wir sind erfüllt von unterbewussten Ängsten und Wünschen/von Ängsten und Wünschen in unserem Unterbewusstsein.

under – below unter

■ **Bedeutungen von *under***
1 *sleep **under** a thick woollen* [ˈwʊlən] *blanket* [= zugedeckt von]
  *a tunnel **under** the river* [= unter … hindurch]

2 *the room **under/below** this one* [= direkt unter, tiefer als]
  *a student in the class **under/below** me* [= „tiefer als" in einer Rangfolge oder Liste]

3 *be **under** 18 years old; **under** 50 km* [= weniger als]

■ **unter, unten**

1 „tiefer als"
Wenn etwas weit unter etwas anderem ist, verwendet man *below*.
auf der Bergspitze stehen und das Tal unter sich sehen ● ● ● *stand on the top of the mountain and see the valley **below** you*

Wenn etwas unter einem Nullpunkt liegt, verwendet man ebenfalls *below*.
unter dem Meeresspiegel ● ● ● ***below** sea level*
unter null, unter dem Gefrierpunkt ● ● ● ***below** zero, **below** freezing*
(weit) unter dem Durchschnitt ● ● ● *(well) **below** average*

2 Wendungen mit „unter"
Sie ist gerade unter der Dusche. ● ● ● *She's just **in the shower**.*
Sie können mich unter dieser Nummer erreichen. ● ● ● *You can reach me **on/at this number**.*
Was verstehen Sie unter „bald"? ● ● ● *What do you **understand by** 'soon'?*

3 „unten", „darunter"
Geräusche aus dem Zimmer unten ● ● ● *noises from the room **below/downstairs***
siehe unten ● ● ● *see **below***
Stundenlöhne von 4 € und darunter ● ● ● *hourly rates of pay of €4 and **below/less***

4 „unten im Haus", „in einem tieferen Stockwerk"
nach unten gehen ● ● ● *go **downstairs***

5 „unten in der Kiste/in der Tasche/auf der Seite"
unten in der Kiste ● ● ● ***at the bottom of** the box*
unten auf der Seite ● ● ● ***at the bottom of** the page*

U

Trouble Spot

understand – hear

1 ...... , or is it still unclear?

   A Are you understanding now   **B** Do you understand now

2 Sorry, but can you speak up a bit? ......

   A I can't hear what you're saying.   **B** I don't understand what you're saying.

3 You just used the phrase 'stick my neck out'. ...... What does it mean?

   A Sorry, I can't understand.

   B Sorry, I didn't understand.

   C Sorry, I don't understand.

4 Let me know fast. – ......

   A What do you understand by 'fast'?

   B What do you understand from 'fast'?

   C What do you understand under 'fast'?

undertaker ≠ „Unternehmer/-in"

1 You need the services of an undertaker ....

   A when someone dies

   B when something is delivered

   C when you want to do business with someone

2 Is Bill Gates *[der erfolgreichste Unternehmer]* of all times?

   A the most successful businessman

   B the most successful entrepreneur

   C the most successful undertaker

unemployment

1 Very often ...... are worse than the economic effects.

   A the social effects of the unemployment   **B** the social effects of unemployment

2 The Wall Street Crash of 1929 not only wiped out the fortunes of millionaires, ... also plunged millions of ordinary people into poverty.

   A the unemployment that followed it   **B** unemployment that followed it

the United States

1 **A** The United States are losing friends at a time when they should be making friends.

   B The United States is losing friends at a time when it should be making friends.

university

1 Sarah did her 'A' levels and left school at 17. ...... , and will have been in her job over five years before most of her German counterparts ....

   A She went to the university for three years ... have even finished the university

   B She went to university for three years ... have even finished the university

   C She went to university for three years ... have even finished university

2 ...... She's a business manager on the administration side.

   A Ali's mother works at the university.   **B** Ali's mother works at university.

3 **A** Marek is a student at Oxford University.

   B Marek is a student at the Oxford University.

understand* – hear* verstehen

■ **nicht in der Verlaufsform**
Understand und *hear* gehören zu den Verben, die man nicht in der Verlaufsform verwendet.
  *Oh, I see. Now I **understand**. (~~Now I'm understanding.~~)* ● ● ● Ach so. Jetzt verstehe ich.

■ *don't/didn't understand – can't/didn't hear*
Mit *don't/didn't understand* drückt man aus, dass man das Gesagte zwar akustisch wahrgenommen hat, aber nicht deuten kann.
  *Sorry, I **don't/didn't understand**. Can you explain what you were saying another way?* ● ● ● Tut mir leid, aber ich verstehe das nicht/habe das nicht verstanden. …
Mit *can't/didn't hear* drückt man aus, dass man etwas akustisch nicht versteht bzw. verstanden hat.
  *It's so noisy that I **can't hear** what he's saying/ that I **didn't hear** what he was saying.* ● ● ● … dass ich nicht verstehen kann, was er sagt/dass ich nicht verstanden habe, was er gesagt hat.

■ *What do you **understand** by 'soon'?* ● ● ● Was verstehen Sie unter „bald"?

undertaker ['----] Leichenbestatter/-in

! **!** **!** ■ **False Friend!**
Undertaker bedeutet nicht „~~Unternehmer/-in~~", sondern „Leichenbestatter/-in".
  *The **undertaker** showed us the coffin.* ● ● ● Der Leichenbestatter zeigte uns den Sarg.
Beachte die englischen Entsprechungen von „Unternehmer/-in":
  erfolgreiche Unternehmer/-innen ● ● ● *successful **businessmen**/**businesswomen***
  der Unternehmer im Kapitalismus ● ● ● *the capitalist **entrepreneur*** [ˌɒntrəprə'nɜː]

unemployment (die) Arbeitslosigkeit

■ **ohne *the* in Aussagen allgemeiner Art**
Unemployment gehört zu den abstrakten Nomen, die in Aussagen allgemeiner Art ohne den bestimmten Artikel verwendet werden.
  *How can we reduce **unemployment** (~~the unemployment~~)?* ● ● ● … die Arbeitslosigkeit abbauen?
Der Artikel ist jedoch zwingend, wenn *unemployment* durch einen Relativsatz oder eine *of*-Fügung näher bestimmt wird.
  *the **unemployment** of the 1930s* ● ● ● die Arbeitslosigkeit der 1930er-Jahre

the United States die Vereinigten Staaten

■ **Singular**
Die Vereinigten Staaten werden als eine Einheit (ein Land) aufgefasst. Deshalb verwendet man *the United States* und die Abkürzungen *the US/USA* wie Singularformen.
  *The **United States** is (~~The United States are~~) at a turning point in **its** history (~~their history~~).* ● ● ●
    Die Vereinigten Staaten stehen an einem Wendepunkt in ihrer Geschichte.

university (die) Universität ▶ study

■ *university* **(als Studieneinrichtung für Studenten/Studentinnen): ohne *the***
University steht im BE ohne den bestimmten Artikel, wenn man ganz allgemein an die Universität als Institution zum Studieren denkt. Im AE wird das Wort *college* verwendet – auch ohne Artikel.
  *go to **university**/be at **university*** ● ● ● auf die Universität gehen/zur Universität gehen/studieren
  *go to **college**/be at **college***
Vergleiche aber:
  *How do I get to **the university**, please?* ● ● ● … zur Universität [= zum Universitätsgebäude]?
  *My brother lives in Bonn. He's (a student) at **the university**.* ● ● ● … Er studiert dort an der
    Universität [= eine bestimmte Universität].
  *teach/work at **the university*** ● ● ● an der Universität lehren/arbeiten [= nicht dort studieren]
In Verbindung mit Eigennamen steht jedoch generell kein Artikel.
  *go/get to **Bonn University**, be a student at **Bonn University**, teach/work at **Bonn University***

U

unless – if … not

1 We will need prepayment to secure your booking ....

   A if you are not paying by credit card

   B unless you are paying by credit card

   C unless you are not paying by credit card

2 It would be much easier ....

   A if we didn't have to take all this luggage with us

   B unless we had to take all this luggage with us

   C unless we didn't have to take all this luggage with us

until/till – by

1 I'll just keep driving round the block ...... and I can find somewhere to park.

   A till someone drives away   B untill someone drives away   C until someone drives away

2 ...... , call the police.

   A If you don't hear from me by midday

   B If you don't hear from me till midday

   C If you don't hear from me until midday

3 A We should know the result by Monday afternoon.

   B We should know the result till Monday afternoon.

   C We should know the result until Monday afternoon.

4 It took ages, ... (just before midnight), we were frozen, hungry and very tired.

   A and by when we finally got there   B and by the time we finally got there

   C and till we finally got there   D and till the time we finally got there

   E and until we finally got there   F and until the time we finally got there

5 Carry on along here ....

   A as far as the Wattler building on the left

   B by to the Wattler building on the left

   C till to the Wattler building on the left

6 We were covered in foam ....

   A from head till foot   B from head to toe   C from the head to the toe

7 [Bis zu 20000 Menschen] are believed to have lost their lives.

   A To 20,000 people   B Till to 20,000 people   C Up to 20,000 people

use (noun)

1 ...... Vicars don't know anything about this sort of thing.

   A What's the use of asking a vicar ['vɪkə]?

   B What's the use to ask a vicar?

   C What's the use that we ask a vicar?

2 ...... I need my laptop. I'll have to go back and get it.

   A It's no use to carry on.   B It's no use carrying on.

   C It's no use of carrying on.   D It's no use that I carry on.

unless außer wenn; es sei denn – **if ... not** wenn ... nicht

■ *unless*

Unless bedeutet nicht einfach „wenn nicht", sondern „außer wenn", „es sei denn".

*You can't get petrol **unless** you buy it on the black market. (= You can only get petrol if you buy it on the black market.)* ● ● ● Man bekommt kein Benzin, außer man kauft es auf dem Schwarzmarkt. (= Man bekommt Benzin nur dann, wenn man es auf dem Schwarzmarkt kauft.)

■ *if ... not*

If ... not und *unless* bedeuten nicht immer das Gleiche. *If ... not* kann man nur dort durch *unless* ersetzen, wo „außer wenn", „es sei denn" einen Sinn ergibt.

*I'll be here at six **if** the plane is**n't** late. = I'll be here at six **unless** the plane is late.* ● ● ● Ich bin um sechs da, wenn die Maschine keine Verspätung hat. = Ich bin um sechs da, außer wenn die Maschine Verspätung hat.

Aber nur mit *if ... not*:

*She'd be a super basketball player **if** she was**n't** so small (~~unless she was so small~~).* ● ● ● Sie wäre eine super Basketballspielerin, wenn sie nicht so klein wäre.

until/till – by bis

■ Die Präpositionen *until* und *till* bedeuten „so lange bis", „die ganze Zeit bis". *Until* und *till* verwendet man typischerweise mit Verben wie *wait*, die eine andauernde Handlung bezeichnen. *Until* und *till* + Zeitangabe drücken aus, wie lange diese Handlung andauert.

*I'll wait **until/till** 8.00, then I'll go home.* ● ● ● Ich warte bis 8 Uhr, dann gehe ich nach Hause.

Until und *till* können auch als Konjunktionen zur Einleitung eines Nebensatzes verwendet werden.

*Keep trying **until/till** the mechanic comes.* ● ● ● Versuch es weiter, bis der Mechaniker kommt.

■ Die Präposition *by* bedeutet „bis spätestens", „nicht später als". Mit *by* drückt man aus, (bis) wann ein Geschehen eintritt, oder man nennt eine Frist, einen letzten Termin.

*They should arrive **by** 8.00 (~~until 8.00~~).* ● ● ● Sie müssten bis (spätestens) 8 Uhr ankommen.

*The essay has to be finished **by** the end of next week.* ● ● ● Der Aufsatz muss bis Ende nächster Woche fertig sein.

Nur in Verbindung mit einem Ausdruck wie *the time* kann *by* einen Nebensatz einleiten.

***By the time** the guests arrived, the food was cold.* ● ● ● Bis/Als die Gäste ankamen ...

Trouble Spot

■ **bis**

1 in räumlichen Entfernungsangaben

Fahre weiter bis zur Kirche. ● ● ● *Drive on **as far as** the church.*

den Tisch bis an die Wand heranschieben ● ● ● *push the table (right) **up to** the wall*

von oben bis unten ● ● ● *from top **to** bottom*

von Kopf bis Fuß ● ● ● *from head **to** toe*

2 „bis (zu)" [+ Mengen- oder Zahlenangabe]

Bis zu 500 Menschen waren dort. ● ● ● ***Up to** 500 people were there.*

bis 50 zählen ● ● ● *count **(up) to** 50*

3 „bis jetzt", „bis heute"

Bis jetzt läuft alles gut. ● ● ● ***Up to now** / **So far** everything has been going fine.*

4 „bis später/bald/morgen"

Bis später/bald/morgen! ● ● ● ***See you** later/soon/tomorrow!*

U

use [juːs] Nutzen, Zweck

■ *what's the use of doing?*

***What's the use of** worrying (~~the use to worry~~ / ~~the use that I worry~~)?* ● ● ● Welchen Zweck hat es / Was nützt es, sich Sorgen zu machen / dass ich mir Sorgen mache / wenn ich mir Sorgen mache?

■ *it's no use doing*

***It's no use** crying (~~no use to cry~~ / ~~no use that we cry~~).* ● ● ● Es hat keinen Zweck/Sinn zu weinen. / Es nützt nichts, wenn wir weinen.

used to

1 A My mum has used to smoke, but she's given up, thank goodness.

B My mum used to smoke, but she's given up, thank goodness.

C My mum used to smoking, but she's given up, thank goodness.

2 A As a cyclist you get used to be treated as a second-class citizen by people in cars.

B As a cyclist you get used to being treated as a second-class citizen by people in cars.

C As a cyclist you get used to treating as a second-class citizen by people in cars.

3 A I'm not used to live in a city any more.

B I'm not used to living in a city any more.

4 A This button here is used to call the emergency services.

B This button here used to call the emergency services.

C This button here is used to calling the emergency services.

usual

1 Which of these two sentences is more likely to be used?

A Is it usual to have to show your passport?

B Is it usual that you have to show your passport?

2 It was [*ein gewöhnlicher Tag*], just like any other.

A a habitual day   **B** an ordinary day   **C** a usual day

3 A Gerry forgot to phone his parents as usual, and they were mad at him as usual.

B Gerry forgot to phone his parents as usually, and they were mad at him as usually.

ventilator ≠ „Ventilator"

1 A ventilator is ....

A a machine that cools you down when it's hot

B a machine used with patients who can't breathe

C an opening that lets fresh air in

2 It can get pretty hot up here in the summer, ... It looks like something out of a South American bar, doesn't it?

A so I bought this air propeller   **B** so I bought this fan   **C** so I bought this ventilator

vest ≠ „Weste"

1 The word 'vest' means ....

A something different in British and American English

B the same in British and American English

2 Can you imagine Sir Wingfield Truman going to a tea party at Buckingham Palace ...... ?

A in a T-shirt and scruffy old corduroy underjacket

B in a T-shirt and scruffy old corduroy waistcoat

used to

■ **used to** ['juːst tə] **do**
I used to do bedeutet „früher habe ich (immer) …". *To* ist hier Teil des Infinitivs.
  *I **used to smoke**, but I gave it up.* ● ● ● Früher habe ich geraucht, aber ich habe damit aufgehört.
  *She **didn't use to like** classical music.* ● ● ● Früher mochte sie klassische Musik nicht.

■ **be/get used to** ['juːst tə] **doing**
Be used to doing bzw. *get used to doing* bedeuten „gewöhnt sein zu tun" bzw. „sich daran gewöhnen, zu tun". *To* ist hier eine Präposition, auf die ein Verb als *-ing*-Form folgt.
  *I'm **used to getting up** (I'm used to get up) early.* ● ● ● Ich bin es gewohnt, früh aufzustehen.
  *Have you **got used to speaking** (got used to speak) English all day?* ● ● ● Hast du dich daran gewöhnt, den ganzen Tag Englisch zu sprechen?

■ **be used** [juːzd] **to do**
Bei der Konstruktion *be used to do* handelt es sich um die Passivform des Vollverbs *use* [juːz] („benutzen, gebrauchen") mit nachfolgendem Infinitiv des Zwecks.
  *Whale blubber **is used (in order) to heat** the dwellings.* ● ● ● Walfischspeck wird verwendet, um die Behausungen zu heizen.

usual ['juːʒuəl, 'juːʒəl,] gewöhnlich, üblich   ▷ ordinary

■ **it's usual (for sb.) to do**
Nach *it's usual* (und *it's normal*) verwendet man in der Regel eine Infinitivkonstruktion, keinen *that*-Satz.
  *Is it **usual to have** to wait so long?* ● ● ● Ist es normal, dass man so lange warten muss?
  *Is it **usual for them to take** so long?* ● ● ● Ist es normal, dass sie so lange brauchen?

Trouble Spot

■ **gewöhnlich**
  Ich fahre nicht meine gewöhnliche [= übliche] Strecke. ● ● ● *I'm not going my **usual** route.*
  Ich komme (für) gewöhnlich um sechs nach Hause. ● ● ● *I **usually** get home at six.*
  Er kam zu spät, wie gewöhnlich. ● ● ● *He was late, **as usual** (as usually).*
  eine Stunde früher als gewöhnlich ● ● ● *an hour earlier **than usual** (than usually)*
  aus gewöhnlicher [= einfacher, normaler] Baumwolle, nicht aus Seide ● ● ● *made from **ordinary** [(BE:) 'ɔːdnrɪ; (AE:) 'ɔːrdnerɪ] cotton, not silk*

ventilator ['ventɪleɪtə] (Be-)Lüftungsvorrichtung; Beatmungsgerät

!
■ **False Friend!**
Ventilator bedeutet nicht „~~Ventilator~~", sondern „Lüftungsvorrichtung", „Abzug" bzw. „Beatmungsgerät".
  *When they built this cellar, they forgot to include a **ventilator**.* ● ● ● … haben sie vergessen, für eine Belüftung zu sorgen.
  *put a patient on a **ventilator*** ● ● ● einen Patienten an ein Beatmungsgerät anschließen
Beachte die englische Entsprechung von „Ventilator":
  an heißen Tagen den Ventilator einschalten ● ● ● *turn on the **fan** on hot days*

V

vest (BE:) Unterhemd; (nur AE:) Weste

!
■ **False Friend im BE!**
Vest bedeutet im BE nicht „~~Weste~~", sondern „Unterhemd".
  *have a shower and put on a clean **vest*** ● ● ● … und ein sauberes Unterhemd anziehen
Die Entsprechung für „Weste" lautet im BE *waistcoat*.
  ein Anzug mit Weste ● ● ● *a three-piece suit (with a **waistcoat** ['weɪskəʊt])*
Im AE allerdings ähnelt der Sprachgebrauch dem Deutschen.
  *put on a clean **undershirt*** ● ● ● ein sauberes Unterhemd anziehen
  *a three-piece suit (with a **vest**)* ● ● ● ein Anzug mit Weste

visit

1 ...... that Robert found out the truth about his grandfather.

  A It was by a visit by his aunt   **B** It was by a visit at his aunt's   **C** It was on a visit to his aunt

2 **A** Is this your first London visit?

  B Is this your first visit in London?

  C Is this your first visit to London?

3 On Sunday morning my parents sometimes ...... , so I have the house to myself.

  A attend a concert   **B** go to a concert   **C** visit a concert

4 I met a Japanese woman in a café this afternoon. ...... I wanted to meet her again, but she's going back home tomorrow.

  A She's attending a conference at the university.

  B She's visiting a conference at the university.

5 One of the questions is certain to be ...... , and I'll have to say that I didn't go to school, but was taught at home.

  A 'Which school did you attend while your parents lived in Britain?'

  B 'Which school did you go to while your parents lived in Britain?'

  C 'Which school did you visit while your parents lived in Britain?'

voice

1 ...... , you can hardly hear him unless you sit in one of the very front rows.

  A He always speaks in such a low voice   **B** He always speaks in such a soft voice

  C He always speaks in such a quiet voice   **D** He always speaks with such a quiet voice

wait

1 What are you doing? – What do you think?! ......

  A Waiting for it to stop raining.   **B** Waiting that it stops raining.

2 ...... from the visa office. They're incredibly slow.

  A I'm still waiting for to hear   **B** I'm still waiting that I hear   **C** I'm still waiting to hear

3 *[Jemanden warten (zu) lassen]* is impolite.

  A Keeping someone waiting   **B** Keeping someone wait   **C** Letting someone wait

4 Mrs Wilcox still doesn't know. *[Ich kann es kaum erwarten]* to see her reaction.

  A I can't wait   **B** I can hardly expect   **C** I can hardly wait

5 *[Mal abwarten]* whether he really reports it to the police. I think he's just bluffing.

  A Let's wait and see   **B** We'll wait   **C** We'll wait for it

wander ≠ „wandern"

1 What is the best paraphrase for 'wandering about the town' in the following sentence?
We spent two hours wandering about the town.

  A looking at the town in a leisurely way, not following a clear plan

  B taking part in an organized walking tour of the town

  C walking all the way round the outside of the town

2 Somebody with a name like Traugott Wandersmann must be *[ein Mitglied in einem Wanderverein]* or a men's choir, or something like that.

  A a member of a hiking club   **B** a member of a wander club   **C** a member of a wandering club

visit 1 Besuch 2 besuchen

- a **visit to** friends ● ● ● ein Besuch bei Freunden
  a **visit to** Berlin ● ● ● ein Berlinbesuch / Besuch Berlins / Besuch in Berlin
  I was **on an exchange visit** to France. ● ● ● Ich war auf einem Schüleraustausch in Frankreich.
  We're just here **on** a short **visit**. ● ● ● Wir sind hier nur kurz zu Besuch.
  on my first **visit** ● ● ● bei meinem ersten Besuch

- **visit** friends / **go to see** friends / **go and see** friends ● ● ● Freunde besuchen
  visit London / **go to** London ● ● ● London besuchen
  visit a sight / **go to** a sight ● ● ● eine Sehenswürdigkeit besuchen
  visit a website ● ● eine Website besuchen

Trouble Spot

- **besuchen [als Zuhörer/-in, Teilnehmer/-in, Schüler/-in usw.]**
  ein Konzert / eine Tagung / einen Vortrag besuchen ● ● ● **attend** a concert/conference/lecture / **go to** a concert/conference/lecture
  die Schule [als Schüler/-in] besuchen ● ● ● **attend** school / **go to** school
  den Gottesdienst besuchen ● ● ● **attend** church / **go to** church
  Die Veranstaltung war gut besucht. ● ● ● The event was **well attended.**

voice Stimme

- speak **in** a loud **voice** (~~with a loud voice~~) ● ● ● mit lauter Stimme sprechen
  a **quiet/soft/low voice** ● ● ● eine leise Stimme
  Keep your voice down, please. ● ● ● Sprich bitte leise.

wait warten

- **wait for sb./sth. to do**
  Wait for sb./sth. to do bedeutet „darauf warten, dass jmd./etwas etwas tut". Im Anschluss an das Verb wait kann man keinen that-Satz verwenden.
  I'm **waiting for her to phone** (~~waiting that she phones~~). ● ● ● Ich warte darauf, dass sie anruft.

- **wait to do**
  I'm **waiting to speak** to her. ● ● ● Ich warte darauf, mit ihr zu sprechen.

Trouble Spot

- **warten lassen**
  Tut mir leid, dass ich Sie habe warten lassen. ● ● ● I'm sorry to **keep** you **waiting.**

- **erwarten** ▷ expect
  Ich erwarte dich dann am Bahnhof. ● ● ● I'll **wait for** you at the station then.
  Ich erwarte Besuch / einen Anruf. [= mit etwas rechnen] ● ● ● I'm **expecting** visitors / a phone call.
  Ich kann es kaum erwarten, dich wiederzusehen. ● ● ● I **can't wait / can hardly wait** to see you again.

- **abwarten**
  Mal abwarten. / Abwarten und Tee trinken. ● ● ● **(Let's) wait and see.**

W

wander ['wɒndə] schlendern, umherwandern

!
!
!

- **False Friend!**
  Wander bedeutet nicht „~~wandern~~", sondern „schlendern", „(ziellos) umhergehen".
  wander round the old town ● ● ● durch die Altstadt schlendern
  Beachte die englische Entsprechung von „wandern":
  Meine Eltern gehen mit ihrem Wanderverein wandern. ● ● ● My parents go **hiking** / (meist BE:) go **walking** with their **hiking** club.

want

1 ...... I really don't feel like going out again just yet.

    A I think I'm wanting a rest now.   **B** I think I want a rest now.

2 **A** They wanted me to give them my passport, but I refused.

    B They wanted that I gave them my passport, but I refused.

    C They wanted that I give them my passport, but I refused.

    D They wanted I to give them my passport, but I refused.

3 My parents suggested that I stay with some friends of theirs, ... I prefer to make my own arrangements.

    A but I didn't want it   **B** but I didn't want to

4 It was the first time the child had been in hospital, and he kept crying, ...

    A "I want home."   **B** "I want to go home."   **C** "I want to home."

5 *[Wir wollten gerade essen]*, when the phone rang.

    A We just wanted to have lunch

    B We were just about to have lunch

    C We were just wanting to have lunch

6 The stupid microphone *[wollte einfach nicht funktionieren]*, so I had to shout.

    A just didn't want to work   **B** just wouldn't work

7 Last time people parked on the grass. ......

    A We don't want it to happen again.

    B We don't want that it happens again.

    C We don't want that it'll happen again.

warehouse ≠ „Warenhaus"

1 A warehouse is ....

    A somewhere you buy clothes

    B somewhere you buy all sorts of things

    C somewhere you store things

2 Out-of-town shopping centres are driving some traditional high-street *[Warenhäuser]* out of business.

    A department stores   **B** goods houses   **C** warehouses

warm – hot

1 ...... I do wish we could open a window.

    A I feel hot.   **B** I feel warm.

2 It was so cold in the conference room. ......

    A We had to keep getting up and walking around to keep hot.

    B We had to keep getting up and walking around to keep warm.

3 ...... is catastrophic. My shower was almost cold.

    A The hot-water system in this house   **B** The warm-water system in this house

4 My granny always used to say, ...

    A "A man needs one hot meal a day."   **B** "A man needs one warm meal a day."

want wollen

■ **nicht in der Verlaufsform**

Want gehört zu den Verben, die man in der Regel nicht in der Verlaufsform verwendet.

*What **does** she **want** (~~What's she wanting~~) now?* ● ● ● Was will sie denn jetzt schon wieder?

■ **want to do**

*I **want to tell** you something.* ● ● ● Ich will dir etwas sagen.

■ **want sb. to do**

Want sb. to do bedeutet „wollen, dass jmd. etwas tut". Im Anschluss an das Verb *want* kann man keinen *that*-Satz verwenden.

*I **want him to go** (~~want that he goes~~) to university.* ● ● ● Ich will, dass er studiert.

■ **want it – want to**

In folgendem Satz bezieht sich *it* auf ein vorangehendes Nomen, auf etwas Konkretes:

*I don't need this penknife. Do you **want it** [= want the penknife]?* ● ● ● Ich brauche dieses Taschenmesser nicht. Willst du es haben?

Im Rückbezug auf einen zuvor genannten Sachverhalt verwendet man *want to*, nicht *want it*.

*I told Tony he could come with us. But he didn't **want to** [= didn't want to come with us].* ● ● ● Ich habe Tony gesagt, er könne mitkommen. Aber er wollte (es) nicht.

In der Wendung *if you want* steht *want* oft allein.

*You can come with us **if you want (to)** (= if you like).* ● ● ● Du kannst mitkommen, wenn du willst.

Trouble Spot

■ **wollen**

1 „gehen wollen", „hinwollen": nicht ohne Verb nach *want*

Ich will raus / nach Hause. ● ● ● *I **want to go** outside/home.*

Lass mich rein! Ich will zu Bob. ● ● ● *Let me in. I **want to go** to Bob. / I **want to speak** to Bob. / I **want to see** Bob.*

2 „haben wollen", „möchte(n)"

Want kann ziemlich direkt klingen; höflicher ist *would like*. Vergleiche:

Du willst wirklich noch einen Toast (haben)? ● ● ● *You really **want** another piece of toast?*

Was möchten Sie (haben)? ● ● ● *What **would** you **like**?*

3 „(gerade) tun wollen" [= im Begriff sein zu tun]

Ich wollte gerade gehen. ● ● ● *I **was just leaving** / I was just **about to leave**.*

4 „nicht tun wollen" [= nicht bereit sein zu tun; sich weigern zu tun]

Das Kind will nicht hören. / Das Kind hört einfach nicht. ● ● ● *The child **won't** listen.*

Die Tür wollte nicht zugehen. ● ● ● *The door **wouldn't** shut.*

---

warehouse ['weəhaʊs] Lager(halle)

! ■ **False Friend!**

Warehouse bedeutet nicht „~~Warenhaus~~", sondern „Lager(halle/-haus)", „(Waren-)Lager".

*the factory **warehouse*** ● ● ● die Lagerhalle (an) der Fabrik

Beachte die englische Entsprechung von „Warenhaus":

das größte Warenhaus/Kaufhaus in London ● ● ● *the biggest **department store** in London*

W

---

warm ['wɔ:m] – hot warm ▷ sharp

■ *Warm* hat die Grundbedeutung „mäßig warm", „angenehm warm".

*a lovely **warm** day at the end of September* ● ● ● ein schöner, warmer Tag Ende September

■ *Hot* hat die Grundbedeutung „heiß", „unangenehm warm", „zu warm".

*I feel **hot**. Can I open the window?* ● ● ● Mir ist (zu) warm. / Mir ist heiß. …

*It's **hot** in here. I'm going to take this jacket off.* ● ● ● Es ist (sehr) warm hier drin. …

Warmes Wasser und warmes Essen bezeichnet man als *hot*, nicht als *warm*.

*a room with **hot** and cold water* ● ● ● ein Zimmer mit Warm- und Kaltwasser

*We eat a **hot** meal in the evening.* ● ● ● Wir essen abends warm.

warn

1 A We were warned to take our money with us and not to leave any in the rooms.

B We were warned to take our money with us and to leave any in the rooms.

waste

1 ...... Let's just do it.

A We shouldn't waste our time thinking about what might go wrong.

B We shouldn't waste our time to think about what might go wrong.

C We shouldn't waste our time with thinking about what might go wrong.

2 A I've wasted six hours for this problem.

B I've wasted six hours on this problem.

C I've wasted six hours with this problem.

way

1 Do you know ...... ?

A a quick way of making all the lines start with a capital letter

B a quick way to make all the lines start with a capital letter

C a quick way to making all the lines start with a capital letter

2 A That's not the way you teach a dog to behave.

B That's not the way how you teach a dog to behave.

C That's not the way that you teach a dog to behave.

weather

1 ...... We just stayed at home.

A It was such an awful weather yesterday. **B** It was such awful weather yesterday.

2 ...... We can't go to the beach if it stays like this.

A What are we going to do by this weather? **B** What are we going to do in this weather?

wedding day – (wedding) anniversary

1 ...... that Jody decided she had had enough and was going to leave William for good.

A It was on her 5th anniversary **B** It was on her 5th wedding anniversary

C It was on her 5th wedding day

week

1 In those days ...... were less than £10.

A a week's wages **B** the wages of a week

2 Has someone thrown out ...... ?

A this week's TV guide **B** the TV guide of this week

weigh

1 The baby is now three weeks old ....

A and is weighing five kilos **B** and weighs five kilos

2 I was at the check-in desk ...... when the fire alarm went off.

A and they just weighed my luggage **B** and they were just weighing my luggage

warn warnen, nachdrücklich ermahnen

■ *warn sb. to do* = „jmdn. ermahnen/auffordern, etwas zu tun"
*I **warned** you **to keep** it to yourself.* (= 'Do this.') ● ● ● Ich habe dich ermahnt/aufgefordert, es für
dich zu behalten.

■ *warn sb. not to do* = „jmdn. davor warnen, etwas zu tun", „jmdm. von etwas abraten"
*I **warned** you **not to tell** Ina.* (= 'Don't do this.') ● ● ● Ich habe dich davor gewarnt, es Ina
weiterzusagen. / Ich habe dir ausdrücklich gesagt, du sollst es Ina nicht weitersagen.

waste verschwenden, vergeuden

■ *waste time doing* ▶ spend
Waste time verwendet man mit einer nachfolgenden *-ing*-Form, nicht mit dem *to*-Infinitiv.
***waste** time/hours **looking** for the keys (waste time/hours to look for the keys)* ● ● ● Zeit/Stunden
darauf/damit verschwenden, die Schlüssel zu suchen

■ *waste time/money on sth.*
Die mit *waste* verwendete Präposition heißt *on*.
***waste** time **on** computer games* ● ● ● Zeit mit Computerspielen verschwenden
***waste** money **on** computer games* ● ● ● Geld für Computerspiele verschwenden

way Art und Weise ▶ far ▶ possibility

■ *way to do – way of doing*
Nach *way* kann man einen *to*-Infinitiv oder *of* + die *-ing*-Form des Verbs verwenden.
*What's the right **way to cook**/ the right **way of cooking** this fish?* ● ● ● Was ist die richtige Art und
Weise, diesen Fisch zuzubereiten?/ Wie bereitet man diesen Fisch richtig zu?

■ *the way (that) you do/ the way in which you do*
Auf *way* kann auch ein Satz mit *that* oder (förmlicher) *in which* folgen, jedoch kein Satz mit *how*.
*I hate **the way (that)**/ **the way in which** (the way how) he talks.* ● ● ● … die Art, wie er redet.

weather Wetter

■ **nicht zählbares Nomen**
Weather ist nicht zählbar. Man kann also nicht *a* davorsetzen.
*What wonderful **weather**! (What a wonderful weather!)* ● ● ● Was für (ein) wunderbares Wetter!

■ *in this/good/bad **weather*** ● ● ● bei diesem/gutem/schlechtem Wetter

wedding day – (wedding) anniversary [ˌænɪˈvɜːsəri] Hochzeitstag

■ *Grit and Pete are getting married today. It's their **wedding day**.* ● ● ● Grit und Pete heiraten heute.
Es ist ihr Hochzeitstag [= der Tag ihrer Trauung/ der Tag, an dem ihre Hochzeit stattfindet].

■ *Julie and Mike married three years ago today. It's their **(wedding) anniversary**.* ● ● ● Julie und
Mike haben heute vor drei Jahren geheiratet. Es ist ihr [jährlich wiederkehrender] Hochzeitstag.

week Woche

■ *this **week's** Observer (the Observer of this week)* ● ● ● der *Observer* (von) dieser Woche
*a **week's** pocket money (the pocket money of one week)* ● ● ● das Taschengeld für eine Woche

W

weigh [weɪ] wiegen

■ **in der Bedeutung „ein bestimmtes Gewicht haben" nicht in der Verlaufsform**
Weigh kann nicht in der Verlaufsform stehen, wenn man sagt, wie viel etwas oder jemand wiegt.
I've been on a diet [ˈdaɪət]. *I **weigh** (I'm weighing) ten kilos less now.* ● ● ● Ich habe eine Diät
gemacht. Ich wiege jetzt zehn Kilo weniger./ Ich habe jetzt zehn Kilo abgenommen.
*How much **do** you **weigh**?* ● ● ● Was wiegst du?
Wenn *weigh* bedeutet „etwas mithilfe einer Waage abwiegen", ist die Verlaufsform möglich.
*I'm **weighing** the parcel to see how much the postage will be.* ● ● ● Ich wiege das Paket …

welcome

1 **A** Welcome in Germany!   **B** Welcome to Germany!

2 ...... It's great to have you back.
   A Welcome home!   **B** Welcome at home!   **C** Welcome by home!
   D Welcome in home!   **E** Welcome to home!   **F** Welcome back!

what

1 **A** The peasant looked at that what remained of his home and started to cry.
   B The peasant looked at what remained of his home and started to cry.

2 ...... Isn't it glorious?!
   A What a wonderful weather!   **B** What for a wonderful weather!   **C** What wonderful weather!

3 I had a blackout. ......
   A I forgot everything I'd learned.   **B** I forgot everything what I'd learned.

when – if

1 We'll open the champagne .... She should be here any moment.
   A if Julie comes   **B** when Julie comes

2 What do we do ...... ?
   A if she doesn't come after all   **B** when she doesn't come after all

3 We'll do what we always do ....
   A if something like that happens
   B when something like that happens
   C when something like that will happen

who – which

1 I'd like to know *[wer von euch]* are coming on the trip to the Shakespeare play next week.
   A which of you   **B** who from you   **C** who of you

2 **A** People which smoke are just plain stupid.   **B** People who smoke are just plain stupid.

3 **A** Anyone who leaves their car unlocked in a place like this is a fool.
   B People who leave their car unlocked in a place like this are fools.
   C Who leaves their car unlocked in a place like this is a fool.

why

1 ...... It's just as quick by public transport.
   A Why take a taxi?   **B** Why to take a taxi?   **C** Why taking a taxi?

without

1 The lorry hit the wall, ...
   A but continued up the road without slowing down
   B but continued up the road without to slow down

2 What we have to do is push the cable through this hole in the wall ....
   A without that it gets stuck   **B** without it to get stuck   **C** without it getting stuck

welcome willkommen

- **Welcome to** England! (~~Welcome in England!~~) ● ● ● Willkommen in England!
  Welcome to Sports Report! (~~Welcome by Sports Report!~~) ● ● ● Willkommen bei der Sportreportage!
  Welcome home! / Welcome back! ● ● ● Willkommen zu Hause! / Wieder da? Willkommen daheim!

what (das,) was; was für (ein/e) ▶ how

- *What* steht auch in der Bedeutung „das, was" allein, d. h. ohne vorangehendes *that*.
  *I was thinking of **what** you told me (~~of that what you told me~~) yesterday.* ● ● ● Ich dachte an das, was du mir gestern erzählt hast.

- Nach *all* oder *everything* („alles") kann *what* nicht stehen.
  everything/all (that) I know (~~everything/all what I know~~) ● ● ● alles, was ich weiß

- Einen Ausruf macht man mit dem Ausdruck *what (a/an)* – nicht mit *what for*.
  What nonsense! (~~What for a nonsense!~~) [nicht zählbares Nomen] ● ● ● Was für ein Unsinn!
  What an unusual design! [zählbares Nomen] ● ● ● Was für ein ungewöhnliches Design!
  What beautiful roses! (~~What for beautiful roses!~~) ● ● ● Was für schöne Rosen!

when – if wenn ▶ as

- *When* entspricht „wenn" in zeitlicher Bedeutung („zu der Zeit, wenn", „sobald").
  *I'll feel happier **when** I know the result of the test.* ● ● ● … wenn ich das Testergebnis kenne.

- *If* entspricht „wenn" in der Bedeutung „falls" (= „im Falle, dass", „für den Fall, dass", „unter der Voraussetzung, dass").
  *I'll help you **if** you want.* ● ● ● Ich helfe dir, wenn du willst.

- In der Bedeutung „jedes Mal wenn", „immer wenn" kann *when* oder *if* stehen.
  *What do your horses do **when/if** it rains?* ● ● ● Was machen Ihre Pferde, wenn es regnet?

who – which wer; der/die/das

- **Fragewort *who* nicht vor *of***
Wenn man fragt: „wer aus einer Gruppe?", verwendet man *which of*. Vergleiche:
  Who knows the answer? ● ● ● Wer kennt die Antwort?
  Which of you (~~Who of you~~) know(s) the answer? ● ● ● Wer von euch kennt die Antwort?

- **Relativpronomen *who* und *which***
Bei Personen steht das Relativpronomen *who*, bei Sachen *which*.
  *I know a lot of **people who** speak English.* ● ● ● Ich kenne viele Leute, die Englisch können.
  *Did you see **the card which** came today?* ● ● ● Hast du die Karte gesehen, die heute gekommen ist?

- **am Satzanfang: *anyone who / the person who / people who***
Am Satzanfang kann *who* in der Bedeutung „der-/diejenige(n), welche(r)" nicht allein stehen.
  Anyone who is late / **People who** are late / **Those who** are late (~~Who is late~~) must stay on at the end of the lesson. ● ● ● Wer zu spät kommt, muss am Ende der Stunde nachsitzen.

why warum, weshalb

- ***why (not)* + Infinitiv ohne *to***
In rhetorischen Fragen und Vorschlägen steht *why (not)* mit einem Infinitiv ohne *to*.
  Why wait? (~~Why to wait?~~) Let's leave now. ● ● ● Warum (sollten wir) warten? …
  Why not write to her? (~~Why not to write?~~) ● ● ● Warum schreibst du ihr nicht? / Schreib ihr doch!

without ohne

- ***without (sb.) doing***
Auf die Präposition *without* folgt ein Verb in der *-ing*-Form – kein Infinitiv oder *that*-Satz.
  *drive all the way **without stopping** (~~without to stop~~) once* ● ● ● … ohne einmal anzuhalten
  *Can't I finish one sentence **without you interrupting** me (~~without that you interrupt me~~)?* ● ● ● … ohne dass du mich unterbrichst?

W

word

1 ...... , you don't want to come with us. Is that right?
  A By other words   B In other words   C With other words

work – job – task

1 ...... in which I'll be able to use my language skills. But I don't want to be a teacher.
  A I want a job   B I want a work

2 Depending on how good you are with your hands, ...
  A there are lots of jobs you can actually do yourself
  B there are lots of works you can actually do yourself

3 ...... and, to be honest, I'm glad it's your responsibility and not mine.
  A It's not a job I like doing   B It's not a task I like doing   C It's not a work I like doing

4 A Which job should we do first?   B Which job should we make first?

5 Please don't walk across the floor in boots like that again. ......
  A It just does extra work for whoever has to do the cleaning.
  B It just makes extra work for whoever has to do the cleaning.

world

1 She's said to be ....
  A the richest woman of the world
  B the richest woman in the world
  C the richest woman on the world

worth: be worth

1 Come on, forget it. ......
  A It isn't worth to worry about.   B It isn't worth worrying about.

2 ...... Or can he go now?
  A Is it worth it for Beng to stay?   B Is it worth that Beng stays?   C Is it worth Beng staying?

write

1 A Please don't write in your books in ink.
  B Please don't write in your books with ink.
  C Please don't write in your books with pens.

2 [Wir müssen vier Tests schreiben] in each half year.
  A We have to do four tests   B We have to make four tests   C We have to write four tests

3 A Sorry, how do you spell the name of the street again?
  B Sorry, how do you write the name of the street again?

year

1 ...... , I qualify for lower insurance premiums.
  A When I'm twenty-five   B When I'm twenty-five years   C When I'm twenty-five years old

2 A Mr Pim only cleans his car once a year.   B Mr Pim only cleans his car once in the year.
  C Mr Pim only cleans his car once the year.

3 How did your friends get on ......? – There were a lot of very good results. We all worked very hard.
  A in this year's exams   B in the exams of this year

word Wort

- *in* other **words** (~~with other words~~) • • • mit anderen Worten, anders ausgedrückt

work – job – task Arbeit

- *Work* ist ein nicht zählbares Nomen. Man kann es also nicht mit *a* oder im Plural verwenden.
  I dream of **work** (~~a work~~) *that is both interesting and well paid.* • • • Ich träume von (einer) Arbeit, die sowohl interessant als auch gut bezahlt ist.
  The house is only half finished. Lots of **work** (~~works~~) *still has to be done.* • • • … Es stehen noch viele Arbeiten an. / Es gibt noch viel (Arbeit) zu tun.

- Zählbare Alternativen zu *work* sind *job* („Stelle" bzw. „Aufgabe") und *task* („Aufgabe").
  Are you looking for **a job**? • • • Suchst du Arbeit / eine Stelle?
  Lydia has **a new job**, *in a hotel.* • • • Lydia hat einen neuen Arbeitsplatz / eine neue Stelle …
  This is **a difficult job / task**. *There are several difficult* **jobs / tasks** *to do today.* • • • Das ist eine schwierige Arbeit/Aufgabe. Heute sind mehrere schwierige Arbeiten/Aufgaben zu erledigen.

- *do* **work** / **a job** / **a task** – *make* **work**
  What **work / job** *do you do*? • • • Welche Arbeit machen Sie? / Was machen Sie beruflich?
  I'm **doing** *an interesting* **job / task** *today.* • • • Ich mache/erledige heute eine interessante Arbeit.
  Pets can **make** *a lot of* **work**. • • • Haustiere können viel Arbeit machen/verursachen.

world Welt

- *the smallest animal* **in the world** (~~of the world~~ / ~~on the world~~) • • • das kleinste Tier (auf) der Welt

worth: be worth [wɜːθ] sich lohnen

- **it's worth doing**
  Nach *it's worth* steht ein Verb in der *-ing*-Form, nicht als *to*-Infinitiv.
  Is it worth waiting (~~worth to wait~~)? • • • Lohnt es sich, zu warten?

- **it's worth sb.('s) doing – it's worth it for sb. to do**
  Hat das Verb nach *worth* ein eigenes „Sinnsubjekt" (z. B. *David*), so gibt es zwei Konstruktionsmöglichkeiten: *worth sb.('s) doing* oder *worth it for sb. to do*. Ein *that*-Satz ist jedoch nicht möglich.
  Is it worth David('s) waiting *any longer*? / **Is it worth it for David to wait** *any longer*? (~~Is it worth that David waits any longer?~~) • • • Lohnt es sich, dass David noch länger wartet? / Lohnt es sich für David, noch länger zu warten?

write* schreiben

- **write in** ink / pencil (~~write with ink / pencil~~) • • • mit Tinte/Bleistift schreiben
  write with *a pen / a pencil / a biro / a felt-tip* • • • mit einem Füller / … schreiben

- **schreiben**
  Morgen schreiben wir eine Mathearbeit. • • • *We're* **doing** *a maths test tomorrow.*
  Ich habe eine Zwei geschrieben. • • • *I('ve)* **got** *a (grade) two.*
  Wie schreibt man das – mit s oder th? • • • *How do you* **spell** *that – with s or th?*
  Guck mal, Anna hat geschrieben. • • • *Look,* **there's a letter / postcard** *from Anna.*
  Er wollte, dass der Arzt ihn krankschreibt. • • • *He wanted the doctor to* **give him a sick note**.

year Jahr; (meist BE:) Jahrgang, Klasse

- *I'm now* **18 years old**. (~~I'm now 18 years.~~) / *I'm now* **18**. • • • Ich bin jetzt 18 Jahre (alt). / Ich bin jetzt 18.
  this year's *holiday* (~~the holiday of this year~~) • • • der Urlaub dieses Jahres
  in (the year) *1066* • • • im Jahre 1066
  once **a year** • • • einmal im Jahr
  I started English in **year three**. *(meist BE)* • • • Ich habe in der dritten Klasse mit Englisch angefangen.

Irregular Verbs

Infinitive	Simple Past	Past participle	
be	*was, were*	*been*	sein
bear	*bore*	*borne/born*	(er)tragen
beat	*beat*	*beaten*	schlagen, besiegen
become	*became*	*become*	werden
begin	*began*	*begun*	beginnen, anfangen
bend	*bent*	*bent*	(sich) biegen; sich beugen
bet	*bet*	*bet*	wetten
bind	*bound*	*bound*	binden, verbinden
bite	*bit*	*bitten*	beißen
blow	*blew*	*blown*	blasen, wehen
break	*broke*	*broken*	(zer)brechen; kaputtmachen
breed	*bred*	*bred*	züchten
bring	*brought* [ɔː]	*brought* [ɔː]	(mit)bringen, (her)bringen
broadcast	*broadcast*	*broadcast*	senden, übertragen, ausstrahlen
build	*built*	*built*	bauen
burn	*burnt/burned*	*burnt/burned*	(ver)brennen
burst	*burst*	*burst*	platzen
buy	*bought* [ɔː]	*bought* [ɔː]	kaufen
cast	*cast*	*cast*	werfen
catch	*caught* [ɔː]	*caught* [ɔː]	fangen, erwischen
choose [uː]	*chose* [əʊ]	*chosen* [əʊ]	(aus)wählen, aussuchen
cling	*clung*	*clung*	sich klammern, festhalten
come	*came*	*come*	kommen
cost	*cost*	*cost*	kosten
creep	*crept*	*crept*	kriechen, schleichen
cut	*cut*	*cut*	schneiden
deal [iː]	*dealt* [e]	*dealt* [e]	handeln (von), sich beschäftigen (mit)
dig	*dug*	*dug*	graben
do	*did*	*done* [ʌ]	tun, machen
draw	*drew*	*drawn*	zeichnen; ziehen
dream [iː]	*dreamt* [e] / *dreamed* [iː]	*dreamt* [e] / *dreamed* [iː]	träumen
drink	*drank*	*drunk*	trinken
drive	*drove*	*driven*	(Auto) fahren; (an)treiben
eat	*ate* [eɪ / BE auch: e]	*eaten*	essen
fall	*fell*	*fallen*	(hin)fallen
feed	*fed*	*fed*	füttern
feel	*felt*	*felt*	(sich) fühlen
fight	*fought* [ɔː]	*fought* [ɔː]	(be)kämpfen
find	*found*	*found*	finden
fit	*fitted/*(AE meist:) *fit*	*fitted/*(AE meist:) *fit*	[größenmäßig] passen
flee	*fled*	*fled*	fliehen, flüchten
fling	*flung*	*flung*	schleudern
fly	*flew*	*flown*	fliegen
forbid	*forbade* [æ]	*forbidden*	verbieten
forget	*forgot*	*forgotten*	vergessen

Irregular Verbs

Infinitive	Simple Past	Past participle	
freeze	froze	frozen	(ge)frieren; erstarren
get	got	BE: got / AE: gotten	bekommen; (hin)kommen; holen; werden
give	gave	given	geben; schenken
go	went	gone [ɒ]	gehen; fahren; werden
grind	ground	ground	zerkleinern, mahlen
grow	grew	grown	wachsen; anbauen, anpflanzen
hang	hung	hung	hängen; [etw.] aufhängen
(regelmäßig:)	hanged	hanged	[jmdn.] hängen
have	had	had	haben
hear [ɪə]	heard [ɜː]	heard [ɜː]	hören
hide	hid	hidden	(sich) verstecken
hit	hit	hit	schlagen, treffen
hold	held	held	(fest)halten
hurt	hurt	hurt	verletzen, wehtun
keep	kept	kept	(be)halten; aufbewahren; weiter[tun]
kneel	knelt / kneeled	knelt / kneeled	knien
know	knew	known	kennen; wissen
lay	laid	laid	legen
lead	led	led	führen, leiten
leap [iː]	leapt [e] / leaped [iː]	leapt [e] / leaped [iː]	springen, hüpfen
learn	learnt / learned	learnt / learned	lernen
leave	left	left	weggehen, verlassen; (zurück)lassen
lend	lent	lent	(ver)leihen
let	let	let	(zu)lassen
lie	lay	lain	liegen
(regelmäßig:)	lied	lied	lügen
light	lit / lighted	lit / lighted	anzünden; beleuchten
lose [uː]	lost [ɒ]	lost [ɒ]	verlieren
make	made	made	machen, bauen; (veran)lassen
mean [iː]	meant [e]	meant [e]	bedeuten; meinen
meet	met	met	(sich) treffen; kennen lernen
overcome	overcame	overcome	überwältigen; überwinden
overtake	overtook	overtaken	überholen
pay	paid	paid	(be)zahlen
put	put	put	stellen, legen, setzen, [wohin] tun
quit	quit / quitted	quit / quitted	verlassen; aufhören
read [iː]	read [e]	read [e]	(vor)lesen
retell	retold	retold	nacherzählen
ride	rode	ridden	reiten; (Rad) fahren
ring	rang	rung	läuten, klingeln; anrufen
rise [aɪ]	rose	risen [ɪ]	(an)steigen; sich erheben; aufgehen
run	ran	run	laufen, rennen; führen, leiten
say	said [e]	said [e]	sagen
see	saw	seen	sehen
seek	sought [ɔː]	sought [ɔː]	suchen

Irregular Verbs

Infinitive	Simple Past	Past participle	
sell	sold	sold	verkaufen
send	sent	sent	schicken, senden
set	set	set	setzen; untergehen [Sonne, Mond]
sew [əʊ]	sewed [əʊ]	sewn/sewed [əʊ]	nähen
shake	shook	shaken	schütteln; erschüttern
shine	shone [BE: ɒ/ AE: əʊ]	shone [BE: ɒ/ AE: əʊ]	scheinen [Sonne]; leuchten
shoot	shot	shot	(er)schießen
show	showed	shown	zeigen
shut	shut	shut	schließen, zumachen
sing	sang	sung	singen
sink	sank	sunk	sinken; versenken
sit	sat	sat	sitzen
sleep	slept	slept	schlafen
slide	slid	slid	rutschen
smell	smelt/smelled	smelt/smelled	riechen
speak	spoke	spoken	sprechen
spell	spelt/spelled	spelt/spelled	buchstabieren
spend	spent	spent	[Geld] ausgeben; [Zeit] verbringen
spit	spat	spat	spucken
spoil	spoilt/spoiled	spoilt/spoiled	verderben; verwöhnen
spread [e]	spread [e]	spread [e]	(sich) ausbreiten; (be)streichen
stand	stood	stood	stehen
steal	stole	stolen	stehlen
stick	stuck	stuck	kleben
sting	stung	stung	stechen
stink	stank/stunk	stunk	stinken
strike	struck	struck	schlagen; treffen [Blitz, Kugel]
strive [aɪ]	strove	striven [ɪ]	sich bemühen, kämpfen
swear	swore	sworn	schwören
sweep	swept	swept	kehren, fegen
swim	swam	swum	schwimmen
swing	swung	swung	schwingen
take	took	taken	(mit)nehmen; (hin-, weg)bringen
teach	taught [ɔ:]	taught [ɔ:]	unterrichten, lehren
tear [eə]	tore	torn	(zer)reißen
tell	told	told	sagen, nennen; erzählen, berichten
think	thought [ɔ:]	thought [ɔ:]	meinen, denken, glauben
throw	threw	thrown	werfen
understand	understood	understood	verstehen, begreifen
upset	upset	upset	erschüttern, verärgern
wake	woke	woken	aufwachen; aufwecken
wear [eə]	wore	worn	[Kleidung, Brille] tragen, anhaben
weep	wept	wept	weinen
wet	wet	wet	befeuchten
win	won [ʌ]	won [ʌ]	gewinnen
write	wrote	written	schreiben

Wordfinder

Die folgende alphabetische Liste führt die englischen „Problemwörter" auf, zu denen *Check it!* nützliche Sprachgebrauchsinformationen gibt.

Die **fett** gedruckten Wörter stehen als Haupteinträge in alphabetischer Reihenfolge auf den Seiten 6–131 bzw. 156–285. Informationen zu den gewöhnlich gedruckten Wörtern findet man in den Einträgen, auf die der orangefarbene Pfeil verweist. TS bedeutet Trouble Spot.

Das Sternchen * kennzeichnet unregelmäßige Verben (vgl. die Liste auf den Seiten 286–288).

A

a
a few ▶ little ▶ pair
a little ▶ little
a lot of ▶ many ▶ much
a.m.
above ▶ over TS
abroad
acceptable
accident
accommodation
according to
account
accuse
across ▶ over TS
act (out) *(verb)* ▶ play
actual
additional
admire
admit
advantage
advice
advise ▶ advice
affect ▶ effect
afraid: be* afraid
after („hinter") ▶ behind TS
after all
after all that ▶ after all
afternoon ▶ morning
against
age
ago
agree
aim *(noun)*
alike
alive
all
all over ▶ everywhere
all together ▶ altogether
allow
allowed: be* allowed to
    ▶ may TS
alone
already
also

alternative
altogether
always
ambulance
among ▶ between
amount
an ▶ a
ancient ▶ old
angry
anniversary ▶ wedding
annoyed
another ▶ other TS
answer *(noun)*
antique ▶ old
anybody ▶ each TS
anyone ▶ each TS
anything ▶ all TS
anywhere ▶ everywhere
apologize
apology ▶ excuse
appear
appetite
apply („sich bewerben")
approach
argue
arms („Waffen")
army
arrange
arrest
as
ask
asleep ▶ sleep*
assure
astronomic(al)
athletic(s)
attempt ▶ try
attend ▶ visit
attitude
autumn ▶ date
average
avoid
aware

B

baby
back *(noun)*
backside
bad
bank
barbecue ▶ grill
be*: I've been to …
be* („werden") ▶ become* TS
be* about to ▶ want TS
be* allowed to ▶ may TS
be* asleep ▶ sleep*
be* supposed to ▶ should TS
be* to ▶ should TS
be* used to ▶ used to
be* worth ▶ worth
beach
bear* ▶ carry
beautiful
become*
beech ▶ beach
before
beginning
behavio(u)r
behind
believe
belong to
below ▶ under
beside
besides ▶ beside
bet* *(verb)*
better („gesund") ▶ healthy
better: had better ▶ had
between
big
bike
birth
blame
blind
boat ▶ ship
book *(noun)*
border
bored: be* bored
born
borrow

289

both
bottom („Boden") ▶ floor TS
boundary ▶ border TS
boyfriend ▶ friend
brave
bread
break („Pause") ▶ pause
breakfast
breast
bring*
bring* up ▶ educate
broil(er) ▶ grill
broken (down)
burglarize ▶ rob
burgle ▶ rob
bus
but („außer") ▶ beside TS
by

call (noun) ▶ phone
calm ▶ quiet
can (verb)
capable
car
carry
cattle
certain(ly)
chance ▶ possibility
change (verb)
chaos
chase ▶ follow TS
chef
chest ▶ breast
choose*
Christ
Christian ▶ Christ
city
classic(al)
clear ▶ sharp
clock
close (verb)
cloth ▶ stuff
coach ▶ bus
coast
cold ▶ fresh
colo(u)r
come*
comment (verb)
competent ▶ unable
complain
completely ▶ fully
concentrate(d)

concept
concerned („betreffend")
condition
confess
confession
confident
congratulations ▶ greet
conscious ▶ aware
consist of
content(s)
continue
control (verb)
cook
cool ▶ fresh
cost* (noun; verb)
countryside ▶ nature
couple ▶ pair
credit
crime
critic
criticism ▶ critic
criticize
cuisine ▶ kitchen
currant
current ▶ actual ▶ currant
customer ▶ guest

damage (noun)
danger
data
date
dead
deadly
decide
decision
deep(ly)
defect
defective ▶ defect
degree
democracy
deny
depend
dependent ▶ independent
describe
desert
deserve
dessert ▶ desert
develop
dictate
die
differ ▶ different TS
difference ▶ different TS

different
difficult ▶ heavy
difficulty
dinner ▶ lunch
discriminate
discuss
dislike
distance
distinguish ▶ different TS
divide
do* ▶ make*
doctor
doctorate ▶ doctor
door
double
doubt
doubtless ▶ doubt
dozen
dressing ▶ sauce
drive* (verb)
driver's license ▶ driving licence
driving licence
drunk
drunken ▶ drunk
during

each
earlier
easy ▶ light
economic(al)
educate
effect
either
elect ▶ choose*
else
email/e-mail ▶ Internet
end
engaged
engine ▶ motor
enjoy
enough
envy
error ▶ mistake TS
escape ▶ flee*
especially
estimated
even ▶ already TS
  ▶ also TS
  ▶ once TS
evening ▶ morning
eventual(ly)

Wordfinder

every ► each ► all TS
every day ► everyday
everybody/everyone
everyday
everyone ► everybody
everything ► all TS
everywhere
evidence
ex- ► earlier TS
exact
exam(ination)
example
except ► beside TS
excuse *(noun)*
excuse me
exercises ► gymnastics
exist
expect
experience *(noun)*
explain
explanation ► explain
express *(verb)*
extra
extract *(noun)*

F

fabric ► stuff
face *(noun)*
fair *(adjective; noun)*
fairly ► quite
fall* *(verb)*
false
family
famous
fancy *(verb)*
fantasy
far
fare ► fair
farther
fast
fat ► thick
fatal ► deadly
fault („Fehler") ► mistake TS
fear
fed up: be* fed up
feel*
female
feminine ► female
ferry ► ship
fever
few ► little
fewer ► less
field

fight *(noun)*
finally ► last: at last
find*
fine *(adjective)*
finish
first *(adjective)*
first(ly) *(adverb)*
fit(*) („passen")
fitness ► gymnastics
flee*
floor
flu
focus: in focus ► sharp
follow
foot
for
for („seit") ► since
forbid*
foresee*
forever
forget*
forgive*
former ► earlier TS
formula
forward(s)
freeze*
freezing ► freeze*
fresh
friend
friendly
frightened ► afraid
from
front („Vorderseite") ► side TS
frontier ► border TS
fry
full
fully
fun
furniture
further ► farther

G

game
garbage ► rubbish
German
get*
get* in/on/off/out of
get* married ► marry
get* used to ► used to
girlfriend ► friend
glass
glasses („Brille")
go*

go* on („weiter-")
go* with („passen zu") ► fit
gone („weg") ► away
good
good (for) („gesund")
    ► healthy
good-looking ► beautiful
govern ► rule
grave *(adjective)* ► heavy
gravy ► sauce
great ► big ► strong TS
greatly
greet
grill *(noun; verb)*
ground („Startverbot erteilen")
ground („Boden") ► floor TS
guest
guesthouse
gymnasium
gymnastics

H

habit
had: I had better …
hair
half
hall
hand
handsome ► beautiful
handy
hang(*)
happen
harbo(u)r
hard
hardly ► hard
hate
have had it ► broken
have* sth. done ► let* TS
have* to ► must
headache
healthy
hear*
heaven
heavy
hell ► heaven
hello: say* hello ► greet
help
hide*
high(ly)
hire
historic(al)
history
hold* *(verb)*

Wordfinder

holiday(s)
homework
hope
hot („scharf") ▸ sharp
hot („warm") ▸ warm
hour
house
household
housekeeping ▸ household
housemaster
housework ▸ homework
how?
human
humane ▸ human
hurt (adjective)

I

idea
if
ill
imagination ▸ fantasy
imagine
impossibly
in addition to ▸ additional
in case ▸ if
in front of ▸ before TS
include
increase
independent
inform
information
injured ▸ hurt
insist on
instead of
instructor ▸ teacher
insure ▸ assure
intense ▸ strong
intention
intermission ▸ pause
Internet/internet
interval ▸ pause
into
introduce
introduction ▸ introduce
involved ▸ concerned
irritate
it's
its ▸ it's

J

jam ▸ marmalade
jar ▸ glass
jealous
jeans
jigsaw ▸ puzzle
job
journey
just

K

keep* („immer weiter-")
kind (adjective) ▸ friendly TS
kitchen
know*
knowledge

L

large ▸ big
largely ▸ greatly
last („dauern")
last („letzte[r/s]")
last: at last
lastly ▸ last
late
lately ▸ late
latest ▸ newest
laugh
law
lay* ▸ lie*
learn(*)
least
leave* ▸ forget* ▸ let* TS
lecturer ▸ teacher
left („links")
lend* ▸ borrow
less
let* („lassen")
let* („mieten") ▸ hire
lettuce ▸ salad
lie* (verb)
life
light („leicht")
like („mögen")
like („wie") ▸ as
like this/that ▸ so
limit („Grenze") ▸ border TS
listen (to) ▸ hear* TS
a little („ein wenig")
little („klein")
live (verb; adjective) ▸ life

living ▸ alive

loan ▸ credit
long
longer: no longer ▸ more
look
look for ▸ search
look forward to
loose ▸ lose*
lose*
lot: a lot of ▸ many ▸ much
lots of ▸ many ▸ much
loud
love (noun)
love (verb)
luck
lucky ▸ luck
lunch

M

machine
machinery ▸ machine
mail ▸ post
majority
make*
male
many
marmalade
marry
masculine ▸ male
match („passen zu") ▸ fit
match („Spiel") ▸ game
material ▸ stuff
maximum
may (do)
mean* (verb)
medium
member
mention
menu
message ▸ phone
meter/metre
middle ▸ medium TS
middle: the Middle Ages
million
mind (verb)
minority ▸ majority
minus
minute
miss (verb)
mistake
mob (verb)
moment
moonlight

Wordfinder

moral
morale ▸ moral
morals ▸ moral
more: no more
morning
most
motor
much
mug *(verb)* ▸ rob
multiply
murder *(noun)*
murderer ▸ murder
music
musical ▸ music
must

N

narrow
nature
near
nearby ▸ near
nearest ▸ next
need *(verb)*
neither
newest
news
next
nil
no („kein") ▸ neither
no doubt ▸ doubt
no longer ▸ more
no one ▸ nobody
no sooner ▸ hard
nobody
noisy ▸ loud
none ▸ neither
nor ▸ also TS
normal ▸ usual
note („Notiz")
nothing
notice („Bekanntmachung")
notice („bemerken")
nought ▸ nil
number

O

o'clock ▸ a.m.
object *(verb)*
obvious
of ▸ from
off ▸ away („weg") ▸ from
offer *(verb)*

oh („null") ▸ nil
old
once
one
only
opinion
opportunity ▸ possibility
opposite
opposition
optimist
ordinary
other
ought to ▸ may TS ▸ should
out of ▸ from
over
overhear*
overlook ▸ oversee*
oversee*
overtake*
own („eigene[r/s]")
own: on my own ▸ alone

P

p.m. ▸ a.m.
package ▸ packet
packet
pair
pajamas ▸ pyjamas
pants
parcel ▸ packet
pardon ▸ please TS
park („parken")
parliament
part („Teil")
party
pass *(verb)*
past ▸ pass
patience
pause *(noun)*
pay* **(for)** *(verb)*
pencil
people
perhaps
permit *(verb)* ▸ allow
persecute ▸ follow TS
person
personal
pessimist ▸ optimist
PhD ▸ doctor
phone
photo(graph)
photographer ▸ photo(graph)
photography ▸ photo(graph)

picnic
picture
pill ▸ tablet
place *(noun)*
play („Theaterstück") ▸ game
play *(verb)*
please
plenty
poem
point *(noun)*
point *(verb)*
police
policy
politics ▸ policy
poor
popular
port ▸ harbour
possibility
possible
possibly: can't possibly
▸ impossibly
post (office)
potato
practice ▸ practise
practise
prefer
prepare
present („anwesend")
pretty („ziemlich") ▸ quite
prevent
previous ▸ earlier TS
price
principal *(noun; adjective)*
principally ▸ principal
principle ▸ principal
prison
prize ▸ price
probably
problem
program
programme ▸ program
progress
promise
pronounce
pronunciation ▸ pronounce
proof ▸ evidence
prospect
protect
proud
public
punish
pursue ▸ follow TS
puzzle *(noun)*
pyjamas

Q

qualify
quantity
quick ▸ fast
quiet
quite

R

rain
raise
rare(ly) ▸ seldom
rather: would rather
rather („ziemlich") ▸ quite
react
reaction ▸ react
ready
realize
reason
receipt
recently
recipe ▸ receipt
recognize ▸ realize
refuse
regret
reign ▸ rule
reject ▸ refuse
related
relevant
remain ▸ stay
remainder ▸ rest TS
remains ▸ rest TS
remember
remind ▸ remember
rent ▸ hire
repeat
repetition ▸ repeat
report
reputation
request (noun)
resist
responsible
rest („Rest")
return („zurückkehren")
rich
ride (noun) ▸ journey
ride* (verb) ▸ drive* TS
right („rechts") ▸ left
right: be* right
rise* (verb) ▸ raise
risk (noun; verb)
road ▸ street
roast (verb) ▸ fry

rob
room („Platz") ▸ place TS
rubbish
rule („regieren")
run* („fahren", „verkehren")
      ▸ drive* TS

S

salad
sale
same: the same
sandwich ▸ bread
sauce
save („retten")
save (up) („sparen") ▸ spare
say*
school
sea
search (verb)
seaside ▸ sea
see
seek* ▸ search
seem
seldom
select ▸ choose*
self: by myself ▸ alone
self-confident ▸ self-conscious
self-conscious
sense („Zweck")
sensible
sensitive ▸ sensible
serious
severe ▸ heavy ▸ strong TS
shade
shadow ▸ shade
shall ▸ should TS
sharp
sheep
shine*
ship
shopping
shorts
should
shout (verb)
shut* (verb) ▸ close
sick ▸ ill
side
silent ▸ quiet
similar ▸ alike
since
size
sky
sleep*

slight ▸ light
small ▸ little
smell (*) (verb)
smile ▸ laugh
smooth ▸ quiet
so
so far ▸ until TS
social
society
soil („Boden") ▸ floor TS
somebody ▸ nobody
someone ▸ nobody
sometime ▸ sometimes
sometimes
soon ▸ already TS
soon: no sooner ▸ hard
sorry ▸ excuse me ▸ please TS
sound („sich anhören")
space („Weltraum")
spaghetti
spare
speak*
special
specialist
specialize
specially ▸ especially
speech
speed (noun)
spend*
spicy ▸ sharp
spoil (*)
sport
spring ▸ date
stadium
stand* (verb)
stationary
stationery ▸ stationary
stay (verb)
steal* ▸ rob
still („noch")
still („ruhig") ▸ quiet
stop
storey
story ▸ storey
street
strong
study (verb)
stuff
subconscious ▸ unconscious
substance ▸ stuff
succeed
such ▸ so
suffer
suggest

Wordfinder

suit („passen zu") ▶ fit
summary
summer ▶ date
sunk
sunken ▶ sunk
support ▶ carry
suppose
sure(ly) ▶ certain(ly)
surprised
suspect *(noun; adjective)*
suspect *(verb)*
suspicious ▶ suspect *(noun; adjective)*
sympathetic

T

tablet
take* („brauchen") ▶ need TS
take* („bringen") ▶ bring*
take* („dauern") ▶ last* ▶ need TS
take* over ▶ overtake*
talk ▶ speak*
tall ▶ big
task
taste *(verb)*
teacher
technique
technology ▶ technique
teenage
tell* ▶ say*
temperature
terrible
terrific ▶ terrible
test *(noun)*
text *(verb)* ▶ phone
text message ▶ phone
than ▶ as TS
thank
thank you ▶ thank
thanks ▶ thank
they („man") ▶ one
thick
thin ▶ narrow TS
think*
thought *(noun)*
threat
throw*
till ▶ until
time („Mal")
time („Zeit")
time: a long time ▶ long
toast

today
tomorrow ▶ today
too
tooth
topical ▶ actual
tour *(noun)*
traffic
travel *(noun)* ▶ journey
travel *(verb)* ▶ drive* TS
trip ▶ journey
trouble
trousers
true
trust
truth ▶ true
try
turn („werden") ▶ become* TS
two: the two ▶ both TS
typical

U

unable
unconscious
under
underpants ▶ pants
understand*
undertaker
undoubtedly ▶ doubt
unemployment
United States
university
unless
until
up to ▶ until TS
up to date ▶ actual
use („Nutzen")
used to
usual

V

valid ▶ actual
various ▶ different TS
ventilator
vest
via ▶ over TS
visit
visitor ▶ guest
voice
vote ▶ choose*
voyage ▶ journey

W

wait
wander
want
warehouse
warm
warn
waste *(verb)*
watch („Uhr") ▶ clock
watch *(verb)* ▶ look
way („Art und Weise")
way: a long way ▶ far
weapons ▶ arms
wear* ▶ carry
weather
wedding day
week
weigh
welcome („willkommen")
well („gesund") ▶ healthy
what
when
which ▶ who
while ▶ during
who
why
winter ▶ date
without
without doubt ▶ doubt
wonder *(verb)* ▶ think*
word
work *(noun)*
work: be* not working ▶ broken
world
worth: be* worth
would ▶ want TS
would like ▶ like ▶ want TS
would love ▶ love
would prefer ▶ prefer
would rather ▶ rather
write*
wrong ▶ false

Y

year
yet ▶ already
you („man") ▶ one

Z

zero ▶ nil

Hinweise für Unterrichtende

Die folgenden Hinweise und Informationen richten sich speziell an Lehrer/-innen und Kursleiter/-innen. Sie ergänzen die in den allgemeinen Benutzerhinweisen (*Frequently Asked Questions*, S. 4/5) vermittelten Informationen zur Zielsetzung, zum Aufbau und zum Einsatz von *Check it*.

Für welche Zielgruppen ist *Check it* geeignet?

Check it eignet sich für fortgeschrittene Lerner ab Stufe B1 des Gemeinsamen europäischen Referenzrahmens für Sprachen. Es berücksichtigt besonders die Bedürfnisse von Schülern und Schülerinnen der Sekundarstufe II an allgemein- und berufsbildenden Schulen sowie von Lernenden der Erwachsenenbildung, die sich auf Cambridge-Prüfungen vorbereiten.

Was leistet *Check it*?

Check it beleuchtet den Grenzbereich zwischen Lexik, Grammatik und Idiomatik und leistet Hilfestellung bei ganz unterschiedlichen Fragen des korrekten Sprachgebrauchs. *Check it* führt Informationen zusammen, die man sonst in unterschiedlichen Nachschlagewerken suchen müsste.

Welches Englisch liegt *Check it* zugrunde?

Check it orientiert sich an der Sprachnorm des *educated (British or American) native speaker* und stützt sich dabei auf Korpusdaten, auf bekannte Wörterbücher wie das *Oxford Advanced Learner's Dictionary* und auf Grammatiken wie die *Longman Grammar of Spoken and Written English*. Wo sinnvoll, wird auch auf stilistische Varianten hingewiesen: Einzelne Wörter und Wendungen werden als formell *(formal)* bzw. informell *(informal)* gekennzeichnet. Außerdem wird zwischen britisch-englischen (BE) und amerikanisch-englischen (AE) Sprachmitteln unterschieden.
Zu beachten ist, dass auch die Sprachnorm gebildeter Muttersprachler ein Kontinuum unterschiedlich akzeptabler sprachlicher Äußerungen erlaubt und *Check it* nicht die Fülle aller denkbaren oder vorfindbaren Ausdrucksmöglichkeiten abbilden kann. Gerade fortgeschrittene Lerner müssen dafür sensibilisiert werden, dass es neben eindeutig fehlerhaftem Sprachgebrauch (z. B. *he suggested to go to the cinema*) auch Formen des Sprachgebrauchs gibt, bei denen die Korrektheit schwieriger zu beurteilen ist (z. B. *typical for Germans*). In der Regel werden nicht allgemein akzeptierte Ausdrucksformen in *Check it* nich vermittelt, auch wenn sie gelegentlich von Muttersprachlern verwendet werden und sich Belege dafür beispielsweise im Internet finden lassen.

Wie lässt sich *Check it* einsetzen?

Check it kann sowohl im Unterricht als auch unterrichtsbegleitend oder zum selbstständigen Üben zu Hause eingesetzt werden. Insbesondere die (rechten) Informationsseiten eignen sich als Hilfsmittel für die Lernenden beim Abfassen von Texten aller Art. Bei der Besprechung und Überprüfung von Schülerarbeiten kann auf die Erklärungen, Regeln und Beispiele dieser Seiten verwiesen werden. In Verbindung mit den Übungen (auf den linken Seiten) können die Informationsseiten in Wiederholungsphasen oder zur Förderung einzelner Schüler/-innen herangezogen werden, z. B. vor oder nach der Leistungsmessung. *Check it* leistet damit auch einen Beitrag zur Individualisierung des Unterrichts.
Die 12 *Checkpoints* in der Mitte des Buches (auf Seite 132–155) bieten die Möglichkeit des übergreifenden, intensiven Übens in einem bestimmten Fehlerbereich, sofern dort ein besonderer Bedarf besteht. Sie können aber auch zur Lernkontrolle eingesetzt werden.

In *Check it* verwendete Abkürzungen und Symbole

jmd.	jemand	fml	formal
jmdm.	jemandem	infml	informal
jmdn.	jemanden	AE	American English / amerikanisches Englisch
jmds.	jemandes	BE	British English / britisches Englisch
sb.	*somebody*	*	unregelmäßiges Verb (s. Seite 286–288)
sth.	*something*	(*)	Verb mit unregelmäßigen **oder** regelmäßigen Formen
		1	Testsatz mit mehr als einer Lösung

John Stevens

Check it!

Lösungsheft

Cornelsen

Inhaltsverzeichnis

Hinweise zum Gebrauch des Lösungsheftes

Das Lösungsheft zu *Check it* enthält alle Lösungen der Übungssätze (linke Seiten des Buches) und der *Checkpoints* (S. 132–155).

Nähere Erläuterungen zu den hier angegebenen Lösungen findet man in den Einträgen auf den rechten Seiten (= Informationsseiten) des Buches.

Das Lösungsheft sollte nur zur nachträglichen Kontrolle verwendet werden, nachdem man die Aufgaben im Buch eigenständig, gegebenenfalls mithilfe der Informationen auf den rechten Seiten bearbeitet hat. Vgl. dazu auch die Hinweise auf den Seiten 4 und 5 des Buches: *FAQ (Frequently Asked Questions).*

Seite 6

a – an 1 *A B E F*, 2 *B*
abroad 1 *A*, 2 *A*
acceptable 1 *B*
accident 1 *B*, 2 *C D*
accommodation 1 *B*, 2 *A C*
according to 1 *A*
account 1 *A*, 2 *A*
accuse 1 *C*

Seite 8

actual ≠ „aktuell" 1 *B*, 2 *B*, 3 *C*, 4 *B*, 5 *C D*
additional – in addition to 1 *B C*, 2 *B*
admire 1 *A*, 2 *A*
admit 1 *B*, 2 *A C D*
advantage 1 *B*, 2 *A*

Seite 10

advice – advise 1 *B*, 2 *B C D*, 3 *C*, 4 *B*, 5 *B*,
  6 *B D*, 7 *A*
afraid: be afraid – frightened 1 *B C*, 2 *B*, 3 *B C*,
  4 *B*
after all – after all that 1 *A*, 2 *B*

Seite 12

against 1 *A*, 2 *A*, 3 *B*, 4 *C*, 5 *B*, 6 *A B*
age 1 *B*, 2 *A*, 3 *A C D*
ago 1 *C*, 2 *B*, 3 *C*
agree 1 *B*, 2 *B*

Seite 14

aim 1 *A*
alike – similar 1 *A C*, 2 *B*
alive – living 1 *B C*
all 1 *B C*, 2 *A*, 3 *A B*, 4 *A*, 5 *B*, 6 *B*, 7 *C*

Seite 16

allow – permit 1 *C*, 2 *B C D*
alone – on my own, by myself 1 *B C*, 2 *C*
already 1 *B*, 2 *B*, 3 *A B*, 4 *B*, 5 *B*, 6 *B*, 7 *C*, 8 *C*

Seite 18

also – too 1 *B*, 2 *D*, 3 *C*, 4 *B*, 5 *B*
alternative 1 *B*
altogether – all together 1 *B*, 2 *A*
always 1 *A*, 2 *A*, 3 *A*

Seite 62

deserve 1 *B*
develop 1 *A*, 2 *B*
dictate 1 *B*
die 1 *B*, 2 *A*, 3 *C*
different 1 *A*, 2 *B*, 3 *B*, 4 *B*
difficulty 1 *A B*

Seite 64

discriminate 1 *B*
discuss 1 *A*, 2 *B C*
dislike 1 *B*
distance 1 *A B*, 2 *C*, 3 *A*, 4 *A*, 5 *A*, 6 *B*
divide 1 *A B*

Seite 66

doctor – PhD/doctorate 1 *A B*, 2 *A*
door 1 *A B*
double 1 *B*, 2 *B*, 3 *A*
doubt – no doubt – without doubt 1 *B*, 2 *C*,
   3 *A C*, 4 *B D*
dozen 1 *A*

Seite 68

drive 1 *D*, 2 *C*, 3 *B*, 4 *B D*, 5 *A D*, 6 *D*, 7 *A*, 8 *C*
driving licence / driver's license 1 *B*, 2 *A D*,
   3 *C*
drunk – drunken 1 *A*, 2 *B*
during – while 1 *B*, 2 *A*, 3 *B*

Seite 70

each – every 1 *B*, 2 *A*, 3 *B*, 4 *B*, 5 *A*, 6 *A*, 7 *D E*,
   8 *B*, 9 *B*, 10 *A B*
earlier 1 *B C*, 2 *A C*, 3 *C*, 4 *A B*

Seite 72

economic – economical 1 *A*, 2 *A*, 3 *B*
educate – bring up 1 *B*
effect – affect 1 *A*, 2 *A*
either 1 *B*
else 1 *C*
end 1 *A*, 2 *B*, 3 *B*, 4 *C*, 5 *B*
engaged 1 *B*

Seite 74

enjoy 1 *A*, 2 *A D*
enough 1 *A*, 2 *A*
envy 1 *A*, 2 *C*
especially – specially 1 *A*, 2 *A B*, 3 *B*
estimated 1 *B*

Seite 76

eventual/eventually ≠ „eventuell" 1 *A*, 2 *B*
everybody/everyone 1 *C D*
everyday – every day 1 *B*
everywhere – anywhere – all over 1 *A*, 2 *B*,
   3 *B*
evidence – proof 1 *B*
exact 1 *A*, 2 *A*, 3 *B*

Seite 78

exam/examination 1 *A C D*, 2 *B C*
example 1 *B*
excuse – apology – note 1 *B*, 2 *C*
excuse me – sorry 1 *B C*, 2 *B*
exist 1 *B*
expect 1 *C*, 2 *B*, 3 *B*

Seite 80

experience 1 *A*, 2 *A*
explain – explanation 1 *B*
express 1 *B*
extra 1 *A C*, 2 *B*, 3 *C*, 4 *B D*
extract 1 *A*
face 1 *C*, 2 *C*

Seite 82

fair – fare 1 *A*, 2 *B*, 3 *A*
fall 1 *C*
false – wrong 1 *B*, 2 *A*, 3 *B*
family 1 *B*, 2 *A B C*
famous 1 *D*
fancy 1 *A*
fantasy – imagination 1 *A*, 2 *B*, 3 *B*

Seite 84

far – a long way – away 1 *A*, 2 *A C*, 3 *C*
farther – further 1 *A B*, 2 *B*
fast – quick 1 *A*, 2 *A*, 3 *B*
fear 1 *A*, 2 *A*
fed up: be fed up 1 *B*
feel 1 *A C*, 2 *B*, 3 *B C*, 4 *B*

Seite 86

female – feminine 1 *A*, 2 *B*
fever – temperature 1 *B*, 2 *C*
field 1 *B*
fight 1 *C*
find 1 *B*
fine 1 *A*
finish 1 *B*
first 1 *C*, 2 *C*, 3 *B*

Seite 88

first – firstly – at first 1 *B*, 2 *A*, 3 *C*, 4 *B D*
fit – suit – go with – match 1 *A*, 2 *B*, 3 *E*
flee – escape 1 *B*, 2 *A*

Seite 90

floor 1 *C*, 2 *C*, 3 *D*, 4 *A*
flu 1 *B C E F*
follow 1 *B*, 2 *C*, 3 *B*
foot 1 *C*, 2 *C F*
for 1 *B*, 2 *A*

Seite 92

forbid 1 *B*, 2 *A*, 3 *B*
foresee 1 *B*
forever – for ever 1 *B*
forget 1 *B*, 2 *A*, 3 *B*
forgive 1 *B*

Seite 94

formula ≠ „Formular" 1 *D*, 2 *C*
forward – forwards 1 *A*
freeze – freezing 1 *A B*, 2 *C*
fresh – cool – cold 1 *A*, 2 *A*, 3 *C*
friend – boyfriend – girlfriend 1 *A*, 2 *B*

Seite 96

friendly 1 *A*, 2 *D E*, 3 *D*
from – of – off – by – out of 1 *B*, 2 *A*, 3 *A*, 4 *C*,
   5 *B*, 6 *C*, 7 *B*, 8 *C*
fry – roast – grill 1 *A*, 2 *B*

Seite 98

full 1 *C*
fully – completely 1 *A*
fun 1 *C*
furniture 1 *A*
game – match – play 1 *A*, 2 *A C*, 3 *B*
German 1 *B*
get 1 *C*
get in / get on – get out of / get off 1 *A*, 2 *A B*

Seite 100

glass – jar 1 *B*
glasses 1 *B C*
go 1 *B*, 2 *B*
go on 1 *A*, 2 *B*
good 1 *A*
greatly – largely 1 *A*, 2 *B*, 3 *A C*

Seite 102

greet – say hello 1 *B C*, 2 *A B*, 3 *B C*, 4 *C*, 5 *C*
grill – broiler/broil – barbecue 1 *A*, 2 *A B*
ground ≠ „gründen" 1 *C*, 2 *B*
guest – customer – visitor 1 *A*

Seite 104

guesthouse ≠ „Gasthaus" 1 *B*, 2 *E*
gymnasium ≠ „Gymnasium" 1 *B*, 2 *C*
gymnastics – exercises – fitness 1 *A*, 2 *A*
habit 1 *A*, 2 *B*
had: I had better 1 *B*, 2 *B*
hair 1 *A*

Seite 106

half 1 *D*, 2 *A*, 3 *A C*, 4 *B*, 5 *B*
hall 1 *A B*, 2 *A*, 3 *B*
hand 1 *B*, 2 *A*
handy ≠ „Handy" 1 *C*, 2 *A B D*, 3 *A C*

Seite 108

hang 1 *B*, 2 *A*
happen 1 *B*
harbour/harbor – port 1 *B*
hard – hardly 1 *A*, 2 *B*, 3 *B D*
hate 1 *B*, 2 *A B*, 3 *A*

Seite 110

headache 1 *B*
healthy – (fit and) well – better – good for
  1 *A*, 2 *B*, 3 *A*, 4 *A*
hear 1 *B*, 2 *C*, 3 *B*, 4 *A*
heaven – hell 1 *C*, 2 *A*

Seite 112

heavy 1 *D*, 2 *C*, 3 *A C*, 4 *E*, 5 *B E*, 6 *A D*, 7 *B*, 8 *B*
help 1 *B*, 2 *A B C D*
hide 1 *B*, 2 *C*

Seite 114

high – highly 1 *A*, 2 *B*, 3 *B*, 4 *A*, 5 *C*, 6 *B*,
  7 *B*, 8 *B*
hire – rent – let 1 *C*, 2 *C D*, 3 *B*
historic – historical 1 *A*, 2 *B*

Seite 116

history 1 *A*, 2 *A*, 3 *B*
hold 1 *A*, 2 *C*, 3 *B*, 4 *A D*, 5 *B*, 6 *C D*
holiday(s) 1 *A*, 2 *B C*, 3 *A*

Seite 118

homework – housework 1 *A C*, 2 *C*
hope 1 *A*, 2 *A*, 3 *B*
hour 1 *B*, 2 *A*
house 1 *B C*, 2 *B*
household – housekeeping 1 *B*, 2 *A*, 3 *C*

Seite 120

housemaster ≠ „Hausmeister" 1 *B*, 2 *A D*
how – what … like? 1 *C*, 2 *B*, 3 *C*
human – humane 1 *A*
hurt – injured 1 *B*, 2 *B*
idea 1 *A*, 2 *A*, 3 *B*

Seite 122

if – in case 1 *A*, 2 *B*
ill – sick 1 *A B*, 2 *B*, 3 *B*
imagine 1 *A*
impossibly – can't possibly 1 *B*, 2 *B*
include 1 *B*, 2 *B D*

Seite 124

increase 1 *B*, 2 *B*
independent – dependent 1 *B C*, 2 *D*
inform 1 *B C D*
information 1 *A*, 2 *B C*
insist on 1 *B*
instead of 1 *C*
intention 1 *A*

Seite 126

Internet 1 *C*, 2 *C*
into 1 *C*, 2 *B*, 3 *B*
introduce – introduction 1 *C*, 2 *D*
irritate ≠ „irritieren" 1 *A*, 2 *C*
it's – its 1 *B*, 2 *A*, 3 *B*, 4 *B*, 5 *A*

Seite 128

jealous 1 *C*
jeans 1 *B C*, 2 *B*
job 1 *A*
journey – trip – drive – ride – voyage – tour –
  travel 1 *D*, 2 *A*, 3 *C*, 4 *B*, 5 *B*, 6 *F*, 7 *D*, 8 *C*

Seite 130

just 1 *B*, 2 *A C*, 3 *C*
keep 1 *A C*
kitchen – cuisine 1 *A B*, 2 *A C*, 3 *B*
know 1 *B*, 2 *C*
knowledge 1 *B*, 2 *B*

Die folgenden Lösungen zu den *Checkpoints* enthalten jeweils einen Verweis auf einen oder mehrere Einträge im alphabetischen Hauptteil des Buches. Beispiel: „keep ▶ hold" bedeutet: Die richtige Lösung ist „keep"; nähere Informationen dazu findet man im Eintrag „hold". Bei einigen *Checkpoint*-Aufgaben (z. B. deutsch-englischen Übersetzungen) gibt es neben den hier angegebenen Lösungen u. U. noch andere, ebenfalls korrekte Lösungen.

Checkpoint 1: Which Word?
Seite 132

A
1. Its grammar ▶ it's
2. The moment passed ▶ pass
3. I'll see you sometime ▶ sometimes
4. The Sahara Desert ▶ desert
5. Think hard ▶ hard
6. the fare to Newcastle ▶ fair
7. most of the housework ▶ homework
8. laid the table ▶ lie
9. The current rate of exchange ▶ currant
10. I lay down ▶ lie
11. I first met her ▶ first (S. 89)
12. At first I couldn't ▶ first (S. 89)
13. You've no doubt heard ▶ doubt
14. to raise doubts ▶ raise
15. The price hasn't risen ▶ raise
16. The principal reason ▶ principal
17. no longer economic ▶ economic
18. basic historical facts ▶ historic
19. a human life ▶ human
20. a musical instrument ▶ music

B
1. take ▶ bring
2. ✓ ▶ greatly
3. remains ▶ rest
4. hot/spicy ▶ sharp
5. a long way ▶ far
6. boiling ▶ cook
7. ✓ ▶ quiet
8. have a barbecue ▶ grill
9. ancient ▶ old
10. go ▶ come
11. listen to ▶ hear
12. shed/building ▶ hall

Seite 133

B
13. lately/recently ▶ last ▶ late
14. buildings ▶ house
15. Stop ▶ let
16. a sick ▶ ill
17. cuisine ▶ kitchen
18. former/previous ▶ earlier
19. jar ▶ glass
20. exercises ▶ gymnastics

C
1. fit ▶ fit
2. Anybody/Anyone ▶ each
3. any[where] ▶ everywhere
4. male ▶ male … female ▶ female
5. imagination ▶ fantasy
6. weapons ▶ arms
7. keep ▶ hold
8. hold ▶ hold
9. stay ▶ stay
10. borrow ▶ borrow
11. false … false ▶ false
12. instructor ▶ teacher
13. border ▶ border
14. frontiers ▶ border
15. expense ▶ cost
16. ground/soil ▶ floor
17. ride ▶ drive
18. left ▶ forget
19. As / (infml:) Like ▶ as
20. loose ▶ lose

Seite 134

D
1. (the) first prize ▶ price
2. You remind me ▶ remember

3 **drunk** ▶ drunk

4 **the murderer** ▶ murder

5 **in the shade** ▶ shade ✗

6 **fell** ▶ fall

7 **with the housework** ▶ homework

8 **the photographer's name / the name of the photographer** ▶ photo(graph)

9 **unconscious** ▶ unconscious

10 **the wrecks of sunken ships** ▶ sunk

11 **defective/broken** ▶ defect ▶ broken

12 **a weekend trip** ▶ journey

13 **a new policy** ▶ policy ✗

14 **How many metres/meters high** ▶ metre

15 **Modern technology** ▶ technique

16 **no further questions** ▶ farther … **close the discussion** ▶ close

17 **a quick lunch** ▶ fast

18 **The injured** ▶ hurt

19 **After all,** ▶ after all ▶ last: at last

20 **vote for** ▶ choose

21 **a note** ▶ excuse

22 **(at) about/around four (o'clock) / about/around fourish** ▶ against ▶ morning

23 **Everybody/Everyone** ▶ everybody ▶ each

24 **gone** ▶ away

Seite 135

E

1 **The nearest bank is ten kilometres/ kilometers away.** ▶ next ▶ distance

2 **Have you heard the latest news?** ▶ newest ▶ news

3 **A/One million – one and six zeros/ noughts.** ▶ nil

4 **We('ve) made a serious/grave mistake.** ▶ mistake ▶ heavy

5 **What you're saying is difficult/hard to believe.** ▶ heavy

6 **We had a long discussion / We talked for a long time – until 10 p.m. / until 10 in the evening.** ▶ discuss ▶ a.m. ▶ morning

7 **Tony is tall. He's 1.96 m (= metres/ meters) tall.** ▶ big ▶ metre

8 **We're in great danger.** ▶ big

9 **How do I get to the station?** ▶ come

10 **Tina is ill/sick? But I saw her only this morning.** ▶ ill ▶ first (S. 89)

11 **What do the letters B.A. after a name / somebody's name stand for?** ▶ behind

12 **It was (in) July and the grass was very long/tall.** ▶ high

13 **Deep snow everywhere.** ▶ high

14 **I have a different suggestion.** ▶ other •

15 **Could you pack this book separately, please?** ▶ extra

16 **Paderborn is a medium-sized town/city.** ▶ medium

17 **We didn't fly direct but via London.** ▶ over

18 **It has turned cold. Take a coat with you.** ▶ become

19 **This shirt is very tight.** ▶ narrow

20 **If you don't hear from me by Friday, tell/inform the police.** ▶ until ▶ inform

21 **We live in a small town near Dresden.** ▶ near ▶ by

22 **My sister works for/at a bank.** ▶ by

23 **Fresh fruit is good for you.** ▶ healthy

24 **Is that your big brother?** ▶ big

Checkpoint 2: Collocations
Seite 136

A

1 **are/were** ▶ age

2 **take** ▶ last (S. 157 unten)

3 **give** ▶ example

4 **had** ▶ picnic

5 **had** ▶ experience

6 **are** ▶ colour

7 **having/taking** ▶ holiday(s) ▶ make

8 **had** ▶ baby

9 **did / are doing** ▶ tour

10 **had / are having** ▶ game

11 **made/taken** ▶ decision

12 **took** ▶ photo(graph)
13 **take/do** ▶ test
14 **is giving/having** ▶ party
15 **making/giving** ▶ speech

B

1 **do** ▶ make
2 **make** ▶ make
3 **do** ▶ make
4 **do** ▶ make ▶ sport

Seite 137

B

5 **do** ▶ make
6 **do** ▶ make
7 **make** ▶ make
8 **do** ▶ make
9 **make** ▶ make
10 **made** ▶ make
11 **done** ▶ make ▶ homework
12 **done** ▶ make ▶ work
13 **make** ▶ make ▶ mistake
14 **do** ▶ make
15 **make** ▶ make
16 **make ... do** ▶ make

C

1 **hard/heavily** ▶ rain ▶ strong
2 **large/great/considerable/tremendous/
   huge** ▶ amount
3 **small** ▶ amount
4 **badly/seriously/severely** ▶ strong
5 **serious** ▶ heavy
6 **small** ▶ quantity
7 **great/ripe old** ▶ age
8 **heavy** ▶ traffic ▶ strong
9 **far** ▶ high
10 **seriously** ▶ heavy ▶ hurt

D

1 **doing** ▶ test
2 **heavy** ▶ strong
3 **quite** ▶ possible

4 **seriously** ▶ serious
5 **make** ▶ cook
6 **putting** ▶ bring
7 **tell** ▶ different
8 **bottom of the sea/seabed** ▶ floor
9 **attend/go to** ▶ visit
10 **dressing** ▶ sauce
11 **instructor** ▶ teacher
12 **Wet** ▶ fresh

Checkpoint 3: False Friends
Seite 138

A

1 *A* ▶ overhear
2 *B* ▶ sensible
3 *C* ▶ blame
4 *B* ▶ irritate
5 *A* ▶ brave
6 *C* ▶ notice
7 *A* ▶ receipt
8 *B* ▶ chef
9 *C* ▶ housemaster
10 *C* ▶ gymnasium
11 *C* ▶ overtake
12 *A* ▶ concept
13 *B* ▶ ordinary
14 *C* ▶ handy
15 *B* ▶ eventual

Seite 139

B

1 **founded/set up** ▶ ground
2 **at the back/rear** ▶ back ▶ backside
3 **What mark/grade** ▶ note
4 **one of the most successful entre-
   preneurs/businessmen** ▶ undertaker
5 **up to date/valid** ▶ actual
6 **save** ▶ spare
7 **the form** ▶ formula
8 **Could you please check** ▶ control
9 **in a restaurant/pub** ▶ guesthouse
10 **very nice** ▶ sympathetic
11 **a brochure** ▶ prospect

12 The audience ▶ public
13 a tray ▶ tablet
14 criticism ▶ critic

Checkpoint 4: Prepositions
Seite 140

A

1 at a later date ▶ date
2 In answer to ▶ answer
3 in your account ▶ account
4 on the afternoon of her 90th birthday
   ▶ morning
5 on the 18th floor ▶ floor
6 spend on food ▶ spend ...
   on average ▶ average
7 in love with someone ▶ love
8 On my brother's bike. ▶ bike
9 pay by credit card ▶ pay
10 up in the sky ▶ sky
11 in such a loud voice ▶ voice
12 at me ▶ throw

B

1 There has been an increase in the
   number of unemployed. ▶ increase
2 I know you don't believe me, but it's
   obvious to me that it's a fake.
   ▶ obvious
3 It's a poem by William Wordsworth.
   ▶ poem ▶ from
4 I'm very proud of you. ▶ proud
5 We made a visit to Berlin. ▶ visit
6 We hope / We're hoping for better
   weather. ▶ hope
7 What do you understand by 'a very
   short time'? ▶ under ▶ understand
8 The café is popular with young
   people. ▶ popular
9 I'm here at Ann's request. ▶ request
10 "We're now travelling at (a speed of)
   180 km/h." ▶ speed

Seite 141

C

1 for ▶ against
2 at ▶ minute
3 from ▶ hear
4 for ▶ reason
5 to/towards ▶ attitude
6 by ▶ from
7 from ▶ before ▶ save
8 of ▶ hear
9 by ▶ by ▶ sea
10 of/like ▶ taste

D

1 on ▶ waste
2 on ▶ comment
3 to ▶ threat
4 — ▶ envy
5 in ▶ accident
6 — ▶ approach
7 — ▶ age
8 against ▶ discriminate
9 by ▶ multiply
10 — ▶ discuss

E

1 Sheila is engaged to a Frenchman.
   ▶ engaged
2 Tom drove/rode into a wall. ▶ against
3 Why are you laughing at me? ▶ laugh
4 Don't write in pencil / with a pencil,
   please. ▶ pencil
5 Ann's brother is in the army. ▶ army
6 What's so special about the car?
   ▶ special
7 What should we do / ought we to do
   in your opinion? ▶ opinion
8 Are you good at chemistry? ▶ good
9 I'll pay the cheque into my account.
   ▶ account
10 Don't shout at me like that! ▶ shout

Checkpoint 5: Articles

Seite 142

A

1. I got some interesting information/ an interesting piece of information ... ▶ information
2. ... in life? ▶ life
3. ... in prison ... ▶ prison
4. ... is absolute chaos! ▶ chaos
5. ✓ ▶ abroad
6. ... speaks excellent German. ▶ German
7. ... interested in politics ▶ policy
8. ... some advice/a piece of advice? ▶ advice
9. ✓ ▶ knowledge
10. ... in nature. ▶ nature

B

1. Most Swiss people understand French. ▶ most
2. I'll give you an extra ten minutes/ ten extra minutes. ▶ extra
3. The bill was debated in Parliament. ▶ parliament
4. We're looking for cheap accommodation. ▶ accommodation
5. Have you found work? ▶ work
6. An estimated 25 million people watch the show every week. ▶ estimated
7. Richard had (the) flu last week. ▶ flu
8. I'm a member of a tennis club. ▶ member

C

1. As a child I was afraid of the dark. ▶ as
2. I'll phone/call you after dinner/supper. ▶ lunch
3. The storm caused great/enormous damage. ▶ damage
4. I'm always an optimist. ▶ optimist
5. We often go on holiday by coach/ on a coach. ▶ coach
6. Mara lives in Grove Road. ▶ street

7. Selim has gone shopping. He'll be back in half an hour. ▶ half
8. European history is a history of war. ▶ history
9. How long will the astronauts stay/are the astronauts staying in space? ▶ space
10. Society is changing. ▶ society

Checkpoint 6: Singular and Plural

Seite 143

A

1. is ▶ news
2. are ▶ number
3. is ▶ United States
4. are ▶ majority
5. are ▶ rest
6. are ▶ glasses
7. is ▶ hair
8. are ▶ police

B

1. The information they've sent me is incomplete. ▶ information
2. These jeans are a really cool colour: purple! ▶ jeans
3. Either day is OK for me. ▶ either
4. It was 32 degrees Celsius, even in the shade. ▶ degree
5. This homework is for Tuesday, not for Monday. ▶ homework
6. Sunglasses are useful when the sun is so low in the sky. ▶ glasses

C

1. Where are my pyjamas/pajamas? *pəˈʤɑːməz* ▶ pyjamas
2. An adult usually/normally has 32 teeth. ▶ tooth
3. I need a holiday. ▶ holiday(s)
4. In New Zealand there are more sheep than people/humans/human beings. ▶ sheep ▶ person

5️⃣ The new building will cost two million euro<u>s</u>. ▶ million

6️⃣ How big are your feet? ▶ foot

7️⃣ Your progress is impressive! ▶ progress

8️⃣ I'll give you some help. ▶ help

9️⃣ Nobody/No one knows you, do they? ▶ nobody

🔟 How many people are coming to the party? ▶ person

1️⃣1️⃣ The Middle Ages are the period from about AD 1000 to AD 1450. ▶ Middle Ages

1️⃣2️⃣ I had a really bad headache and couldn't go to school. ▶ headache

Checkpoint 7: Word Order
Seite 144

A

1️⃣ A ▶ both

2️⃣ B ▶ opposite

3️⃣ B ▶ ago

4️⃣ B ▶ include

5️⃣ A ▶ all

6️⃣ A C ▶ please

7️⃣ A ▶ all

8️⃣ A B ▶ quite

9️⃣ B ▶ especially

🔟 A ▶ minus

1️⃣1️⃣ A ▶ double

1️⃣2️⃣ B ▶ each

B

1️⃣ The students concerned will have to resit the exam in January. ▶ concerned

2️⃣ Do you know the Evans family? ▶ family

3️⃣ I don't think we'll need more than half a day. ▶ half

4️⃣ It was too easy a task for the students … ▶ too

5️⃣ We always have eight lessons on Monday. ▶ always

6️⃣ What else can this machine do? ▶ else

7️⃣ I've lost both my contact lenses. ▶ both

8️⃣ The other parents present were asked to leave the room. ▶ present

9️⃣ The party will probably be a disaster. ▶ probably

🔟 On Wednesday we had already collected over €250. ▶ already

1️⃣1️⃣ I've done four exams in the last week alone. ▶ alone

1️⃣2️⃣ I think we've waited a long enough time. ▶ enough

Checkpoint 8: that-Clauses and Clauses with "dass"
Seite 145

A

1️⃣ Will there be enough time (for me) to go home and change first? ▶ enough

2️⃣ ✓ ▶ time („Mal")

3️⃣ ✓ ▶ feel

4️⃣ I don't trust Arnold to be there when he said he would. ▶ trust

5️⃣ ✓ ▶ irritate

6️⃣ We can't allow people to drink alcohol at school. ▶ allow

7️⃣ The party was organized without him knowing anything about it. ▶ without

8️⃣ Fatima will never forgive Daniel for lying to her. ▶ forgive

9️⃣ I wouldn't want you to get the wrong impression. ▶ want

🔟 ✓ ▶ suspect (verb)

B

1️⃣ Damian apologized for being late. ▶ apologize

2️⃣ I'd like you to join us/to come (with us). ▶ like

3️⃣ We don't want you to pay for us. ▶ want

4️⃣ Martin accused us of breaking our promise. ▶ accuse

5️⃣ Ann has offered to take/drive us to the airport. ▶ offer

Seite 146

A

1. finding/making ▶ practise
2. being ▶ deny
3. worrying/thinking ▶ stop
4. taking ▶ suggest
5. going/to go ▶ love
6. being ▶ dislike ... being/to be ▶ prefer
7. trying ▶ advice
8. eating ▶ finish
9. being ▶ imagine
10. cleaning/to be cleaned ▶ need
11. to get up ▶ need
12. sitting/lying/standing ... watching ▶ remember
13. getting up/working ▶ enjoy
14. sitting ▶ avoid
15. to come/go/play/sit/eat ▶ like
16. losing ▶ risk
17. seeing ▶ miss
18. looking ▶ resist
19. talking ▶ go on
20. to take ▶ advice
21. seeing ▶ forget
22. to bring/take/pack ▶ forget
23. taking ▶ mind
24. to have to ▶ regret
25. going ▶ fancy

Seite 147

B

1. of hacking ▶ capable
2. of paying ▶ point
3. in persuading ▶ succeed
4. on paying ▶ insist
5. for looking after ▶ thank
6. from criticizing ▶ prevent
7. in waiting ▶ sense
8. of winning ▶ confident
9. for stealing ▶ punish
10. to living ▶ used to

C

1. of getting lost ▶ fear
2. of/in using ▶ advantage
3. of getting ▶ intention
4. of reducing ▶ effect
5. making ▶ problems
6. ✓ ▶ used to
7. of seeing ▶ hope
8. of taking ▶ possibility
9. of having ▶ idea
10. (in) finding ▶ difficulty
11. ✓ ▶ idea
12. finding ▶ trouble
13. of phoning ▶ habit
14. of winning ▶ thought
15. ✓ ▶ intention

D

1. Anna confessed to finding Jem "really sweet/cute"/confessed that she found Jem "really sweet/cute". ▶ confess
2. We look forward/We're looking forward to having you here as our guest. ▶ look forward to
3. I'm not used to walking/going that/so far. ▶ used to
4. David admitted (to) knowing about the problem/that he had known about the problem. ▶ admit
5. I object to paying for something (that) I don't need. ▶ object

Seite 148

A

1. quite far/so far/too far/awfully far/a long way ▶ far
2. to be found ▶ find
3. before/earlier ▶ ago
4. It isn't permitted ▶ allow
5. with great concentration ▶ concentrate
6. 6 o'clock/6 p.m. ▶ a.m.
7. the same size ▶ same: the same

8 in such a friendly way ▶ friendly

9 I promise (you) ▶ promise

10 Just ▶ fine

B

1 The last *thing* I did ... ▶ last

2 ... many *people* didn't have ... ▶ many

3 ... why he doesn't greet *me* ... ▶ greet

4 Last *but* not least ... ▶ least

5 Roger can *speak* Spanish very well ...
▶ can

6 ... the only *thing* I can advise you
to do ... ▶ only

7 ... makes *you* fat. ▶ thick

8 ... – all *the* people were ... ▶ all

9 ... she thanked *me* ... ▶ thank

10 ... I warned you *not* to buy it. ▶ warn

Seite 149

C

1 I left home two minutes too late and
missed the bus, so was *late* for school
again. ▶ late

2 ... I could remember *none* of my
English / I could*n't* remember *any* of my
English and said practically nothing.
▶ nothing

3 It's fully understandable that they
made so many mistakes. They were
completely/absolutely exhausted.
▶ fully

4 I've spent *a lot* and don't have much
money left now. ▶ much

5 It's an impossibly difficult task. We *can't
possibly* ask them to do it on their own.
▶ impossibly

6 We have a lot of time; it's still *many*
weeks before we have to make a
decision. ▶ many

7 Don't formulate your question *like that*.
It sounds so impolite, you know. ▶ so

8 I wanted *none* of my friends to know /
I did*n't* want *any* of my friends to know,
so I told nobody. ▶ nobody

9 I'd like to have my own room.
Unfortunately I've never had *my own
room / a room of my own.* ▶ own

10 You seldom see a leopard in the wild.
It's a very *rare* sight. ▶ seldom

11 *Which* of you can tell me the answer?
Come on, who knows? ▶ who

12 We arrived *pretty/rather/quite/very*
late because of the snow. But plenty of
others did too. ▶ plenty

D

1 What time should I suggest *to them*?
▶ suggest

2 The whole plan seems completely crazy
to me. ▶ seem

3 Sorry, could you repeat that last number
to/for me, please? ▶ repeat

4 David admitted his mistake *to his boss.*
▶ admit

5 ... I'm not going to dictate it *to you.*
▶ dictate

6 Can you describe the criminal *to/for us*?
▶ describe

7 They bet *us* that we couldn't do it. ▶ bet

8 I apologized *to the teacher* for my bad
behaviour. ▶ apologize

9 ... I'd better explain *to you* the layout of
the building / explain the layout of the
building *to you.* ▶ explain

10 I asked *the man* his name. ▶ ask

11 This milk tastes sour *to me.* ▶ taste

12 "... We didn't mean to spoil the evening
for you." ▶ spoil

Seite 150

E

1. (for) a long time ▶ long
2. (that) I've played ▶ time („Mal")
3. abroad ▶ abroad
4. an average of £7 an hour / £7 an hour on average ▶ average
5. a maximum of €400 ▶ maximum
6. a medium-sized country ▶ medium
7. be foreseen ▶ foresee

F

1. it ▶ know
2. so ▶ afraid: be afraid
3. it ▶ forget
4. so ▶ suppose
5. — ▶ say
6. — ▶ try
7. — ▶ forget
8. so ▶ think
9. — ▶ know
10. —/so ▶ say
11. — ▶ want
12. so ▶ hope

Seite 151

G

1. paid ▶ pay
2. dying ▶ die
3. ✓ ▶ potato
4. repetition ▶ repeat
5. tried ▶ try
6. developed ▶ develop
7. ✓ ▶ regret
8. ✓ ▶ public
9. envied ▶ envy
10. altogether ▶ altogether
11. receipt ▶ receipt
12. pronunciation ▶ pronounce

H

1. advice ▶ advice
2. beach ▶ beach
3. independent ▶ independent
4. died ▶ die
5. advise ▶ advice
6. beech ▶ beach
7. pyjamas/pajamas ▶ pyjamas
8. marmalade ▶ marmalade

Checkpoint 11: Topic Boxes
Seite 152

A

1. search engine ▶ Internet
2. the file ▶ Internet
3. 20 years old ▶ age
4. nought/zero ▶ temperature
5. bookmark ▶ Internet
6. lie in / have a lie-in ▶ sleep
7. Three times two is / Three twos are ▶ multiply
8. the fourth of April / April the fourth ▶ date
9. sleep on it ▶ sleep
10. doing/taking ▶ school
11. go to bed ▶ sleep
12. The spring / Spring ▶ date

B

1. up ... answer ▶ phone
2. down ▶ ill
3. miss ▶ lunch
4. failed ▶ school
5. lower ▶ temperature
6. (A) Happy ▶ greet
7. picked ▶ ill
8. bite (to eat) ▶ lunch

C

1 Get well soon! ▶ ill
2 Don't fall asleep! / Don't go to sleep!
   ▶ sleep
3 Good luck with your driving test!
   ▶ greet
4 Congratulations on (passing) your
   driving test! ▶ greet
5 Many happy returns! ▶ greet
6 What's the date (today)? ▶ date
7 What's the temperature? ▶ temperature
8 It's one degree above zero.
   ▶ temperature

D

1 We got up at dawn. It was just after
   four / a little after four. ▶ morning
2 At five o'clock sharp we left the hut and
   began to climb. ▶ morning
3 At about/around eleven / About/around
   eleven(ish) we reached the summit.
   ▶ morning
   It was hot, in the upper twenties / nearly
   thirty degrees. ▶ temperature
   I was tired and almost dying of thirst.
4 One of the others asked me if he could
   use my mobile (phone) / cell phone to
   make a quick phone call / if he could
   make a quick phone call on my mobile
   (phone) / cell phone. ▶ phone
5 It was Alfred, an old school friend of
   mine. We're the same age. ▶ age
   We started school together and left
   school together. ▶ school
6 I said, "OK, here (you are). I'll have/take
   a nap / have a snooze." ▶ sleep
7 I gave him my mobile (phone) / cell
   phone and lay down.
   I fell asleep / went to sleep at once /
   immediately and slept for 30 minutes.
   ▶ sleep

8 When I woke up, Alfred was still on the
   phone to his girlfriend / Alfred was still
   speaking/talking to/with his girlfriend
   on the phone. ▶ phone
   At the end he said, "And give my love
   to your parents." ▶ greet
9 I was pissed off.
   Alfred's girlfriend was over 1000 kilo-
   metres/kilometers away – on holiday in
   Denmark. ▶ distance
   I said, "Thirty multiplied by eighty
   is/equals 2400. / Thirty times eighty is
   2400. / Thirty eighties are 2400.
   ▶ multiply
   You owe me 24 euros."
10 It was just before five / It was nearly
   five / It was coming up for five when we
   got back to the hut / when we were
   back in the hut. ▶ morning
11 I was ravenous. I was absolutely
   starving. "What's for dinner/supper? /
   What are we having for dinner/supper?"
   I asked. ▶ lunch
12 "Not much," was the answer. "Unless
   you want to go shopping / go to the
   shops." "No, thanks," I said.
   The nearest supermarket was two
   hours' walk away. / It was two hours'
   walk to the nearest supermarket.
   ▶ distance
13 I tried to get/go to sleep. After twenty
   minutes the burbling of the stream
   outside sent me to sleep. ▶ sleep
14 Then my mobile (phone) / cell phone
   rang. I answered it. ▶ phone
15 It was Alfred's girlfriend. She wanted to
   speak/talk to/with Alfred.
   "Happy holidays / Have a nice holiday,"
   she said to me. ▶ greet
   I couldn't get/go back to sleep. ▶ sleep
16 For supper/dinner there was a tin/can of
   sardines, fried egg(s) and raspberry
   yoghurt. ▶ lunch

Checkpoint 12: Correcting Texts

Seite 154

A

The Rolls Royce was built in 1929 but *for* (▶ since) many years – *at least* (▶ last; at last) twenty, maybe more – it had stood in a garage *doing* (▶ make) nothing.

Then one day, *in* the late afternoon (▶ morning), a rich *businessman* (▶ undertaker) came and bought it for a *large/great* amount (▶ amount) of money and *took* (▶ bring) it away. He was the owner of a *mobile phone/cell phone* (▶ handy) factory. He decided that he didn't want to *leave* (▶ let) the car at the *back/rear* (▶ back ▶ backside) of the factory, where *nobody/no one* (▶ nobody) would see it *among* (▶ between) the *parked* (▶ park) cars of his 380 employees. But he didn't trust *people to leave* (▶ trust) the car *alone* (▶ let). So he *had* (▶ let) a glass box built *in front of* (▶ before) the factory building, *on* the main road (▶ street), where everybody *was* (▶ everybody) able to see the car. He wanted *people to stop* (▶ want) and admire it and *think that he was* (▶ hold) a nice, old-fashioned person.

Only once in the years that followed *did the car leave* (▶ only) the box: when the factory owner's daughter got married *to* (▶ marry) a nice young man from eastern Europe. The young *couple* (▶ pair) went away in it on their honeymoon. But the car was *stolen* (▶ rob) from outside the first hotel they stayed at, just outside London – and was never seen again.

B

Three weeks ago (▶ ago ▶ before) I *passed* (▶ driving licence) my driving *test* (▶ driving licence). And now I have *a/my* (driving) licence (▶ driving licence) and want to buy a car. But which one? People *who* (▶ who) have *a lot of/lots of/plenty of* money (▶ much) have no difficulty *(in) deciding* (▶ difficulty) on a model (▶ decide). But when you're still *a* student (▶ study), you can't spend a lot of money *on* a car (▶ spend). I asked all of my friends to *tell* me (▶ say) what they *think/thought* (▶ mean). I wanted *them to give* (▶ want) me *some* good advice (▶ advice). I don't want to risk *buying* (▶ risk) the *wrong* model (▶ false). But I *don't have to/don't need to/needn't* (▶ need ▶ must) *make/take/arrive at/come to/reach* a decision (▶ decision) yet.

At the moment (▶ moment) I can *borrow* (▶ borrow) my mother's car *most of the* time (▶ most). But not my father's. He always warns me *not* to drive (▶ warn) too fast. When he sits *next to/beside* me (▶ beside), he gets *nervous* (▶ become) when I do more *than* (▶ as) 60 miles *an/per* hour (▶ hour).

Last week I *missed/didn't see/overlooked* (▶ oversee) a traffic light. It can happen *to* (▶ happen) *anyone/anybody* (▶ each), can't it? My father didn't *say* (▶ say) anything but he looked *at* me (▶ look) *like* (▶ as) a *murderer* (▶ murder). I thought: how can *my* own (▶ own) father be so mad at me? The *moral* (▶ moral) of this story is: always let your father *drive* (▶ let).

Seite 182

most 1*A*, 2*A C*, 3*A*
motor – engine 1*A*, 2*B*
much – many – a lot of – plenty of 1*A*, 2*A C*,
  3*A*, 4*A*, 5*A B C*
multiply 1*A*, 2*B C*, 3*A C*

Seite 184

murder – murderer 1*C*, 2*A*
music – musical 1*A*, 2*B*
must – have to 1*B*, 2*A B*, 3*B*
narrow 1*D*, 2*A*, 3*C*, 4*B C*
nature 1*A*, 2*B*, 3*C*
near – nearby 1*B*

Seite 186

need 1*B*, 2*A B*, 3*B*, 4*B C*, 5*B C*
neither – none – no 1*A*, 2*C*, 3*C*, 4*A*, 5*C D*

Seite 188

newest – latest 1*A*, 2*B*
news 1*B C*, 2*B*
next – nearest 1*A*, 2*B*, 3*C*
nil – zero – nought – oh – love 1*B D*, 2*B C*,
  3*A C*, 4*B*, 5*C D*, 6*B C*

Seite 190

nobody/no one – somebody/someone 1*C*,
  2*B*, 3*A*, 4*A*
note ≠ „Note" 1*A B C D*, 2*A B*
nothing 1*A*, 2*A C*
notice ≠ „Notiz" 1*B*, 2*A*, 3*B*

Seite 192

notice – realize/realise – remember – note
  1*B*, 2*C*, 3*B*, 4*A*
number 1*A*, 2*B*, 3*B*, 4*B*
object 1*B*, 2*C*
obvious 1*B*
offer 1*A B C*, 2*B*

Seite 194

old – ancient – antique 1*A*
once 1*A*, 2*C D*, 3*B D*, 4*B C*, 5*B*
one – you – they – people 1*D*, 2*B C*, 3*A C*
only 1*A*, 2*C*, 3*B C*

Seite 196

opinion 1*C*
opposite 1*A*, 2*A*
opposition 1*C*, 2*D*
optimist – pessimist 1*A*
ordinary ≠ „ordinär" 1*B*, 2*A C*
other – different 1*C*, 2*B*, 3*B*

Seite 198

over 1*B*, 2*B C*, 3*A*, 4*A*, 5*A*, 6*A*, 7*D*, 8*B*
overhear ≠ „überhören" 1*C*, 2*A C*
oversee ≠ „übersehen" 1*A B*, 2*B*, 3*B C*

Seite 200

overtake ≠ „übernehmen" 1*B C*, 2*B*, 3*B*
own 1*B*, 2*B*, 3*A C*
packet ≠ „Paket" 1*A B C*, 2*A C*
pair – couple – a few 1*A*, 2*A*, 3*D E*

Seite 202

pants 1*C D*
park 1*A*
parliament 1*B*
part 1*B*, 2*A C*
party 1*B C D*, 2*A*
pass – past 1*B*, 2*B*, 3*B*

Seite 204

patience 1*C*, 2*A*
pause – break – interval/intermission 1*A*,
  2*B*, 3*B C*
pay 1*A*, 2*A*, 3*A*, 4*B*
pencil 1*B D*
people 1*A*, 2*B*, 3*B*, 4*D*

Seite 206

perhaps 1 *B*
person 1 *B*
personal ≠ „Personal" 1 *C*
phone 1 *C*, 2 *C*, 3 *A*, 4 *A*, 5 *A D*
photo(graph) – photographer –
  photography 1 *C D*, 2 *B*, 3 *B*, 4 *B*, 5 *C*

Seite 208

picnic 1 *B D*
picture 1 *A*, 2 *B*
place 1 *B*, 2 *C*, 3 *A*, 4 *B*
play 1 *B D*, 2 *B*
please 1 *B*, 2 *B*, 3 *A C D*, 4 *B C*, 5 *A*

Seite 210

plenty 1 *B*, 2 *B C D*
poem 1 *A*
point *(verb)* 1 *A*, 2 *C*
point *(noun)* 1 *B*, 2 *B C*, 3 *A*, 4 *A*, 5 *A C*
police 1 *A*
policy – politics 1 *A*, 2 *C*, 3 *B*

Seite 212

poor 1 *B*, 2 *B*, 3 *A*
popular 1 *C*
possibility – chance – opportunity – way
  1 *A*, 2 *A B*, 3 *C*, 4 *A*
possible 1 *B*, 2 *B*
post – mail – post office 1 *A*
potato 1 *A*

Seite 214

practise/practice – practice 1 *A*, 2 *C D*
prefer – would prefer 1 *C*, 2 *B*, 3 *A B*
prepare 1 *A*
present 1 *A*
prevent 1 *A C*
price – prize – cost 1 *B*, 2 *A*, 3 *C*
principal – principally – principle 1 *B*, 2 *A*,
  3 *A*, 4 *B*

Seite 216

prison 1 *B*, 2 *C*
probably 1 *C*, 2 *B*
problem 1 *A*
program – programme 1 *A B*, 2 *A*
progress 1 *A*
promise 1 *B*, 2 *A C*
pronounce – pronunciation 1 *C*
prospect ≠ „Prospekt" 1 *B*, 2 *A*

Seite 218

protect 1 *A C*
proud 1 *B*
public ≠ „Publikum" 1 *A*, 2 *B C*, 3 *A*
punish 1 *C*
puzzle 1 *A*, 2 *B*
pyjamas/pajamas 1 *B*, 2 *B C*
qualify 1 *C*
quantity 1 *D*

Seite 220

quiet – silent – calm – smooth – still 1 *B*,
  2 *B C*, 3 *A*, 4 *A*, 5 *D*, 6 *A*
quite – pretty – fairly – rather 1 *A B C E*, 2 *B*
rain 1 *A B D*, 2 *A*
raise – rise 1 *B*, 2 *A*, 3 *C*

Seite 222

rather: would rather 1 *A*, 2 *A*
react – reaction 1 *C*
ready – finish 1 *A*, 2 *B*
realize/realise – recognize/recognise 1 *B*, 2 *A*
reason 1 *A B C*, 2 *B*
receipt ≠ „Rezept" 1 *A*, 2 *B*, 3 *A*

Seite 224

recently 1 *A*
refuse – reject 1 *B*, 2 *A*
regret 1 *B*, 2 *B*
related 1 *B*
relevant 1 *B*
remember – remind 1 *B*, 2 *A*, 3 *C*, 4 *B*, 5 *B*, 6 *A*

Seite 226

repeat – repetition 1 C, 2 B
report 1 B
reputation 1 A
request 1 A, 2 B
resist 1 B
responsible 1 A
rest 1 B, 2 A

Seite 228

return 1 B
rich 1 B C D, 2 B
right: be right 1 A
risk 1 A, 2 A
rob – mug – steal – burgle 1 B C, 2 C, 3 A
rubbish/garbage 1 B
rule – govern – reign 1 A B, 2 C, 3 B C

Seite 230

salad – lettuce 1 A, 2 B
sale 1 C, 2 C
the same 1 B
sauce – gravy – dressing 1 B, 2 A
save 1 C, 2 C
say – tell 1 B, 2 B, 3 A C, 4 A, 5 D

Seite 232

school 1 A, 2 A, 3 C, 4 A
sea – seaside 1 A, 2 D, 3 B C D
search (for) – look for – seek 1 A, 2 C, 3 D
see 1 A, 2 B C, 3 C

Seite 234

seem 1 B, 2 A, 3 B
seldom – rare(ly) 1 A B, 2 A,
self-conscious ≠ „selbstbewusst" 1 B, 2 B
sense 1 B
sensible ≠ „sensibel" 1 B, 2 B
serious 1 B
shade – shadow 1 B, 2 A

Seite 236

sharp – hot/spicy – in focus/clear 1 C, 2 A B,
  3 A, 4 B
sheep 1 A, 2 A
shine 1 C
ship – boat 1 A, 2 A B, 3 A
shopping 1 A
shorts 1 A, 2 A C

Seite 238

should – ought to 1 A D, 2 B, 3 A, 4 A, 5 B,
  6 B, 7 B C, 8 B
shout 1 A, 2 C
side 1 B, 2 C, 3 B

Seite 240

since – for 1 C, 2 C, 3 C
size 1 A C
sky 1 B
sleep – be asleep 1 C, 2 A, 3 B, 4 B E, 5 A B C,
  6 B, 7 A, 8 B

Seite 242

smell 1 B, 2 B
so – such – like this/that 1 D, 2 B, 3 C, 4 A, 5 A
social – social-minded 1 A, 2 B
society 1 B
sometimes – sometime/some time 1 A B,
  2 A
sound 1 C, 2 B

Seite 244

space 1 A
spaghetti 1 B
spare ≠ „sparen" 1 A, 2 B
speak – talk 1 B, 2 B C
special 1 A
specialist 1 B
specialize/specialise 1 C
speech 1 A C

speed 1 *A*

spend ≠ „spenden" 1 *B*, 2 *A*, 3 *A*

spoil 1 *A*

sport 1 *A*

stadium ≠ „Stadium" 1 *B*, 2 *A*

stand 1 *A*, 2 *A*, 3 *A*

stationary – stationery 1 *B*, 2 *A*

stay – remain 1 *B*, 2 *A C*, 3 *B*, 4 *A*

still 1 *B*, 2 *B*

stop 1 *A*, 2 *B C*, 3 *A*, 4 *B*

storey – story 1 *A B*, 2 *B*

street – road 1 *A*, 2 *B*, 3 *A*, 4 *B C*, 5 *B*, 6 *A*,
  7 *B C*, 8 *C*

strong 1 *C*, 2 *B*, 3 *A B*, 4 *D*, 5 *A*, 6 *B C E*, 7 *A B*,
  8 *A*

study 1 *B C*, 2 *A E*, 3 *B C*, 4 *A B*

stuff ≠ „Stoff" 1 *B*, 2 *A*

succeed 1 *B*

suffer 1 *C*

suggest 1 *A B*, 2 *A*

summary 1 *C*

sunk – sunken 1 *B*, 2 *A*

suppose 1 *B*, 2 *B*, 3 *B*

surprised 1 *B*

suspect – suspicious 1 *A B D*, 2 *A*, 3 *A*

suspect *(verb)* 1 *B*

symbol 1 *B*

sympathetic ≠ „sympathisch" 1 *C*, 2 *C*, 3 *A*, 4 *B*

tablet ≠ „Tablett" 1 *C*, 2 *A B*

task 1 *A*

taste 1 *C*, 2 *B D*, 3 *C*, 4 *A*, 5 *B*

teacher – instructor – lecturer 1 *C*, 2 *B*, 3 *A B C*

technique – technology 1 *B*, 2 *A*

teenage 1 *B*

temperature 1 *D*, 2 *C*, 3 *B*, 4 *B C*, 5 *A*

terrible – terrific 1 *B*, 2 *A*

test 1 *A*, 2 *B*

thank – thank you / thanks 1 *A*, 2 *B C*, 3 *A*

thick – fat 1 *A*, 2 *A B*, 3 *B*

think 1 *B*, 2 *A*, 3 *B*, 4 *C*, 5 *C*

thought 1 *A*

threat 1 *B*

throw 1 *B*, 2 *B*, 3 *C*

time („Zeit") 1 *C*, 2 *C*, 3 *B*, 4 *A*, 5 *A B*, 6 *D E*,
  7 *A D*

time („Mal") 1 *B*, 2 *B*

toast 1 *A*

today – tomorrow 1 *A*, 2 *C*, 3 *A*

too 1 *B*

tooth 1 *A*

tour 1 *A C*

traffic 1 *B*, 2 *A*

trouble 1 *B*, 2 *A*

trousers 1 *A*, 2 *A C*

true – truth 1 *B*, 2 *B*

trust 1 *A*, 2 *B*

try – attempt 1 *B*, 2 *B*, 3 *A*, 4 *A*, 5 *C*, 6 *A*

typical 1 *A*, 2 *B*

unable – incompetent – able – competent
  1 *A*, 2 *A B*

unconscious – subconscious 1 *B*, 2 *B*, 3 *A*

under – below 1 *A C*, 2 *B*, 3 *A*, 4 *A*, 5 *A*, 6 *B*,
  7 *A*, 8 *A B*

P-Nummer: 963118